Ballencelve

Gabriele Marcotti is the world football correspondent for *The Times* and UK correspondent for the *Corriere dello Sport*. He is also a columnist for *Sports Illustrated* and his work appears regularly in *La Stampa* and the *Sunday Herald*. He is a regular pundit on BBC Radio Five Live. His books include *The Italian Job: A Journey to the Heart of Two Great Footballing Cultures*, co-written with Gianluca Vialli, which was shortlisted for the William Hill Sports Book of the Year award in 2006, and *Paolo Di Canio: The Autobiography*. He lives in London.

D1100641

www.**rbooks**.co.uk

Also by Gabriele Marcotti

Paolo Di Canio: The Autobiography
(co-written with Paolo Di Canio)

The Italian Job: A Journey to the Heart of
Two Great Footballing Cultures
(co-written with Gianluca Vialli)

CAPELLO

The Man Behind England's World Cup Dream

Gabriele Marcotti

BANTAM BOOKS

LONDON • TORONTO • SYDNEY • AUCKLAND • JOHANNESBURG

TRANSWORLD PUBLISHERS
61–63 Uxbridge Road, London W5 5SA
A Random House Group Company
www.rbooks.co.uk

CAPELLO
A BANTAM BOOK: 9780553825664

First published in Great Britain
in 2008 by Bantam Press
an imprint of Transworld Publishers
Bantam edition published 2009
Bantam edition reissued 2010

196.801

Addresses for Random House Group Ltd companies outside the UK
can be found at: www.randomhouse.co.uk
£12.°⁰ The Random House Group Ltd Reg. No. 954009

The Random House Group Limited supports The Forest Stewardship Council
(FSC), the leading international forest certification organisation. All our titles
that are printed on Greenpeace approved FSC certified paper carry the FSC
logo. Our paper procurement policy can be found at
www.rbooks.co.uk/environment

Typeset in 11/14pt Berling by
Falcon Oast Graphic Art Ltd.
Printed in the UK by CPI Cox & Wyman, Reading, RG1 8EX.

2 4 6 8 10 9 7 5 3 1

To Jennifer, my light, and Luisa, my soul.
And to Filippo (*ti guardo, sempre . . .*)

Contents

Acknowledgements

Fabio Capello was appointed England manager on 14 December, 2007. The fact that you are holding this 130,000-odd word text in your hand many months later would have been impossible without the help of a veritable army of people.

I have to start with David Luxton, my agent at Luxton Harris, who turned an idea into reality (and a book contract) in record time. I first met David years ago when he was stacking the shelves at the legendary SportsPages Bookshop on Charing Cross Road. We've come a long way, mate.

There is no way I could have packed so much of Fabio's life into this book without the help of my researchers, above all Pierluigi Pardo, of Sky Italia, and Andrea Ramazzotti, of *Corriere dello Sport*. Both are not just creative, talented journalists but also true professionals who know the meaning of hard work.

I also owe a big 'thank you' to Aurelio Capaldi of RAI, a model professional himself, whose own 'Capello file' of cuttings got the ball rolling. Sid Lowe, a gifted and creative writer, and José Luis Guerrero were invaluable in helping piece together Capello's Spanish period. Benjamin Adler was a huge help in procuring interviews with a number of the French sources I spoke to. Stefano Melegari kindly did yeoman work digging around in the archives of AC Milan and *Forza Milan* magazine and he has my never-ending gratitude. Nick Michlewicz was the first person to read my draft and his input was both valuable and incisive. And Kevin Danton, who clearly missed his calling and should have been a historian, was invaluable in researching the Bisiacheria, the land that produced Capello.

Other colleagues who added valuable tiles to the Capello mosaic were, in strict alphabetical order: Marco Ansaldo, Fabrizio Aspri, Guillem Balague, Roberto Beccantini, Paolo Brusorio, Duncan Castles, Alessio Di Francesco, Furio Fedele, Giancarlo Galavotti, Graham Hunter, Alfredo Pedulla, Alberto Polverosi, Filippo Maria Ricci, Piero Torri, Annalisa Turel and Jonathan Wilson. A special mention to two veteran journalists who, years ago, inspired me to get into this line of work: Mario Sconcerti and Alberto Cerruti.

The folks at Transworld, from publishing director Doug Young to my editor, Giles Elliott, one of the most patient people you're ever likely to meet (and another SportsPages veteran), were instrumental in turning this whole thing around in record time. Thanks must also go to Katrina Whone, who handled the production, picture editor Sheila Lee, Roger Field and John English, my very laid-back copy editor.

And how about all the people who gave up their time to speak to me about this book? I owe them all a big 'thank you', including those who, for a variety of reasons, I can't name. Again, in alphabetical order, a heartfelt grazie/thank you/merci/dankeschön/obrigado to: Rafael Alkorta, José Altafini, José Emilio Amavisca, Vincent Candela, Pierfilippo Capello, Franco Causio, Franco Ceravolo, Giorgio Chinaglia, Fulvio Collovati, Luigi Colombo, Mario Corsi aka Marione, Olivier Dacourt, Oscar Damiani, Marco Delvecchio, Bruno De Michelis, Gianni Di Marzio, Stefano Eranio, Giovan Battista Fabbri, Fabrizio Ferron, Adriano Galliani, Massimo Giacomini, Toni Grande, Fernando Hierro, Francisco Lima, Marcello Lippi, Luciano Moggi, Giovan Battista Monti, Stefano Nava, Enrique Ortego, Silvano Ramaccioni, Edy Reja, Sebastiano Rossi, Luciano Spinosi, Miguel Torres, Jacopo Volpi and Ray Wilkins.

My thanks also go out to the twenty or so people who spoke to me on condition of anonymity. You know who you are and I thank you.

Finally, I owe a major debt of gratitude to my wife, Jennifer, whose patience and understanding as I locked myself away for hours in writing this opus was nothing but phenomenal.

Author's note

On a hot July night in 2006, minutes after Italy had won the World Cup, I was interviewed by *TalkSport*. As the players celebrated on the pitch just a few yards away, I said: 'I hope England wins the World Cup. I hope you get to experience what it feels like.'

I still feel that way. I have come to love this country and its people for the opportunities it has afforded me and my family. And I am proud of the fact that a fellow Italian, Fabio Capello, is in charge of the England team.

Capello is no guarantee of success. But he's about as close as you can get in football. That alone made him a fascinating subject.

But, in researching this book, I found more. Much more. I found a man who has witnessed up-close so many of the seminal moments in the game over the past forty-five years. A man who has grown and adapted to the changes which have swept across not just football, but Europe as well. A man who is at peace with himself, despite making choices – and occasionally errors – which made him, at times, deeply unpopular.

Writing a biography about a living person is not easy. You're asked to chronicle somebody's life, knowing that, no matter how much research you do, there is someone (in my case, someone who lives less than a mile away from my house) who knows the truth – or, at least, his version of the truth – better than you.

I did the best I could. I enlisted the help of trusted researchers and spoke to as many people as I could. Invariably, everyone has an opinion on Capello, some positive, some negative. When the dust settled, I found that I and my researchers had spoken to more than 120 people.

My job was putting all that into some kind of coherent narrative. I gave myself a few ground rules. For every anecdote or story I was told, I tried to get confirmation from at least two primary sources. Sometimes this was possible, sometimes it wasn't (and, indeed, I could have written a whole other book with the stories that turned out not to be verifiable). One of the things I found in researching this book – and something which will make me forever suspicious of biographies, particularly of those who are long dead – is that the same incident is remembered differently by different people.

Except where otherwise stated, every quote in the book comes from a direct interview, conducted either by me or one of my researchers. I have tried to minimize the use of anonymous quotes, but, in some cases, I had no choice. People have strong feelings when it comes to Capello, there are no two ways about it. And football is, ultimately, a small world.

One more thing. You won't find much in here about

Capello's childhood or his family life (his wife Laura, his sons Edoardo and Pierfilippo, his mother Evelina). I wanted to respect their privacy and, as an outsider, the brutal truth is that I was never going to get an accurate picture of Capello's private life. What's more, I didn't really care. The one exception is his father, Guerrino, who, by all accounts, was a central figure and a major influence on his life.

Regardless of whether you like Capello or not, regardless of whether you think he is a good manager or, indeed, a good man, I hope you learn something from this book. And I hope you will find that this is a fair and balanced portrayal of one of the most successful men in the history of football.

Introduction

Wednesday, 21 November 2007. Italy, who have already qualified for Euro 2008, are playing the Faroe Islands in Modena. Nine minutes have passed in the second half, the Azzurri are winning 3–0, and the meaningless game is slowly petering out like a run-of-the-mill friendly.

Up in the stands, Marco Civoli, the lead commentator for RAI, the Italian state broadcaster, is told that England are losing by two goals at home to Croatia in their decisive European qualifier. He quickly thinks of a way of breaking the news to his summarizer, Fabio Capello.

As the cameras offer up a close-up of Simone Perrotta, the Italy midfielder, Civoli says, 'Well, Perrotta, he was born in Ashton-under-Lyne. Which, of course, is in England . . . England, who are losing at home to Croatia! Fabio, were you expecting that? It's not a full-time score, of course . . .'

'No, I thought England could have done much better throughout this qualifying campaign,' Capello replies. 'They've proved themselves to be a team with good players who don't know how to express themselves. Or, at least, in my opinion, they don't live up to their potential.'

'OK, yes-or-no question: would you ever manage England?'

'Well . . . that would be quite a challenge, eh? That would be something . . . Well, I'm the right age for it . . .'

Odds are, Capello (despite suspecting that – barring a miraculous comeback – Steve McClaren would soon be out of a job) wasn't thinking of throwing his hat in the England ring. Rather, he was honestly saying what he had said a number of times before: he wanted the England job. He had come very close to getting it some seven years earlier and he knew that, at sixty-one years of age, his window of opportunity was closing.

Some young men enter the priesthood as teenagers and devote their life to God. Capello had entered football and given himself to the game. And, all in all, it had been good to him. He became a top-drawer international player, he won league titles and international caps.

After retirement, he paid his dues, first working with youngsters and, later, learning about the business side of sports management. And, when he turned to coaching, he dominated. He replaced a legend in Arrigo Sacchi at Milan and rewrote the record books. He went to Real Madrid and became the first Italian manager to win the title in a major European league. He delivered another title to Rome, a city which seemed genetically pro-grammed to underachieve. He moved to Juventus and flattened the opposition, keeping his team in first place for two consecutive years, start to finish, while winning two league titles. And then he returned to Madrid, breaking the longest dry spell in half a century and delivering another league title in the most difficult of circumstances.

His CV was there for all to see. Yes, he had tasted failure as well. As a player, he lost one European Cup final, as a manager, he lost a further two. His two titles at Juventus were stripped amid the worst scandal in Italian football history, though he felt strongly that what was achieved on the pitch could not (and should not) be taken away. But these were details. Or, rather, these were the setbacks which made his victories all the sweeter.

There was one thing left to do. One mountain left to conquer. The World Cup. But it wasn't just about winning it. Sixteen different managers had won the World Cup, most recently his countryman – and long-time sporting rival – Marcello Lippi. No, he would win the World Cup in a way that had never before been done. He would deliver the World Cup at the helm of a foreign team. And not just any team: England, the country who had invented the game only to see it pass it by, the nation groaning under forty-plus years of underachievement.

That would be his crowning achievement. That would be his legacy.

Capello would make history. Again. And in such a way that his record could never be bettered, only equalled.

CHAPTER 1

Pieris

When you're born at a crossroads, you at once belong to everyone and no one.

Fabio Capello was born into one of the bloodiest, most diverse and most disputed corners of the Old World. A gateway between East and West, a place where history was written both on the backs of its inhabitants and those who were just passing through.

He is a child of the Bisiacheria, an area of some forty square miles in the north-east corner of Italy, but culturally and historically distinct from the larger Friuli-Venezia Giulia around it. It's unclear where the term 'Bisiaco' (the name given to local inhabitants) comes from. One theory is that it's derived from the Latin *bis acque*, which means 'between waters', a reference to the nearby Isonzo and Timavo rivers. Others suggest that the term comes from the Slovenian *bezjok*, meaning 'refugee'. Lying as it does on a largely flat floodplain close to the waters of the Adriatic Sea, the Bisiacheria has long been a logical entry point to Italy for any traveller from the

East. Indeed, back in Roman times, this is where the border crossing was and where customs duties were collected.

In 1420, the area, which previously had enjoyed some level of independence as a city-state, came under the control of the Republic of Venice. The Venetians, with their booming maritime trade, exploited it as an important land-based alternative for commerce with the East. Indeed, for nearly four hundred years, invaders from the Ottoman and Austro-Hungarian Empires were regularly repelled just a few miles from where Capello was born. The Venetians were defeated in 1814 and the area fell to the Austrians, who remained in charge until the end of the First World War. In fact, it was during the Great War that the Bisiacheria was the scene of some of the most brutal fighting, as Italian, Slovenian and Austro-Hungarian forces struggled for control. It officially became Italian territory after the armistice of 1918, but peace was not to last long. The Second World War was around the corner.

This time, the battle-lines were a lot less clear. Italy was an Axis power, allied to Germany and Japan. In July 1943 Benito Mussolini, the Italian dictator, was overthrown and a new government led by General Pietro Badoglio took control. After initially announcing that Italy would 'continue to fight side-by-side with our Germanic ally', Badoglio changed his mind, and on 8 September 1943 signed a proclamation which 'ceased all hostilities' towards Allied troops.

While Badoglio saw it as 'ending the war', it was, in fact, a disastrous decision that threw the country into complete chaos. The Italians were in limbo: they had turned their backs on the Germans but had yet to negotiate anything with the Allies, against whom they had been fighting until the previous day. Badoglio, King Victor Emmanuel and most of the cabinet fled Rome and repaired to Brindisi, in the heel of the Italian boot, one of the few places which was controlled neither by Allies nor by Germans. The Germans, who had been preparing for such a scenario since Mussolini's arrest in late July, sprang into action. They unleashed 'Operation Achse', which saw German Wehrmacht divisions (many of whom had been transferred to Italian soil in the meantime) take over key cities in northern and central Italy, including Rome.

As far as the millions of Italian soldiers (and their generals) fighting abroad were concerned, Badoglio's move effectively left them high and dry. They were given no real instructions. Some were told to return home, but, amidst the chaos, this bordered on the impossible. Others were told to 'take up arms' against the Germans with whom they had been often fighting side-by-side until the week before. Given that the Germans controlled logistics and supplies for the Axis, it was a losing proposition from the start. And the German reaction was often violent and brutal. Many were executed (including some 4,000 Italian soldiers on the Greek island of Kefalonia), many more were rounded up and sent to prison camps in Germany.

Among the latter was Guerrino Capello, Fabio's father, who had been an officer with an artillery division on the eastern front. Like many, he nearly starved to death in the camps. Indeed, when he finally returned home to Pieris in the late summer of 1945, many failed to even recognize him. The once strapping Guerrino weighed a mere forty-eight kilos, just over one hundred pounds. It may have been the realization of how lucky he was to be still alive, unlike so many of his comrades. It may have been the will to buckle down and start again now that the horror was behind him. Or it may simply have been that after six years of hatred and violence, it was time for some love.

Whatever the case, Fabio Capello was conceived around that time. And on 18 June 1946 Guerrino's wife, Evelina, gave birth to a healthy baby boy. The Italian Republic had only been created on 2 June that year and, until 14 September 1947, the area was controlled by the British Army's Third Survey, based in nearby Trieste, which meant that Capello missed out on being 'born British' by sixteen days.

And, if you believe in destiny, perhaps you could have predicted that this little boy would grow up to one day manage England. Among the British troops in the area were a fair few who had played professional football before the war. The local military authorities thought it would be a good idea to keep the footballers together and so a number of them were stationed in Pieris and would have trained on the town's pitch, just a stone's throw from where Capello was born. Among them was Stan Mortensen, who would go on to become a legendary centre-forward for Blackpool and England, scoring twenty-three international goals in twenty-five appearances. And, to this day, he is the only man to have scored a hat-trick in an FA Cup Final (unfortunately for him, it happened in 1953, in what would famously be remembered as the 'Matthews final' and his feat would be somewhat overshadowed).

There is zero concrete evidence that Capello saw Mortensen going through his paces in Pieris but it's tempting to picture the scene. Who knows? – maybe the infant Fabio Capello was there at pitch-side, perhaps in his mother's arms. Given that Guerrino was heavily involved with the local football club, it stands to reason that he would have been around. And, maybe, just maybe, he would have wanted to show off his baby boy to the future England centre-forward.

The war may have been over, but the Bisiacheria into which Capello was born was hardly a halcyon place. In fact, it would take the best part of a decade to return to normality. The area had always been a melting pot of Italians, Slovenians, Slavs and Austrians, but now it was in danger of boiling over. Tensions between left and right – between the Communists and the Christian Democrats – were rife all over Italy, but in the Bisiacheria there was another twist: nationalism. Many, primarily those of Slovenian descent, sympathized with Josip Tito, the Communist leader of the nascent Yugoslavia, who had led the partisan resistance to the German occupation. They saw this as an opportunity to break away from Italy and return to the pre-1918 status quo. The Italian-speakers in the area naturally grew apprehensive. On 30 June 1946 the pro-Tito Slovenians halted the Giro d'Italia cycle race, pelting the riders with stones as they approached Pieris. The violence soon escalated, not just in the Bisiacheria, but all the way down the Adriatic coast to Trieste. It wasn't open street fighting, it was uglier and more sinister. People would 'disappear' from one day to the next, only to turn up a week later, with a bullet in the back of the head, in the *foibe* – the typical sinkholes which dot the area from the Bisiacheria down to Trieste. By some estimates, as many as two thousand were summarily executed by Tito sympathizers, some of them Fascists who had backed the Germans, but also many whose only crime appears to have been that they wanted the Bisiacheria to remain Italian.

Many went into hiding, though not Guerrino. A popular and respected figure in Pieris – he was both a schoolteacher and the local football coach – he remained above the fray, trying instead to bring the two factions together. By the early 1950s the situation had stabilized, not least because the iron curtain came down just a few miles from Pieris, separating the West from Communist Eastern Europe. The Bisiacheria slowly bounced back. Monfalcone, a few towns over from Pieris on the Adriatic coast, became an important shipbuilding centre and the economy recovered. But while wealth and development hit the area, the bloody past was not forgotten. Nor is it forgotten to this day.

By 1962 the teenaged Capello left Pieris for good. I'm always a bit sceptical when we ascribe too much importance to a person's origins as a way of explaining their personality. We create regional stereotypes and then we look for confirmation, whether it be dour Yorkshiremen or wheeler-dealer cockneys. And Italy is no different. People from Friuli are seen as introverted, humourless, workaholic, tough, unemotional, light years away from the generic Italian stereotype. Depending on your point of view, you may feel that Capello is a typical 'Friulano'. But, if he is, it's a coincidence, because he is, in fact, Bisiaco. And it's something he'll always carry with him.

That said, it's equally true that Capello has spent the past forty-six years away from Pieris and the Bisiacheria, nearly half of them in Milan. Those who know him describe him as an 'urban animal', a man most at home in big, metropolitan cities, whether Milan or Madrid.

His love of city life and all it offers probably defines him as much as his origins in the Bisiacheria. Yet there is little question that, like all of us, he has not managed to fully free himself from the environment in which he spent his early, formative years. Capello left the Bisiacheria. But the Bisiacheria did not leave him.

CHAPTER 2

Spal

Had he been born forty years later, Capello's route into professional football might have been different. Until the age of sixteen, he played in the youth ranks of his local side, Pieris. These days, Capello, who began making waves from a young age, would probably have been snapped up by one of the professional clubs in the area, most likely Udinese or Triestina. He would still have lived at home, it's just that, rather than walking to training after school, the club would have sent a minivan to collect him.

Instead, he stayed where he was, not least because his father coached the local side. It soon became clear, however, that it was time for him to go to the next level. Scouts had seen him play a number of times; it was a question of who got to him first and who could convince Guerrino.

Perhaps it wasn't surprising that the man to take Capello into the big time was Paolo Mazza, the president of Spal, a small club from Ferrara, in central Italy. Gianni Brera, one of Italy's greatest twentieth-century journalists, had nicknamed him *Il Rabdomante* (the 'Diviner') for his uncanny talent-spotting abilities. That knack for uncovering hidden gems among lower division players and identifying the promise of youngsters helped Spal rise all the way to Serie A, where they would remain for thirteen seasons.

But Mazza was much more than just a wheeler-dealer president. Born in 1901, he had been a lower division footballer who later said: 'If my skills matched my love of the game I would have been the greatest player in the world.' He went on to manage Spal and eventually moved up to sporting director and then, in 1946, the presidency. Despite this, he remained the classic jack-of-all-trades at the club. He was just as likely to help the groundsman repair the divots in the pitch or the kit manager hang the shirts to dry as he was to drive three hours to watch some fifteen-year-old or negotiate the sale of one of his starlets to a bigger side.

Spal may have been a small club, but it thought and acted like a big one. In fact, in some ways it anticipated and pioneered innovations which would later become the norm. Mazza insisted on building a dedicated training centre for the club's youth teams – the Centro Giovanile di Addestramento – anticipating what would become commonplace many years later. Such was his profile in the game that the Italian FA begged him to take the position of assistant manager at the 1962 World Cup in Chile, despite the fact that he hadn't actually coached or managed in some twenty-five years. At least not officially: in practice, he was always out there, watching, training and dispensing what he called 'advice' (and others might have called 'unwanted interference'). Yet despite his larger-than-life figure, he was also reserved, businesslike and highly professional.

This probably played a big part in convincing Guerrino that his beloved son would be in good hands, even if it meant moving some 140 miles away. It was the summer of 1962. Mazza arrived at Capello's home, just a few days after the long and exhausting trip back from Chile. He was disappointed (Italy were controversially knocked out in the first round) and shattered, but he knew there was no time to waste. Other clubs had been sniffing around Capello.

The deal was done quickly, both with the family and with the club. Pieris would receive two million lire, just over £500 at the time. Capello would move at the end of the summer, when he would be enrolling in a local school. It would take a few days for the paperwork to go through, but, as far as Guerrino was concerned, it was a done deal.

Then, a day or two later, another visitor showed up at the Capello home: Gipo Viani. Viani was already a legend. He had been a visionary coach at Bologna, where he was among the first to pioneer the use of a sweeper and often played without a centre-forward, preferring instead to attack via the flanks and with runners from midfield. In 1956, he had moved to Milan, winning two league titles before moving into the role of sporting director. Milan were a club on the rise; that very season they would win their first of seven European Cups. It wasn't the kind of club used to hearing the word 'no'. Especially not when the great Viani himself travelled to your home, rather than merely sending an emissary.

Guerrino invited him in and opened a bottle of wine.

He wasn't going to deny Viani his hospitality. But there was no question about him changing his mind, not after committing himself to Mazza and Spal. Viani insisted. He outlined how young Fabio would be joining one of the biggest clubs in the world, how in a few years he'd be playing for the European champions. But Guerrino would not budge. His word was more important.

'So? Do something, tell Mazza that, on the day he came to see you, you were confused . . . or that you were drunk,' Viani said. 'The papers have yet to be filed – make something up and you can get out of it.'

'I gave him my word.' Guerrino held firm. Milan might have been able to offer more, both in terms of Fabio's future as well as a transfer fee for Pieris. But he was old school. A handshake was his bond.

We can only wonder what might have happened if Capello had landed at Milan in 1962, as a youngster, rather than in 1976, as a veteran on his way down. He may still have turned into a great footballer and an even greater manager. But a number of people in his life – from his wife, Laura, to his best friend in football, Edy Reja – probably would not have been a part of it.

Capello arrived in Ferrara that autumn and, on one of his very first days, he wandered into the club offices and was introduced to a lanky wide-eyed kid, roughly his own age. 'You guys are from the same neck of the woods, I'm sure you'll get along fine,' they were told.

The boy was Reja. He was some eight months older than Capello and he too had just arrived. He hailed from Gorizia, a few miles up the road from Pieris and was of Slovenian descent. Both were midfielders and, together, they would form the heart of Spal's youth team in the 1962–63 season.

They also became inseparable off the pitch. That first year they boarded together in a room above the club offices. 'And then, for three years, we moved in with Teresa and Amelia,' Reja recalls. It may have been the 1960s, but this was not a case of two young bucks sharing some free-love pad with their girlfriends. Teresa and Amelia were, in fact, elderly spinsters who took in boarders to make some extra cash.

Reja and Capello shared a room and their days followed a familiar routine. Reja would go to school in the morning, they would meet for training and then Capello would go to school in the afternoon. They would get together for dinner around eight o'clock. And then their paths would diverge.

'I would stay up and watch television with the spinsters, he would go to bed,' says Reja. 'Most nights, by nine, nine thirty at the latest, he'd be asleep. He was single-minded that way.'

The spinsters treated them as if they were the sons they never had. And they were territorial too. 'One of them liked me, the other one preferred Fabio,' says Reja. 'Sometimes we'd lie in bed and listen to them bicker over which one of us was the finer, more upstanding young man.'

Even then, Capello was obsessively tidy and organized. He put all his energy into school and football.

'There was an obvious focus about him,' says Reja. 'He was very competitive, always pushing himself. And he always wanted to win. It was like that on the pitch, but also in whatever he did. Whether we played tennis or went swimming, it always turned into a competition.

'I have to say, if he became what he is today, it's because he always had that attitude. I can't say I was quite as obsessive. And maybe that's part of the reason why he did so well.'

Reja, who enjoyed a long career in Serie A and Serie B and went on to become a successful manager, most recently at Napoli, was no slouch himself. It's just that it was difficult for anyone to match Capello's drive.

That second season, 1963–64, was to be a big one for Capello. Not only did he make his first-team debut, but he met the love of his life. It was storybook stuff. Capello would ride a city bus to school and one day he spotted Laura. One thing led to another. And now, forty-five years later, they're still together.

The two friends would both marry in 1969, within a few weeks of each other. But, at the time, Capello was preoccupied with turning his brief encounters on the bus into a proper courtship. He soon discovered the perfect ruse to see as much of Laura as possible. He volunteered to take the daughter of his youth-team coach, Giovanbattista Fabbri, to and from school. And he often went to Fabbri's home for dinner. Given that Laura lived just around the corner, the arrangement worked very well.

'He'd come to see me, we'd have dinner and then he'd leave, but I knew he was going to see Laura,' says Fabbri. 'I didn't mind. It was all very innocent, those were different times. And besides, given the effort he put into his schoolwork and his football, there was nothing to worry about.'

Capello and Laura would often double-date with Reja and his girlfriend, Livia. 'I owe Fabio a lot,' says Reja. 'Because Laura and the woman who would become my wife, Livia, were close friends and remain close to this day. Although, initially, Fabio had an easier time than me. Before I got to know her, I would always see Livia with this other guy and so I assumed she had a boyfriend. And so I kept my distance. It was only later that I discovered that the guy she was always with was actually her twin brother.'

The two couples spent a lot of time together and would regularly summer in Grado, on the coast, not far from Pieris. They would borrow Guerrino's little boat and spend days out on the lagoon, fishing and snorkelling.

'It seems silly today, when I look back it was just an ordinary little boat with an outboard motor, nothing special,' recalls Reja. 'And it's not as if we did anything amazing. But to us, it seemed wonderful. Out there, on the water, in a boat . . . those were some of the happiest times of my life.'

These days, they obviously don't see as much of each other, though the wives speak often. But, whenever they can, they go back to Grado and eat at Nico, the seafood restaurant they've been patronizing for nearly half a century. It's one of the few times Capello allows himself to become sentimental.

Imagining Capello as a teenager is not easy to do. Those who knew him at the time say that, beneath the workaholism and competitiveness, there was a fun streak. 'He was intoxicated with football,' says Fabbri. 'I can't count the times he'd be over for dinner and we'd end up taking the ball out and playing right there in my front room. I loved it, though my wife didn't always appreciate it.'

But Fabbri wasn't just an excuse to see Laura. He genuinely has a special bond with him. When I interviewed Capello in October 2007, he said that Fabbri, along with Helenio Herrera, who worked with him at Roma, was the manager who influenced him the most. To this day, Fabbri keeps two stuffed pheasants in his house, a gift from the young Capello: 'He was sixteen or seventeen when he shot them.' Hunting was a passion Capello shared with Guerrino. Whenever he went home, father and son would set off, guns in hand. Anything they shot would either get stuffed or eaten. Nothing went to waste.

'After going home to see his family, he'd often return with a bag full of little birds that he had shot and he'd bring it to our house,' says Fabbri. 'My wife would cook them up with some red wine and some polenta.'

Fabbri also seemed to bring out the fun-loving side of Capello, the one few – apart from his closest friends – ever saw. Fabbri surprised him one day with a special training routine, aimed partly at improving his technique, partly at helping him loosen up.

'It worked like this,' says Fabbri. 'I'd put him on a bicycle and have him pedal towards the goal. Then I'd send over a cross and he'd have to head it in, without falling off the bike. Then, we'd switch over. I'd be on the bike and he had to put in a cross accurate enough to reach me, wherever I decided to cycle.'

On the pitch, Capello was making strides as well. The transition from Pieris to Fabbri's youth team was a bit bumpy to begin with. Mazza came down to watch some of his early training sessions and, after a particularly poor outing, was distinctly unimpressed.

'I'm thinking I might have made a mistake,' he told Fabbri. 'They say people from Friuli are tough and resilient. This guy looks like he's made of ricotta.' The 'Diviner' seemed to be doubting his own judgement. But Fabbri was having none of it.

'Trust me, this kid is going to make it,' he said. 'You'll see . . .'

Whatever else one might think of Capello, whether you like him or hate him, it's safe to say that it was probably the last time anyone compared him to ricotta cheese: 'soft', 'creamy' and 'somewhat flavourless' are not adjectives you would associate with him. In any case, Fabbri decided to prove his point. He invited Mazza along to watch the youth side's next game. And, just for that one match, he played Capello out of position. Rather than his usual central midfield role, he was deployed as a holding midfielder, with strict instructions to take the opposing number ten out of the game. He fulfilled the task with gusto, supplying crunching tackles and turning in one of the most physical performances of his career. Mazza was duly impressed. Fabbri gloated.

What was he like as a player? He sat in front of the back four, dictating play and imposing himself on the midfield. He had an uncanny ability to read the play and pick out passes. He was two-footed, strong in the air and in the tackle. His only obvious weakness was a lack of pace. I've asked dozens of former teammates to compare him to present-day players and they've come up with a wide-ranging selection of names: Massimo Ambrosini, Esteban Cambiasso, Patrick Vieira, Michael Carrick, Pep Guardiola, Demetrio Albertini . . . plus a half-dozen others, including Daniele De Rossi, my personal choice. What stood out about the young Capello though was his personality.

'From day one he told his teammates what to do, how to move, where to go . . . it's a cliché, but, even as a kid, he was a manager on the pitch,' says Fabbri. 'He had ability, but he also had a confidence and a poise you rarely see. And he wasn't afraid to make himself heard. He'd often tell me, his boss, what to do. Always politely, of course, but firmly.'

He spent two seasons in the youth team. In his second, they won the Italian youth championship. The senior side, however, were doing poorly and so, that spring, Fabbri was promoted to the first team. With Spal sliding towards relegation, he called up some of his youngsters, including Capello, who made his debut on 29 March 1964, a 3–1 loss to Sampdoria. They went down that season, with Capello making four appearances. But the following year they came straight back up and the young midfielder from Pieris began getting more and more time in the side.

The veterans had mixed feelings about Capello's rise. On the one hand, he was clearly a gifted player who could contribute to the team. On the other, he was seen as Mazza's 'pet' and some were jealous. Particularly because, for all his ability and intelligence, he had a major flaw . . .

'Back then, there were no substitutions,' says Gianfranco Bozzao, a defender in Capello's Spal. 'And, early on, Fabio simply lacked stamina. Or maybe he didn't know quite how to pace himself. But what would happen is that he would play twenty minutes all-out and then his energy would wane. And we pretty much had to "carry" him the rest of the way. We didn't mind, he was worth it.'

One of the players 'carrying' Capello was none other than Edy Reja. His workrate had won him a space in the side and, in 1965–66, their first year back in the top flight, Spal were counting on their teenaged midfield to help them stay up.

'Fabio was tough and committed, but, at the time, he had some limits in terms of endurance,' Reja said in a 2003 newspaper interview. 'He was even booed sometimes by our own fans, despite being the resident starlet. And so we all worked hard for him. One thing I always could do was run all day. I didn't mind sacrificing myself for him. It allowed him to take a breather occasionally. We understood this, we had to protect him because he was too important to us. Our whole side revolved around him.'

The club felt Capello needed to fill out and grow physically stronger. But they weren't about to lock him in a gym for six months. Back then, if you were good enough, you played. And others would have to adjust. Reja and Capello were even called up to the Italian Under 23 side, as mere nineteen-year-olds, such was the regard in which they were held. And Capello, even at that tender age, was named Spal's penalty-taker. Confidence was never his problem.

That year, Spal alternated moments of brilliance with drops in form, as you would expect from a very young side. On 12 September 1965, they produced their first shock of the season, winning 2–0 away to Roma at the

Stadio Olimpico. It was something of a coming-of-age party for both Capello and Reja. 'We dominated them and both of us played very well,' Reja recalled in 2003. 'We beat Roma at home as well that year [2–1]. We knew we had impressed them. It was clear, especially for Fabio, that he would be getting offers from bigger clubs.'

Spal managed to stay up on the last day of the season. They came back from two goals down at Brescia to draw 2–2, thus avoiding a relegation playoff against Sampdoria. It was a triumph for a young team put together on a shoe-string budget.

The following year was not so fortunate for Capello. He suffered a bad injury to his left knee, one which would never fully go away and would dog him for the rest of his career. Sports medicine back then was rudimentary, both in terms of diagnosis and treatment. As far as specific rehab work was concerned, forget about it: you hurt your knee, the doctor would fix it and you'd be out on the pitch again. Capello ended up making just sixteen appearances. And without him pulling the strings, Spal looked lost and slid down the table.

Then Roma came calling. Capello was moving to the big time: a metropolis of three million, an 80,000 seat stadium, fans who demanded ownership of their stars, a media that introduced itself into every sinew of a player's life. Things were about to change radically.

For Capello, it spelled the end of a key chapter in his life. In those five years in Ferrara, he had grown to become a man. He had discovered that he was, in fact, good enough to make a living playing professional football and that he could do it at the highest level. He had left his family and, especially, his father. He had forged two of the most influential relationships in his life: Reja, who would become one of his very closest friends, and Laura, with whom he would share the rest of his life and start a family.

His reference points in life were shifting. Guerrino had always been the hub of his life and would continue to be there. They would continue to write long letters to each other, twice a week, with unfailing regularity. But, as inevitably happens when we grow up and strike out on our own, he would now be sharing that role as mentor. Throughout, he followed his son closely – coming down to watch him train as a player and then, later, watching him lead training sessions when he worked with the kids at Milan, right up until his death in 1982 – but always from a distance, at least when it came to the professional sphere.

'Signor Guerrino was a great man,' Reja told me. It was curious but telling how he addressed his best friend's father, a man he had known for twenty years, with the more formal 'Signor'. 'Just being in his company was stimulating. I remember when he came to visit, he was always somewhat detached, respectful of our space and what we did. He played a big role in our lives, especially Fabio's of course, but he was never invasive, he was never one of those fathers who could not let go.'

I have no idea whether Guerrino was familiar with the work of Khalil Gibran, or whether he even read poetry. But I like to think he would have appreciated the following lines from Gibran's 'On Children':

You are the bows from which your children
As living arrows are sent forth.
The archer sees the mark upon the path of the infinite,
And He bends you with His might
That His arrows may go swift and far.
Let our bending in the archer's hand be for gladness;
For even as He loves the arrow that flies,
So He loves also the bow that is stable.

And then there was Laura. Those who know the couple well – that rare inner circle – say you cannot overestimate the impact of Laura on Capello's life. It's not just the usual cliché about the 'great woman behind the great man'. What many forget is that Capello went through some very difficult times, particularly as a player. Laura centred him, focused him, settled him.

In writing this book, as I've said, I made it a point to be respectful of Capello's private life. I did not try to speak to his octogenarian mother, I did not track down his boyhood friends or delve too far into his family. I wanted to keep it in the professional sphere. But Laura's contribution ought not to be overlooked. To this day, even when he is away from home, they speak four or five times a day. The relationship between a man and his life partner ought to remain private. That said, if you want to begin to understand Capello, you have to be at least aware of Laura and the relationship which began to bloom way back in the mid-1960s.

His life was changing for the better and so too was the larger world around him. After suffering through the aftermath of the Second World War, Italy was back on its feet.

The economy was booming, there was a new optimism. The legacy of the war was still fresh on everyone's mind, the memory of the folly that had been the latter years of Mussolini's regime was very real. But there was also a desire to look ahead. For those years, right up to 1967, life was largely good. The country was growing and there was a certain innocence. When Reja, earlier in this chapter, talked about his summers with Capello, out fishing in Guerrino's boat, and how it seemed like the most extraordinary and wonderful thing in the world, he's not just talking about some Huckleberry Finn/Tom Sawyer childhood memory. He's reflecting the mood of an entire nation. An innocent nation, one which had yet to confront itself with what was to come: terrorism, drugs, the escalation of the Cold War. But also women's liberation, changing social attitudes (divorce only became legal in Italy in 1970), rock and roll, the counterculture.

When Capello left to join Roma in 1967, it wasn't just his world that was changing. The wider world was as well. For ever.

CHAPTER 3

The Eternal City

When Capello arrived at Roma in 1967, he found a club which had been punching well below its weight. But then, that was nothing new. They were the biggest club in Italy's capital, they had a fiercely passionate support and yet they had won just one league title in their history (and that came during the war, when there really wasn't much to celebrate). Think Newcastle United – if Newcastle had been in the top flight for all but one year of their history and if Newcastle had a catchment area that was ten times greater.

Apart from that one *scudetto*, Roma's trophy room was bare, save for the odd Coppa Italia and the Inter-Cities Fairs Cup, the precursor to the UEFA Cup (which, curiously, Newcastle also won). The fans did not take underachievement well. Some blamed some kind of grand conspiracy on the part of the wealthy Northern clubs. Others suffered in silence, knowing that next season would, most likely, bring more heartache. Still others vented their legitimate anger at the club, blaming mismanagement for their regular humiliation.

They had been relegated once before, in 1951, but the true low point came perhaps during the 1964–65 season, three years before Capello's arrival. Everyone knew the club was heavily in debt, but few could have imagined the scale of the problem. After training one January afternoon, manager Juan Carlos Lorenzo decided he couldn't take it any more. He announced that the club was broke, that there was no money to pay players and that there probably wasn't any money to travel to the next fixture, away to Vicenza. The supporters were angry, but, typically, sprang into action. They organized a fundraising event at the Sistine Theatre in Rome and invited Giacomo Losi, the club's captain and longest serving player. Several old-time Roma fans told me that the sight of Losi, the hometown hero, wandering through the theatre aisles, bucket in hand, collecting donations as he fought back tears was one of the most humiliating sights in the club's history. At the same time, it encapsulated Roma and its supporters.

With the help of a new president, Franco Evangelisti, Roma avoided bankruptcy and returned to respectability. By the time Capello signed for the club in 1967, enthusiasm was mounting. In addition to the future England manager, they signed Franco Cordova, an elegant midfielder, Giuliano Taccola, a promising and popular centre-forward, and, above all, Jair, the Brazilian winger who had already won two European Cups with Internazionale. Quick and unpredictable, Jair had been part of Brazil's 1962 World Cup winning squad and probably would have played a major role alongside Pelé, if he hadn't had the misfortune of being kept out of the side by a certain Garrincha.

The season began on a high. After eight matches, Roma were unbeaten and in first place. Capello had played his part, most notably scoring the only goal in a stunning 1–0 victory over Juventus. (Throughout his career, he had a knack for doing well against his previous or, in this case, future clubs.) But then he injured his left knee again, the same one he had hurt at Spal. Opinions vary, but it's more than likely that the original injury had never properly healed. The club sent him to Paris for two weeks of treatment with a then famous – if unorthodox – doctor, who had treated everyone from the French rugby team to prima ballerinas. He would concoct mysterious foul-smelling ointments made of herbs, chemicals and goodness knows what else, and patients had to apply them for up to eighteen hours a day. One day, Capello ended up in a famous Paris nightspot with an ointment-filled bandage on his knee. The smell was so foul that several patrons demanded he leave immediately.

In any case, it may have been a coincidence, but without Capello Roma went into free-fall and tumbled down the table. They finished in tenth place, just five points from relegation in the sixteen-team Serie A. Manager Oronzo Pugliese, who had been mercilessly booed by supporters following a 6–2 home defeat to Inter, was sacked. To replace him, Evangelisti, the club president, made the boldest of moves. He turned to Helenio Herrera, the wizard, the man who had turned Inter into a world-wide force in winning two European Cups. Herrera did not come cheap: his £150,000 a year contract made him easily the highest paid manager in the world at the time. But he was already one of the greatest managers in the history of the game. And, from Capello's point of view, he would prove to be a tremendous influence.

Herrera was unique, one of the most colourful figures football has ever seen. His father was a well-known radical Spanish anarchist who was forced to flee to Argentina at the turn of the century. Herrera was born in Buenos Aires, but, at the age of four, his parents emigrated to Morocco, where his father continued his political activities, attempting to organize anarchist work collectives, much to the amusement of the French colonial authorities. Herrera grew up in poverty in Casablanca, but developed into a decent footballer, eventually moving to Paris and winning a handful of caps for France as a defender. He turned to management immediately after retirement, leading – among others – the Spanish clubs Atlético Madrid, Deportivo La Coruña, Sevilla and Barcelona, and Belenenses of Portugal.

Herrera came to Inter in 1960 and his unorthodox methods immediately made a splash. It wasn't just his strict discipline and his mania for controlling the private lives of his players (he would send minions to do 'bed-checks' in their homes during the week) which set him apart. He had favourite slogans (such as Class + Preparation + Intelligence + Athleticism = Championships) which he would plaster on billboards around Inter's training ground and make the players chant repeatedly, mantra-like during sessions. Most of all, he pioneered the infamous *ritiro*, or pre-match retreat. For a Sunday game, he would get the squad together on a Thursday and lock them up in a remote country hotel, away from temptation.

This manager, this quirky cosmopolitan product of six nations in three continents, became a key figure in Capello's development. 'Herrera taught me to never fear an opponent,' Capello told me, in October 2007, 'to channel my determination in the right way. And, most importantly, he showed me that, if you could find confidence inside you, you always stood a chance to win.'

Let's see . . . if you buy into the stereotyped image of Capello, the parallels between him and Herrera become obvious. Both defensive-orientated specialists, un-compromising, single-minded, strict disciplinarians – they do, in some ways, seem cut from the same cloth. But, in fact, as you'll find out reading this book, there's a lot more to Capello than that. And there is more to Herrera than the capsule definition as the man who turned *catenaccio* into a household word. One basic difference, for example, is that, unlike Capello, Herrera was very close to his players, demanding their undivided attention before, during and after training sessions. He was very physical, with the habit of touching their chests, one by one, as they filed on the pitch. It was his way of telling them that 'heart' mattered. By contrast, Capello was – and is – far more aloof.

In Herrera's first season, Capello, finally fit, was a fixture in midfield, chipping in with six goals. One of them came against Juventus, on 16 February 1969, as Roma snatched a 2–2 draw away to the defending Serie A champions. Once again, Capello had scored against a former or future club: 'Yes, it happened throughout his career,' says Luciano Spinosi, a defender in that Roma side. 'I don't know why, but it's uncanny. Then again, Fabio rarely got the big matches wrong.'

The season, however, was scarred by an unexpected and senseless tragedy. On 15 March Roma were in Sardinia, where they were set to face Cagliari the next day. That night, Taccola, the rangy centre-forward who had arrived the year before, told the team doctor that he had a bad headache and a high fever. Despite having trained normally the previous day, Herrera kept him out of the lineup. After the match, a scoreless draw, the doctor proceeded to give Taccola a painkilling injection in the dressing room. Within seconds Taccola collapsed, just steps away from Capello. The doctor frantically tried to revive him, an ambulance was called and, by the time it arrived, he had slipped into a coma. That night, he passed away. The causes of his death remain shrouded in mystery; Taccola had suffered from high fevers and headaches for most of the season and, in some quarters, it was suggested that, had the medical staff acted sooner, none of this would have happened.

Unsurprisingly, Taccola's death had a variety of knock-on effects and not just because Roma had lost their top scorer. The aftermath soured the relationship between Herrera and Alvaro Marchini, who had replaced Evangelisti as president a few months earlier. Marchini, a proud Communist who had fought with the partisans against the Germans during the war, had said that Herrera's massive contract was 'immoral' and 'scandalous' and attempted to have it rescinded.

Herrera, never one to shy away from a fight, fired back with equal venom and the two reached an uneasy truce, probably because the side were doing well. But Taccola's death infuriated and pained Marchini. In his version of events, when he heard the news of his young centre-forward's collapse, he immediately rang Cagliari's Sant'Elia stadium and asked to speak to Herrera to find out about Taccola's condition.

According to Marchini, Herrera simply confirmed that Taccola was in a coma and then insisted on discussing the game itself and how the team would replace the player. To Marchini, Herrera's behaviour went beyond the single-mindedness of a manager worried about his side; it spilled over into gross insensitivity and 'lack of humanity'. A young man had just died and Herrera wanted to talk about football. As for Capello, at twenty-one, he had seen death up close, just like his father before him during the war. It was not something you easily forgot.

After the trauma and the shock of what happened, Roma recorded just two league wins the rest of the season and finished in eighth place. However, things went much better in the Coppa Italia. They cruised through the competition and qualified for the final group stage which saw them pitted against Cagliari, Foggia and Torino. As tournaments went, it was a bit anticlimactic. The vagaries of Italian scheduling meant that it was played in June, dragging the season out needlessly. By the time Roma travelled to Foggia in the final group game, it was 29 June, a full six weeks after the end of the Serie A season. What's more, they had virtually already won the competition. Roma were on seven points, with a goal difference of +4. Foggia were on five points, with a goal difference of –2. This meant that, to not win the Cup, they would have had to lose by a three-goal margin against a Serie B side. With Herrera in charge, that was never going to happen. Roma hit on the break and came away with a 3–1 victory.

'Most of us had never won anything, so we had a massive celebration in the dressing room and under the showers, where we had a massive group hug,' says Luciano Spinosi. 'Capello celebrated as well, in his own way. He was like that even then, he never got carried away. It was his first piece of silverware as a professional, but he was probably already thinking of what was to come next.'

Spinosi and Capello grew close that year. Reja remained his dearest friend – for a while it looked as if he too would join Roma, though it never came to pass – but Capello got on well with Spinosi. So much so that, when he and Laura married that very summer, he asked him to be a witness.

By all accounts, those were happy times for Capello off the pitch, perhaps the happiest as a player. He and Laura, who joined him in Rome as soon as they were married, made a home for themselves in the Balduina neighbourhood, on the north-western outskirts of Rome. The Balduina, on the slope of Monte Mario, is Rome's highest point, and, from there, the city spills out in all its beauty.

While its history goes way back – Dante Alighieri made reference to Monte Mario in Canto XIV in the 'Paradiso' of his *Divine Comedy* – until the early twentieth century it was largely undeveloped. The housing boom took off after the war, as Rome's population escalated. Roma's former president, Count Francesco Marini-Dettina, had been one of the early real estate developers and many Roma players, including Capello, ended up living in one of his properties.

It's worth taking a step back to note just how 'normal' a

footballer's life was back then. It wasn't uncommon for employers – whether they be factories or banks or government institutions – to provide housing for their employees. And a lot of it was built in the Balduina, which was ripe for development in the 1950s. In that sense, Capello and the other Roma players were not that different from the supporters who cheered them on in the stands, right down to the fact that most of them took the bus to work (well, training).

The following season, 1969–70, began under a cloud. Herrera, the autocratic, highly paid manager, and Marchini, the Communist president, remained at loggerheads. The players were caught in the middle. At twenty-three Capello wasn't going to take sides either way, but it was clear that, professionally, he owed a lot to Herrera.

'Herrera believed in me, despite the injuries which had dogged me prior to his arrival,' he said in a later interview. 'He taught me a lot about many things and, tactically, I really improved under his tutelage. I think he is the greatest foreign manager Italy ever had. He influenced so many people and took our game as a nation to a different level.'

Increasingly, Capello was taking Roma by the hand and growing as a leader. He was very much Herrera's man on the pitch, the guy who would execute the manager's wishes. One match stands out in the mind of Giovanni Battista Monti, who for three decades would serve as Milan's team doctor and develop a close relationship with Capello. It was 16 October 1969, Roma were visitors at the San Siro.

'We were the reigning European Champions and they came here and beat us 3–2,' he recalled. 'Peiró [Roma's Spanish striker] scored two, Capello the other. But what I remember most was that they taught us a lesson in football. Capello was simply perfect that day, dominating the pitch.'

Once again, Capello was scoring against past or future teams. What made the pill somewhat harder to swallow for Milan was that everyone knew that, seven years before, on the day of Viani's famous visit to Pieris, they had come tantalizingly close to signing him.

'His technique was exceptional, he was a gifted passer who could put the ball anywhere he liked,' says his teammate Fausto Landini. 'I think he had a natural sense for the rhythm of a game. Coupled with his strong personality, it made him a natural leader. He always wanted to win and, if he had something to say, he said it, during or after the game. Sometimes it could get unpleasant, but most of us knew that he was simply trying to get the best out of us.'

Occasionally, it would spill over. Spinosi remembers another match which left Capello raging at everyone after the final whistle. Roma were hosting Sampdoria at the Stadio Olimpico. They battered them from the first minute, with Spinosi opening the scoring, followed by Capello and Braglia. Then, an hour or so into the game, Roma fell apart. Samp roared back, scoring twice and grabbing the equalizer with four minutes to go.

'I was just glad the game was over,' recalls Spinosi. 'We played so well for so long and then it all went wrong. If we had played just two more minutes, I'm convinced they would have scored again. Momentum had shifted entirely.

Fabio's reaction was different. I too was angry, but also relieved that we had got a point. He was absolutely furious, he was ranting at all his teammates both as we walked off the pitch and all through our time in the dressing room. Like I said, he hated to lose.'

Roma's form continued to be erratic in the league, brilliant one week, unwatchable the next. After a 2–0 loss at Sampdoria in March, Marchini finally pulled the plug on Herrera. The personal acrimony between the two had, of course, been significant. But now, the lack of forward progress in the league gave him the perfect excuse. Luciano Tessari came in on an interim basis.

Yet for many, there was still a lot to look forward to. Roma had done well in the Cup Winners' Cup, reaching the semi-final against Poland's Gornik Zabrze. The first leg, played on April Fools' Day at the Stadio Olimpico, finished 1–1. Capello put Roma ahead in the return leg, poking in the rebound after his own penalty was saved. Gornik stormed back to equalize, taking the game into extra-time. Wladimir Lubanski netted for the Poles to give them the lead, before Francesco Scaratti, a hard-nosed fullback, smacked a late, late goal into the Gornik net. It finished 2–2. These days, with a score like that, Roma would have qualified on the away-goals rule. But, back then, away goals in extra-time did not count double. The tie would be heading to a replay in a neutral venue.

Roma's players knew this, which is why they were somewhat muted at the final whistle. Nando Martellini, the man doing commentary for Italian television, did not. He assumed that Roma had qualified on the away-goals rule and proudly announced that they were in the Cup-Winners' Cup final, before signing off. Hundreds of thousands of Roma fans, believing Martellini was correct, spilled out on to the streets to celebrate. Those were the days when – much more than now – if the man on television said something, it had to be true. And so Roma fans awoke the next morning not only facing the uncertainty of a replay, but also with the humiliation of having celebrated the night away for no good reason.

UEFA had determined that the deciding match be played in Strasbourg. Gornik took the lead, Capello – who else? – equalized from the spot, calmly side-footing it past the keeper. The match stayed deadlocked at 1–1 even after extra-time. After 330 minutes of football had been played, neither side had the supremacy.

UEFA's solution to those situations probably seems absurd nowadays: a coin toss. But, corny as it sounds, those were different times. Winning was important, but there was little at stake, apart from prestige and satisfaction. Compared to today, people were perhaps a bit more accepting about things outside of their control. There was a slightly greater fatalism, a greater sense that if it was not meant to be, it was not meant to be.

Thanks to YouTube, anyone can see what happened to this day. The pictures are grainy and black-and-white, but the silliness of the occasion is evident. The cameras show a large crowd of people gathered around someone, presumably the referee. There are players, coaching staff, police, hangers-on, a fetching woman in a miniskirt. You can clearly see the coin rise up into the air, dozens of heads following its flight, and landing on the pitch. Then, seconds later, the Gornik players erupt in celebration, as if they had just won the World Cup.

Roma and their fans were gutted. It had turned into a season to forget. But the worst was yet to come. Marchini, already unpopular after his row with Herrera, felt he needed to balance the books. Out of the blue, he sold Capello, Spinosi and Landini, three of Roma's rising stars, to Juventus. It was the footballing equivalent of raising the white flag.

Roma supporters had had enough. Marchini was threatened and had to obtain police protection. Flags and season tickets were tossed on to bonfires outside the Stadio Olimpico. There were marches and demonstrations. It was 1970, after all, and in those days people loved a mass protest. But it was to no avail. The deal was done. Capello was touched by the outpouring of sympathy, if a little disturbed at the vehemence of the reaction. He had come to love Rome, his first son Pierfilippo was born there, his family were settled. 'I implored the club not to sell me,' he would say in a later interview. 'But the club needed the cash. I was very sad to leave.'

However depressed he might have been, he knew that Juventus – then, as now – were almost impossible to turn down. He had turned twenty-four at the end of the season. He had to accept that the time was right to go to the next level.

CHAPTER 4

Juventus, Team of the Seventies

Turin and Juventus were a world apart from what Capello had experienced before. The northern city has a regal, reserved air about it, as befits Italy's former capital. In a country which has often been divided and ruled by foreign powers, the Piedmont region – except for a spell under Napoleonic rule – managed to remain largely independent.

This was an aristocratic city and he had landed at the most aristocratic of clubs. Juventus, known as the *Vecchia Signora* or 'Old Lady', was Italy's most popular and successful team. Which, in some ways, was somewhat curious since, at the time, Italy was undergoing an anti-Establishment backlash. And yet Juventus were very much the Establishment. They were owned by the Agnelli family who, in turn, own FIAT, the car manufacturer, Italy's largest employer, as well as *La Stampa*, which, at the time, was the country's second most read newspaper. (Again, full disclosure: I am a regular contributor to *La Stampa*.) They also had strong interests in property, banking and insurance.

It was something of a cradle-to-grave situation. You lived in a house owned (or built) by the Agnellis. You went to work in the Agnellis' factory. You read the Agnellis' newspaper. You banked at the Agnellis' bank. You drove cars manufactured by the Agnellis' company. When you died or fell ill or your house was burgled, the Agnellis' insurance company would step in. And, of course, in your spare time, you supported the Agnellis' football team.

At least, that was the cliché. In fact, it was more complex than that. Many locals, perhaps not wanting to live in an Agnelli World, chose to support Torino, Juventus' cross-town rivals. It was one area of their life which they could control. More importantly – and, perhaps, amazingly, for a club with such strong local ties – Juventus' fan base stretched up and down Italy. Poll just about any city in Italy (with the possible exception of Milan and Rome, each of which is home to two big clubs) and you'll find that Juve are either the best or second-best supported team (usually after the local side).

Romy Gai, Juve's former commercial director, put it best. A few years ago, he told me: 'In 1897, when a group of students from Turin founded the club, they could have called it Torino, but they chose a totally nongeographic word, Juventus. Though they probably didn't realize it at the time, it was a brilliant marketing choice. It disengaged the club from territorial issues. In a world where many are so proud of their roots, you could freely support Juventus without supporting Turin, which might be a rival to your own city.'

Gone was the localism of Rome, a city intensely pre-occupied with itself (not that you can fault them for it; it is, after all, the Eternal City). In its place was a club which thought and acted on a national, if not global scale. A club which thought of itself as a class apart. And, in many ways, they were.

Capello arrived at Juventus just as the side was undergoing a youth movement. The previous season they had finished third, but the choice was made to go in a different direction and freshen up the squad. Juve brought in some of Italy's best and brightest. Capello, twenty-four, defender Luciano Spinosi, twenty, and striker Fausto Landini, nineteen, arrived from Roma. Twenty-year-old forward Roberto Bettega returned from his loan spell at Varese, while winger Franco Causio, twenty-one, was acquired from Palermo. All but Landini would go on to become Italian internationals, amassing more than 150 caps and 33 goals between them.

They went with youth on the managerial front as well, handing the job to Armando Picchi who, at thirty-five, became the youngest Juve manager in history, a record he holds to this day. He had hung up his boots just a year earlier, but was already considered some kind of prodigy, partly due to the career he had enjoyed as a player. He had been the captain of Helenio Herrera's legendary Inter side, winners of two European Cups and, in Herrera's *catenaccio* system, had redefined the position of *libero*, or sweeper.

The experience of working under Herrera was something Picchi and Capello had in common, though it wasn't always a smooth ride. Their relationship was rocky at times and they clashed on more than one occasion. Part of the problem may have been that Capello had been used to

Herrera, an older, highly successful manager who was already a legend in his own time. Picchi, on the other hand, was just eleven years his senior: indeed, Capello had even played against him a few years earlier.

'Did they get along?' says Spinosi. 'Well, let's just say they both had very strong personalities. But Picchi was, ultimately, in charge. He knew what he was doing. He knew when to listen to Fabio, when to let him get his way and when to crack the whip.'

Complicating matters in those first few months was the fact that Capello clearly missed Rome and Roma. For a man who loves to travel and has seamlessly adapted to a variety of environments, it seems incredible that he felt homesick for a city which wasn't his own and in which he had spent just three years. As Capello admitted years later in a newspaper interview, in his first few months he was often sad and sulky. Picchi had made him a regular, but his performances on the pitch were somewhat erratic, to the point that, one day, Gianni Agnelli, the club's owner, said: 'This Capello, he's not bad, but he's always so grumpy and sad. He's obviously thinking of Rome all the time.'

Picchi's young side started slowly, as could be expected. In early January 1971 they were stuck in eighth place, though Capello's performances had begun to improve. But then, tragedy struck.

For most of the season, Picchi had been making the daily three-hour round trip to Milan to tend to his wife Francesca, who was gravely ill. The strain began to show and Picchi started to complain about fatigue and back pain, both of which got progressively worse. So much so that when Juventus travelled to Bologna by train on

6 February 1971, Picchi spent the entire trip lying down on the floor of the carriage. The image of Picchi struggling, fighting against an internal – and as yet unexplained – malaise was seared in Capello's mind.

The following day, Juventus were defeated 1–0 in a heated match which saw Causio sent off. Picchi, normally so calm and controlled, completely lost his cool. He remonstrated with the referee during the match and was eventually given his marching orders. He made things worse by initially refusing to leave the pitch. And, when he did, he came back out to abuse the official.

His behaviour was shocking precisely because it was so out of character. But what almost nobody knew was that, by this stage, the disease had taken control of his body. The searing pain, coupled with the stress and worry over his wife and exhaustion from weeks of sleepless nights, had driven him to breaking point.

The following Wednesday would be a very eventful day. Picchi took charge of what would be his final training session, not least because the Italian FA took a very hard line towards his behaviour in Bologna. He was slapped with a two-month ban, which, frankly, seems outrageous today, when managers regularly get away with far worse. The seriousness of his condition was, of course, no mitigating factor: the FA were not aware of his state. That very same evening he deteriorated further and spent the night in hospital.

On Thursday, Picchi, looking 'tense' and 'unhappy' (according to a report in *La Stampa*), watched Juventus train from a distance. He told reporters that he felt 'much better' physically and that he felt very sorry about his long ban. Witnesses at the time say he looked ill and worn out. In any event, he spent another night in hospital. That same day, Capello, who knew that Picchi had been unwell but clearly had no idea of the scope of his illness, criticized his manager and teammates in an interview with *Corriere dello Sport*, a Roman newspaper. Capello admitted that he did not feel settled in Turin and that many of the players were 'selfish' and more preoccupied with themselves than the team. The criticism of Picchi was implicit but nonetheless obvious.

The next morning, Friday, Picchi was diagnosed with a rare spinal disease, possibly 'of cancerous origin', aggravated by the stress he had put on himself in looking after his wife. Juventus were stunned. The fact that, on that same day, Capello's outburst against Picchi appeared in the press only made matters worse.

Club president Giampiero Boniperti convened an emergency meeting with general manager Italo Allodi. They would need to appoint a new manager, partly because of the ban and partly because Picchi needed time to recover. And, of course, Capello would have to be disciplined. Juventus would not stand for a young player criticizing the manager, let alone when the manager in question was a beloved legend like Picchi who, on top of everything else, was laid up in hospital.

They asked Capello to explain his remarks. He simply said that it was a private conversation with a 'friend' and that he had no idea that his words would end up in the newspaper. The club did not buy his excuse and decided that he would be banished to the reserves and would not play again for Juventus that season.

That same day, Picchi dragged himself out of the hospital and went to see Boniperti. He looked pale and weak – it was as if the illness had grabbed him all of a sudden and was slowly sucking the life out of him. Nevertheless, he had one last task to accomplish as Juve boss. He pleaded Capello's case and asked Boniperti not to ban him. Capello was a young man, he said, who had made a mistake. And Picchi said he believed Capello's words – though hurtful – were motivated by genuine concern for the team and the way things were going. Boniperti was sceptical, but eventually granted Picchi his final request as manager: instead of a ban, Capello would receive a heavy fine. Later that evening, he visited Capello at the Villar Perosa training ground and had a long chat with him. Capello was touched by what Picchi had done. He had placed the good of the team above whatever resentment he may have had for Capello's public insubordination.

It may well be that on that cold February day, Capello learned a lesson which would stay with him for the rest of his life. A manager has to put the team above everything else. And, if it means occasionally putting your pride to one side, so be it. One of the themes of his management style – as we'll see later on – is never to hold grudges, never to let personal feelings, particularly bad ones, get in the way of coaching decisions. Even if it means putting up with the occasional spot of abuse from your star player.

The following morning, Cestmir Vycpalek, the club's youth team coach, was appointed Juventus manager. Everyone wished Picchi a speedy recovery. That day, Juventus defeated Verona 2–1. Capello, who would have been nowhere near the pitch if Picchi hadn't stepped in, scored the winner, nine minutes from time. The win was, naturally, dedicated to Picchi and his return. It never came to pass. On 26 May 1971, after receiving the last rites from his parish priest, he died at just thirty-six years of age.

For the rest of the campaign, the club made an executive decision. They asked the press to respect Picchi's privacy and not report on his illness. And so they did. The players knew he was unwell, but there were no updates, no progress reports and, except for one occasion, no visits. As for the fans, they only had a vague idea of what was happening. They just knew that Picchi had taken time off to recover, possibly from exhaustion. And that Vycpalek was now in charge.

Juventus clawed their way back up the table and would eventually finish fourth. But it was in Europe where they were truly making a splash. They advanced all the way to the final of the Inter-Cities Fairs Cup, knocking out Barcelona along the way (Capello got on the scoresheet in the 4–2 aggregate win). Their opponents were Don Revie's Leeds United, a side which combined technique and physicality thanks to the likes of Billy Bremner, Peter Lorimer and Johnny Giles. The Serie A season ended on 23 May and Juventus, as was the custom in those days, were immediately sequestered to a hotel in order to focus on the final five days later, away from any type of distraction. By this point, Capello's role within the side had grown. Despite being still just twenty-four he was older than many others in the side and he imposed his personality in the dressing room.

Some of his teammates at the time go so far as to say that he became like an adjunct manager, laying out tactical plans on how to defeat Leeds and, effectively, taking over from Vycpalek. The latter did not seem to mind. The Czech coach had spent the last ten years working with amateur sides. He arrived at Juve almost as an afterthought, thanks to Boniperti, who had played with him immediately after the war. Capello would later call him 'a great psychologist, who knew just what buttons to push'.

Not everyone appreciated Capello's input. After all, he was just a player, and a young one at that. And yet here he was, forty-eight hours before a European final, seizing power and trying to decide the team's tactics and formation. This was not his job. Things grew heated, tempers rose. Vycpalek sagely mediated and, slowly, most of his teammates came around to Capello's way of thinking.

Thus, on 26 May 1971 Juventus arrived at Turin's Stadio Comunale for the first leg of their final against Leeds. Almost at the same time, just a few miles away, Picchi passed away. Club officials chose not to tell the players until later. As they took to the pitch, a violent thunderstorm engulfed the ground. The rain got so bad that, early in the second half, with the game deadlocked at 0–0, the referee had no choice but to call everything off. It was as if the heavens had decreed that there was no football to be played on the day of Picchi's passing. For the second time in two years Capello was close witness to a premature and senseless death in football.

UEFA hastily arranged a replay two days later. Juventus twice took the lead, the second time thanks to Capello, but Leeds stormed back to clinch a crucial 2–2 draw. It was a surreal atmosphere, with players and supporters still in shock and mourning. Five days later, at Elland Road, Juventus and Leeds battled to a 1–1 draw and the Yorkshire club became the first side to win a European trophy thanks to the away-goals rule.

Juve made few changes that summer. It was felt that, given the trauma of Picchi's death, it was best not to upset the squad too much. Besides, the young side had shown its mettle with the European final and the fourth place finish.

Off the pitch, Capello and his young family were finally finding their niche in Turin. Laura taught in a school – yes, those were the days when WAGs didn't mainly occupy themselves with partying and shopping – and was soon expecting their second child. With so many young players in the side, there was an active if discreet nightlife among the Juventus set. A lot of it centred around a restaurant called I Due Mondi, which was better known as 'Da Ilio', after the owner's nickname. Capello participated, but only to a point. Unlike many of the players he was already married and a father and, besides, he often liked going to bed early.

Some of his teammates pointed to the fact that Capello looked and acted older. Indeed, except for the glasses and a few more wrinkles, he looks today uncannily like those photographs from the early 1970s. One former teammate told me he was not really part of the group, but was nevertheless very influential, 'like an older brother'. Another, Causio, put it like this: 'You could see immediately that he had the mentality to be a manager or a club executive. He didn't think like a player, he was very close with the coaching staff and other club officials. We got on well, even though, of course, as everyone knows, he has a certain type of personality. Still, he was very much one of our leaders.'

And, sometimes, a leader needs to be somewhat detached from those who follow him. And Capello was, though he was by no means a hermit or a recluse. As another former teammate put it: 'He spoke to everyone and listened to everyone. But there were very few guys among his teammates with whom he was close.'

One guy with whom he did spend a lot of time was Luciano Spinosi, whom he introduced to hunting. 'He dragged me along to get my licence,' Spinosi recalls. 'It became a passion of mine, just as it was his great passion. Occasionally, we were joined by Boniperti. Those were special days.'

It may seem strange that Capello, at twenty-five, would opt to spend his free time with his club president, Boniperti, a man nearly twenty years his senior. But, even then, Capello seemed to enjoy the company of the powerful and the important. And Boniperti was certainly both, at least within Juve. He wasn't just the president, he was the club's greatest ever goalscorer and had made more appearances for the *bianconeri* than anyone else. A one club man, he was the homegrown element in what came to be known as Juve's 'Magic Trio' in the late 1950s, when he lined up alongside the flamboyant Argentine Omar Sivori and the Welsh 'gentle giant', John Charles. One teammate likened Capello to those precocious schoolboys who skip a year and are more comfortable around teachers and adults than they are around their friends. Another said that, if you didn't know him, you could think he was 'sucking up' to those who mattered: Boniperti and other members of Juve's board.

Still, in those first two years, Spinosi was definitely one of his closer friends. Indeed, when Spinosi got married, Capello was his witness. But when they stepped on to the pitch they ceased being friends and became teammates. Or, to put it perhaps more appropriately, work colleagues.

'On the pitch he is a winner,' Spinosi says. 'That's true today and it was true back then. And he wasn't the kind of winner who felt the need to endear himself to others. He knew what he wanted and he knew how to get it and he wasn't going to let anyone stand in his way or distract him from it.'

'He was also the kind of guy who had to always be right, especially during games,' adds Spinosi. 'When I disagreed with him, he just clung more passionately to his views and grew more angry. Eventually we would tell each other to fuck off. But then, after the match, come what may, it usually ended in an embrace.'

The 1971–72 season represented Capello's definitive consecration as a top drawer central midfielder. For the first time in his career he was injury-free, missing just one game in Serie A, and that was through suspension (he was sent off on the opening day of the season). He also chipped in with a career-high nine goals in the league (including two against Roma, continuing his curious habit of scoring against his former or future clubs), as Juventus cruised to the title.

After a slow start, Juve took over first place on 5 December and stayed there the rest of the season, except for one week in April, when Torino went top. They did this despite losing Bettega, their bright young striker, just after the halfway mark. In the UEFA Cup (as the Fairs Cup was now called), their progress was halted at the quarter-final stage by Wolverhampton Wanderers, who defeated them 3–2 on aggregate. Indeed, there was an English stranglehold on the competition that year, with Tottenham Hotspur beating Wolves in the final.

Towards the end of the season, Capello finally received his call-up to the Italian national team. Many felt it was long overdue, but coach Ferruccio Valcareggi was somewhat hesitant. He had a very settled side and remained loyal to the players that had helped Italy win the European Championships in 1968 and reach the World Cup final in 1970 (losing 4–1 to the legendary Brazil side of Pelé, Rivelino and Carlos Alberto).

For Capello, the satisfaction was bittersweet. On 2 May 1972, Vycpalek's son, Cestmir Jr, had tragically died in a plane crash. Once again, the shadow of death hung over Capello and Juventus, just as it had less than a year earlier, with Picchi's passing. The reserved Vycpalek did his best not to let it affect the side. But there was no question it had left a mark on everyone.

Italy had rolled through the European Championship qualifying phase without losing a game, before facing Belgium in a two-legged quarter-final. The first leg, played in Milan, was a disappointment as the Azzurri were held to a goalless draw. Valcareggi decided to make changes for the return, calling up both Capello and Spinosi to a gifted side which featured Gigi Riva, Italy's all-time leading international scorer up front, Sandro Mazzola in the hole and the legendary Giacinto Facchetti at the back. It wasn't enough. Italy went down 2–1 in Brussels. Capello made his debut, coming on as a substitute, but it wasn't much of a consolation. The heavy favourites and defending champions were out.

Still, just over a month shy of his twenty-sixth birthday, Capello had finally cracked the national team. Unsurprisingly, he would prove very hard to dislodge, going on to start Italy's next nineteen internationals, including the 1974 World Cup.

That summer, Juventus reinforced their squad even further, raiding Napoli for their goalkeeper and striker. Dino Zoff was just thirty and was in the prime of his career. Ten years later he would become the first forty-year-old to win the World Cup, captaining Italy in Spain. José Altafini on the other hand remains one of the most colourful figures in world football. Born in São Paulo, he was the son of Italian immigrants and was the typical precocious phenomenon, with crowds lining up to see him even as a sixteen-year-old. In Brazil he was known as Mazola, a nickname given him for his physical resemblance to the legendary Valentino Mazzola, star of the great Torino side which won five straight Serie A titles in the 1940s and was snuffed out in the Superga air-crash in 1949.

Altafini was called up to the Brazilian national team for the 1958 World Cup at the tender age of nineteen and, had it not been for a certain seventeen-year-old named Edson Arantes do Nascimento (better known as Pelé), he would have been the *Seleção*'s teenage sensation. Brazil duly won the World Cup and he made the move to Italy immediately afterwards, joining AC Milan. With the *rossoneri*, he went on to win two league titles and the 1963 European Cup (in which he scored 14 goals, which is still a record), before moving to Napoli in 1965. His international career with Brazil stalled when he moved across the ocean – back then, the Brazilian FA were reluctant to call up overseas players – so, in 1961, taking advantage of his dual nationality, he opted to play for Italy. At club level, he would go on to become the third all-time leading scorer in the history of Serie A.

But, by the start of the 1972–73 season, Altafini was thirty-four and many felt his inevitable decline had begun. Vycpalek, however, still felt he could contribute. On the pitch, he carved out for himself the role of super-sub, notching nine goals, despite regularly coming on midway through the second half of matches. Off the pitch, the club felt he would be a calming influence on Capello. It was no coincidence that the two were made to room together.

The idea was that Altafini's laid-back jocularity would balance out Capello's intensity, while perhaps Capello could learn a thing or two from the old master. It worked. While they did not become close friends, they got along just fine and Altafini's influence added another weapon to Capello's arsenal. For the first time since Herrera at Roma, he was in close contact with a genuine world class superstar, a legend who had won everything there was to win at club and international level. The difference was that, unlike the driven, detail-obsessed Herrera, Altafini was more relaxed, more willing to share a joke or a prank, while remaining a serious and effective professional. And, of course, Altafini, despite being older, was Capello's peer in the sense that they were teammates.

There was more than one path to success. The burning, single-minded intensity of Herrera was one way. But there was also the Altafini way. Each has to choose his own path and Capello knew that he was closer to Herrera. Yet now he better understood the Altafini way. It was an experience that would prove invaluable to him years later as a manager, especially when dealing with some of football's freer spirits. When asked about his relationship with Capello, Altafini's words, tellingly, are measured, rather than effusive. 'There was lots of reciprocal respect between us,' he says. 'Fabio is a very intelligent man. You could tell, even then, that he wanted to go far. And he did go far. Very far.'

Juventus lived up to their billing that season, coming within a whisker of completing an incredible Treble: Serie A, Coppa Italia and European Cup. And yet they had to fight every step of the way. The domestic campaign was one of the tightest and most dramatic in history. Juventus and Milan were joint leaders at the halfway mark, with Inter and newly promoted Lazio a single point behind. Zoff proved to be the most astute of signings, keeping nine consecutive clean sheets in setting a new record.

Milan began to pull away, however, and by early April, they enjoyed a three-point lead over Lazio and five points over Juve. A week later, following a 4–1 home win over Palermo and Milan being held at home by Cagliari, the team held a players-only meeting in the dressing room to discuss the situation. They had already won the title the year before; what really mattered to many was the European Cup, where they had reached the semi-finals.

They had beaten Derby County in the first leg, but a tricky trip to the Baseball Ground lay in wait. Making up four points in the final five matches against a side like Milan seemed an impossible task, especially since Lazio were also lurking in second place. Would it not make more sense if they took their foot off the gas in Serie A and, instead, concentrated on Europe?

Remember, this was in the days before large squads and luxury travel. It would have been a legitimate choice. And one championed by a portion of the dressing room. 'We talked among ourselves and then we all decided to make a pact: come what may, we would battle on with every ounce of strength in every single game,' recalls Causio. 'Capello, of course, was with us. We were not going to give up.'

A wise decision. Including that win over Palermo, the *bianconeri* reeled off three straight victories, while Milan were dropping points, including a controversial 2–1 defeat to Lazio at the Stadio Olimpico. With three games to go, Milan's lead was down to a single point over Lazio and two over Juventus.

Juventus were away to Atalanta, while Milan travelled to face Torino and Lazio were at Bologna. Atalanta, fighting to avoid relegation, were a physical side and the game soon turned heated. Try as they might, Juventus couldn't find an opening. Then, minutes before half-time, it came thanks to a brilliant piece of lateral thinking from Altafini. As Juventus prepared to take a free kick from a wide position, the ageing Brazilian took up a position near the penalty spot. Meanwhile, Capello was being marked at the edge of the penalty area, ready to make a run. As the ball came in, Capello and his marker dashed towards the six-yard box. Altafini stepped right into the path of Capello's marker. In the inevitable collision, both were knocked to the ground but the upshot was that Capello found himself unmarked and duly buried the free header. Like a pic, or block, in basketball, one teammate had put his body on the line for the benefit of another. (Years later, playing for Chelsea, John Terry would do something similar.)

Now, Altafini was neither a bruiser nor a dirty player. At his age, he tended to avoid physical contact. But he had sacrificed himself for the team. And he had done it with creativity and imagination. Capello, celebrating his goal, made a beeline for Altafini. Another lesson learned. Creativity and flair can combine with physical prowess and courage to provide unexpected results. Winners do what it takes to win, even if it means going against their very nature as players.

Juventus went on to win 2–0, while Lazio were held to a 1–1 draw. Meanwhile, in Turin, Milan found themselves two goals down, before scraping back to a 2–2 draw with minutes to go. Some newspapers speculated that Torino, not wanting their city rivals Juve to win the title, had allowed Milan back into the game. Most Juve players took it in their stride. Had Torino really wanted to hurt them, they would have gone all the way, letting Milan win.

As it happened, all three sides won the following week, setting up a dramatic finale. Going into the last day of the season, Milan were hanging on to a one-point lead over Lazio and Juventus. The *rossoneri* were away to Verona, Lazio were away at Napoli and Juventus travelled to Roma. It was to be one of the most dramatic ninety minutes in the history of Serie A.

Verona, needing a win to be sure of avoiding relegation, raced out to a 3–0 lead in under half an hour, eventually going into the break 3–1 up. Napoli and Lazio were scoreless at half-time, while Roma, who also were in danger of going down, had taken the lead over Juve. As it stood at half-time, Milan and Lazio were headed towards a one-game playoff to determine the Italian champions (goal difference was not considered in awarding the title back then). Juventus were stuck in third place. The Juve players were angry and gutted as they walked off the pitch. The scoreboard at the Olimpico came to life and the half-time score from Verona flashed on the screen: Verona–Milan 3–1.

'That's when many of us got really angry,' recalls Causio. 'We were convinced they were putting up the wrong score to mock us. We figured there was no way Milan could be losing like that. We all walked off cursing Rome and the Romans. Even Capello.'

Only when they got to the dressing room were they told that, no, in fact, they weren't the victims of some cruel Roman joke. Milan really were two goals down. Which meant that, if Juve could turn it around, they could grab the title. Boniperti, the president, walked into the dressing room. His face was bright red. The normally reserved and understated Boniperti (think Sir Bobby Charlton, only with a full head of hair) was furious. 'If you don't win this game, I'm going to eat all of you for breakfast tomorrow,' he said.

Short and sharp. After Vycpalek had given his

instruction for the second half, Capello gave a brief team talk, reminding the players of the pact they had made six weeks earlier. Vycpalek sent on Altafini as a substitute in an effort to turn things around. And, on the hour mark, the veteran super-sub found the back of the net. Some ten minutes later, word came from the bench: Milan were now 5–1 down. If the results didn't change, there would still be a one-game playoff, only it would involve Juventus and Lazio, who were still drawing 0–0 in Naples.

Everything happened very quickly. With three minutes to go, Antonello Cuccureddu scrambled the ball into the Roma goal. Less than sixty seconds later, Oscar Damiani (who would move to Juventus in the summer of 1974) scored the winner for Napoli. The fact that Milan pulled two goals back against Verona proved to be entirely irrelevant. Juve were champions again under the most dramatic of circumstances. The promise the players had made to themselves and to each other had been kept. They battled and they won.

But the celebration did not last long. They returned to Turin and, two days later, took off again, this time for Novi Sad, in Yugoslavia. Having overcome Derby, there was a European Cup final in Belgrade against mighty Ajax to prepare for.

Juve were a traditional club and, in those days, Italian sides believed in the *ritiro*, a sort of monastic retreat before big games that Helenio Herrera devised in the sixties at Inter. They holed up in a hotel on the outskirts of Novi Sad and trained under bootcamp conditions. Early to bed, early to rise, long training sessions, one phone call home a day, a strict ban on going into town. And, most of all, long, long hours spent thinking about the game.

'We were there all week long,' recalls Altafini. 'It was like being in a bunker. We were trapped, we couldn't wait to get out.'

Causio describes the week as 'hell'. 'I felt like beating my head against the wall, I was, at once, wound up, bored silly and mentally and physically exhausted,' he says.

'I was injured, but travelled with the team anyway,' says Spinosi. 'That hotel was a nightmare. It used to be a castle and it had all these tiny single rooms, which felt like prison cells. We were stuck there. We couldn't even really talk among ourselves because the lights-out curfew was strict and we were all in our own little rooms, which made us all feel even more alone. It was really a horrible week.'

And then, on the eve of the game, they ran into the Ajax team. They showed up tall, blond and confident. They had long, permed hair (in striking contrast to Juventus, who until the early 1990s, demanded that players keep their hair short) and big muttonchop sideburns. They were accompanied by their pretty wives and girlfriends. The Juve players were envious and looked at them wistfully. They had spent so much time away from their families and here came the Dutch, who presumably got to party until the night before and had sex that very morning. Oh, and there was no Slavic Addams Family Castle with cloister cells for Ajax. They stayed in a five-star hotel with a casino and gambled the night away.

Ajax had won the European Cup two years running and were looking for the hat-trick. The spine of the team featured many of the stars who would dazzle the World Cup a year later as part of Rinus Michels' 'Clockwork

Orange' side. They weren't just the inventors of Total Football, they were its highest exponents. And, with the likes of Ruud Krol, Johnny Rep, Johan Neeskens, Arie Haan and, of course, Johan Cruyff, they oozed class.

That night, Juve were taught a footballing lesson. Rep's header beat Zoff after just four minutes and it was pretty much game over from there on. Ajax toyed with them, dominating them tactically, physically (the week in Novi Sad left them completely burnt out) and technically.

'That final simply came too early for us,' recalls Causio. 'We were worn out from the long season and we simply lacked the experience to compete with Ajax, who had already won it twice. I could only think to myself that if it had come a year or two later it would have been a different story.'

Another Juve player underscored Ajax's dominance like this: 'We could have played for another six hours and we would not have scored. And, in the unlikely event that we did score, we felt that they would just come back and get another. They were simply a class apart.'

After the match, insult came on top of injury. As the Juve squad sat on the team bus, stewing with sadness and anger, they watched as Barry Hulshoff, the Dutch captain, strolled over to the Ajax bus. He had a gorgeous woman on his arm and was carrying the European Cup by one of its handles, as if it was some kind of cheap luggage. Capello watched in silence as Hulshoff flipped the Cup over to the kitman, who chucked it into the baggage compartment of the bus. Hulshoff then turned, smiled and wandered over to the casino.

'They just left the Cup there as if it was some kind of

bauble and went back to the casino to gamble,' says Spinosi. 'It was incredible. And, for us, a real humiliation.'

It may have been incidents such as these which prompted Capello never to dwell on victories (or defeats, for that matter). Juventus had worked so hard to get to the final. Ajax had treated the European Cup as no big deal – at least outwardly – and, once it was won, it got put away along with the sweaty socks and dirty jerseys. And the players moved on to their women, their gambling, their partying. Was it disrespectful? No. They had earned the right to behave that way. What mattered was winning, not how you celebrate. And, as soon as one goal was reached, they moved on to the next. That's how winners behave.

Capello took that night to heart. And it may explain why none of the thirty-plus trophies he has won in his career as player and manager are prominently displayed in his home, but instead are locked away somewhere away from sight. Winners don't need baubles to remind them they have won.

CHAPTER 5

That Wembley Goal

Juventus' season still wasn't over. That year, the Coppa Italia again rumbled on into June, a somewhat senseless epilogue to a long and punishing season. The last eight were split into two groups of four, who played each other home and away, with the group winners squaring off in the final. A further complication was the fact that the Italian FA had arranged two high-profile friendlies right in the midst of it all.

Having begun the semi-final group stage, Capello, along with his international teammates, left to join up with the Italian national team. On 9 June 1973 they took on mighty Brazil, the world champions, at Rome's Stadio Olimpico, coming away with a 2–0 victory, with Capello providing the second. Five days later, in Turin, they were set to take on England in a fixture arranged to celebrate the seventy-fifth anniversary of the Italian FA. England, managed by Sir Alf Ramsey, featured the likes of Bobby Moore, Emlyn Hughes, Allan Clarke and Martin Peters.

Appearing on RAI, Italy's state broadcaster, for a pre-match interview, Capello spoke about taking on the English. Again, it's uncanny how, but for the absence of glasses and fewer wrinkles, he looked virtually identical to the way he does now.

Hearing the young Capello speak, it's interesting to note how he avoids the usual footballer clichés and talks with confidence, looking straight into the camera. 'With the national team there is a whole different set of issues compared to club football,' he says, gaze unflinching. 'You only meet up once in a while and, naturally, you don't have the same team spirit that you have at club level. Not to mention that, in friendlies like these, you don't have the same stimuli or incentives that you have when there is something at stake. Like I said, the national team is a wholly different challenge.'

Read now, those words seem eerily prescient. And yet, in this age of sponsors, hype and TV rights, it seems unthinkable that a national team player – before a prestige friendly no less – would come out and talk about a lack of motivation and the issues facing a somewhat divided dressing room. Then again, maybe we were all a lot more honest in the early 1970s.

He did devote a word to his opponents, betraying perhaps the admiration he always had for the English game: 'They are the masters of football, period. Beating them would be tremendous. About as good as it can get.'

Which is exactly what happened. Italy won 2–0 and Capello again found the back of the net, latching on to a header in the area and striking it first time with his left foot. Thirty-four years later, on 16 December 2007, during his last appearance on *La Domenica Sportiva*, Italy's version of *Match Of The Day*, he confessed that he had actually mis-hit the ball: 'I wanted to put it in the opposite corner,' he said. 'I guess I was a bit lucky.'

It was a historic win. On their ninth attempt, the Azzurri had at last defeated the country that had gifted football to the world. And Capello had played a key role.

He had almost no time to reflect on it because, three days later, Juve were back in the Coppa Italia, away to Inter. They went on to win the group, setting up a final against none other than AC Milan. The media billed it as Milan's opportunity for redemption after throwing away the title on the last day of the season. Inside the Juve dressing room it was seen as a cruel reminder that, had things turned out differently in Belgrade, they would have been going for an unprecedented Treble. Juventus took the lead with Bettega, but Milan equalized thanks to a penalty converted by Romeo Benetti. Extra-time yielded no goals and it went to spotkicks, which Milan won 5–2. It was something of a subdued day. Juventus were still reflecting on the Treble which had gone up in smoke. For Milan it was scant consolation after what had happened in Verona.

The side remained relatively unchanged that summer and Juve were favourites to retain the title in 1973–74. But Italian football in those first few months of the season was overshadowed by another event, one that took place at Wembley Stadium on 14 November 1973. The Azzurri travelled to London on a massive wave of media interest. They had not lost a game in eighteen months and had not even conceded a goal in nine games. And they were to play at Wembley, a venue whose halo of magic, mystery and awe had been drilled into Italian minds since before the war. The days preceding the game had been the usual blend of jingoism and mild xenophobia. When one English columnist commented that the visitors would be cheered on by '20,000 Italian waiters' – a reference to the many Italian immigrants who had settled in London in the late 1960s – the Italian press seized upon it, turning it into a rallying cry.

'I wanted to beat England so badly,' Lazio striker Giorgio Chinaglia, who started up front, says. 'Partly because of my history [Chinaglia was raised in Wales], partly for those 20,000 Italian waiters.'

It was the first time under the Twin Towers for Capello and most of his teammates. Rather than being intimidated though, they seemed galvanized by the occasion, particularly the noisy support they got from the Italian supporters, many of whom were based in England. The home side started well and ratcheted up the pressure for much of the game, but Italy hung in there.

'We were really suffering at Wembley,' Causio recalls. 'The game was played at a high pace, they just kept coming, it was like one of those western films, where the soldiers are penned into the fort and the Indians attack them from all sides. It was physically and mentally exhausting.'

Chinaglia's recollections echo Causio's. 'That wasn't a friendly match, it was a real battle,' he says. 'Not a dirty game, but one played at the highest intensity. Nothing like the friendlies you see today. England played very well, our goalkeeper Zoff pulled out some real miraculous saves that day.'

And then, four minutes from time, came that historic goal. But let's let Chinaglia describe it.

'England were on the attack and, in those situations, my job was to be on the shoulder of the last defender, so that, if we won the ball, I could provide an outlet and hold the ball up,' he says. 'I was wide right, almost on the touchline. We won the ball and it quickly came to Spinosi. I'm not sure if he had seen me, but I knew that he would know exactly where I was, because our tactical instructions had been clear.

'The second he struck the ball in my direction, I took off into space,' he continues. 'I went down the whole right flank, I took a quick glance at Peter Shilton in the England goal and I smacked it as hard as I could.'

Many have debated whether Chinaglia's was a shot or a cross.

'Let's just say it was a "shot-cross" . . . I thought I could beat Shilton, but I also knew that if he parried it, there was a good chance a teammate would be up there to turn it in or get a foot to the ball on the way in,' he says.

Which is what happened. Capello, after sprinting halfway up the pitch, stretched out to meet the ball, striking it with the sole of his boot.

'I joked that, given how close he was, there was no way he could miss,' says Spinosi. 'But in fact, you have to credit Fabio for being there.'

Indeed, Capello, not the quickest player, had produced a lung-bursting run in the final minutes of a tense and tiring game. And he had correctly anticipated both Chinaglia's run and where he would put the ball. It was a goal that embodied both his determination and ability to dig deep, as well as his capacity for reading the game. Capello would later tell friends: 'Had I missed that goal, I could never have shown my face in public ever again.'

Chinaglia remembers watching the ball trickle into the net. 'I was frozen in time,' he says. 'Everything slowed down after Fabio made contact. It felt like an hour had passed before the ball crossed the line.'

Looking back, it seems a bit bizarre that this match is considered so important in the history of Italian football. It seems to have acquired a life of its own. True, Italy had never before beaten England on English soil. Then again, until five months earlier in Turin, they had never beaten England anywhere, in any competition. Nor was Capello's goal – as some have written – the first by an Italian at Wembley. On 6 May 1959, Sergio Brighenti and Amos Mariani had both scored in a 2–2 Wembley draw against an England side which included Billy Wright and Bobby Charlton.

Furthermore, while it's always special to record a win against a prestigious national side like England, those were, in fact, tough times for the Three Lions. Three years had passed since Mexico 1970 (when many felt England were even stronger than when they won the World Cup in 1966) and, since then, they had struggled. They were knocked out of the quarter-finals at the 1972 European Championships and, more surprisingly, had failed to qualify for the 1974 World Cup. It was the first time in England's history that this had happened and it occurred despite the fact that they were in a relatively manageable group featuring Poland and Wales. Indeed, less than a month earlier, the Poles had held them to that infamous 1–1 draw at Wembley, sealing England's exit.

And yet, to the Italians, it was as if they had won the World Cup.

'Without question it was the most important goal of Fabio's career and it helped us to a fantastic victory,' says Spinosi. 'He became something of a folk hero, not just in Italy, but especially to Italians living abroad, whether in England or elsewhere. I think some of it might have had to do with the fact that, at club level, Italian sides always seemed to do badly in England. But, with that goal, he became a kind of symbol of what Italians could achieve abroad. And I think he loved that.'

A symbol of what Italians could achieve abroad. Remember that phrase. It will come up again later, when we look at Capello's return to Madrid and some of the bitterness which followed.

Domestically, Juve's season was somewhat understated. They finished second, two points behind Lazio, but, in fact, they spent most of the year playing catch-up. It was Lazio's first-ever *scudetto* and, for Italian football, it was quite a shock to the system. Just two years earlier Lazio had been in Serie B, but buoyed by Chinaglia, who led the scoring with twenty-four goals, and a charismatic coach like Tommaso Maestrelli, they proved that the previous year's third-place finish was anything but a fluke. Capello had another fine season and his stature in the game was growing, on and off the pitch. He had become a father for the second time the previous year when Edoardo was born and Turin was now very much home to his young family.

Still, one objective loomed large in his mind: the 1974 World Cup. Objectively, he had probably been good enough to get into the 1970 side, but, especially back then, Italian football was rather conservative when it came to handing out caps to youngsters (not that, at twenty-four, his age in 1970, Capello was exactly a kid). But all that was in the past. This was going to be his World Cup. And he was in excellent company. Five other Juve players – Zoff, Spinosi, Causio, Francesco Morini and Pietro Anastasi – had also been called up.

More importantly, there was reason to believe that Italy were among the favourites to win the tournament. They had lost just one competitive match since the 1970 World Cup final four years earlier (the 2–1 defeat by Belgium when Capello made his debut). With Zoff in sparkling form, they had not conceded a goal since 20 September 1972 – nearly nineteen months – keeping clean sheets against the likes of Brazil, West Germany, Sweden and England (twice).

They had the irrepressible Chinaglia up front alongside the prolific goalscorer Riva. Gianni Rivera, a former European Footballer of the Year, teamed up with Sandro Mazzola to provide flair; between them, the pair had won four European Cups. At the back, Tarcisio Burgnich and Giacinto Facchetti, stalwarts of Herrera's legendary *Grande Inter*, marshalled a seemingly impregnable defence. And then, of course, there was the unbeatable Zoff in goal.

As impressive as Italy looked on paper, however, there were serious cracks beneath the surface. Capello's interview a year earlier in which he spoke of how it was difficult to build a club-like team spirit in the national side had been prescient. The squad was split into a number of different clans. 'We at Lazio had just won the title, but there were only three of us in the squad: myself, Pino [Giuseppe] Wilson and Luciano Re Cecconi . . . and the other two weren't given a chance,' says Chinaglia. 'The clubs had far too much influence – the more powerful ones lobbied for their players.'

On top of that, some felt that serious mistakes were made in the build-up, particularly when it came to fitness. 'We went there as favourites, but in reality our physical condition was awful,' says Spinosi. 'Everybody else seemed to run more than us. Furthermore, everyone wanted to play. Everyone. Those who were left out grumbled, egged on by the press. Those who played were fearful of losing their spot.'

There was probably another, equally important, factor. Too many key players were, simply put, on the downside of their careers. Rivera, Mazzola and Facchetti were all in their early thirties, Burgnich thirty-five. What's more, many of them were clearly battle-weary by this stage.

The opening game saw them matched against Haiti, a side making their first ever World Cup appearance (and one which would concede fourteen goals in three games). Yet problems manifested themselves straight away. With two strikers plus the two flair players Rivera and Mazzola in the side, a tremendous strain was placed on Romeo Benetti, the only holding midfielder, and Capello, who was forced to cover far more ground than he was used to. The Haitians weren't particularly good, but they were big and strong and ran themselves into the ground.

Thus, when Capello and his teammates walked into the dressing room at half-time it was still goalless and the many Italian supporters in the crowd were starting to grumble. But things would quickly go from bad to worse. In the first minute of the second half, Manno Sanon, the Haitian centre-forward, latched on to a clearance, accelerated past Burgnich and slipped the ball past Zoff – the first time he had been beaten for a full 1,147 minutes.

Italy were stunned. They recovered to win 3–1, but the damage had been done. The press wanted scapegoats. One obvious target was Chinaglia, who, upon being substituted with twenty minutes to go, made an obscene gesture towards the coaching staff. Also under fire were Rivera and Mazzola: just like four years earlier in Mexico when the manager thought he had resolved the issue by giving them one half each, many felt they simply could not be accommodated in the same side, especially with two genuine strikers up front.

An already strained atmosphere, despite the win, grew even more tense. Up next were Argentina, who had suffered a shock defeat to Poland. Valcareggi, the Italian national team manager, knew he had to punish Chinaglia, but at the same time, perhaps fearful of depriving himself of his most in-form striker, he was unwilling to take a public stand. And so a compromise solution was reached: Chinaglia was officially 'injured' for the Argentina game.

'What injury?' says Chinaglia. 'They dropped me because of what happened, but they didn't have the courage to say that was the reason.'

Still, Italy got away with a 1–1 draw against the Argentines. Capello, in particular, looked galvanized and was one of the more impressive players. The slower, more technical approach from the South Americans suited the Azzurri just fine.

This set up a final group game against Poland. The Poles had already qualified; a draw would have allowed both teams to advance, while letting Poland top the group. Some newspapers, especially in Argentina, speculated that a stitch-up was a 'foregone conclusion'. Rumours that FIAT were ready to show their gratitude by opening up a new truck manufacturing plant in Poland were doing the rounds. Still, Valcareggi wasn't taking chances. He dropped both Riva and Rivera, two of the resident legends, for the more dynamic Anastasi and Causio (two more Juve players, bringing the total to six and prompting more whispers of the Turin club's undue influence over national team affairs). Neither Riva nor Rivera would play another minute for Italy.

Poland weren't fazed in the slightest. In fact, towards the end of the first half, they scored twice. So much for the 'stitch-up'. With Italy reeling, Valcareggi took off Chinaglia (whom he had restored to the side) at the half-time interval. Cue more recrimination and acrimony. Capello popped up with a goal four minutes from time, but the match slipped away from them. When Italy returned home, they were greeted by an angry mob, pelting them with rotten tomatoes.

Capello, along with Zoff, was spared much of the bile. 'And rightly so,' says Chinaglia. 'He was above it all, he just focused on playing. He wasn't involved in the clans and the mindgames and the lobbying.'

Capello's relative aloofness from his teammates served him well at that World Cup as he was largely above the factionalism and the backbiting. While he was a Juve player and close to both Zoff (who would become a close lifelong friend, almost on a par with Reja) and Spinosi, all three were somewhat removed from the politics which went on behind the scenes. Zoff was the unquestioned number one and had a reserved, almost taciturn personality. Spinosi, at twenty-four, was one of the younger members of the group and kept a lower profile. Capello did, however, develop a friendship with the rambunctious and outspoken Chinaglia, one that persists to this day. Again, this may seem like a bit of a contradiction. Chinaglia, like his Lazio teammates, was an outsider, a gate-crasher at the Azzurri's World Cup party. Both had big personalities, but Capello was the more measured, knowing which fights to pick and which to avoid. Chinaglia, on the other hand, was always in the firing line. Yet Capello loved Chinaglia's spirit and fearlessness. And, in some ways, having an ally among the Lazio clan didn't hurt him either.

'Fabio is and will always be a very good friend,' Chinaglia says. 'Neither of us cares what people think. I'll always be identified with Lazio, I was even president of the club at one point. He's a Roma guy, but, even when he was manager of Roma, we would regularly go out to dinner. Some frowned upon that. We didn't care.'

The biggest change for Juventus that summer involved the manager. Carlo Parola joined from Novara to replace Vycpalek at the helm. Parola had been Boniperti's teammate and was Juve through and through. He wasn't a high-profile manager, but the club believed one wasn't needed. They were well organized in every department, the squad was solid, they would once again be competitive.

Oscar Damiani, a tricky winger, added balance to the midfield. And, at the back, there were two new faces. Both would become outstanding defenders, though their styles were as different as Ann Widdecombe and Kate Moss.

Claudio Gentile was one of the roughest, toughest man-markers in the history of the game. Part of the Gentile legend has it that when Kevin Keegan went up to collect his European Footballer of the Year award a few years later, Gentile, who was in the audience, whispered to him: 'Had I been marking you this season, you would never have won this award.' Whether this story is true or apocryphal is difficult to determine, but it is certainly in keeping with the tough-guy attitude which made Gentile so popular among certain supporters. Gaetano Scirea was Gentile's polar opposite. A mild-mannered sweeper, he was graceful and elegant in his movements. He was proud of the fact that, throughout his career he was never sent off or even suspended, a rare achievement for a defender in those days.

After a slow start to the 1974–75 season, Juventus took over first place in week six, 10 November 1974, and never looked back. Napoli, who would finish second, provided the most sustained threat, but they were summarily dispatched in the head-to-head encounters: an incredible 6–2 shellacking in Naples in December and, four months later, a famous 2–1 win in Turin, with the 36-year-old Altafini, a former Napoli hero, coming off the bench and scoring the winner two minutes from time against his old club, forever earning himself the nickname *Core 'ngrato* ('ungrateful heart'), after the classic Neapolitan song.

There was a small hiccup on the penultimate day of the

season, as Juve were surprisingly beaten 4–1 by mid-table Fiorentina, but the title was wrapped up on the final day with a 5–0 trouncing of Vicenza, who were already relegated.

In the UEFA Cup they knocked out sides such as Ajax (something of a revenge for the European Cup three years earlier) and Hamburg, before stumbling over Twente in the semi-final. They somehow contrived to lose both legs, 3–1 in Holland, 1–0 in Turin.

'It would have been nice [to win the UEFA Cup], but we weren't overly bothered,' says Causio. 'What was important to us was winning back the *scudetto* and, while we were in first place, Napoli were always threatening. Twente outplayed us, but, in any case, winning the UEFA Cup would have been the cherry on top, not the cake itself. And we wanted the cake.'

Meanwhile, Capello was developing a passion for what would become one of his other great loves off the pitch: contemporary art. And, again, just as he had with Chinaglia, he formed a bond with someone who, on the surface, appeared to be his polar opposite: the newly arrived Damiani. Nicknamed 'Flipper' (the Italian word for Pinball), he was a brash, flamboyant, extrovert winger. Not surprisingly perhaps, he went on to become a very successful agent and a fixture on Italian football chat shows, where he often appears wearing bespoke suits with outrageous pinstripes and hand-made crocodile shoes.

'I'm a dandy dresser, even more so back then,' says Damiani. 'Fabio, of course, was a lot more reserved. But we would regularly go shopping together. We both got into men's fashions at the same time. I introduced him to Paggin, my favourite men's store in Vicenza. And, while he stuck to the more sober styles as you would expect, he really liked the shop and went back for many years.'

But where they really hit it off was in the art world. They were both fascinated by the Arte Povera movement, which created works of art, primarily sculptures, using rubbish and other discarded items. Michelangelo Pistoletto, one of the most prominent exponents of the movement, had a gallery in Turin and the pair spent considerable time there, mixing with the local art scene.

Two events that summer foreshadowed the fact that Capello's time in Turin might soon be coming to an end. On 8 June 1975, while playing for Italy against the Soviet Union in Moscow, Capello injured his knee once again. Except this time it was his right knee, the one which had been – relatively – healthy. He would miss the start of the following season and, while his layoff wasn't as long as expected, Juventus officials were becoming increasingly worried about him.

The other event was the signing of a promising central midfielder named Marco Tardelli (you may remember his celebration after his goal in the 1982 World Cup final). He was a few months short of his twentieth birthday but his ability was already obvious. Quick and dynamic, he covered lots of ground and popped up regularly in the opposing penalty box. Capello remained the first choice, as the versatile Tardelli was often deployed at rightback, but it was clear that the young buck would soon be providing plenty of competition.

That season, the league championship was an all-Turin affair, pitting Juventus against their city rivals. Juve had the pedigree and the experience, but Torino had a pair of strikers who seemingly scored at will: Ciccio Graziani and Paolino Pulici would combine for thirty-six goals that season.

They were knocked out of the European Cup early following a 4–2 aggregate defeat at the hands of Borussia Mönchengladbach, which meant they could focus entirely on retaining the league title. And as late as 21 March 1976, with nine rounds to go, Juventus had a five-point lead and looked unassailable at the top of the table. And then the wheels came off. A defeat at Cesena, coupled with a Torino victory at home to Roma, cut the lead to three points going into the Turin derby. Juventus lost 2–1, but it didn't matter: a flare, fired from the Juventus end, hit the Torino goalkeeper Luciano Castellini, and Torino were awarded the match. The next week brought another defeat – their third on the bounce, 0–1 at Inter – allowing Torino to take over at the top. Juventus bounced back with a laboured 2–1 win over relegation-threatened Ascoli (Altafini, the old master, came off the bench and scored), but the problem was that Torino kept winning too. Still, they somehow hung in there and, going into the final day of the season, they were just one point back. Torino were held 1–1 at home by Cesena, but Juventus, against all odds, were defeated by the only goal at Perugia. Knowing that their rivals had slipped up only made defeat more bitter.

Capello made twenty-seven league appearances that year, notching three goals. Not a bad individual return, but, privately, Juve were starting to have serious concerns over him. It wasn't so much about his performance: he was still a regular for Italy and still gave everything he had on the pitch. Rather, the concern was his health.

His knees remained in bad condition; the only reason he did not miss more games was that he would simply grit his teeth and play through the pain. He also suffered from a recurring sports hernia (also known as 'Athletic Pubalgia'), for which he was often given painkillers. Capello's own stubborn determination may have aggravated the situation: he wanted to play so badly that, on occasion, he probably pushed himself too far.

'Fabio's body did not always support him the way it should have,' says Spinosi. 'Because he was – and is – a fighter, he just battled his way through the pain. I remember games when he would run around as if everything were OK. Then, in the dressing room, the pain was so strong that he could hardly sit down.'

The club reluctantly decided it was time to move him on. Tardelli deserved more playing time and it was best to sell Capello now, when he could still command a good price. Obviously, they did not advertise his condition. Instead, when asked about why he was being sold, they said 'It's a tactical decision. We no longer want to play with a traditional midfield *regista* ['organizer']. That position is going out of fashion.'

Which, to some degree, was true. The midfield playmaker, sitting in the middle of the park, dictating play, acting as the side's metronome, was becoming extinct. The game had become faster and more physical, central midfielders were asked to cover more ground. It was also felt that to have a guy in that role made the side somewhat predictable, as most of the attacking possession went through him at some point. In addition, a new manager, Giovanni Trapattoni, was on his way in and he preferred having two holding midfielders.

Still, there is little question that concerns over his health were a big part of the reason why Juventus was willing to axe Capello. He had just turned thirty, hardly an old man, but, as one source put it: 'His birth certificate said he was thirty, but his body was that of a forty-year-old. Admittedly, his brain was that of a fifty-year-old with a PhD. But his brain alone could not get him around the pitch quickly enough.'

Boniperti, the president, sealed the deal with his Milan counterpart, Vittorio Duina, on a flight to Rome. Capello would join the *rossoneri* in exchange for Romeo Benetti, a holding midfielder and fellow Italian international, plus 100 million lire in cash (around £40,000 at the time). It was a huge story. Imagine Chelsea swapping John Terry for Rio Ferdinand plus cash and you get the picture. The pair had done well together for Italy, with Benetti acting as a hardman to Capello's playmaking. And now, one was traded for the other.

Capello, of course, knew why Juve were letting him go. And he was disappointed. But he had learned never to look back, only forward. Milan were ready to build a side around him. They were an equally big club. He would prove the critics wrong, not that he cared about what they said or wrote. Fifteen years after Gipo Viani had sat in his father's kitchen, desperately trying to persuade him to join Milan, Fabio Capello would finally become a *rossonero*.

CHAPTER 6

Back to the Kids

The Milan side Fabio Capello joined in the summer of 1976 was light years away from what we know Milan to be today. Apart from the red and black colours, the San Siro and the Milanello training ground, it might as well have been a different club. For a start, money was often tight, as they struggled to keep up with Juventus and Inter.

More importantly, they hadn't won a league title in eight years and that hunt had turned into something of an obsession. In Italy, when a side wins ten league titles, they get to stitch a gold star on their jersey. Milan had been stuck on nine *scudetti* since 1968 and the pursuit of the *Scudetto della Stella* – the 'star' *scudetto* – consumed the club and its owners. It's not as if the previous eight years had been unsuccessful – they had won the Coppa Italia twice, a European Cup, the Cup Winners' Cup (against Leeds United in 1973), a World Club Cup and had finished second three times in that time period – it's just that, without a domestic title, it all felt somewhat empty.

The previous season they had finished third, without ever really challenging for the title. But they had a new owner, Vittorio Duina, who brought in a new manager, Pippo Marchioro. He had made a name for himself at provincial clubs, winning promotion with Como and taking little Cesena all the way up to sixth place. Upon arriving at Milan, he said: 'For me, this is the chance of a lifetime. When I walk away, it will be either as a fool or a king.'

The side still featured Gianni Rivera, the former Golden Boy of Italian football, who was thirty-three, but had the lithe body and boyish looks of a man ten years younger, as well as a top-notch goalkeeper in Ricky Albertosi (kept out of the national side by the untouchable Zoff). Capello was pencilled in as the man who would pull everything together and make the side function. First, however, he had to pass his medical.

Giovanni Battista Monti, the club's team doctor, remembers the first time he examined Capello. Monti told him his knee was in bad shape and said he was amazed he had not gone under the knife. Capello looked him in the eye, squared his jaw and said: 'Look, I've had this same messed up knee all my life. I managed to play with this very same knee and win titles and trophies. If this knee stood me in good stead all these years, no matter how messed up you think it is, it will surely last me another few seasons.'

Medically, Capello was right. His knee was in pieces, but it had been that way for a long time. Impressed with Capello's determination and self-assuredness, Monti gave him a pass on his medical, though he did wonder how

Capello had been able to sustain all that pain for all those years.

'Everyone was excited by the swap,' recalls Fulvio Collovati, a promising young defender at the time who would go on to win the 1982 World Cup. 'Benetti was a great player, but he was a holding midfielder and a year older, whereas Capello had real quality. It looked like Milan had the best of the deal. But, of course, Benetti was fit and healthy. Capello struggled. I can still see him now with giant icepacks on his knees. It seemed as if whenever he wasn't on the pitch, he had that icepack with him.'

Milan's season soon turned into a nightmare. The side – Capello apart – struggled to understand Marchioro's sometimes overly elaborate tactical instructions. They won their opener (2–1 over Perugia, with Capello scoring his only goal of the season) and then went nine straight without a win. An even worse spell – ten consecutive games without a victory – was to follow in the second half of the season, leaving them in the relegation zone with just two games to go.

Marchioro got the bullet and the club, desperate for a turnaround, recalled the legendary Nereo Rocco to save them. Rocco was the manager who had led them to two European Cups in the 1960s. Like Herrera, he had mastered the art of the *catenaccio*. Unlike Herrera he was funny, witty and likeable, a figure known for his bons mots, such as, 'Whatever you see moving on the pitch, just whack it. If it happens to be the ball, too bad.' By that point, however, Rocco was seventy-four and had officially retired several years earlier. Still, his mere presence gave the side an instant lift and Milan won their last two games, avoiding what would have been the first relegation in their long and glittering history.

Some solace did come from the Coppa Italia. Milan reached the final, where they defeated Inter 2–0 (Capello was injured and did not feature). Nevertheless, it was pretty obvious to all: Milan would have to rebuild. Again.

It had not been an easy campaign for Capello. He may have been handed 'the keys to the team', but he found the chaos around him difficult to deal with. Duina was in the process of stepping down to make way for a new president, Felice Colombo. Marchioro had shown he was not the man to lead a side like Milan, especially when the going got tough and the press and supporters began to criticize him. Capello was also used to being a leader, but Milan was very much Rivera's team. On top of everything else, Capello's knee flared up again and he found that, as he got older, the pain got more and more difficult to bear.

That season also saw his final appearances for the Italian national team. He played well in a 2–0 home win over England, a World Cup qualifier played in November 1976. The next game, 22 December 1976, a 1–2 loss to Portugal in Rome, would be his last. Again, the official line was that, tactically, Italy were better off without an old-school playmaker. But there is reason to believe his injuries – which by this point had become known to all – played a significant part. Besides, Enzo Bearzot, the Italy boss, was building a side for the 1978 World Cup and he opted to go with youth. Less than a year after his final appearance for the Azzurri, his place had been taken by Marco Tardelli, just like at Juventus.

Off the pitch, the transition to Milan had been smoother than the one to Turin six years earlier. Capello moved to Legnano, a few miles from the Milanello training ground, and Laura and the kids seemed to enjoy themselves. His father, Guerrino, was able to visit more frequently, often turning up at training. He was always careful not to tread on anyone's toes and would often stand on an adjacent field, watching the youth team train and chatting to its coach, Italo Galbiati, who years later would become Capello's right-hand man.

Capello was somewhat detached from his teammates at that stage, preferring to spend his free time away from football. He had befriended a few local art dealers and added to his growing collection. He may have had his interests outside the game, but he was determined not to go quietly. The last time he had suffered through a relegation battle, he was a teenager at Spal; to find himself in this situation at a club like Milan was shameful. The following season would be different. It had to be.

After the Marchioro disaster, Milan opted for a safe pair of hands to lead the club: Nils Liedholm. Nicknamed 'the Baron', the Swede had been one of the club's greatest ever players, spending twelve years at the club and anchoring Milan's famous Gre-No-Li frontline with Gunnar Gren and Gunnar Nordahl. Upon retiring from football in 1961, he immediately went into management, starting as an assistant at Milan, before taking over two years later. He bounced around a number of clubs, big and small (including Fiorentina and Roma), building a reputation as a soft-spoken, likeable boss who preferred carrots to sticks.

The club had an ulterior motive in bringing in

Liedholm. There was little money to spend, so they decided to push their own home-grown youngsters. Other managers might not have accepted this, but the affable Liedholm took it in his stride. It proved to be the right decision, as the likes of Collovati and a scrawny seventeen-year-old named Franco Baresi began featuring in the first team.

It's worth taking a small detour to describe just how Franco Baresi ended up at Milan, if only for two reasons: it changed the course of history (for both Inter and Milan) and the man who made it happen was Italo Galbiati who, for seventeen years (and counting), has been Capello's right-hand man on the training ground. In 1969, shortly after his retirement, Galbiati did some work with Milan's youth academy. A year later, he took a job with crosstown rivals Inter, where he developed a reputation as an excellent talent-spotter: his finds included goalkeeper Walter Zenga and midfielder Beppe Baresi. Now, the latter had a younger brother, Franco, who was quick and moved very well on the pitch, although he was a bit on the small side. In 1974 Franco famously scheduled a trial at Inter. Just before he was due to turn up, Galbiati told the club that he did not feel comfortable assessing Franco, because he had a conflict of interest: he was moving to Milan that summer. The club didn't believe him, but, nevertheless, instructed another coach to assess the youngster. The rest is history. The other assessor got it all wrong: he felt Franco was just too small.

Galbiati was delighted. A few months later, both were at Milan and Franco Baresi would go on to win six Serie A titles, three European Cups and, with Italy, the 1982

World Cup, while amassing 716 appearances with Milan and a further 81 with Italy. His brother Beppe became a very good footballer and an international, but Franco went on to be a legend. And, since then, Milan fans have delighted in rubbing Inter noses into this very fact.

Liedholm was an instant success. He energized the club, bringing some much needed enthusiasm back to the fans and players. By December, Milan had won seven straight and were top of Serie A, with a three-point lead. Capello was fit – or as fit as he could get in those days – and his experience, vision and tactical intelligence helped settle the young side. Milan tailed off somewhat in the spring and eventually finished fourth. But the foundations had clearly been laid.

For Capello it was a satisfying campaign, probably his best at Milan and his finest in several years. He missed just two league starts and chipped in with three goals, including a dramatic late winner at Roma (continuing his streak against his former clubs). At the same time, he was learning a lot from Liedholm, a man who probably ranks just beneath Fabbri and Herrera among Capello's main influences as a manager.

Liedholm was an interesting case because he was *in* Italian football, but not *of* it. He had been in Italy since the age of twenty-seven and obviously knew the Italian game inside-out. At the same time, probably precisely because he was foreign, he was always able to view things with a detached critical eye, free from bias or prejudice. An independent, free-thinking man, he was one of the first to have the courage to introduce zonal marking in Italy, at a time when everyone played man-to-man with a sweeper.

Capello was at once fascinated and eager to learn from him. Playing under him was a crash course in the zonal marking system. While in South America it had been popular since the 1930s, in Europe it had been largely discarded in favour of sweepers and man-marking. Experiencing it as a player no doubt helped Capello years later when he would take over from Arrigo Sacchi, who believed in an even more radical version of the 'zone'.

But the respect between the two was clearly mutual. Liedholm was impressed with Capello's natural ability to see the way play would unfold on the pitch.

'Capello would sit in the middle of the park and the ball would always go to him,' he said in a 1999 interview with *Gazzetta dello Sport*. 'There are some players who go to the ball. And others, far fewer, where the ball goes to them. The ball went to Fabio. Always. There was no secret to it, beyond the fact that he always knew where the ball was going to go. And he made sure he was there to meet it.'

As much as Liedholm loved Capello's natural instincts as a footballer, the following season it became obvious that his body simply couldn't keep up with his mind. Injuries limited him to just eight appearances as, in 1978–79, Milan finally won their long-awaited tenth title.

Some teammates cruelly called him the 'traffic cop' because he spent a lot of time standing in the middle of the pitch, barking orders and moving his arms, but rarely seeing the ball. 'He loved to give orders, especially to the younger players,' says Collovati.

His enemies saw him as a bit of a bully, substituting words and commands for the fact that he could no longer do it consistently on the pitch. At the same time, others I spoke to indicated that, while it was clearly painful for him to accept his diminished role in the side, his bossy attitude was actually born of a genuine desire to share his experience and help his teammates. 'He was no longer a regular, but I think he really wanted to help out any way he could,' says Collovati. 'And sometimes he could be sweet; he dubbed me the "painter" because he said I would "paint the pitch" with my passing from the back.'

Liedholm left that summer, lured back to Roma, whom he had managed before. He told people that his job was done and he wanted a new challenge. In his place, Milan chose Massimo Giacomini, a promising young manager who had won two straight promotions with Udinese.

Rivera retired at the end of the season, amidst much fanfare. The title was a fitting way for him to bow out. Privately, some Milan executives hoped that Capello would do the same. The club's medical staff had serious and legitimate concerns over his knees. In the summer of 1979 there was talk of retirement, perhaps with an eye towards getting him involved in youth coaching – it was obvious, even then, that his tactical awareness and intelligence could turn him into a top-flight coach. But Capello would not budge. He was thirty-three, he was a professional, he had always been single-minded about leading the life of an athlete. He had battled through pain and injuries before, he was not about to give up.

As the months wore on, it became obvious that the 1979–80 season would be no kinder to him than the previous campaign. The press and the supporters were starting to murmur. Yes, he had been loyal to the club and, yes, it was admirable that he would put his body on the line and play hurt, but surely there was a point when it became detrimental to the team. To be fair, he wasn't really a drag on the side, as he rarely got on the pitch. But, when he did, there were too many times when his presence hurt, rather than helped, the side.

'Capello was clearly unsettled at that point,' recalls Giacomini. 'He was frustrated, he wanted to play, but he had few opportunities with us that season. He gave his all in training and was always very respectful towards me. But the fact was he was struggling, because he was a proud man.'

Sometimes, after Giacomini would announce the starting eleven and Capello's name, typically, wasn't there, he'd take the manager aside and say: 'Look, I feel really good this week, I'm in great shape. Maybe, if you have a spot, you can throw me in there . . .'

Giacomini would smile and say: 'Yeah, I saw you, you looked good out there. We'll see . . .'

But his number was hardly ever called. This was the moment every athlete fears – the realization that his or her powers are on the wane. Some choose to go out at the peak of their ability. Some soldier on in the hope of coaxing one final swansong from their battered bodies. Capello was among the latter, even as the press grew increasingly hostile.

His mind was as sharp as ever, his ability to read the game, to spot the opportunities, to anticipate the play, all of that was still there. As was his technical ability: he could still thread a pass through the gaps, some of which only he could see; he could still hold it up, he could still put the ball pretty much where he wanted.

But he simply was no longer the athlete he had been. His mind would will something to happen, his feet were ready to make it happen, but the rest of his body too often could not or would not follow. He had never been the quickest, but, with the searing pain in his knees, he slowed down even further. One newspaper commented that 'he played from a standstill'. Another, that he was good 'for fewer and fewer minutes' every week.

One journalist who clearly felt Capello's time was up was Alberto Cerruti, a promising young reporter for *Gazzetta dello Sport*. Capello, who for much of his career would appear pretty much immune to the critics, was clearly affected by Cerruti's writing.

'I'll admit that I was needling him over the fact that his career was coming to an end,' Cerruti told me. 'It showed on the pitch, he was struggling.'

On 11 December 1979, the eve of Milan v Napoli, a replay of a match which had earlier been abandoned due to fog, Capello decided to confront Cerruti. It was a cold, wintry day at Milanello, the club's training ground, and, by five-thirty, when Cerruti was making his way back to the car park, it was already dark. Cerruti heard footsteps on the gravel and, the next thing he knew, Capello was upon him.

Capello shoved the journalist to the ground. Punches were thrown. And then, as he stood over his victim, a livid Capello said: 'Do you still have the courage to say to my face what you've been writing in your newspaper? Go on, tell it to my face.'

Cerruti was stunned and lay there in shock for a minute or two. It wasn't the physical injuries he sustained, which were negligible, it was the way the situation had transpired. Before he knew it, Capello had disappeared into the darkness.

What is curious about this episode is not the incident itself. Capello, like everyone, occasionally loses his temper. And while his solid build and often aggressive demeanour make him more menacing than most, he is not a violent man. By all accounts, this was an isolated and unexpected loss of control and Capello did apologize afterwards.

What is remarkable, though, is what developed between Cerruti and Capello over the next thirty years. For the next decade, they had little contact, as Capello worked in Milan's youth academy and then went on to become general manager of Mediolanum. But in 1991, when he took over the first team, he began to forge a special relationship with Cerruti, one which continues to this day. Indeed, Cerruti is among the very small circle of journalists that Capello seems to trust and respect implicitly.

'I appreciated the fact that he never held a grudge over what happened earlier and that we now have a rapport based on mutual respect and esteem,' says Cerruti, who went on to become *Gazzetta*'s chief football writer. 'I'm proud of my relationship with him. I think it shows that, whatever Capello's character and personality may be like, he has this incredible ability to move on and look forward, never behind.'

Indeed, it's a theme which would come up time and again in his career. Capello may be undiplomatic, aggressive, sometimes even rude. And on occasion, as happened with Cerruti, he clearly oversteps the mark. But he rarely if ever harbours grudges. Something happens, good or bad, and he moves on. Just as he doesn't dwell on victory or on defeat, he never looks back. Every day is a blank slate in his relationship with others. The past is irrelevant. It's all about the present and the future.

That year was a turning point for the whole club, not just Capello. On 23 March 1980 the 'TotoNero' betting scandal erupted. Betting on sport was illegal in Italy at the time, but there were plenty of underground bookmakers willing to take action. It emerged that some of them had ties with players and even chairmen. Fourteen arrests were made. Along with Lazio, Milan were the hardest hit club: goalkeeper Albertosi, midfielder Giorgio Morini and striker Stefano Chiodi all received bans ranging from six months to four years, as did club president Felice Colombo, who was banned for life.

Milan's season petered out. They would finish third, but were punished with relegation to Serie B, along with Lazio. That spring, Capello went to see Dr Monti, Milan's club doctor. 'You were right, I need to quit football,' he told him.

'Fabio had yet to make that decision public,' says Monti. 'I appreciated the fact that he came to me first.'

The realization had finally hit him all at once. His future was no longer as a player. But Capello did have one last hurrah.

'It was the last week of a season to forget,' says Giacomini. 'We were away to Lazio at the Stadio Olimpico. Fabio was on the bench, we were two–nil up, so I sent him on. It was the right thing to do, the right send-off after the career he had. I just felt bad that, when I worked with him, he had so many physical problems. He was limping noticeably even that day, although on the pitch he gave his all.'

When Capello came off the pitch for the very last time, it was somewhat understated. He didn't receive the standing ovations or newspaper tributes that were accorded others. But he didn't care. A new chapter in his life was about to begin.

'We all agreed that he was a massive resource to the club and it didn't take long for us to offer him a spot on the coaching staff, working with kids,' says Giacomini. 'You would have to have been blind not to see that he had all the qualities to manage.'

Nature had given him tremendous gifts, both physical and mental. The former had left him. He was now going to build a career with the latter. Which, as it turned out, were as sharp as ever.

CHAPTER 7

Laying the Foundations

For the first time in his career, Capello went into pre-season training preoccupied not with himself, but with others. He was now in charge of eighteen kids in Milan's Allievi d'Eccellenza side, a fancy name for the Under 17s. Italo Galbiati, his future right-hand man, was looking after the Under 19s.

Growing up with a father like Guerrino, who was not just a coach but a schoolteacher as well, he always had an affinity for youngsters and teaching. In fact, in his last years at Milan, when he was more often than not injured, he made a point of wandering over to the youth players' training pitches. An old interview which appeared in *Forza Milan*, the club's official magazine, way back in 1980 reveals an innocent, wide-eyed Capello, brimming with an enthusiasm which, today, is frankly hard to imagine.

'I could have kissed them all, one by one!' he says, reflecting on a victory in a youth tournament. 'Seeing these kids work, learn and grow, right here, under my very own eyes . . . well, it's magical. I just try to teach them what I can. I am a happy man right now. I feel like I'm really accomplishing something meaningful. Far more than when I played. And, as you know, I had a fair bit of success as a player.'

It's hard to figure out what to make of those words. Was he being honest? Was he maybe sucking up a little bit to the club? Was he just a little bit carried away?

Whatever the reason, Capello evidently threw himself into his new job with gusto. His father, Guerrino, would drop in regularly, always watching quietly and respectfully from the sidelines, before grabbing a quick chat with his son after training.

'I remember one training session where we played a small-sided match and he [Fabio] decided to join in,' Giuseppe Incocciati, the team's centre-forward, recalled in a 2000 newspaper interview. 'I went in hard and kicked him on the knee. He stopped for a second and I immediately apologized. And then he said, "It's fine, go for it, kick away, kick away."'

On the pitch, Capello's boys attained success right away, winning two invitational tournaments and then the regional title. In the meantime, his relationship with Galbiati continued to grow. Capello looked up to the veteran youth team coach and seemed to want to soak up as much of his knowhow as possible. Galbiati was just pleased to have someone to bounce ideas off.

The following season, Capello's kids went one better. They dominated the regional competition and qualified for the national finals. They faced Bari in a two-legged final for the Italian Under 17 title. After losing the first leg in Milan 0–1, they found themselves two goals down at half-time in the return. Capello made two changes at the interval and they stormed back to win 3–2, winning the crown on the away-goals rule.

That year, 1982, also saw the passing of Guerrino. He had been without question the single biggest influence on Capello's life. As you would expect, Capello was not outwardly emotional. Whatever grieving he did was largely internal. But he would later tell a friend that he was above all grateful for the fact that he got to know his father so well; it was a luxury not everyone enjoyed. Those few, simple words summed up his gratitude towards his father. Which is probably how Signor Guerrino would have wanted it.

In 1982–83 Capello was promoted to the Primavera – or Under 19 side – the highest level of youth football in Italy. (Galbiati had moved on to the first team as an assistant.) That season also saw him try his hand at writing. In researching this book, I came across an article by Capello in the November 1983 issue of *Forza Milan* in which he assesses – of all things – English football. He could not have imagined that, twenty-five years later, he'd be coaching England, of course. But it's still a fun read which provides a rare insight into Capello's vision of football at the time.

In it, he describes Bryan Robson as 'surely by far the best midfielder in Europe'. Glenn Hoddle, on the other hand, is described as 'supremely talented' but 'maddeningly inconsistent'. He also provides a critique of England's attacking strategy: 'There seems to be an insistence on taking the ball up the wing to provide crosses into the box. And yet, the two England strikers, Luther

Blissett and Trevor Francis, are both pacy players, who, in my opinion, would benefit more from quick through balls hit into space. Especially since both are rather ordinary in the air.' There's also, bizarrely, a special appreciation for, of all people, Paul Walsh, who at the time played for Luton Town: 'He's a quick and tricky player who is very dangerous in the penalty area . . . in terms of characteristics, he strikes me as more Latin than Anglo-Saxon.'

Back to Capello and his youth team. Season 1983–84 was set to be triumphant, but ended in heartbreak. They lost just twice in the league, reaching the final against Roma, winners of the southern section. A series of injuries and suspensions had robbed Capello of five regulars. To make matters worse, that Roma side featured no fewer than six players who would go on to make more than 200 Serie A appearances. In fact, three of them, Giuseppe Giannini, Angelo Di Livio and Fabrizio Di Mauro, would later become full Italian internationals. Capello's Milan lost the first leg in Rome 1–0 and then battled to a 2–2 draw at home. They also reached the Coppa Italia final, going down to Torino over two legs.

Fabrizio Ferron, who would later enjoy a long career in Serie A for Atalanta and Sampdoria, was Capello's starting goalkeeper that season, though he missed the final through injury.

'He was very serious, very professional,' he recalls. 'He demanded respect. We would train for ninety minutes and he absolutely demanded all-out concentration and effort. It wasn't about the quantity of the training, it was about the quality. What struck me was that he was always so sure of himself. He never doubted himself, at least not in front of us. But he backed it up with his ability as a manager: he would read the game exceptionally well and give us very detailed instructions. And when, as a player, you're given detailed instructions, you carry them out and they work well, you learn to listen to your boss.'

The following season, 1984–85, Capello added two promising defenders to his Primavera side: Billy Costacurta and Paolo Maldini. Not too shabby, given that they would go on to make more than 1,500 appearances for Milan and a further 180 odd for Italy. They went on to win the Coppa Italia that year, defeating Torino on penalty kicks in the two-legged final.

'We were a phenomenal side,' recalls Ferron. 'Nine of us went on to play in Serie A. You have to give credit to Capello, not so much for winning the cup, but for the way the players developed afterwards.'

Capello had the habit of getting all the boys together under a big tree at Milanello before and after training. He would ask them what they hoped to get out of the upcoming session and, afterwards, do a post-mortem of how things went. 'They were kids, but he treated them like adults, he spoke to them eye to eye,' says Giovanni Battista Monti, Milan's team doctor. 'And he listened to them, he made each of them feel important. Even the youngest ones.'

Among the 'youngest ones' was, of course, Maldini. At the start of the season he had just turned sixteen, making him a full three years younger than many of his teammates and opponents. The fact that his father, Cesare, had been a Milan legend brought an extra layer of expectation and, according to some, preferential treatment. He wasn't about to get any from Capello though.

'He was as tough on Maldini as he was on all of us,' says Ferron. 'Besides, I think it became pretty obvious just how good Maldini was. His father's name had nothing to do with it.'

Maldini was in and out of Capello's youth team, often joining the first-team squad where, at the tender age of sixteen, he made his Serie A debut (as a rightback, no less) on 20 January 1985. Their relationship was one of mutual respect, rather than outright affection.

Indeed, the October 1985 issue of *Forza Milan* features a spread on the young phenomenon breaking his way into the Milan side. A number of people are interviewed and all of them wax lyrical to different degrees. Capello's assessment is telling: 'The kid has plenty of personality, technique, good elevation. And he's fearless on the pitch, which is important. He does the same thing with the first team that he did with me in the youth team: he does what is strictly necessary. That's what's important. He needs to work hard, but, as far as I'm concerned, he's a player.' That's it. No comparisons to his dad, no suggestions that he will go on to break records, no talk of precocious talent. Simply a straight assessment of a young professional.

Capello's final season with the Primavera, 1985–86, was one of transition. He had to integrate eight new players into his squad, which was far from easy. That season, he also got his full coaching badge at Coverciano, Italy's football academy, completing his final exam with flying colours.

Everything changed at Milan on 20 February 1986, the day the Berlusconi Era began. Silvio Berlusconi, a television and property magnate, acquired the club from

Giussy Farina, under whose stewardship Milan had accumulated large debts, both towards banks and towards the tax man.

Berlusconi would go on to become a controversial and flamboyant politician (and, on three occasions, Prime Minister of Italy), but, at the time, he was merely a very wealthy entrepreneur. He had revolutionized commercial television in Italy, building up the country's first national private networks, and had become immensely popular. Some of his advisers had warned him against buying a football club for fear that he would alienate fans of other teams, who might then not tune into his networks. But Berlusconi saw beyond that. He had cultivated an image of glamour and success and understood better than most that if he could replicate that aura on the sporting stage, it would only add to his prestige. Even those who hated Milan for footballing reasons would still secretly admire the club if it were successful and, just as importantly, if it achieved success in the right way.

He knew that he could tap into the 'feelgood' factor sweeping Italy in the mid-1980s. It was a time of excess and consumption around the Western world and Italy was no different. The economy was, once again, booming (though in the background the national debt was also spiralling at the same time). People wanted glamour and success. And he was ready to provide it.

Capello sensed that Berlusconi offered a whole world of opportunity. Farina's tenure had been marked by debt, scandal and a sense that Milan were stumbling along, trying to make it from one season to the next. Berlusconi was different. He didn't live day-to-day, he had grand designs.

Milan finished seventh that year, but Berlusconi promised the 1986–87 season would be different: it would be the year of Milan's rebirth, the year Milan set off on a journey that would make it 'the greatest club in the world'. He was true to his word. That summer saw Milan embark on a spending spree unseen since the 1960s. In came winger Roberto Donadoni, goalkeeper Giovanni Galli and strikers Daniele Massaro and Giuseppe Galderisi. The latter three were Italian internationals, Donadoni would soon win his first cap.

Nils Liedholm, who had returned to the club in 1984, was retained as manager to provide some continuity. Capello realized he had a chance to impress. By that point he had established himself as one of the most respected youth coaches in Italian football. But in some ways he faced a dilemma. He was forty years old and felt he was ready to try his hand at management. In fact, some felt he was wasted working with kids.

At the same time, with Berlusconi on board, this was probably the wrong time to leave, especially if it was going to mean working his way up from a lower division side. He opted to give it another year, while making his ambition clear. He wanted to do some work with the first team and offered to join Milan in their pre-season training camp at his own expense. Liedholm had no objection. In fact, he was happy to have Capello around. Berlusconi and his right-hand man, Adriano Galliani, who would take the role of chief executive, were impressed. They loved the fact that Capello was willing to go out on a limb. They promptly went even further. Not only did they send him to pre-season training, they made him Liedholm's assistant.

It was a turbulent campaign. With the new signings on board, Milan alternated highs and lows on the pitch. Much of the season was spent between third and sixth spot, a healthy distance behind Diego Maradona's Napoli, who were dominating the league. The club accepted that this would be a transition year, but they nevertheless had two basic objectives: to get into Europe and to win, or at least come close, in the Coppa Italia.

Both were essential parts of Berlusconi's grand plan for the club. He envisioned worldwide tours, a global fan base, a chain of club shops, prestige friendlies . . . all things we now take for granted but which, at the time, were revolutionary. And it was crucial to him to maintain his image of success, a type of Midas who excelled in any venture he chose. Milan looked as if they were going to fail on both counts.

On 25 February 1987 they hosted Parma in the first leg of the second round of the Coppa Italia. Parma had just been promoted to Serie B and were managed by a former shoe salesman-cum-football revolutionary: a certain Arrigo Sacchi. 'We played them off the park that night,' Sacchi told me years later. 'We won 1–0, but we were first to every ball and, literally, they didn't know what hit them.'

Berlusconi was impressed by this bald-headed hyper-active manager and his brand of football, so unlike anything he had seen. Parma pressed high up the pitch, they pushed their defenders right up to the halfway line, moved as a unit and defended using a pure zone, where players seemed to move in perfect synchronicity. He made what turned out to be one of the most crucial mental notes in the history of football.

Milan won the next two games in the league, moving into a tie for second. But then they gained just one from their next four, slipping down to joint fifth. Liedholm was looking increasingly tired and weary. When an irate fan threw a rock at the Milan dugout, shattering the glass next to the manager, Liedholm probably knew he'd had enough. And the club felt the same way. The return leg of the Parma tie in the Coppa Italia was up next (yes, the vagaries and eccentricities of the Italian fixture list meant it was played five weeks after the first leg). Milan felt they had to make a tough decision: the stakes were simply too high.

Galliani summoned Liedholm to the Sala del Focolare – the fireplace room – at the Milanello training ground. The manager probably knew what was coming. The atmosphere was sombre and somewhat tense. Galliani, hoping that Liedholm would willingly bow out, said, 'Look, you need to give me a hand here . . .'

The elderly Swede extended his arm towards Galliani, palm up, and said: 'Sure. Here, go ahead, take it . . .'

It was silly and childish and oh-so-funny. It was also vintage Liedholm. The Swede knew that there were times when it was best not to take yourself too seriously. Galliani was there to give him his marching orders. Milan's mind was made up. So why not break the tension with the kind of joke an eight-year-old might make?

Liedholm pre-empted Galliani's thoughts. 'It's become all a bit too much for me,' he said, according to a January 2000 interview in *Gazzetta*. 'You need another manager. And you already have him right here, under your nose: Capello.'

The popular Swede bowed out with class.

'I was disappointed that Liedholm wasn't allowed to continue,' recalls Ray Wilkins, who had arrived at the San Siro in 1984 with fellow England international Mark Hateley. 'And, had it been at a smaller club, he would have continued. But the stakes were too high after Berlusconi's arrival. Nils was fabulous, we all had the utmost respect for him. But we players knew that Fabio was ready.'

Even back then, Capello was seen as someone who would crack the whip. And he did, from the very first training session. 'He was extremely aggressive in his coaching style and his attitude towards the game,' recalls Wilkins. 'Nils was relaxed in training and in team talks, maybe a bit too relaxed. Fabio's approach was totally different. He wanted winners around him, he wanted success. It was pretty evident.'

At his very first training session, Capello held a team meeting and asked the players to share their thoughts on the club's situation, what had gone wrong and how things could improve.

'All of a sudden, [Francesco] Zanoncelli gets up and says, "I think I should get more playing time,"' defender Filippo Galli recalled years later in an interview with *Gazzetta dello Sport*. Zanoncelli was nineteen at the time, a seldom used defender who would make just six appearances that season. But his confidence clearly struck a chord with Capello, who put him straight into the starting eleven for the following league match.

It's somehow fitting that Fabio Capello's managerial debut should have come in the second leg of the Coppa Italia tie against Sacchi's Parma. The two men will forever be linked with Milan and the Berlusconi revolution (but more of this later) and, of course, it would be Capello who replaced Sacchi at the helm of the club in 1991. The contrasts are obvious as we shall see, but on that warm April evening it was Sacchi who had the last laugh. Milan, despite creating numerous chances, were held to a 0–0 draw and Parma went through.

Berlusconi, smitten with Sacchi, began sounding him out for next season. Capello got on with the job of getting Milan into Europe. The main problem was that too many players seemed demotivated. Some of the 'star signings' made in the summer – Galderisi and Bonetti – had disappointed. Others, like Donadoni and Massaro, were struggling under the weight of expectation. Of the 'holdovers' from the pre-Berlusconi era, some were understandably deflated. The likes of Agostino Di Bartolomei and the two foreigners, Wilkins and Hateley, realized there would probably be no space for them in Berlusconi's 'new' Milan.

Capello's tenure in the league began well. In addition to starting the youngster Zanoncelli, he recalled Wilkins and Hateley, who had seen their roles diminish under Liedholm. Hateley duly scored the winner against Torino on 12 April 1987. Capello also made his mark in another way. At half-time, he sent on Galderisi, one of the summer's star signings whose season had turned into a bit of a nightmare. After just fourteen minutes, he took him off again. 'I knew that I would get a lot of stick for substituting a substitute,' Capello said after the match. 'But I don't care. I just wanted to win and we did.'

Then came an understandable away defeat against

league leaders Napoli and a resounding 4–1 win over Roma. By this stage of the season, with Napoli shaping up for a league and Coppa Italia Double, it became evident that to ensure a UEFA Cup place for the following season, Milan had to finish fifth in Serie A. The pressure on Capello was intense as he tackled the climax of the campaign.

Mid-table Como at the San Siro were next, in the penultimate game of the season. A win would have just about wrapped up Europe, as it would have left the *rossoneri* joint fourth, with a two-point margin over Roma and Sampdoria. Instead, they were held to a scoreless draw, which left them just a single point clear going into the final match of the season.

According to Milan lore, it was after this 0–0 draw that Berlusconi opted to make the bold choice of calling upon Sacchi for the following season. Capello was highly regarded by Berlusconi and his crew, but it was felt Milan needed to be truly different, to have a style and an ethos which clearly set them apart. Sacchi, the revolutionary, had that. Capello, with just a few games under his belt, did not. It's unclear to what degree Capello knew that, come the end of the season, regardless of what happened, he'd have to hand the first team back. Officially, he was the interim manager, but it's obvious that he was ambitious and was hoping for a chance.

Either way, a Milan victory in the last game of the season would have guaranteed European football. And their opponents were more than manageable: Udinese, dead last and mathematically relegated to Serie B a month earlier. It finished – again – 0–0. Come what may, Milan could not break down Udinese's defence. With Roma losing to Avellino and Sampdoria defeating Torino, Milan were facing a one-game playoff in Turin against Samp for that crucial European place.

Morale was dipping. Milan had failed two 'match points' and momentum had swung the other way, into the hands of a bright young Sampdoria side, led by Gianluca Vialli and Roberto Mancini, Italian football's two rising stars. It had been a long season, Milan were running on fumes. Nevertheless, Capello buckled down and on 23 May 1987 Milan grabbed their place in Europe with the 1–0 victory coming late, very late: in the final minute of extra time, Daniele Massaro rose to meet Mauro Tassotti's cross to score the winner. More than celebration, it was all about relief.

But Capello's work was not finished. Milan's players hung around and, in June, competed in something called the 'Mundialito'. It was very much a made-for-TV competition: Berlusconi's networks had no football rights whatsoever and he wanted to see to what degree it would be a marketable commodity for his broadcasting empire. So he proceeded to organize a 'prestige' friendly tournament, inviting Paris Saint-Germain, Barcelona, Porto and Inter. Capello stuck around to manage, and duly won the competition, which followed a round-robin format. From a sporting perspective it was a bit of a sham, but it nevertheless represented Capello's first trophy as a manager.

In some ways, it was remarkable that Capello was even still a part of the club. With Sacchi on his way in, he received offers from elsewhere. But he remained loyal.

Some saw it as a lack of ambition. How wrong they were. In fact, Milan had big plans for him.

At the time, Berlusconi was a big believer in psychological profiling. The concept was simple: employees would undergo a battery of tests of all kinds and those who scored highest would be put on a fast track to top management which might include Master's courses, language training and rotations through every department of his company.

'The idea was to identify those with exceptional potential and then give them the tools they would need to become top-level executives,' says Bruno De Michelis. Today, the imposing De Michelis is the scientific coordinator at MilanLab, the club's state-of-the-art medical facility. Back then, he was a consultant to Berlusconi's companies and had begun to work with the football club as well. The colourful De Michelis, a psychologist and former two-time European karate champion, is a pioneer in assessing and strengthening the mental potential of individuals, teams and workplaces. Rather than doing it through psychoanalysis and motivational psychobabble, he uses instruments which measure and stimulate brain activity. At the time, he helped design aptitude tests aimed at assessing the full potential of an individual.

Capello was given the same battery of assessment tests that fresh MBAs working in Berlusconi's television or property companies would receive. And he scored exceptionally high. So much so that, when Berlusconi was told his results – which, coincidentally, was shortly after hiring Sacchi – according to a source he said: 'Goodness! I knew he was good, I never knew he was that good. Had

I known, maybe I would have given the Milan job to him.'

It was too late, of course. Yet Milan felt Capello could still be a valuable asset. But where? And how? Berlusconi said: 'We'll worry about that later. In the meantime, let's send him to school.' Which is what happened. Capello was sent on a year's worth of intensive executive training, alongside the bright young things of the Berlusconi business empire. It involved classes in English and French, but also courses in accountancy, business administration, human resources and finance.

'And we also sent him on workshops in things like interpersonal communication, team-building, stress management, risk assessment, problem solving, negotiation . . . everything you would expect for a high-level executive,' says De Michelis.

Capello embraced the opportunity, even though it meant taking a break from football. The fact that Berlusconi believed in him enough to send him on such a course meant a lot to him. It's one thing to be self-assured and to be confident in your intelligence (a trait which some saw as arrogance), quite another to have one of the most successful entrepreneurs in the world believe in you, a forty-year-old ex-footballer who, but for a few months, had only ever worked with kids – to the point of investing a whole year's worth of resources in your personal development in fields wholly unrelated to football or even sport.

That year, 1987–88, was a chance for Capello to not only study the nuts and bolts of running a business and working within a large corporate structure – qualities which, increasingly, would become necessary in club football – but also to hone his personal skills, communicate more effectively and learn principles of team-building and leadership. Obviously these were qualities which in large part he already had, but the course allowed him to think of them in a more structured way.

'Look, a donkey won't turn into a thoroughbred, no matter how many courses you send him on,' says De Michelis. 'Fabio obviously already had that skill set within him. But, thanks also to the spirit and enthusiasm with which he approached that year of study, I think he was able to better master the ability that was already there. And perhaps use it in a more efficient way. Let's put it this way: you can use a stone to drive a nail into a wall. But, obviously, it's better to do it with a hammer. Many sportsmen have just stones at their disposal. Fabio now has a range of high-precision hammers.'

It also – though Capello may disagree – boosted his confidence and broadened his horizons. He had crossed from the blue-collar world of football to the white-collar world of business and he had more than held his own. Indeed, he felt very much at ease in that context.

'I'm glad I did it because I see many things in a different light,' he said in the January 2000 interview quoted earlier. 'I understand the business side of football. I'm not going to be blinded or intimidated by numbers and balance sheets. I have a better appreciation for the problems of others and how they can be solved.'

On the pitch, Sacchi, after some initial scepticism, was true to his billing, delivering the 1987–88 *scudetto*. The side was pretty much that of the year before, with the addition of Carlo Ancelotti in midfield and the Dutch duo of Ruud Gullit and Marco Van Basten (who missed most of the campaign through injury). Despite the fact that Milan had to come from behind to snatch the title from Maradona's Napoli (a dramatic 3–2 win in Naples on the third-to-last weekend of the season sent them on their way), it was very much seen as Sacchi's success. His revolutionary brand of football was all the rage, not just in Italy but elsewhere too. Capello quickly fell out of the limelight, but that suited him just fine.

While Berlusconi was revelling in winning the league title, he wasn't forgetting about Capello. In fact, he had an ambitious project lined up for him. For some time he had been fascinated with the idea of clubs like Barcelona or Real Madrid, who fielded teams in a variety of sports, from basketball to water polo. He felt that, under his tutelage, the Milan brand could grow along the same lines, achieving success in multiple sports. And, ultimately, it would achieve levels of popularity (and, therefore, sponsorship) which would allow each sport to be not just successful, but self-sustaining as well.

Thus was born the 'Polisportiva Mediolanum', with Capello as General Manager, responsible for everything from approving budgets to sponsorship deals to marketing to personnel decisions. He had a staff of some forty people working under him. Mediolanum began with a volleyball team (Gonzaga Milano) and an ice hockey team (Diavoli Milano); the following year it added a baseball team (CUS Milano) and a rugby club (Amatori Milano). In each case, Berlusconi took over existing clubs and brought them within the Mediolanum fold.

The idea was to have a two-prong approach. On the one

hand, it was to push 'minority sports' to young kids on a participatory basis: a laudable initiative for which Mediolanum hoped eventually to get government support (it never did). On the other hand, Berlusconi wanted his clubs to win straight away, believing that success, coupled with his ability as a salesman, would drive interest in those sports.

This whole process wasn't without a degree of controversy. While some of the clubs were in financial difficulty and welcomed the approach, others were happy with their semi-professional status. Supporters weren't too pleased either when many teams abandoned their traditional kit for designs inspired by Milan's black-and-red logo.

Then there was the fact that Berlusconi pumped a large amount of cash into the Mediolanum clubs in an effort to achieve instant success. Capello found himself in charge of sizeable budgets which, overnight, shifted the balance of power in the respective sports. To cite but one example: the rugby club brought in David Campese, arguably the greatest winger in the history of the game, a man who would retire with 101 caps and sixty-four tries in Test matches for Australia (the latter was a world record until 2006). They also raided opposing clubs, bringing in no fewer than five Italian internationals, including fly-half Diego Dominguez. To the purists, they were wrecking long-established traditions. To the bean-counters, they were driving up costs and wages to unsustainable levels.

Capello oversaw the first three years of the Mediolanum project. When he left, in 1991, they were well on their way. They would end up winning Italian titles in rugby, baseball and ice hockey, while the volleyball club would win the European Cup Winners' Cup. By the mid-1990s, however, Berlusconi – who had not seen the necessary financial return to justify the spiralling costs of full-fledged professionalism – pulled the plug. It was a sudden and unpopular decision which affected all the clubs badly. The baseball club nearly went bankrupt and opted for relegation to the fourth division, where costs were much lower. Rugby was folded into another club, Calvisano. The hockey side effectively did the same, moving some 200 miles away to Courmayeur. And the volleyball side, unable to meet its wage commitments, was forced to release all its players and reform in the lower divisions.

Of course, by that point Capello was long gone. Certainly, he can't be held responsible for the long-term failure of the project. If anything, one would question Berlusconi's decision to spend wildly on sports which clearly could not be viable at certain levels of investment. In fact, according to a source, on more than one occasion Capello wondered about the financial wisdom of giving these clubs massive budgets. He nevertheless has fond memories of his time at Mediolanum. He gained first-hand knowledge of other sports and learned not just about technique and training methods, but also the differences in spirit and ethos between, say, rugby or ice hockey on the one hand, and football on the other.

'I think he inevitably picked up certain elements from other sports,' says De Michelis. 'For example, he was struck by ice hockey, a sport which is, of course, faster and more dynamic than football, but where good teams move around the ice as one, in perfect synchronicity. The question became, can you transfer some of that to football? And how? Intelligent people don't just invent things on their own. They look at what others do. And they copy the best bits.'

Now, it's not as if Capello's training methods today are borrowed wholesale from (or even based on) what he saw on the baseball diamond or the volleyball court. Rather, those experiences got him thinking about the commonalities between the two, particularly the way space was covered on the field of play and the way different positions interacted with each other.

The Mediolanum experience, like his year of advanced study, had added to his skill set. Now, however, it was time to capitalize. He was now forty-five years old, he missed football, he was itching to show what he could do. The call came straight from Berlusconi: Sacchi was leaving, did he want to take over Milan?

In a heartbeat.

CHAPTER 8

In the Footsteps of Sacchi

On 19 June 1991 the media assembled at AC Milan's headquarters in Via Turati for Capello's unveiling. According to reporters present that day, Milan's press office was going into overdrive. They scurried around among the media representatives, speaking to each one by one.

'Guys, please, go easy on him . . .' they pleaded. 'Give him a chance, don't criticize him right away . . . And please, don't say that he's just a yes-man and that Berlusconi is the real manager . . .'

With hindsight, it seems extraordinary just how badly the media misread the situation. Today, calling Capello a 'yes-man', a stooge, a puppet of the owner or, as the Milan correspondent for *Corriere della Sera*, Italy's biggest newspaper, put it, 'the man from Berlusconi's human resources office' would appear ludicrous. Even his harshest critics concede that, whatever else he may be, he is very much his own man. Like Michael Fish failing to predict the Great Storm of 1987, the media's powers of prediction were way off that day.

And yet, to some degree, you could see where they were coming from. Sacchi had left under a storm, slamming the door behind him. He had been sacked after four seasons in which Milan won a league title, two European Cups, two World Club Cups and, just as important, displayed a brand of football which was innovative to the point of being revolutionary and, on some nights, entertaining to the point of being magical.

Yes, Sacchi could be stubborn and abrasive. And he had made certain demands of the club, which had rankled with Silvio Berlusconi and Adriano Galliani. He felt that Milan wasn't doing enough to support him in the transfer market. In his first year, 1987–88, they had acquired the Dutch triumvirate of Marco Van Basten, Ruud Gullit and Frank Rijkaard (who would arrive a year later, when Serie A increased the number of places for foreigners from two to three). After that, it was slim pickings. Milan had focused on adding youngsters (only one of whom – striker Marco Simone – would have any real impact) and squad players. Thus, the starting eleven in his last season was identical, except for Rijkaard, to the one he used in 1987–88.

He wanted wholesale changes. According to reports, he felt that players such as Mauro Tassotti (thirty-one at the time) and Carlo Ancelotti (thirty-two) were nearing their expiry date. More generally, he felt that 'a cycle of success had come to an end' and a shake-up was necessary. One that would bring fresher, hungrier players who could counter the fact that, while Milan stood still, other clubs were strengthening year on year.

Milan agreed a shake-up was needed. But what he could

never have imagined was that the shake-up began (and ended) with him. Berlusconi felt that, with Sacchi's help, they had created a near-perfect system, which only required some tweaking. And if Sacchi wasn't willing to do it, he'd get somebody else to do it.

But there was another factor as well. The club felt that, at times, Sacchi pushed his players too hard, that his maniacal quest for 'perfect football' took too much out of the team, physically and, especially, mentally. After winning the title in 1987–88, they had placed third and then, twice in a row, second, but, in both of the latter cases, it was felt Milan should have won the *scudetto*. The runners-up spot in 1989–90 was an especially harsh blow, as Milan's defeat in Verona (just like sixteen years earlier) handed the title to Napoli at the end of a crazy ninety minutes which saw a furious Sacchi sent off, along with Billy Costacurta, Rijkaard and Van Basten. The popular theory was that Sacchi heaped so much psychological pressure on his players that, at the crucial hurdle, they would fall. Someone with a slightly more pragmatic attitude, someone who knew what buttons to push and when, someone who would not smother the players – that's what was needed.

Yet at the time the media were largely with Sacchi. They felt Berlusconi was simply unwilling to spend more money on the side. And that he couldn't fathom someone outspoken who regularly said no to him. Berlusconi's own ego, they claimed, was getting in the way of Sacchi doing his job. Indeed, the situation was uncannily similar to that at Chelsea in September 2007, when the club parted company with Jose Mourinho, another outspoken and self-assured manager who had enjoyed tremendous success.

And, as was the case at Chelsea – who turned to Avram Grant – the guy chosen to replace a legend was seen as a 'company man', a toady who would fulfil the owner's every whim. Again, outrageous as it seems today, back then, Capello was the Grant of his day.

'Fabio was greeted with lots of scepticism and zero enthusiasm,' says Silvano Ramaccioni, who had the title of 'team manager' at Milan but who was a sort of jack-of-all-trades behind the scenes. 'Sure, he had been a great player, but he had disappeared from view in the previous years, when he went on his training courses and, later, at Mediolanum. Some questioned whether he had kept up with football, they wondered whether he even had the desire to be a manager, given that he had chosen to spend so long away from the game.'

In some ways, it's understandable. In football, it's often out-of-sight, out-of-mind. Capello's coaching CV consisted of five seasons of youth football, nine months as an assistant and seven competitive matches as interim manager. What's more, for the previous four years he had been away from the game. And now, there he was, taking over a powerhouse side who had won two European Cups in the past three seasons. Then again, Berlusconi liked to make bold and unorthodox choices. When he opted for Sacchi, back in 1987, the media were equally nonplussed. At the time, he had four seasons of management under his belt, three of them in the third division and one in Serie B, when he led Parma to a respectable, but not earth-shattering, seventh-place finish. And of course, unlike Capello, Sacchi had never played competitive football. In fact, when Sacchi arrived, the joke at Milanello was that he wouldn't stick around to eat *panettone*, the traditional Italian Christmas cake.

So, from Berlusconi's perspective, this was nothing new. They had taken a chance before, they were doing it again. It had worked out before, and – as we all know – it worked out again.

But it's worth noting the climate around Milan at the time. Sacchi wasn't just a successful manager, he was seen as a kind of prophet, a genius and an innovator who had turned the game on its head. The line that was spun was that he was the iconoclast, the Messiah of football who had been crucified by the rich and powerful Berlusconi, perhaps scared that Sacchi would fully redefine football. And, by contrast, Capello was depicted as the polar opposite: the lackey, the toady, who had seized the place of the righteous Sacchi by sucking up to the powers-that-be.

'Every morning I look in the mirror and I tell myself that Capello is the single greatest insult to the coaching profession. I am ashamed that he is a Serie A manager, and, therefore, a colleague of mine.'

Harsh words? You bet. They were spoken by Franco Scoglio, a Serie A manager whose career had mirrored Sacchi's. He had never played professionally, but instead was a teacher turned coach, who had worked his way up from youth football all the way to Serie A. He too thought of himself as a tactical visionary, often saying that he drew inspiration from Uruguayan football of the 1920s, albeit updating it with his own ideas, which he often explained lacing them with literary and cultural references. He did enjoy some success initially (though, obviously, Sacchi was on another level), though many eventually came to see him as something of a blowhard. Either way, his disdain for those like Capello who, in his opinion, had cut corners and been handed Milan on a silver platter was obvious. As he saw it, a mortal sin had been committed against Sacchi and all those who, like him, wanted to 'reinvent' football.

Looking back, Sacchi had been truly different. He was responsible for arguably the greatest tactical innovation since Rinus Michels' 'total football' in Holland in the early 1970s. The bald former shoe salesman with the intense, almost wild eyes and obsessive-compulsive mannerisms can justifiably claim that he changed the game for ever. Like most prophets, his message was later processed, reworked and made more palatable by others, but there can be little question that almost every manager who has followed him in the past two decades has taken something from him. He was the idealist who tried to impose his own utopia on football. Those who followed – Capello among them – took the core of the message and adjusted it to their own needs. But there is no question who the source was: Sacchi.

When I went to see him in the spring of 2008, he was a tiny bit mellower than I remembered him – as one of his ex-players might have said: 'He was set to eight, not his usual eleven' – but the aura was still there. When he spoke, he was like a preacher, though not in an annoying sense, but, rather, like a man with an incredible need to explain himself.

One of his core beliefs was that, if you could synchronize movement and positioning, you could achieve a 'multiplier' effect. If your team moved as one, each player continuously adjusting to what was happening, it would be almost like playing with thirteen or fourteen players, rather than eleven. Thus, Sacchi had a counter-measure for every possible scenario on the pitch. So, for example, if the opposing fullback passed to the winger on the right-hand side of midfield, the whole team read-justed. And when the winger passed it inside to a central midfielder, they would all readjust again. Always co-ordinated, always in unison. And it was the same when Milan had possession.

'And then there was our pressing game, of which we had four or five different varieties, based on the situation,' Sacchi told me. 'But it was always a collective, harmonious effort.'

Such was Sacchi's faith in the power of tactics that he would challenge his players to a little game. He would take his back four, plus the goalkeeper – all of whom had been drilled in his defensive philosophy – and have them defend one of the goals against ten outfield players.

'They had fifteen minutes to score,' he says. 'There were ten of them – great players, mind you, Gullit, Van Basten, Ancelotti, Donadoni and so on – against five of us. The only rule was that, if they lost possession, they would have to restart inside their own half. Beyond that, they could do what they liked. And, you know what? In all my time there, they never once managed to score. Never. Even though it was ten against five! Why? Because the five were following my instructions. That's how I convinced the foreigners, Gullit and Van Basten, that they should believe in my way of doing things.'

Sacchi's idea was that tactical prowess would inevitably

improve the players and, by extension, the team. And so he drilled as much tactical knowledge and scenarios into his men as possible, demanding that they follow the instructions to the smallest detail. The day before a game, he would line up his starting eleven on a full-size pitch and have them simulate a match . . . with an imaginary ball.

'I would run around and say, "The ball is here, what do you do?"' he says. 'Or, "indirect free kick" from there. Or, when we were in possession, the players would have to pass the imaginary ball to each other, while reacting against imaginary opponents I conjured up on the spot. Somebody watching us would have thought we were crazy. But it worked, as it drilled certain concepts into the players' brains which would then become second nature.'

But wasn't it about putting eleven robots on the pitch?

'Quite the contrary,' says Sacchi. 'I gave them the tools of what they should do, but they were the ones who, in a split second, would have to assess the situation, decide what scenario we were facing and react accordingly. They had to use their brains for that. I am like a scriptwriter and director in one. I give them the screenplay and the instructions, but it's up to them to interpret the role.'

'Of course, all of this was extremely demanding, both physically and mentally,' he adds. 'That's why I think we trained harder than anybody else.'

The last point is extremely telling. And it was one of the factors that had concerned Berlusconi and Galliani. Sacchi's football was so intense, so taxing, that the players could only execute it to the highest level maybe a dozen or so times a year. Those performances – like the 5–0 annihilation of Real Madrid in the 1988–89 European Cup semi-final second leg – stand out. But it was nearly impossible to replicate that every week, precisely because it was so exhausting. Of course, even when Milan did not reach those heights, they still ground out good results, as evidenced by the two second-place finishes. But, Sacchi's critics said, that was down to having world class players, not the system of play. Or, put another way, Sacchi's football worked when Milan played well and were 100 per cent fit. On those days, they were truly out of this world. But when they weren't in top form, Milan were, once again, ordinary.

Capello, it was felt, was the man who could bridge that gap, who could add consistency, even at the expense of Sacchi's occasional brilliance, to the side. Plus, as some have noted, Capello wouldn't overshadow Berlusconi, as Sacchi often seemed to do.

Back to Capello's first day. He could sense the scepticism in the air. He would have to win everybody over. Not because he particularly cared what others thought, but because he knew well that if people did not believe in him, his job would be that much more difficult.

Among the very first words out of his mouth were these: 'I am proud and honoured to follow in the footsteps of Sacchi who, in my opinion, is the greatest manager in the world.'

It was a clear message that he was respectful of Sacchi's work. And it was also a sign of humility towards those who remembered him as a player and were convinced he would bring his cocksure attitude into management as well.

He knew he wasn't going to get much help from Berlusconi in the transfer market. If the president wasn't willing to spend money for Sacchi, who had won two European Cups, he sure as heck wasn't going to do it for him. Not initially, anyway. Thus, his squad was largely unchanged, with two notable exceptions: Demetrio Albertini, a promising young midfielder, returned from a loan spell with Padova in Serie B. Despite his tender age, Capello would show no hesitation and stick him straight into central midfield, in place of the ageing Ancelotti. And Francesco Antonioli, a promising goalkeeper, returned from a season on loan at another Serie B club, Modena.

Thus Capello knew he wouldn't be able to bring in 'his guys'. Which presented a bit of a problem. I remember interviewing Arsène Wenger a few years ago and him telling me: 'Too many veteran players in a dressing room can be a ticking time bomb for a manager. Especially if those players had already been successful under someone else.'

Which was the situation Capello was facing. Five of the starting eleven were twenty-nine or older. They had excelled under Sacchi and, while it wasn't always plain sailing in terms of personal relationships, they all knew that they had been a part of something truly special. And now, here was the 'president's man', coming in to take his place.

Capello had, of course, worked with Maldini and Costacurta at youth level. He had played with Baresi, and Donadoni had been there back in 1986–87, when he was Liedholm's assistant. But they all knew him as part of the 'old' Milan, the pre-Sacchi-revolution Milan. Gaining their trust was going to be tricky.

He revealed a little bit about how he did it in a February 2001 newspaper interview. On his first day, he called a team meeting and addressed his players.

'They said most of you are finished, that your time has passed and that Milan should be torn down and built up again,' he said, looking each one in the eye. 'I know in my mind and in my heart that this is not true. I know that we can win again as a group, I know you can all last another five years, at least. I know this because I played at the highest level until I was thirty-four and I know that it can be done. I want you to prove to all the naysayers who don't believe in you that they are wrong. That you do have a future and that we can win together.'

As an icebreaker, it worked. Capello had turned the issue around. He had reminded them that it was Sacchi who wanted them gone, not he. And that, in fact, he had accepted the job because he thought he could make it work.

'It was a clever thing to do and we bought into it,' one Milan player, who asked for anonymity, told me. 'He probably would have been better off not citing himself as an example though, given that his career nosedived after he turned thirty-one and that, while he may have played until he was thirty-four, the last two seasons he contributed very little. Fortunately, I don't think most of the guys knew what had happened to Capello at the end of his career. So rather than focusing on that, they focused on the main part of his message, that they were not, in fact, finished.'

With most of the starting lineup established, the main conundrum for Capello was in goal, where the choice was between the returning Antonioli and Sebastiano Rossi, a reserve the previous season. The club were leaning towards Antonioli, a gifted goalkeeper who ticked all the boxes: he was athletic, aware and unflappable. Plus, he was homegrown, unlike Rossi, whom Sacchi had insisted upon signing in the summer of 1990.

Rossi was the kind of goalkeeper who tended to divide public opinion. At 6ft 7in he was a giant of a man who dominated his area in the style of Peter Schmeichel. But he was often not easy on the eye and his style was sometimes unorthodox. He was strong-willed, vocal and occasionally there were flashes of a fiery temper, which led one teammate to describe him as 'difficult, very difficult. Though deep down, he meant well. Very deep down.'

'It wasn't easy for me, because I was coming from a small club like Cesena,' he says. 'My first season I struggled a lot, then slowly I was given a chance. My personality? Let's just say I was a lively boy . . .'

Capello's mind leant towards Antonioli, who had the better range of skills. But his heart screamed out for Rossi. He loved the big goalkeeper's passion and intensity, the way he played goalkeeper as if it were an attacking position. He may have been Sacchi's hand-picked choice, he may occasionally have infuriated teammates with his outbursts, he may have been objectively not as good as Antonioli, but to Capello it didn't matter; the intangible qualities and personality he brought to the game made all the difference. Rossi got the starting job.

Milan were banned from Europe that year, punishment for what had happened in Marseille the previous March in the quarter-finals of the European Cup. Having drawn the first leg 1–1, Milan were a goal down a few minutes from the final whistle when one of the Stade Vélodrome's floodlights went out. The referee halted play and then, a few minutes later, decided there was still enough light to continue. But, by that point, Galliani had taken all the players off the pitch and refused to play on. He was obviously hoping for a replay, but UEFA was having none of it. The final result stood and Milan were kicked out of Europe for the 1991–92 season.

In some ways, it suited Capello just fine, because it allowed him to focus on winning back the *scudetto*. Which is exactly what happened, and in the most emphatic manner. Milan tore through the season and finished eight points clear at the top. They did so without losing a single game. Not one.

'Out of all of Fabio's many achievements, I still think that was the single most difficult,' says Silvano Ramaccioni. 'Because it's the kind of record which will live for ever, in the sense that it can't be beaten, only equalled. It had only happened on one other occasion, at Perugia in the late 1970s, a year I remember well as I was sporting director there at the time.'

Van Basten, at the peak of his powers, led all scorers with twenty-five league goals in thirty-one games. The previous season injuries had limited him to just eleven in thirty-one. Albertini settled neatly into the midfield role, progressively taking the baton from Ancelotti. And the defence was as impregnable as ever, conceding just twenty-one goals. As for entertainment, well, Capello's Milan hit the back of the net seventy-four times, which is thirteen more than Sacchi's Milan had ever achieved. Along the way, they put five past Sampdoria (the defending champions) and Napoli and an incredible eight past mid-table Foggia away from home on the final day of the season.

'The foundation was, of course, Sacchi's Milan, but Fabio was clever about how he built on it,' says Ramaccioni. 'Defensively, it was still about pressing, the flat back four and the offside trap. But in the final third, players had more opportunity to express themselves. And I think he also created a slightly different climate, one less pressurized than the team experienced under Sacchi.'

Van Basten agreed. Years later, he would say: 'Capello gave us more freedom than Sacchi, but also more responsibility. And we also varied the pace of our game more, which meant we would sometimes have pauses which gave us time to think. We still pressed, but we did it with more intelligence and it was definitely less demanding physically.'

One quirk which made him different was the way the team prepared for matches. The night before games, he would have long individual chats with those who would start. Then, on matchday mornings, he would give his tactical instructions, usually by writing things out on the wipe-erase board. The idea was that if you told a player something, he could feign attention and perhaps not listen fully. But if you wrote it down, you forced the player to at least read it once. And, consciously or not, the concept would stick in his mind.

The only defeat that year came in the Coppa Italia semi-final against Juventus. After a scoreless first leg which Milan dominated, a goal by Totò Schillaci, Italy's hero at Italia 90, condemned Capello to his first defeat as

Milan manager. It came on 14 April 1992, a full ten months after his arrival.

The critics who had so questioned his appointment the summer before were silenced. Those who had said he wasn't fit to carry Arrigo Sacchi's clipboard had to eat crow. 'Sacchi's football was innovative, no question about it,' Capello said that summer. 'But, as with all things, it can be improved upon.' Asked about the criticism, he replied: 'Nothing can hurt me. I let everybody think what they like and then I get on with the job. I let my results do the talking. I don't seek vengeance in words. My revenge comes on the pitch.'

Some pundits did point out that, while Sacchi was clearly wrong in believing the current Milan crew were finished, it was nevertheless true that Capello had won with Sacchi's Milan. The formation and tactics – apart from the tweaks mentioned above – were largely the same, as was the personnel. And, of course, Capello had yet to be tested in Europe.

Capello accepted this. But he also knew that now he could approach Berlusconi from a position of strength. He had held up his end of the bargain, he had delivered the *scudetto* without lavish spending in the transfer market. He had shown that the 'old guard' still had gas in the tank. Now, however, he needed Berlusconi's help. It was time to open up the wallet and strengthen the team.

Berlusconi duly responded in the most emphatic way. He broke the world transfer record in bringing in Gigi Lentini, a powerfully built goalscoring winger from Torino. The sheer size of his transfer, thought to be around £15 million, shocked public opinion, including the Vatican, whose official newspaper called the fee 'an offence against the dignity of work'. Nando De Napoli, a hard-tackling holding midfielder and former Italian international, arrived from Napoli, while Stefano Eranio, another Italian international, joined from Genoa.

And then there was the issue of foreigners. The Italian FA had relaxed their rules on the matter. While clubs could still field no more than three foreign players at one time, they could in fact have as many as they liked on their books. Milan, despite already counting on Gullit, Van Basten and Rijkaard, added another three. Jean-Pierre Papin, the reigning European Footballer of the Year, was signed from Marseille, while Dejan Savicevic, the mercurial virtuoso from Montenegro joined from Red Star Belgrade. Finally, there was the player Capello was most excited about: Zvonimir Boban.

The Croatian midfielder had actually been signed the previous summer from Dinamo Zagreb but, because of the rules on foreigners, Milan had shipped him on a season-long loan to Bari.

Boban had made headlines two years earlier, in May 1990 at the Yugoslav Cup Final between Dinamo and Red Star Belgrade. The country was beginning to fall apart, tensions were running high between Croats and Serbs and there had been fighting between the two sets of supporters: nationalism masquerading as football. The Delije, Red Star's hardcore supporters (led by future war criminal Zeljko Raznatovic, aka Arkan), stormed the pitch in an effort to get at their Croatian counterparts, the BBB (Bad Blue Boys), who themselves spilled on to the playing field. The predominantly Serb police stepped in and their tactics were particularly heavy-handed. Many neutrals described it as one-sided policing, with Dinamo fans getting hit by batons and teargassed. Boban, one of the few players remaining on the pitch, initially tried to restore order, pleading with police to calm down. When he saw police beating a member of the BBB who was lying prone on the ground, he lost it. He struck a police officer and then, as they chased him around the pitch, decked another one with a flying karate-kick worthy of, if not Jackie Chan, at least Eric Cantona. That kick – in addition to becoming a YouTube classic – instantly made Boban a legend among Croatian nationalists. It also, symbolically, marked the beginning of the war between Croatia and Serbia which would ultimately result in the break-up of Yugoslavia.

As for Boban, he initially faced a prison term but ended up receiving 'merely' a six-month ban. For a time, it looked as if his career would go off the rails. The many Western clubs who were queuing up to sign him got cold feet. How do you gamble on a guy who attacks a police officer in a public arena? But Capello saw things differently. Boban's skills were obvious. And, more importantly, Boban struck him as an intelligent youngster, albeit one who had been caught up in something far bigger than himself and had made a serious mistake. He wasn't about to write him off.

Competition for places naturally intensified. Eranio and Lentini were a threat to both Donadoni on the right and Alberigo Evani on the left. De Napoli, like Boban, was an alternative to both Rijkaard and Albertini (Ancelotti had retired that summer). And, up front, Van Basten and Gullit had to deal not just with Marco Simone, the promising youngster nicknamed 'Peter Pan' who would win his first cap that season, but also Papin, one of the best strikers in the world. Finally, there was Savicevic, who looked like the squarest of pegs in Capello's round holes. He was an immensely gifted number 10 who had previously floated behind the strikers, strolling about the pitch and, as one journalist put it, 'creating magic but only whenever the Muses inspired him to do so, which rarely was more than once or twice per game'. Nobody had any clue where he might fit in.

Complicating matters further was the fact that the foreign players were also competing against each other, regardless of position, since only three could be included in the matchday squad. Potentially, it was a gigantic headache, with Capello having to take into account not just a player's ability, but his passport as well. And knowing that, every week, he'd have to tell three of his best (and best paid) players to watch from the stands.

Yet Capello had wanted it that way. Milan's football was still largely based on Sacchi's vision, which meant it was physically very exhausting. He felt he needed a deeper squad, partly to cope with injuries, partly to implement what in Italy is known as 'turnover' (or squad rotation). Papin was something of an insurance policy against Van Basten's injuries: the Dutchman's ankle had held up beautifully the previous year, but there was no guarantee it would last. As for Savicevic, he was obviously an unorthodox player whose workrate was suspect and who had no natural role in the Milan side. But Berlusconi adored him and, after all, he was the guy who paid the bills. Capello knew and accepted that. Which is why he tried to turn a negative into a positive. Finding a way to take Savicevic and turn him into a productive member of the squad was a huge challenge and one which probably went against his nature as a manager. But, if he could find a way to do it, he would improve his range of skills even further and become an even better boss.

Today, squad rotation is taken for granted. It is seen as part-and-parcel of the modern game – any big club wishing to compete both domestically and in Europe has to do it to some degree. But, back then, it was a novel concept which stunned the footballing world (which was as conservative in the early 1990s as it is today). That year, Capello's Milan became the first side in history to employ wholesale rotation in an effort to generate competition among players and minimize the effects of fatigue.

The season could not have begun any better. Milan won their first seven Serie A games, equalling the record. And they did it resoundingly. Among the streak were a 5–4 win at Pescara, a 5–3 home victory against Lazio and an incredible 7–3 away win at Fiorentina. A few weeks later, they followed it up with a 5–1 win at Napoli, in which Van Basten scored four.

The media were stunned. Milan were on track to rewrite every record book. They had played sixteen games in all competitions – Serie A, Coppa Italia, Champions League – winning fourteen and drawing just two. They had scored fifty-four goals – an average of three and a half per game – and conceded fourteen.

But Capello was not entirely happy. Milan were leaking too many goals: two against Serie B Ternana in the Coppa Italia, three each against Fiorentina and Lazio, four against

Pescara. While everyone was praising him, he felt a bit uncomfortable. Milan were unbalanced and it showed. Yes, they were getting away with it because of the incredible firepower up front, but what happened if the strikers had a bad day?

Part of the problem lay in the flanks. Previously, he, like Sacchi, had counted on Evani and Donadoni, wide men who were gifted going forward but were also familiar enough with Milan's tactical needs to do a job defensively as well (indeed, both had been there since Day One of the Sacchi era). Now, however, he was using Lentini and occasionally Gullit, Massaro or even Savicevic in wide areas. These players were too good to leave out, but, by shoehorning them into the lineup he was forcing them to do things they had never done before.

Going back to the tried and tested – Evani and Donadoni week in, week out – was not an option. The club had invested too much in Lentini and, besides, Capello could tell that, even though he had his inconsistencies, he also had a tremendous amount of potential. And so he came up with Plan B, dropping Rijkaard and Albertini that little bit deeper and creating what was going to become one of his hallmarks: what the Spanish called the 'double pivot', two central midfielders who would break up play and pull strings from deeper positions. This had the dual effect of providing more cover for the back four while allowing the wide midfielders licence to continue doing what they had been doing, getting forward and effectively acting as auxiliary strikers.

Capello also made a goalkeeping change, albeit a forced one. Antonioli had been very impressive in pre-season training, while Rossi had looked somewhat erratic. With a portion of the public still doubting Rossi's ability, especially compared to the elegant Antonioli, Capello gave the job to the latter. Rossi was dejected and angry. He was told that 'his time would come' but, of course, that's what reserve players always get told. Everything changed on 29 November when Milan played away to Juventus. Antonioli got hurt and Rossi came on as a sub.

'That was the game when I finally silenced the critics and won the job for good,' Rossi says. 'I came on and saved a penalty from Gianluca Vialli, preserving our 1–0 win.' It was vintage Rossi. He was so fired up and so aggressive, so one Milan player told me, that he seemed to gobble up the whole face of the goal with his body – there was nowhere for Vialli to put the ball.

'After the game, there were no special congratulations from Capello, no thank you for what I had done,' says Rossi. 'He simply walked up to me, half-smiled and punched me lovingly in the arm. It was his way of show-ing affection, I guess. And it meant a lot to me.'

A few weeks later, in December, Van Basten went down again to injury. Again, it was his ankle and the doctors' verdict left little room for hope: the Dutchman would miss at least five months. In some ways, the cloud had a silver lining. Van Basten's absence allowed the manager to give the other foreigners more playing time. Before that, Rijkaard and Van Basten effectively started every game, which meant there was only one slot for Papin, Gullit, Boban and Savicevic. Now there were more opportunities. Papin responded by scoring regularly (he would end the season on thirteen goals in twenty-two appearances) and it certainly took some of the pressure off in terms of team selection.

Increasingly, it was becoming an issue. Nobody likes to sit on the bench (or, worse, in the stands) but as the season wore on, players began to grumble. One of them was Gullit. The Dutchman had been an integral part of Sacchi's Milan and even in Capello's first season he had done his bit. Now, however, he was fighting for a place in the side every week. Striker one week, benched the next, wide right in midfield the next and up in the stands the week after that. For a former European Footballer of the Year who, at age thirty, felt that he had plenty of football left in him, it was very humiliating.

In terms of pride, he hit rockbottom one day when the club announced the travelling squad for the next game. Gullit thought he had heard his name and duly boarded the team bus with all his kit. Capello noticed him on the bus and, to avoid an uncomfortable public scene in front of his teammates, sent Ramaccioni to tell him to get off. It was supposed to be low-key, but, in fact, everyone knew what was going on. Especially since everyone could count and they had all noticed that there were already three foreign players on the bus. Gullit trudged off, head bowed, spirits in the gutter.

'I don't know why Fabio didn't go and tell him himself,' one Milan player told me. 'Some of my teammates felt it was cowardly to send Ramaccioni to do his bidding. I don't think that was it. I think he genuinely didn't want to embarrass him and thought this would be a better way.'

Later, Capello did vent his anger on Ramaccioni, whose responsibility it was to notify the players in the matchday squad. 'Like all rows with Fabio, it quickly passed,' he says. 'But I did learn my lesson. From then on, I simply posted the team sheet and let players find out for themselves if they were in or out.'

Gullit soon had another row with Capello and, this time, they got right into each other's faces, before players and staff pulled them apart. For Capello, it was all over and forgotten very quickly. For Gullit it was another sign that, from his perspective, the situation was unsustainable.

'That's the thing about Fabio, he might blow up and have a row with someone, but, half an hour later, it's as if nothing happened,' says Ramaccioni. 'He has this incredible ability to move on, to never harbour a grudge. He really doesn't care about the past, only what's up next.'

Things were also tough for Simone, the young starlet known as 'Peter Pan'. He had won his first international caps that season, but simply could not find space in the side. His agent, Oscar Damiani, Capello's old friend and teammate from their years together at Juventus, hoped that he could put in a good word for his client. If he didn't want to play him, fine, but at least perhaps he would let him go elsewhere?

Capello's answer was an emphatic 'no'. In a nutshell, Simone wasn't good enough to get into the side ahead of the likes of Van Basten, Papin and Massaro. But he was also too good to be allowed to leave and strengthen a rival club. If Simone didn't like it, tough. He was paid to train and be ready to play if called upon. He didn't have a right to start and he certainly didn't have a right to demand a move, not as long as he was under contract.

'Yes, it was quite a row,' Damiani recalls. 'He wouldn't

budge one inch. And he was brutally honest. But that's the thing about Fabio, he'll say things directly to your face. Diplomacy is certainly not his strong suit. I mean, we were friends, but he was absolutely frank and brutal with me. Our relationship didn't come into it.'

Eranio was another who had hoped for more playing time. He was signed as a right-sided midfielder but knew from day one that he would be facing stiff competition in the shape of Donadoni and Lentini. So he did his best to adapt, offering to play rightback or central midfield, what-ever Capello needed. He had been a regular for Italy for the past eighteen months (under – ironically – Sacchi, who had taken the job in October 1991), but he had the humility to try and become a jack-of-all-trades. He had to. It was the only way to get on the pitch. Still, he bore no grudges.

'I think everyone had a run-in with him at some point,' he says. 'But the great thing about him is that he doesn't care who you are or what reputation you show up with. If you don't prove you're good enough in training, you won't play. He chooses his team based on the moment, who's doing well, who isn't, who's fit, who's not. Nobody is untouchable. And that way, everyone felt they had a chance, even the guys who hardly ever played.'

Of course, it's easier to do that when results are going your way and, at the time, they certainly were. Capello's first Serie A defeat didn't arrive until 21 March 1993, a one-goal loss at Parma. Coupled with his thirty-four-game undefeated streak the previous season, it meant that Milan had gone an incredible fifty-eight league games without loss. It's a run which probably won't be broken for some time: Arsenal's 'Invincibles', by comparison, managed forty-nine games, which is a full two months of matches fewer.

Capello took the defeat in his stride. And why shouldn't he? By that point, Milan had an eleven-point lead in Serie A: in the era of two points for a win, it was simply an enormous margin. It was obvious to all that they wouldn't be caught and, in fact, they weren't.

'We didn't dwell on the streak,' says Rossi, whose contribution would be decisive. He saved two penalties – in draws against Foggia and Atalanta – which could have broken the run. 'We didn't even think about it. We lost and we moved on.'

The Coppa Italia, where they had fielded an under-strength team (or about as under-strength as Milan could be in those days) for much of the season, saw them knocked out in the semi-finals by Roma. But nobody was too bothered. With Serie A virtually in the bag, the focus had shifted to the Champions League, which was in its inaugural season.

Milan dominated like no team before or since. On their way to the final, they won ten out of ten games, knocking out the likes of Porto and PSV Eindhoven along the way. They scored twenty-three goals in those ten games, conceding just one – and that was a disputed penalty converted by Romário.

Marseille lay in wait in the final, in what promised to be a bit of a grudge match, given events the year before. There were obvious parallels between the two sides. Marseille was owned by Bernard Tapie, who some saw as a French version of Berlusconi. The flamboyant millionaire businessman had taken control of Adidas and acquired a controlling share in Marseille. Like Berlusconi, he would later go into politics (unlike Berlusconi, he would go to prison for tax fraud as well). Tapie pumped vast amounts of money into Marseille, building a side which featured the likes of Marcel Desailly, Fabien Barthez (still with a full head of hair), Didier Deschamps, Rudi Völler and Alen Boksic (and, before his move to Milan the previous summer, Papin as well).

Capello, as ever, had tough choices to make with his starting eleven. The biggest was up front. Van Basten had returned from injury a month earlier. The doctor's verdict had been cautious: he had sustained so much damage to his ankle that there was really no way of telling whether or not he could play until he stepped on the pitch. And, even then, he would always be at risk. Van Basten, who knew that every game might be his last, wanted to play, of course. And Capello wasn't about to stop him.

But with Van Basten occupying one of the two spots up front, what to do with the other? Gullit said he was fit and desperately wanted to play. But he hadn't featured in more than a month and, besides, when Capello had used him, it was mainly on the right side of midfield. Papin was fired up to face his old teammates – he had left the French club under a cloud – but he was only just back from a six-week layoff. He had played the previous weekend in the league – a 1–1 draw in Cagliari – but was substituted and did not look right. With Rijkaard – as ever – untouchable in midfield, there was just one slot left for foreigners. Capello chose Papin, but, not believing he could last the ninety minutes, left him on the bench, with the speedy

Massaro up front. A sulking Gullit had to watch from the stands.

Milan had the upper hand in the first half. Van Basten, clearly suffering, struggled to move around the pitch, but the rest of the side were flying. Massaro wasted a few good chances. And then, entirely against the run of play, Marseille took the lead. With one minute to go in the first half, referee Kurt Röthlisberger awarded a dubious corner kick to Marseille. Abedi Pele stepped up to take it and his cross was met by Basile Boli, whose looping header beat Rossi. Milan were stunned.

Capello sent on Papin soon after the break, but Marseille grew in confidence and, led by a brilliant Desailly, protected the lead effectively. By this point, Van Basten's ankle had given way, anything other than a light trot clearly unsustainable. Capello stuck with him. So much for the idea of the cold, heartless coaching automaton. While he has never admitted it, it's hard to believe that it was anything other than an emotional choice. Both Papin and Van Basten were unfit, yet both soldiered on, believing – along with Capello – that qualities such as drive, heart and class could get the best of something as basic as fitness. They were wrong.

Four minutes from time, Capello puts an end to Van Basten's suffering. The fourth official holds up two yellow signs: '14' and '9' (the electronic board was still some years away). Van Basten looks toward the bench, face blank, mouth slightly open. His face tightens. Maybe he knows it's all over. Maybe not. A quick jog towards the sidelines, the final demands made of his knackered ankle. A quick handshake with Stefano Eranio, his replacement, a brush of Capello's arm and a nod as he trots past. And then nothing.

Marco Van Basten, the greatest centre-forward yours truly has ever seen, would never play football again.

'We dominated them that night,' says Rossi. 'That's all I remember from that game. That's all I choose to remember. We created so many chances, especially in the first half. I remember walking into the dressing room at half-time: nobody could believe we were losing. But that's football, I guess.'

Milan were gutted. Boli's goal was the only one from open play they had conceded all season long. There were some recriminations over Röthlisberger's officiating, in particular the granting of that corner kick, though frankly it seems a bit excessive to suggest a decision like that was part of some premeditated conspiracy. Yet a few years later, more disturbing facts emerged. Just four days before the Champions League final, Jacques Glassman, a defender at French first division club Valenciennes, blew the whistle on the fact that forty-eight hours earlier, he and two teammates had been offered bribes to lose their league match with Marseille. A full inquiry followed and Marseille were later stripped of the title and relegated (though they were allowed to keep the Champions League crown). Tapie eventually went to prison.

Nor was it lost on Milan that Röthlisberger, the Swiss referee, would also see his career and reputation tarnished. In 1996 FIFA banned him for life after allegations that he had tried to influence a fellow match official in a Champions League match between Auxerre and Grasshoppers. Capello had lost his first European final to a club which had fixed a match six days earlier. And that game was officiated by a referee whom football's governing body would later find guilty of corruption. You can see why, looking back, they would be just a little bit upset.

That summer, Capello knew the club had some rebuilding to do. As dominant as Milan had been, he knew this was no time to rest. As he has often said, 'I'd rather sit down and work on long-term problems, real or potential, when things are going well. It's a lot harder to fix things when things are already going badly.'

Rijkaard, such a steady performer over the years, was allowed to return home to Ajax. At thirty-one, he probably had a few more good years in the tank, but the club felt they wanted to reward his loyalty and allowed him to go home. Gullit, whose relationship with Capello remained strained, especially after being left out in the Champions League final, was also allowed to leave, albeit only on loan. He was a favourite of Berlusconi and the decision to send him to Sampdoria on a season-long loan smacks of a 'just in case' attitude from the Milan president. Yes, Gullit was unlucky under Capello and, right now, Capello had the upper hand, but, in football, you never know . . . should Capello leave or be sacked, Berlusconi wanted to be sure he could get Gullit back. Van Basten would remain under contract for another two years, undergoing lengthy and exhausting rehabilitation programmes, but all to no avail. The Dutch Era was over.

Christian Panucci, a gifted defender, arrived from Genoa. He was still just twenty, but his versatility – he could fill any position in the back four – appealed to Capello who felt he needed some cover for his veteran defence. He also signed two promising – if, until that point, disappointing – foreigners, Brian Laudrup and Florin Raducioiu. Both raised a few eyebrows. The Dane Laudrup was undoubtedly talented, but – perhaps unsettled by the inevitable comparisons to his brother, the legendary Michael – had been a flop the previous year at Fiorentina. The pacy Romanian Raducioiu had bounced around three different clubs, without really making his mark. Both looked like gambles and, frankly, you had to wonder if Milan, a club where competition for places was fierce and regular playing time hard to come by, was the right place for such calculated risks.

In fact, behind the scenes, there was considerable belt-tightening going on. Panucci was the only sanctioned purchase. The dumping of Gullit's wages, plus the sale of Rijkaard and Evani – still reliable at age thirty – had generated enough funds to sign Laudrup and Raducioiu. It seems incredible that Milan, after winning the *scudetto* and reaching the Champions League final, should have been hamstrung financially. But these were the days before huge TV deals and massive Champions League prize money. Milan had spent heavily in previous seasons; now it was time to rein things in.

Capello had no choice but to accept this, though he wasn't entirely happy about it. And he was even more annoyed in August, when Lentini suffered serious injuries after crashing his Porsche on the motorway. He had changed a tyre and was reportedly driving in excess of 110 miles per hour (nearly three times the recommended limit) with the spare. It was a stupid and very dangerous thing to do. And it permanently soured the relationship between him and Capello. One thing was not holding grudges. Quite another needlessly putting your own life and that of others at risk.

The media did not exactly feel sorry for Capello or Milan. Surely that was the whole point of having a deep squad. In fact, in certain positions Capello did not have quite as many options as he would have liked, particularly in central midfield, where Boban had taken over from Rijkaard alongside Albertini.

The Croat was more of a box-to-box type and he struggled in the deep-lying role. Still, Milan ground out results. They kept clean sheets in each of their first seven league matches and, by early October, they were top of the table. But there had been warning signs. In the Champions League, Milan struggled to overcome little Aarau, winning 1–0 in Switzerland and then settling for a scoreless draw at the San Siro. Albertini missed both games through injury and Capello tried both reinventing Eranio in a central role and dusting off the ageing De Napoli to replace him. Neither plan worked.

Then came three straight disappointing results in the league: two 1–1 draws (away to Foggia and home to Juventus) and then a 3–2 defeat at Sampdoria. The latter was particularly stinging. Milan were 2–0 up well into the second half but were unable to hang on to the lead. And, to make matters worse, none other than Gullit scored Sampdoria's winner twelve minutes from time.

It was obvious to Capello that the Boban–Albertini partnership was far from impregnable. And, while they could get away with it, they had no cover. What would happen if one of them got hurt?

He got to find out the following Sunday, when Boban limped off in a 2–1 win over Inter in the Milan derby. The prognosis wasn't good: out for three months. Now what? Parma had reached Milan at the top of the table. And, in a few weeks' time, the group stage of the Champions League would kick off, pitting the *rossoneri* against Werder Bremen, Porto and Anderlecht: hardly a cakewalk.

Capello spoke to Galliani. Something had to be done. But there were two problems: the transfer window closed in forty-eight hours. And there were no transfer funds available. Franco Tatò, whom Berlusconi had placed in charge of the club's finances while he embarked on his political career, had frozen all budgets.

'So I picked up the phone and called Tapie [owner of Marseille],' says Galliani. Tapie, perhaps realizing it would be difficult for Marseille to escape unscathed from the match-fixing charges, agreed to do business.

'We reached a deal quickly, £4.5 million, quite a bit of money in those days,' Galliani recalls. 'I had to make a decision on the spot, so I approved it without telling Tatò. Predictably, he was furious. I spent the next few weeks avoiding him . . . fortunately, by the time he caught up with me, Berlusconi had seen what Desailly could do and he backed me.'

Desailly arrived a few days later and went straight into the lineup. He had previously been deployed primarily in central defence, but Capello immediately saw his potential as a deep-lying midfielder. What some now call the 'Makelélé role' was actually pioneered by Desailly.

'He was like a sweeper in front of the defence,' says Ramaccioni. 'He wasn't given any specific marking duties, his job was simply to win the ball whenever it was nearby. Even when he did not get near the ball, he contributed. Opponents were forced wide, nobody wanted to come into his sphere of influence. Our defenders slept soundly at night thanks to him.'

His arrival was a masterstroke. And, as it turned out, a necessity. Albertini got injured in Desailly's very first game and missed the next six weeks. Which meant both of the men pencilled in as starting midfielders at the beginning of the season were out at the same time. Capello shuddered to think what would have happened if Desailly had never arrived and he had to face the next set of games without his first-choice pairing.

It's hard to overstate the impact he had. Desailly's arrival signalled the shift from the collective 'total football'-inspired game seen under Sacchi and in Capello's first two seasons. Instead, there now was a clearer definition of roles and a greater specialization as well.

'Desailly stiffened up our midfield, but he also changed the way we played,' says Eranio. 'He replaced Rijkaard who had more quality and would get forward more. Now we had a guy who did a disproportionate amount of defensive work. This took some of the defensive pressure off the other players, who felt more free to push on.' Tactically, it was a huge departure for Capello. Having achieved success with one system – his variation on Sacchi's approach – he was now taking a radical step in a different direction.

'I don't think a manager should have just one system of play,' he told me in an October 2007 interview. 'I think he should be familiar with several, so that he can choose the one that best suits his players.'

Meanwhile however, Capello was struggling with his strikers. Van Basten was nowhere near returning, Papin had a succession of niggling injuries that would limit him to just eighteen league starts. Raducioiu and Laudrup had both been disappointments. The relationship with Simone continued to be rocky, not least because he seemed unable to find the back of the net: he would score just three league goals that season.

Savicevic, meanwhile, still looked like a fish out of water in Capello's system, at least before Desailly's arrival. The purists loved his elegance, his sublime technique and his creativity, which is why he earned the nickname, *Il Genio*, 'The Genius'. But if he was a genius, he was a misunderstood one. His languid movements on the pitch irked the coaching staff, who expected workrate from everyone in the lineup. And his self-indulgence, particularly in front of goal, was maddening: amazingly, for a player of his talent, he would not score a single league goal all season. All of which left the 32-year-old Massaro as the only reliable option up front. Not coincidentally, he was nicknamed *Provvidenza* – 'Providence' – for the way he always seemed to find the net at crucial moments.

On 6 December 1993 the team flew out to Tokyo for the World Club Cup. Because of Marseille's domestic corruption scandal, UEFA chose Milan, the losing finalists, to represent Europe in the clash with the South American champions, São Paulo. The Brazilian side, brilliantly led by the legendary Telê Santana, was tough and talented, boasting the likes of Cafu, Leonardo, Müller and Juninho, plus a 'golden oldie' like Toninho Cerezo pulling the strings in midfield. The year before, they had come from behind to teach Johan Cruyff's Barcelona, the so-called 'Dream Team', a footballing lesson.

Milan were slight favourites, at least on paper, though, between absentees and rows, Capello had plenty on his plate. In addition to the long-injured Van Basten and Lentini, Eranio, Boban and Simone were also unavailable.

Then there was a major issue involving Savicevic. *Il Genio* was in a decent run of form. The coaching staff agreed that he was the right man to face São Paulo, who would play a slower, more technical brand of football. Plus, with Simone and Van Basten both unavailable and Massaro shunted to the wing, he was the only tried and trusted option to partner Papin up front. Savicevic, however, had a two-match FIFA ban hanging over him after being sent off with his national team.

Shortly before boarding the plane for Tokyo, Capello was informed that the ban would apply: Savicevic could take no part. During the flight, he explained the situation to him: both were dejected, but there was nothing he could do. He also took Raducioiu aside and told him he would start. The young Romanian had been used sparingly, partly because of the three foreigners rule, partly because he was simply not performing. While he had scored the winner, in a rare start the previous Sunday against Torino, it was obvious to all that he was out of his depth.

The night before the match, Capello announced his starting lineup to the team, confirming to Raducioiu that he would, indeed, start. The very next morning, a fax arrived at Milan's hotel from FIFA headquarters in Zurich. The game's governing body had taken another look at the situation and decided that Savicevic's ban did not apply to club competition, even in FIFA-sanctioned matches. He would serve his suspension with his national side and thus was free to play.

Everyone assumed this meant that he would go straight into the side. Instead, Capello made a very unpopular decision: he stuck with Raducioiu. Years later Capello would say: 'I thought about it long and hard, but ultimately I felt I couldn't play Savicevic, not after telling Raducioiu he would start. As a manager, I would have played Savicevic. But as a man, I had to play Raducioiu. And I am a man first.'

Savicevic was furious. He complained direct to Berlusconi in no uncertain terms. Savicevic had flown all the way to Tokyo to be with his teammates and, when it emerged he could play, he was denied a place. Privately, according to a source, he told teammates that he never again wanted to play for Capello. Galliani had to go into overdrive to mediate the situation.

So much for Capello's supposed win-at-all-costs mentality. Certainly the way he handled this incident seems entirely inconsistent with his image. On this occasion, the word he had given to Raducioiu trumped everything. Even if it meant diminishing Milan's chances of victory. Why put a promise made to a minor squad player above the good of the team?

I have no neat explanation for this, beyond the fact that Capello is not a machine, but a human being. And human beings grow and evolve over time. We are not always rational beings, we do not always follow our own precepts or, indeed, our own personalities. Maybe Capello did feel genuinely bad for Raducioiu. Maybe he felt he could win even without Savicevic. Maybe it was a temporary lapse of reason. In any case, that would be the very last time Capello announced the starting lineup on the eve of the game. From that moment forward, he would wait until a few hours before kickoff.

As it happened, it was a wide open game, with São Paulo twice taking the lead through Palinha and Cerezo and Milan twice coming back with Massaro and Papin. Raducioiu struggled, as many had predicted. Then, four minutes from time, Cerezo hit a ball over the top into Milan's penalty box. Rossi got there first, but failed to push it away and Müller, lightning quick, deflected it into the net.

'I partly blame the pitch and the fact that the ball took a funny bounce,' says Rossi. 'But I also blame myself. I was first to the ball, I should have had it.'

It was a long and disappointing flight back. The media speculated over the fallout between Capello and Savicevic. Even Berlusconi was called into the fray, speaking with Savicevic on several occasions in an effort to mend the relationship. Capello went on as if nothing had happened. Savicevic played the full ninety minutes in Milan's next match, a 2–1 home win over Cagliari. Capello had, typically, moved on.

'The way he handles the squad is unquestionably one of his greatest assets,' says Mario Ielpo, Milan's reserve goalkeeper at the time. 'He doesn't hold grudges, he just looks forward all the time. Capello can do this kind of thing, because he's somewhat detached from the players. He doesn't try to be their friend and, in doing so, is more free to make his decisions.'

Milan began the new year with an incredible defensive streak. While they continued to have trouble scoring, they weren't conceding either. Rossi kept a clean sheet at Reggiana on 2 January. Thus began a run which would continue until 27 February at home to Foggia. Nine consecutive games without conceding a goal.

Going into that match, Rossi's goal had not been breached in the league in three months, since 19 December against Cagliari. The streak stood at 863 minutes, just forty shy of Dino Zoff's record, which he had set at Juventus in 1973 (ironically, with Capello as a teammate).

When the clock hit thirty-nine minutes and Rossi was just sixty seconds away from the record, the entire crowd rose to their feet and began counting down the seconds – 'Sixty, fifty-nine, fifty-eight . . .' – before erupting in a standing ovation.

'Honestly, I didn't even notice, I was so focused on the game,' says Rossi. 'My teammates had to tell me during a break in play. I just wasn't thinking about it. I wouldn't say I didn't care about the record, but I really wasn't too bothered. I just wanted to set it and move on. Looking back, I'm proud of it, though obviously it's an honour which I need to share with all my teammates. And, I guess, it would have been a shame not to break the record, having come so close . . . a bit like going to Rome and not seeing the Colosseum.'

A gorgeous long-range effort from Foggia's Igor

Kolyvanov finally broke the run mid-way through the second half. Rossi's record stands to this day. Milan went on to win 2–1, maintaining a six-point lead at the top of the table, and ultimately secured the title two months later, at home to Udinese. Capello was three from three. No team had won three straight *scudetti* since the 1940s, when the legendary Torino side, the one which was snuffed out in the Superga air crash, won five in a row. Along the way, Milan had set a new record: fifteen goals conceded in thirty-four matches, the fewest ever in an eighteen-team top flight.

Milan were undefeated in the Champions League – conceding just two goals along the way – though their run was less impressive than the previous year. They topped the group stage thanks to a scoreless draw away to Porto on the final matchday. It was a crucial result given the format of the competition. That season, the top two sides in each group advanced, but the group winners had the luxury of playing the one-legged semi-final at home.

On 27 April 1994 they demolished Arsène Wenger's Monaco 3–0, in front of a capacity crowd at the San Siro, setting up the final against Cruyff's Barcelona. That night, however, would prove to be bittersweet. Costacurta was sent off and Baresi, who was one booking away from a ban, was cautioned. Milan would have to face the mighty Barça without their first-choice defensive partnership.

Cruyff had turned Barcelona into a veritable powerhouse. They were in the process of winning their fourth consecutive Liga title and, two years earlier, they had won the Champions League, beating Sampdoria at Wembley. The Dutchman could count on a star-studded side which the Spanish press had dubbed the 'Dream Team' – Romário, Hristo Stoichkov, Pep Guardiola, Jose Maria Bakero, Txitxi Beguiristain, Ronald Koeman – they were immensely talented from top to bottom. And they suited Cruyff's approach perfectly. Everyone could pass, everyone was comfortable on the ball, which meant they kept possession for ages, toying with their opponents, before upping the tempo and shooting at goal with startling ease. Cruyff's impact on the Spanish game was almost as significant as Sacchi's had been a few years earlier. The purists saw it as a triumph of skill, creativity and flair over tactics, strength and athleticism.

They had cruised through the competition, dispatching Porto with an emphatic 3–0 in the semi-finals and looked to be the favourites in Athens. In fact, Cruyff himself had announced that he was 'certain' that they would be returning with the Cup.

The press, particularly in Spain, had come up with their own script. Here was Cruyff, the paladin of bright attacking football, taking on Capello, the negative curmudgeon who had wrecked Sacchi's 'perfect machine' by turning it into a modern-day reworking of the most horrible form of *catenaccio*. The fact that Milan had conceded just fifteen league goals wasn't something to be proud of, it was a sign of their own destructive tendencies and their inability to play football the way it was meant to be played.

Capello was very much the villain. He could, of course, have pointed out the injuries which had robbed him of Papin, Boban, Lentini and Van Basten for much of the season. And he could have reminded them that this very same Milan side had actually been Serie A's top scorers in the two previous seasons and it was only necessity which forced him to rework the side. But that wasn't his way. He chose to let the pitch do the talking.

Perhaps his mind had wandered back to that other European final, Ajax v Juventus, back in 1973, when he had faced Cruyff as a player. That day, Ajax had played them off the park and done it with a confidence and a nonchalance that only the most consummate of winners can display. Twenty-one years on, he was not going to let the humiliation of that night affect him. This time, he vowed, he was going to be the one carelessly chucking the European Cup about.

But first, he had to figure out his lineup. Boban was fit again, which meant he could put the Croat in midfield alongside Albertini and switch Desailly into central defence, plugging one of the two holes left by the suspensions of Costacurta and Baresi. Indeed, he experimented with Desailly in that role in a warm-up friendly, with disastrous results, prompting some of his teammates to suggest the Frenchman played badly on purpose, so that Capello wouldn't shift him from midfield, a position he had come to enjoy. Whatever the case may be, Capello called upon the reliable veteran Filippo Galli and Maldini to come in as his defensive partnership, with Panucci playing wide on the left. Until that point, Panucci had played leftback just once that season, but Capello was confident that he had the technique and athleticism to do the job. Skipper Tassotti was at rightback.

Boban was deployed on the left wing. Capello was impressed with the way he had taken to a new, wider role after returning from injury and finding his old spot taken by Desailly. The young Croat had lived up to his billing: he had a combination of confidence, determination and intelligence that Capello loved.

Up front, with Papin still sidelined, Capello opted for Massaro and Savicevic. Yes, the same Savicevic who, a few months earlier, looked set to walk out on the club. The languid genius who played the game at his own pace and, for long stretches, appeared to be in his own world. After the incident in Tokyo, Capello and Galbiati had worked very hard to bring him back into the fold. He became a virtual first choice after their row, either on the flank or up front, and some Milan players noted that the coaching staff seemed to go soft on him. Or, rather, they seemed more tolerant of his idiosyncrasies than they were with others.

With hindsight, the reasons for this become clear. Having spent eighteen months trying to get Savicevic to train and run as hard as the others, they understood it was to no avail. Some things he just couldn't or wouldn't do. When they had Van Basten or Papin or even Lentini fully fit, they could afford to take a hard line with him, because they had alternatives. But by January of that year, Van Basten's return was nowhere in sight, Papin was continually breaking down and Lentini, while fit, lacked sharpness (and, some felt, desire). Milan needed quality and the ability to unlock opposing defences, something Savicevic could provide, even if it came at the expense of the workrate and team play that Capello craved.

'Without question, Savicevic is the player with whom I had the most rows,' Capello said in an interview years later. 'He hardly trained, he hardly worked. And, when he was on the pitch, everybody else had to work twice as hard to make up for him. But he was an exceptional talent. And we turned him into a superstar.'

That was another difference between Capello and his predecessor. It's unlikely that Savicevic would have got anywhere near Milan's starting eleven in Sacchi's time. But Capello – in case you had not figured it out by now – is a pragmatist. He redesigned Milan to suit this one player, asking all of his men to work harder so that *Il Genio* could strut his stuff.

After fifteen minutes of trading punches, Milan took over and smothered Barcelona, with Savicevic outshining everyone on the pitch. In the twenty-second minute he took a loose ball, accelerated towards the Barça goal, beat a defender and, just as it appeared as if he was going to walk it into the net, dinked the ball across the face of the goal to the waiting Massaro who buried it. Just before half-time it was 2–0. Donadoni made a brilliant run down the left as Savicevic ghosted towards the near post drawing three defenders with him. Donadoni cut it back for Massaro who slammed it home. Savicevic then made it three with an outrageous piece of skill: a perfectly weighted lob from near the touchline which eluded the desperate Zubizarreta in the Barça goal. Savicevic then hit the post, before Desailly later made it 4–0. The *rossoneri* coasted to victory in the last thirty minutes.

Barcelona – and especially Cruyff – had been humiliated. Capello, to this day, considers that game his 'masterpiece'. So much for those who had predicted a cautious, counter-attacking Milan. Capello beat Cruyff at his own game.

But there was also a metaphorical significance to Milan's three goalscorers that day. Each had been transformed by Capello that season. Massaro had been a reserve for most of his eight seasons at Milan. Now, on the eve of his thirty-third birthday, Capello had reinvented him as a centre-forward and the club's top goalscorer. Desailly was a defender bought as an emergency quick-fix whom Capello turned into the most dominant holding midfielder in the world. And then, of course, there was Savicevic. After a season of rows, ups-and-downs and underachievement, Capello had unleashed him in the biggest game of all, giving him total licence to do as he pleased.

Capello has long cultivated the image of a man who dwells neither on victory nor defeat. That night, however, was different. Milan celebrated in the team hotel until the wee hours. By four o'clock, everyone had moved on, except for Capello and Galliani.

'Normally we're partial to wine, not spirits,' says Galliani. 'But that night in Athens, everything just kept flowing. Finally, at six o'clock in the morning, we decided it was time to retire to our rooms.'

They were going up in the lift when Capello turned to Galliani and said: 'By the way, what did we do with the cup?' Galliani's expression turned from jubilant to terrified. They had it with them in the dressing room, they had it with them on the team bus, they took it with them at the bar . . . and now it was gone!

'Christ!' Galliani said. 'I must have left it downstairs at the bar!'

'Well, you're the chief executive, it's your responsibility,'

Capello said with a smile, before getting off at his floor.

Galliani rushed back down, only to find that the trophy was gone.

'I ran around in a flat panic,' Galliani recalls. 'Finally I found a maid. As it turned out, she had taken it and put it in the lost and found. I grabbed it, hugged it and kissed it like a long-lost child. I wasn't going to let go of it for anything in the world.'

'I was staying in a two-room suite and my wife at the time was sleeping in one bed,' he adds. 'I'm not sure what happened, but I ended up in the other bed, with the cup. My ex-wife tells me that she found me in bed, still holding tight to that cup.'

Galliani had literally slept with the European Cup. And, with Capello on board, he had vivid dreams of winning it again and again . . .

CHAPTER 9

Still Rolling

The summer of 1994 was one of change at Milan. By now, all but the most incurable optimists had accepted that Van Basten was not coming back. Indeed, he would spend another year attempting a return before finally throwing in the towel and retiring in the spring of 1995. Papin, too, was finished, at least according to Milan's medical staff. The club nevertheless managed to get some money back for him by selling him to Bayern Munich: their judgement was vindicated as a string of injuries limited him to just twenty-seven appearances over two seasons.

Milan needed a big name centre-forward to replace them. They got one on the cheap, by welcoming back Gullit after his season-long loan at Sampdoria. Everyone was aware of the friction between the Dutchman and Capello, but Gullit had just enjoyed his best season in years, notching fifteen Serie A goals and leading Sampdoria into third place. Surely, the club felt, Capello would find a way to make it work: it was in everyone's best interest to do so.

The other notable signing that summer was an extravagant, if volatile, winger named Paolo Di Canio. He was coming off a stellar season for Napoli, highlighted by an outrageous goal against none other than Milan, in which he made Baresi and Maldini dance like puppets on a string. (Check it out: it's on YouTube.)

Milan did not get off to a good start that year. Milan's internationals, the likes of Baresi, Maldini, Costacurta, Tassotti, Albertini, Donadoni and Massaro, returned exhausted and off-form after the 1994 World Cup, which had seen Sacchi's Italy side advance all the way to the final, where they were defeated on penalty kicks by Brazil. Gullit, the man who was supposed to solve all the problems up front, was not happy, despite scoring three goals in the first month. The Dutchman was expecting some sign of affection or gratitude or even just reconciliation from Capello. Instead, he got nothing. As for Capello, he gave him nothing because there was nothing to give. It was Gullit who had asked to leave in the first place. Now that he was back, Capello had expected him to get on with it, just like any other player. Realizing Gullit's return had been a mistake, Galliani quickly engineered a swap deal with Sampdoria, trading the Dutchman for Alessandro Melli, a promising striker. Gullit's return 'home' had lasted just eight league games.

After ten weeks of Serie A, Milan had already lost three league matches – as many as they had lost in the entire season the year before – and were ten points back in tenth place. Inter had knocked them out of the Coppa Italia. And they were stuttering in the Champions League as well, having been beaten home and away by Louis Van

Gaal's young Ajax side in the group stage. To make matters worse, in the group match against Salzburg, the opposing goalkeeper Otto Konrad was hit by a bottle thrown from the stands. Milan were deducted two points and had to play the next two games in a neutral venue. This meant they had to win away at Salzburg in the final group game to go through.

It was the toughest moment of Capello's managerial career to that point. And he was learning some valuable lessons. Squad rotation, which had generally served him well in the past, was getting more difficult for some players to accept. In some ways, this was obvious: it's easier to accept being left out if the team keeps winning. Now that they were struggling, some players were grumbling and the media were beginning to question his decisions.

'For him, it was simple: you had to accept his decisions, no matter who you were,' says Eranio. 'And, for him, rotation in certain positions, especially up front and on the flanks, was a fact of life. We had to accept it, we had no choice.'

Capello's detached style cut both ways. On the one hand, players interpreted it as the manager being fair and even-handed with everyone. On the other hand, some saw him as cold and heartless. Sacchi, for all his quirks, was warm and affectionate. He would talk the players' ears off whenever he saw them, to the point that one player told me that he made it a point to avoid Sacchi around Milanello, 'otherwise I'd be stuck listening to him for an hour'. Capello never made small talk and rarely exchanged more than a gruff greeting, unless it was a 'work' situation: a training session or team meeting.

Different players recounted the 'Capello' experience in different ways. In his autobiography (which I co-wrote), Paolo Di Canio saw the manager's stance as part of a manipulative master-plan. 'Fabio Capello was brilliant,' he writes.

> He knew how to motivate us, how to pit us against each other in a healthy way. This does not mean that I liked him, because I didn't . . . I have come to realize that, with a few very rare exceptions, to be a successful manager you have to be mean, tough and often a little unfair . . .
>
> He would tease me, coax me, tell me that I'd play the following week and then leave me out. I think he did it as a way of motivating both me and the players against whom I was competing. That's what intelligent managers have to do. They can't be friends with players, they can't always be good people.

Another example of this can be seen in his treatment of Stefano Nava, a reserve defender who got very little playing time. Nava eventually grew frustrated and asked to be transferred. Capello told him he was not for sale, at any price. Yet, still, he didn't get into the side. That said, Capello was good at throwing players the occasional bone: in Nava's case, he sent him on with six minutes to go in Athens in the Champions League final. The game was already won – Milan were 4–0 up – but Nava will now be able to tell his grandkids that he played in (and won) a European Cup final.

'In my case, it was obvious that he thought Rossi was the better goalkeeper,' says Ielpo, Milan's reserve netminder for three seasons. 'He didn't have to explain it to me and, well, he didn't. But he still managed to make me feel important and he used me whenever he could, in friendlies or in the UEFA Cup. And he made sure my contract was renewed. These are little things, but they mattered.'

Rossi, a Capello loyalist, sees the issue slightly differently. 'I would look into his eyes and see that, deep down, he wanted to be a friend, he wanted to be affectionate with us,' he says. 'But, at the same time, he did not want to show it. I think [his detachment] is actually one of his stronger traits. There were times when I really struggled. I wouldn't go so far as to say he was there for me, but, when it was really necessary, I sensed that I had his support. And that was important.'

Opinions differ wildly when it comes to the issue of a player's personal relationship with his manager. Ask most Chelsea players who worked under Mourinho (well, maybe not Andriy Shevchenko) and they will tell you that there was a genuine friendship and even love between themselves and their boss. Capello's relationship is closer to the other end of the spectrum.

I asked myself if this was part of Capello's management style or whether it was simply a continuation of his personality: after all, by his own admission, he has very few friends in football. Even as a player he was often somewhat detached in the dressing room. So I turned to a guy who knows a thing or two about management: Marcello Lippi, whom some describe as the anti-Capello.

'I think you have to do what fits your personality,' he told me. 'The manager doesn't necessarily need to be a friend. What matters is that he be a guide. That's what players want and need. They already have plenty of mates, if they've made it to a big club, they also have plenty of desire. What they crave is a guide, someone to show them the way. How you show them the way is up to you. There is more than one path to success.'

Back to late November 1994. In the space of seven days, Milan faced two huge games. First, the World Club Cup in Tokyo, which saw them take on Argentina's Vélez Sarsfield, winners of the Copa Libertadores. Then, the do-or-die clash in Salzburg with a place in the Champions League quarter-finals at stake.

Everything went wrong in Tokyo. Milan started on the wrong foot logistically. Capello had scheduled a double training session a few days before the match, with a rest at the team hotel in between. But due to the distance to the training ground as well as Tokyo's diabolical traffic jams, that day Milan ended up spending more hours (four) on the bus than they did training (three). Capello stuck with his veterans, many of whom were clearly exhausted and clearly not match-fit. Little Vélez Sarsfield won 2–0 and Costacurta was sent off late in the game.

'I've said this many times, but that was the single worst performance of my career,' Costacurta would say later in a television interview. 'I cost us the game. I gave away a stupid penalty for the first goal, I gifted them the second goal with a silly backpass and then I got myself sent off. It took me a long time to live that down, especially since they were a decent side, but one we should have beaten.'

By this point, the media were on Capello's case as were some of the fans. Milan hadn't been this poor in nearly a decade. Cracks had begun to appear in Capello's relationship with some of the veteran players as well. They were worn out and Capello seemed distant to some. But there was no time to think about it. Salzburg were up next and any result other than a win would see Milan, the defending champions, out of Europe before Christmas.

Capello dug deep in his tactical arsenal for this one. Knowing Milan had to get the three points, he started with a 4-3-3. Then, after Massaro (who else? 'Providence' strikes again) put Milan ahead he switched to a 4-4-2 before ending with a 5-4-1, a hyper-defensive scheme which Milan had not employed since the early 1980s.

'We used three different tactical formations depending on the phase of the game,' Capello said in the post-match press conference. 'I'm proud of my players that they were able to do that, though, of course, we did not play particularly well, I'll grant you that.'

It was an ugly win, but an important one. Regenerated in the knowledge that their season was still alive, Milan kicked it up a gear domestically. They went on an undefeated run of eleven games in all competitions, winning the European Super Cup along the way (they beat George Graham's Arsenal 2–0 on aggregate in the days before it became a season-opening one-off game played in Monaco). Simone had established himself as a reliable goalscorer (he would finish the season with seventeen in Serie A), as Milan dispatched Benfica and Paris Saint-Germain to advance to the Champions League final in Vienna against Ajax.

If they weren't already, Ajax had that season established themselves as Capello's bogey-team, beating Milan twice in the group stage. And, of course, Capello's bad memories of Ajax dated back to the 1973 European Cup final. Milan had a clear edge in terms of experience, but Van Gaal's side were dynamic and gifted and played an intoxicating brand of attacking football. He had a good blend of experience (Danny Blind and Frank Rijkaard, back to haunt his former club) and youth (Clarence Seedorf, Edgar Davids, the De Boer twins and Patrick Kluivert).

Van Gaal's expansive football was predicated on the use of old-school wingers, something which, increasingly, was disappearing from the European game. In Finidi George and Marc Overmars he had two wide men who could get behind fullbacks and, because they stayed up, rather than doubling back to help the midfield, they made it very difficult for Milan's own fullbacks Panucci and Maldini to push on and help the side going forward.

Milan's pedigree again made them favourites, but, as was the case in Tokyo, they arrived exhausted, both mentally and physically. There was just one notable absence, but it was a big one: Savicevic. *Il Genio* was essential in matches like these, because he allowed Milan to focus on defending and shut up shop, knowing that at some point he was likely to create an opening. Without him, Capello relied on Simone and, of course, 'Providence' Massaro: still quality strikers, but also men who needed either service or an opposition slip-up to score goals.

Milan's gameplan that day was to deny Ajax the flanks – Donadoni and Boban, deployed wide, spent much of the game helping the fullbacks defend Finidi and Overmars – while looking to make a breakthrough down the middle, perhaps in the second half, when the *rossoneri* usually upped the tempo. That blueprint backfired. While Overmars and Finidi were largely neutralized, it came at the cost of attacking wing play and Milan struggled to impose themselves. And when Van Gaal sent on two gifted eighteen-year-olds in the second-half – Kluivert and Nwankwo Kanu – their size and energy made all the difference. Milan hung in there until five minutes from time, but had to capitulate when Rijkaard found Kluivert, who rode Baresi's tackle before beating Rossi.

'Their goal may have come late, but they deserved to win,' Capello would later admit. 'We were never really in the game, we were just too worn out by that stage of the season.'

The media agreed. And, in some quarters, Capello was attacked. What was the point of having a big squad if Capello simply played the same men in the big games? Why had he made no changes until after the Ajax goal, with just five minutes to go? Especially when it was clear that Van Gaal's substitutions had re-energized Ajax and when he had a guy like Lentini – who may have been an acquired taste, but was still the world's most expensive footballer – on the bench? Also, how was it possible that Milan always seemed tired in big games? And why did they pick up so many injuries?

All this blame was laid at Capello's door. Some of it was fair, some probably a case of the press looking for reasons to explain the defeat, when, perhaps, the truth was that Ajax were simply better than they were given credit for – they would go on to reach the final again in 1996 and the semi-final in 1997, only to lose both times to Marcello Lippi's Juventus. One fashionable theory was that Capello put too much pressure on his players, particularly in training sessions. They were so tightly wound, they simply could not recover, mentally or physically.

'Well, that was certainly a difference compared to Sacchi,' says Nava. 'Before, we might have trained longer at times and sometimes it was physically more intense, but there were pauses, there were moments of relaxation too. Capello wanted each training session to be just like a match. Same tension, same intensity, same build-up, same concentration. And maybe there is some truth in the fact that, as a result, we picked up more injuries and, when it came to the games themselves, we were a little more worn out. But it also made us tougher. When I started managing, Capello was an inspiration and I copied his methods. But, of course, as a player, some of us viewed these techniques a bit differently.'

Milan had finished Serie A in fourth place and the trophy cabinet contained only the European Super Cup, and another Italian Super Cup. Capello had shown that he was not, in fact, an all-conquering managerial machine. He too could make mistakes. This message was not lost on Galliani. Milan's chief executive had developed a close relationship with Capello – every week, they and their wives would dine together at L'Assassino, a legendary Milanese restaurant – but he had a job to do. And the question of whether Capello had lost his edge seemed a relevant one to him.

There were other issues too. Relations had become strained with some players, including some members of the 'old guard'. It was respectful, but primarily businesslike, professional and frosty. And while this suited

Capello just fine – indeed, it was part of his approach – it was a stark contrast to the Sacchi Era. And, finally, deep in the back of his mind, there must have been another question. Milan had the best players in the world, they were the wealthiest club in the wealthiest league. They were the best organized club, they had state-of-the-art facilities, top-notch medical staff . . . could it be that Capello was not really as central to Milan's success as some would have him believe? Could it be that Milan were such a great club that another manager could lead them with equal success? Perhaps someone with a slightly less abrasive personality, someone who was a bit more media-friendly, someone who would smile a little bit more often?

Those issues weighed heavily on Galliani's mind when he met with Capello that spring to discuss a new contract. Capello had a year left and, when he went in, he told Galliani in no uncertain terms that he expected a pay rise and a three-year deal which would take him through 1999. To him, it seemed only fair. In four years he had delivered three league titles, a European Super Cup, three Italian Super Cups and a Champions League crown. Plus, he had taken Milan to the final on two other occasions. He had done this without making excessive demands in the transfer market and while working with a squad whose size was unprecedented in the history of the game. He had been at Milan for fifteen years – as player, coach and manager – plus another four working directly for Berlusconi, the club's president. Surely it was time for the club to show some loyalty.

'I want a gesture from the club that shows you have

faith in me,' Capello told Galliani. 'After what we've achieved together, I think I've earned it.'

Galliani felt that Capello was asking Milan to have 'blind faith' in him. He couldn't bring himself to do it. 'I can give you a three-year contract extension,' he said. 'But we need to put in a performance-related clause for the club's protection.'

That clause was simple. Capello would get his deal (and a hefty pay rise), but the club had the option to void the contract at the end of each season if Milan failed to win either the *scudetto* or the Champions League.

To Capello it was nothing less than a slap in the face. This was the gratitude the club was showing for what he had achieved? Effectively, Galliani's offer meant that he had to prove himself again, every single season. Even calling it a three-year contract was a joke. In fact, this was an annual deal, with the club holding all the cards if he failed to deliver silverware.

Capello was far from happy. He told Galliani he would see out his current contract – which had one season left to run – and then evaluate the situation. Unless, of course, Galliani wanted to sack him then and there, in which case they could talk about compensation.

Capello's words made Galliani very uncomfortable. But it was too late to go back. He put his faith in Capello's professionalism, though he was concerned about what the future might bring.

'But the fact was that I was afraid of giving him a full three-year deal,' Galliani now says. 'Was it a mistake? Maybe. But, at the time I felt I could not blindly commit the club's future to Capello. And that's why I put in those performance clauses.'

Galliani told himself that everything would be fine. Capello would go back to his winning ways and they would simply proceed year by year, as they had always done. But, just in case, he also put together a Plan B. Acting through intermediaries, that same June he contacted Oscar Washington Tabárez. The Uruguayan manager was something of a legend in South America, having guided the likes of Boca Juniors and Peñarol. He had just concluded a season in Italy, taking unheralded Cagliari to a respectable ninth place. Milan sealed a gentleman's agreement, whereby Tabárez would remain on stand-by, just in case things did not work out with Capello.

Thus Milan embarked on their summer transfer campaign knowing that Capello was potentially a lame duck manager. Transfer spending had always been done by committee at Milan, with Galliani and sporting director Ariedo Braida handling all negotiations. Then, of course, there was Berlusconi, the man who ultimately wrote the cheques: generally he would tend to defer to the football men, occasionally he put in his two cents, which, as you would expect, invariably became law. Managers had varying degrees of input based on their status. Capello would normally have had a fair amount of say but, given the uncertainty over his future, this summer was somewhat different.

Indeed, Milan's transfer spending brought a decidedly mixed bag. It was obvious that the club needed a new centre-forward, especially since 'Providence' Massaro, who was now thirty-four, had been sold to Roma. George

Weah, signed from Paris Saint-Germain, fitted the bill neatly. Capello would have liked another genuine striker: instead, he got not one, but three, number 10s: Tomas Locatelli, Paulo Futre and Roberto Baggio. The trio joined Di Canio and Savicevic bringing to five the number of what Italians call *fantasisti* – deep-lying attacking midfielder/forward hybrids who are at their best in a free role. For a team managed by someone like Capello it was – at least on paper – about five too many.

By their very nature players such as these do not easily fit into tactical schemes. They may be great entertainers, blessed with outstanding skill, but too often their workrate is suspect. Capello had made things work with one such player – Savicevic – in the side. And he had managed to get some level of productivity from Di Canio, a player with whom he rarely saw eye to eye. But what was he supposed to do with the others?

Locatelli, acquired from Atalanta, had just turned nineteen. He had a bright future, but at that age, what he needed most was playing time, which was exactly what Capello could not provide. But if Locatelli was one for the future, rather than the present, Futre was decidedly one for the past. At twenty, he had been considered Europe's answer to Diego Maradona, thanks to his pace and outrageous dribbling skills. But that was a decade earlier, before he was hit by a succession of injuries. By the time he was twenty-seven, Atlético Madrid had given up on him. He moved to Reggiana, not exactly a big Serie A club, where he managed just thirteen appearances over two seasons. And now, there he was at Milan, with his two bad knees. Apparently, Berlusconi was a big admirer.

And that's how Futre became Capello's hot potato.

Then there was Baggio, potentially the biggest headache of all. He may have been one of the greatest players Italy has ever produced, but he was also one who – despite his low-key personality – always found himself at the centre of controversy, which, it must be said, tended not to come from him but from others. Baggio's problem was that just about every manager he ever had struggled to find a rational place for him in the side, short of absolving him of all defensive and pressing duties, getting the rest of the team to work for him and letting him do whatever he liked (which, to be fair, is what some managers did, with mixed levels of success). And so Baggio was forever dogged by endless debate: Was he a striker? Was he a midfielder? Was he an attacking midfielder? Despite playing for clubs of the size of Milan, Inter and Juventus in his career it's fair to say that he really enjoyed only a season and a half of success at the highest level of club football. Instead, some of his best football came at smaller clubs, late in his career, such as Brescia and Bologna, when the whole side was built around him.

The year before, at Juventus, he had missed five months of the *scudetto*-winning season. His injuries, coupled with the fact that Juventus felt they had a ready-made replacement in a young Alessandro Del Piero (who perhaps was not in Baggio's class in terms of ability, but made up for it by offering pace, athleticism, workrate and tactical discipline), meant that when Milan came knocking, they almost bit Galliani's hand off. Juve's medical staff felt that while Baggio was still just twenty-eight it was an 'old' twenty-eight, given the injuries he had suffered earlier in his career.

Milan probably had other reasons for gambling on him. Apart from Maldini, the club did not really have a marketable face that could drive some of their commercial ventures. Baresi was thirty-five. Albertini and Desailly played unglamorous positions. What they needed was someone like the Gullit or Van Basten of old: a world class superstar who was also confident and charismatic. Baggio, a convert to Buddhism, had a massive following in Asia. At the 1994 World Cup, he carried Italy all the way to the final. Plus, he had the right look, at once recognizable and desirable. He was easily the most famous Italian footballer in the world and, the club reckoned, would be a hit in Milan's worldwide marketing campaign.

All this was great, but it didn't really do Capello any favours. With Baggio on board, he would be under pressure to play him. And, furthermore, Berlusconi was expecting him to fit both Baggio and Savicevic – two very similar players – in the same lineup, behind Weah. Doing so also effectively meant giving up on wingers, which did not bode well for Donadoni, Lentini and Di Canio.

It all amounted to a massive tactical headache, made worse by the fact that Capello knew Baggio represented a no-win proposition. As many an Italian manager discovered, if you play Baggio and don't win, you're an idiot for playing him. And if you don't play Baggio and don't win, you're an idiot for leaving him out. The only solution, Capello realized, was not to worry about Baggio and simply win. That way, nobody could criticize him.

Which is pretty much what he did. Milan led the whole way through, from Week 1 to Week 34. Apart from his defence and the ever-reliable Albertini–Desailly pairing in

Capello first played in Serie A for Spal, a club from the central Italian town of Ferrara.

Roma brought Capello his first piece of silverware and a taste of city life.

Above: Pulling on the Juventus shirt in 1970.

Right: Capello strikes a pose in training.

Having words with keeper Roberto Tancredi in 1970.

Pietro Anastasi's goals helped Juve to the *scudetto* in 1971–72.

Capello's club performances led to international recognition. He is pictured here with Gianni Rivera in a World Cup qualifier against Sweden.

14 June 1973: Italy's first win against England. Capello fires home as Martin Peters watches; the Italian later called the goal 'a bit lucky'.

Always have a man on the post. Wembley, 14 November 1973.

Above right and right: Capello's famous goal for the *azzurri* at the home of football sparked scenes of celebration among Italians at home and abroad.

1974 World Cup: Italy prepares to take on Haiti in Munich. Dino Zoff conceded his first goal in 1,147 minutes in the 3–1 win.

Pavel Kazakov lectures Capello during the 1–1 draw with Argentina. Defeat to Poland then sent the *azzurri* home to a rotten-tomato welcome.

Left: Milan, 1976: the start of Capello's long association with the *rossoneri*.

Below: 1978–79 brought the *scudetto della stella* a tenth Serie A title and the first since 1968. The middle row features young defenders Fulvio Collovati and Franco Baresi (*third from left and right respectively*), coach Nils Liedholm (*centre*) and Capello (*far right*).

Above and below: Capello's long-standing knee injury would curtail his career but his experience, vision and tactical intelligence helped settle the young Milan side. 'He always knew where the ball was going to go,' said Liedholm.

At home with wife Laura and sons Pierfilippo and Edoardo in the late seventies.

midfield, nobody started more than three-quarters of Milan's league games. Capello chopped and changed his front four, depending on form, availability and opponent, carefully doling out playing time to the likes of Weah, Savicevic, Baggio, Di Canio, Simone, Eranio and Donadoni in such a way that, even though they may not all have been happy, all felt involved.

He was helped by the fact that, in Weah, he had a devastating attacking force. It wasn't so much the Liberian striker's goalscoring – he ended up with eleven in the league – it was his sheer workrate along the frontline. He didn't need service to be effective, his mere presence forced defenders to key in on him, giving Baggio, Savicevic, Simone or whoever else was up there with him time and space to operate. The fact that he had tremendous stamina and often sacrificed himself when Milan did not have possession – one newspaper report described Weah as being 'a one-man pressing machine' – helped keep the balance of the side, allowing Capello the luxury of fielding Baggio and Savicevic together on a number of occasions – something which the media said he would not be able to do.

'Everything clicked that season,' one Milan player told me. 'Defensively we were close to perfect, maybe even better than when we set the record for fewest goals conceded. He knew when to gamble a bit, maybe by playing Savicevic wide left or leaving Baggio in there behind Weah and Simone. And he knew when to play it safe.

'From the midfield up, we were clearly not a well-assorted team,' he added. 'Capello knew that, but he still found a way to make it work. He squeezed as much as he could out of us and, I suppose, you have to give him credit for that. Though that was also the season when it became more difficult to paper over the breakdown in relationship which some players had with him.'

The old stereotype – that success wipes away controversy and ill-feeling – held true that season, but only to a point. Capello maintains the uncertainty over his future did not affect him, but it's difficult to see how that could be the case. In January 1996 he was contacted by Lorenzo Sanz, president of Real Madrid. Capello politely told him they would speak later on. But then, in March, Sanz came to see him again. And this time, word got out.

'We knew something was afoot,' says the Milan player. 'Personally, while I had my differences with him, I felt the club made a mistake in not granting him the extension he wanted. And they compounded it in the transfer market in those years, perhaps because they did not consult him the way they should have or did in the past. It's not a co-incidence that, between '95 and '98, we made a series of transfer blunders.'

On the training pitch, Capello was his usual self, at least outwardly. He clung to his usual routines and superstitions which, by that point, had become legendary at Milanello. Speaking to Milan players of that period, you get a picture of the quirky, superstitious Capello. One who insisted that the same three journalists ask the same question in the exact same order every Friday, at Milan's televised press conferences. One who would always hold his weekly press conferences in the same spot: outside, under the ivy at Milanello, even when it was snowing. One who turned Ramaccioni into a kind of good luck charm: on charter flights, Capello would always sit – depending on God knows what – in either seat 3A or 4A (the left-hand side of the plane, by the window) and Ramaccioni would have to sit directly behind him. Ramaccioni also had to have a cup of coffee with Capello on the eve of every match. And he always had to be the last person to board the team bus.

He also apparently didn't want anyone to write anything in red ink and was maniacal about players leaving their flip-flops lying around the dressing room. 'It bordered on obsessive-compulsive disorder,' one player told me.

Most of the squad and staff found these quirks amusing, more than anything else. And some, like the jovial Ramaccioni, milked it a little bit. Under Sacchi, a half-dozen or so peacocks freely roamed the grounds at Milanello. After Capello's arrival, they were gone. Whether it was Capello who had them removed or not remains a mystery. Ramaccioni joked that, if the peacocks were gone, it must have been because Capello 'ate them'.

Football and superstition go hand in hand, of course. But it does seem extraordinary that a man like Capello, known for his rational, detached approach, should have been so superstitious. By all accounts, it's a trait which has abated considerably. Few of the players who were with him at Roma remember particular superstitious quirks and, by the time he was at Juventus and Real Madrid (the second time around), they seemed to have disappeared from his daily routine.

In any case, by mid-March 1996, Milan hit another major road bump and, for the first time in years, the fans turned on Capello and the players. First, they lost to Inter in the derby, 1–0. After a Serie A players' strike (not the best PR move) wiped out the next weekend's fixtures, they travelled to France to take on Bordeaux in the quarter-finals of the UEFA Cup. They were 2–0 up from the first leg and there was no reason to believe that it wouldn't be just a formality. Bordeaux, however, brilliantly marshalled by a young midfielder named Zinedine Zidane (who, back then, had yet to reveal his monk's tonsure), hammered Milan 3–0, sending them crashing out of the competition.

The supporters took it very badly. The following week, Milan entertained Parma. As the team bus approached the San Siro, it was pelted with rocks and rubbish. Inside the stadium they were greeted with angry banners taking them to task for the defeat against Bordeaux and reminding them that it was the supporters who paid their wages. Things went from bad to worse when Baggio missed a penalty after eleven minutes. And, while Milan eventually won 3–0, they exited the pitch to a chorus of boos. The fans had a point to make and they made it.

The anger wasn't so much about the two consecutive losses. It was more about what the supporters considered to be a directionless team, one that kept winning unconvincingly, one sagging under the weight of its supposed superstars and their enormous wage packets. And, of course, they wanted to know what was going on with Capello.

Berlusconi was horrified: 'They shouldn't be acting like this,' he said. 'Not after everything we've done for them.'

The players were dumbfounded. Milan had an eight-point lead by that stage. What were they expecting? A resounding 6–0 win every week? Capello's reaction was unexpected.

'The fans have every right to be upset with us,' he said after the game. 'We should be grateful that they care enough to do this. These are the same people who filled the San Siro fifteen years ago, when we were relegated to Serie B.'

He had, for the first time, broken ranks publicly with the club and the players. Was he trying, as some suggested, to curry favour with the supporters? Probably not. Even when things were going well, Capello always had a luke-warm rapport with the fans compared to, say, the initial years of Sacchi's regime. They weren't the ones employing him; he saw no reason to go out of his way to cater to them.

Besides, he knew that he would be leaving the club in a few months (in addition to Real Madrid, Parma had also shown strong interest in his services). There was no reason to suck up to the fans at this stage. If he wanted to do a 'man of the people' act, he should have thought about it years ago.

More likely, he was as frustrated as they were. Not for the results, they only mattered to a point. Rather, he was annoyed at the direction the club had taken, the ease with which they were going to let him go. As for the players, maybe he felt they needed a kick up the backside as well. He had juggled the squad and found a way to make things work, but too many of them were taking too much for granted.

Boban was a case in point. The Croatian midfielder had been injured since mid-February, but by mid-April he was almost fully recovered. On 24 April, Croatia were due to play against England at Wembley for the first time. Boban, ever the patriot, asked to be released. Milan's medical staff agreed, on the condition that he didn't actually play in the game. He could join his international teammates at Wembley, he could walk out with them, but under no circumstances was he to take part.

Instead, Boban started the game, coming off at half-time in the scoreless draw. Capello was furious. Boban had ignored a direct order. Upon his return to Milan, Capello sent him to train with the youth squad and left him out of that Sunday's match against Fiorentina, which Milan won 3–1, sealing their fifteenth *scudetto*, the fourth under Capello.

Boban had evidently counted on Capello's understanding: after all, his manager had fond memories of Wembley and he would understand how important a place it was to an international footballer. And, perhaps, he figured Capello wouldn't mind: the title was virtually wrapped up, and, besides, Capello was leaving anyway. At this point, what did he care?

Capello would later say that until the very last day of his employment with Milan, he would give his all to the club and do what was best for them. And that meant punishing Boban, no matter how unpopular it made him.

Indeed, that attitude continued well into June, when Milan embarked on a post-season tour of China. The club's internationals missed the tour, while other players knew they were playing their final games for Milan. Nobody seemed to really care: nobody, that is, except Capello. In one friendly match, Capello decided to make a substitution ('To preserve our tactical equilibrium,' according to Di Canio, the player who was to come off). This incensed Di Canio, who in his autobiography claims he and Capello got into a furious row. Details vary – Di Canio's account of what exactly transpired is slightly different from that of other eyewitnesses – but it ended with Di Canio storming out of the stadium at half-time. Even then, even after committing to Real Madrid, Capello was not about to sacrifice his professional beliefs to suit the whims of a player. Even then, he wanted to win and stick to his principles. The day after winning the title, Capello announced that he would be leaving.

'It's my decision to go, I made it a month ago,' he said. 'They [Milan] offered me a three-year contract, but with the kind of clauses that made it very clear to me that they did not truly have faith in me. But that was obvious to me anyway, since I knew they had approached Tabárez a year ago.'

'I think I did my bit,' he added. 'Everyone said we were finished and we won the title. Everyone said I couldn't find a way for Baggio and Savicevic to play together and I did.'

The players' reaction was mixed. Lentini, who had received very little playing time after his injury, was very critical: 'The way Capello treated me was disgusting.' Rossi, on the other hand, told me: 'I felt as if my world was collapsing all around me. I never believed the rumours. But he told me that he wanted to take me with him to Real Madrid. And that made me feel better. Not because I wanted to go to Real [he turned down a move to Spain], but because it meant he believed in me.'

But perhaps it's Stefano Nava who summed it up best: 'We all argued with him, we all had our moments when we hated him. But deep down, if we're honest, we're all immensely grateful to him.'

For those too young to remember, it's worth noting just what Serie A was like in the Capello years of the early to mid-1990s, and what winning an Italian championship meant. It truly was the greatest league in the world by some margin in those years.

Just about everybody who was anybody in the game tried their hand in Serie A during that period. Every single European Footballer of the Year between 1980 and 2000 played in Italy at some point, with the exception of the Russian Igor Belanov. In fact, it's easier to list the greats from the 1980s and 1990s who did *not* make the jump to Serie A than those who did. Hugo Sánchez, Kenny Dalglish, Emilio Butragueño, Alan Shearer, Romário, Ronald Koeman, Michel, Gary Lineker . . . and perhaps a few others. Had it not been for the limits placed on foreigners, it's safe to say that even more stars would have made the jump into Italian football.

And they weren't just piling into the big clubs. Gheorghe Hagi was at Brescia. Dragan Stojkovic and Preben Elkjaer Larsen at Verona, Enzo Francescoli at Cagliari, Zico at Udinese, Müller at Torino, Igor Shalimov at Foggia. But then, so many Italian clubs could claim to be 'big'. No fewer than seven different Serie A sides reached European finals in the period 1991–96. This was no fluke; Italian sides dominated European club football throughout the eighties and nineties: Serie A clubs reached the European Cup final twelve times in the sixteen years between 1983 and 1998; they won eight of eleven UEFA Cups between 1989 and 1999.

It was against this backdrop that Capello won his four Serie A titles in five seasons. And it was this achievement that led Sanz, the Real Madrid president, to claim: 'We have just signed the greatest manager in the world.'

CHAPTER 10

The Real Deal

Lorenzo Sanz had promised a 'revolution' and he duly delivered.

The construction magnate had been elected president of Real Madrid on 26 November 1995, replacing Ramón Mendoza, who had been forced to step aside after it emerged that the club had accumulated an enormous amount of debt under his tenure. Sanz had been Mendoza's vice-president, but the two were cut from a very different cloth. The patrician Mendoza, trained as a lawyer, was effectively a politician who treated Real Madrid like a public utility. Keeping the supporters – i.e. his voters – happy appeared more important than things like budgets, sponsorship and some of the cruder commercial aspects of the game. If Real needed something to be done, there was always money to be found, if not in the club's coffers then by leaning on banks to provide more and more lines of credit.

Sanz, on the other hand, was a former lower league footballer who had gone on to amass a fortune in property and construction in Spain's first post-Franco economic boom. He was a practical man, more aggressive and self-assured than the gregarious Mendoza. Like his predecessor, he wasn't overly concerned with Real's books – institutions like Real Madrid simply did not go bust, any more than the government, the police department or the royal family did – but he was well aware that the club's commercial potential was largely untapped.

To do this, however, Real needed to get back to winning ways. Since 1990 they had won just two trophies, a Spanish league title and a Spanish Cup. And, when he took over, they were mired in yet another disappointing campaign, one which would see them finish a lowly sixth, seventeen points behind Atlético Madrid. While the first half of Mendoza's tenure had been very successful, Real had fallen away badly. It wasn't just the lack of silverware, it was the fact that, since 1990, arch-rivals Barcelona, brilliantly marshalled by Johan Cruyff, had won four consecutive Liga crowns, as well as the European Cup. They had become the epitome of success, Real was becoming a by-word for faded glory. The point was driven home even further in 1995–96 when the title went – after nearly two decades of futility – to Atlético Madrid, Real's basketcase neighbours from the capital's working-class southern districts.

Something had to change. And it had to happen quickly. Hiring Capello was only part of the equation. That summer Real Madrid went on a spending spree, most of it occurring before Capello's arrival. Much of the cash to fund the purchases came not from the club, but through financing arranged by Sanz, a necessary measure given that more than a few banks had become wary of extending credit to what was becoming an insatiable financial black hole.

Sanz raided two of Real's direct opponents – Sevilla and Valencia – to secure two brand new frontmen: Davor Suker, lethal in the penalty box, and Predrag Mijatovic, gifted and unpredictable. Between them, they had scored forty-four Liga goals the previous year and, together with Real's own wunderkind, the eighteen-year-old Raúl, who had notched nineteen the previous year, they seemed certain to guarantee goals galore. The precocious Clarence Seedorf – still just twenty but with a European Cup with Ajax already under his belt – added quality to the midfield, while the back four were bolstered by a pair of new fullbacks, Carlos Secretário from Porto and a stocky, lightning-quick Brazilian blessed with a vicious left foot: Roberto Carlos, from Inter Milan.

As was the case at Milan, Capello's input on these signings was somewhat limited. Some were made before he put pen to paper, others were described as 'club priorities'. Roberto Carlos, on the other hand, was a player Capello requested and had fully endorsed. And, in some ways, this may seem counterintuitive. In Serie A the knock on the Brazilian was that he was simply 'too attack-minded'. At Inter, his marauding runs and long-range shooting made him a fan favourite, but he would occasionally get caught out, prompting some observers to say that 'he lacked tactical discipline and rigour'. What would a supposedly defence-obsessed disciplinarian like Capello want with someone like Roberto Carlos?

In fact, as the player himself explained in a 2007

interview, Capello had specific plans for him. He didn't view him as a defensive weapon, but as an attacking one, albeit from deep-lying positions.

'Capello wanted me with him in Spain, after seeing me at Inter,' Roberto Carlos said. 'But it wasn't about defensive football. From the beginning, he wanted me to attack and go forward. We had Rafael Alkorta in central defence, he was very quick and read the play very well, so he could cover my back. Thus Capello told me I should attack instead of worrying too much about my defensive work.'

In fact, as we'll see later, Roberto Carlos became a key element of a tactical scheme involving Raúl, Mijatovic and Hierro which Capello's Real employed to devastating effect. As for Inter, the ease with which they let Roberto Carlos go remains a symbol of the club's futility in the 1990s. The Brazilian went on to become a fixture at the Bernabéu for eleven seasons: during that time span, Inter featured no fewer than twenty-eight different leftbacks.

As ever, Galbiati joined Capello in Madrid. But it was felt he could use a local assistant as well, so he asked José Martinez Pirri, the club's general manager, to recommend a replacement. Sanz was impressed: Capello had made a number of demands of the club, but asking them to provide one of their own for his staff was seen as a sign of humility and respect for the club's history.

'And so Pirri recommended me,' says Toni Grande, who joined Capello's staff. 'It all happened very quickly. I had been working with the feeder club and at youth level. Now, all of a sudden, there I was, not just in the top flight, not just at Real Madrid, but working alongside someone like Capello. I had to pinch myself.'

One of the first things that struck Capello upon his arrival was the difference in pre-season training between what he was used to at Milan and what had been the norm at Madrid. Physically, many of the players were unused to the kind of hardcore fitness regimen which Capello wanted to implement. The game in Spain was played at a slower pace, it was more about technique and movement than power and athleticism. Equally, there was less of an emphasis on tactics. Capello had to change that if he was going to get Real to play his brand of football.

And most of the players were not averse to being whipped into shape. The holdovers had been through the trauma of the previous campaign, the controversy over Mendoza's departure, the daily crucifixions in the voracious Madrid press, the criticism from the supporters. As for the new-comers, for most, Real was their first experience of the big-time, which made them far more malleable to a new manager, even one who promised to make them sweat.

'That was exactly our reaction: "There's a drill sergeant in charge now, he's going to sort us out, we're going to have to work like mad, but we're going to win,"' says José Amavisca, at the time a young midfielder at the club. 'His pedigree made him a virtual guarantee. And so we all bought into it. If a lesser coach had tried to make us do the same thing, I'm not sure it would have worked. But with Capello we were absolutely sure that we would win something and if that meant running a thousand miles, well, we'd run a thousand miles. Because you know that in the end it's going to be different.'

That emphasis on fitness and athleticism set him apart from most of his Liga colleagues. Although Cruyff had left Barcelona that summer, his philosophy – which included aphorisms like 'Why run yourself, when you can let the ball run instead?' – had infected most of Spanish football.

'The whole pre-season camp was horrible in terms of the amount of work we did,' says Fernando Hierro. 'Seriously, it was the toughest of my career. I remember we trained twice a day for fifteen days straight before he gave us an afternoon off. We were delighted. The club had arranged for us to visit a nearby town for a few hours. As it happened, the bus driver got lost, which meant we spent three hours driving around aimlessly . . . and that was supposed to be our time off! We returned to tell him that we were more exhausted than we would have been if we had trained. But, of course, he just put us back to work the next day.'

Capello also put an emphasis on defensive organization. This did not mean simply telling players to hang back, but synchronizing their movements when they did not have possession.

'The thing that struck me most was one day in pre-season when he got the four defenders and the goalkeepers and he took them off to a different pitch, while we stayed and trained with one of his assistants,' says Amavisca. 'I'd never seen that before. After about an hour, he called over the holding midfielder [Fernando Redondo] and they all worked together for another half-hour or so. And then he called another eight of us over and said: "Right, I want you guys to try and score against my defence."'

It was a variation on what Sacchi had introduced at Milan nearly a decade earlier. (In this, Capello has always been very open, admitting: 'I've stolen ideas from almost everyone. If I see something working, I try it out and see if it works for me.') 'Well, it was virtually impossible,' recalls Amavisca. 'We'd be attacking, eight against five, and it just wouldn't work. And, if we did happen to score, he would explode and yell at his defenders, even though you would think that, in an eight v five, the eight would score sooner or later.'

'That gave him real credibility in our eyes, because it was an instantaneous improvement, it wasn't a case of somebody trying to improve over time,' adds Amavisca. 'We could see the difference it made straight away. We believed in him because he did things in training which showed instant progress.'

Capello also made a point of working on technique, especially with younger players. When I interviewed Capello for my book *The Italian Job* (which I co-wrote with Gianluca Vialli), he came down squarely with those who believe that formerly great players have a natural edge when it comes to coaching, because they have a better sense of the mechanics of a player's technique. Indeed, when I sat down again with him in October 2007, he cited just such an example from his time working with Clarence Seedorf at Real.

'You can always improve a player's technique, but you have to understand exactly what the weak points are and what he could be doing differently,' he told me. 'And you have to do it while making it clear to him that you're trying to improve him, not merely exposing his weaknesses. With Seedorf, after several months of working with him I asked him: "Do you think you can shoot [on goal]?" He replied: "Yes, very well, in fact." I told him: "Maybe so, but you can only do it one way." And I worked with him to get him to shoot in different ways: with the outside of the boot, with the laces, with the instep. I think he learned a small lesson that day. I was able to do it because I had an understanding of the mechanics of striking a ball and the technique involved. But, also, because Seedorf is an intelligent man who understood what I was trying to do.'

The belief that players can continue to improve their skills, even in mid-career, has been a hallmark of Capello's time as a manager. At Real, he laid on extra sessions every day for players to work on individual technique.

'He'd send his assistants out on the pitch with a bunch of balls for a half-hour or so after training,' says Hierro. 'Anyone who wanted to work on individual skills could do so. It was optional but you could tell it was important. And it was unstructured, each player could work on whatever he wanted, whether it was his weaker foot or headers or whatever. The regular training session was for the team; this was for the individual. Italo Galbiati was a big part of this. His knowledge of technique is exceptional and we soon saw results.'

Capello's belief that players can improve stems from two important experiences earlier in his career.

'I was lucky that I played professional football at a very high level and that I spent six years coaching at youth level,' he said in a newspaper interview. 'It taught me to build upon my knowledge of the technical aspects of the game and it allowed me to understand the right way to teach it. You can improve even when you're thirty years old. If the basic ability is there, you can help a player grow and improve.'

The fans, at least initially, jumped on the Capello bandwagon. Much like twelve years later, when he would take over the England team, the papers were full of stories of Capello the Disciplinarian, the drill sergeant who had turned pre-season training into boot camp. As often happens after a disappointing season, the public craves a tough guy who will 'whip things into place'.

The press, on the other hand, were a little less enamoured. He broke with long-standing tradition by banning the media from the club's hotel during pre-season (previously, outside of training, journalists had mixed almost freely with the players). No more. If the press wanted to find something out, they would go to him, rather than asking a player over a bowl of cornflakes at breakfast or in the lift.

'It took a while to break certain habits in Madrid,' Capello would say years later in a newspaper interview. 'Photographers and journalists were used to being at pitch-side. Agents and hangers-on would wander into the dressing room whenever they liked. To have any kind of privacy, we couldn't train at the training ground, we had to lock ourselves into the Bernabéu . . . are you kidding me? I had to put an end to that and I did. As for the supporters, I think they liked the fact that I cracked the whip and was demanding of the players. They saw that I had a plan.'

Capello was very much 'the Boss', something which had

not always been the case at Milan, where he was dealing with players who had already enjoyed success, where Galliani spoke out almost as often as he did, where Berlusconi loomed large over the club. At Madrid, the focus was entirely on him.

'I don't like the term drill sergeant, but it's true that he imposed himself very quickly,' says Toni Grande. 'We weren't used to it. The way he carried himself, you knew he was in charge. The moment he walked into a room, all the focus shifted to him. He dominated just by his presence.'

'It was strange to see him control everything in the way that he did, because at a club like Real Madrid players are normally given a certain degree of freedom and he changed that,' says Amavisca. 'On the first day, he came in and banned mobile phones. I mean, totally. Even if it was a four-hour bus journey. And then there was the food. We used to have the occasional ice cream, but now that was totally off-limits too. He would walk by at meal times and make sure nobody was eating something they were not supposed to be eating. He determined when players should go to bed and made sure it was strictly enforced. Still, no one doubted that was right: no one questioned that he was the one in charge.'

This was Capello in his micro-management phase. This was the workaholic Capello. This was the Capello who had no hesitation about taking on the club and its customs. 'He didn't want the club's directors and their entourages travelling with us,' says Amavisca. 'In fact, he didn't want them with us at all, not in the dressing room, not in the hotel. And that was a big step at a club like Real

Madrid. Anything that could be a distraction was banned. I even remember that he hated it when the club had special pre-match tributes to former players. I think this would later contribute to his deteriorating relationship with Sanz and the other directors.'

In some ways, it was a bit like Jose Mourinho's Chelsea a decade later. The manager was the club, from Alpha to Omega. And sometimes this manifested itself in other ways. He had the habit of whistling loudly to attract a player's attention on the pitch. Grande noticed this and began doing the same.

'So one day he takes me aside, looks me straight in the eye and says: "Toni, I'm the only one here who whistles at the players, OK?"' says Grande. 'That was it. I never did it again.'

By late August, Capello was generally pleased with the team's progress. But there remained one glaring problem: goalkeeper. The previous season, Francisco Buyo, the long-time number one, had alternated with Santiago Cañizares, whom many touted as the club's future. At twenty-seven, the home-grown Cañizares had bounced around several clubs on loan, and many believed he was ready to take over as the starter. Not Capello. He felt that, at just under six feet, Cañizares lacked the size to command the penalty area. The club were not so convinced, the media even less so. They started writing that Capello was 'obsessed with height' and failed to appreciate that Cañizares had other qualities which made him a very good goalkeeper (and, to be fair, Cañizares would go on to enjoy an exceptional career at Valencia).

Capello was undeterred. After trying to bring over

Sebastiano Rossi from Milan, he began calling around, just as the transfer window was beginning to close. An old friend would prove decisive.

'He rang me up with forty-eight hours left in the transfer window and told me he needed a goalkeeper,' says Oscar Damiani, his former teammate at Juventus, who went on to become a successful agent. 'I hit the phones immediately and found that Illgner was available. It was very tough negotiation with very little time. At two o'clock in the morning, just as the window closed, we managed to seal it.'

Bodo Illgner had been something of a goalkeeping prodigy, making his debut for Germany at the age of twenty and helping them win the World Cup in 1990. Tall and rangy, he was considered one of the better goalkeepers around, but had repeatedly rebuffed offers to leave Cologne, the club where he had come through the ranks. Despite the fact that Cologne were basically a mid-table side, he had always said he was happy there and saw no reason to move to a bigger club. But when the call came from Real Madrid, even he couldn't say no. 'There are bigger clubs and then there are bigger clubs,' he would joke years later, explaining why he suddenly agreed to a move.

By mid-October, Real Madrid were in a head-to-head battle with Barcelona at the top of the Liga table. Yet, at least as far as public perception was concerned, Real were seen as little better than workmanlike. Barça, by contrast, looked like all-conquering champions. Even without Cruyff, the Catalans remained a formidable force, retaining his principles of possession, creativity and all-out attack. The new Phenomenon of world football, Ronaldo, led the frontline and the presence of Luis Enrique, Luis Figo and Pep Guardiola behind him ensured he got plenty of service. The purists were in love with Barcelona, while Real looked like the ugly stepsister: solid, matronly and decidedly unspectacular. Even when Real did turn on the style, as they did on 19 October, beating Real Sociedad 6–1, Barcelona found a way to overshadow them: the following day, they put eight past Logroñés. To his critics, Capello was sterile and lucky, nothing more.

'I think the reality is that his arrival was a bit of a shock to the system,' says Hierro. 'We had to get used to him, and his methods and personality were very different from what we had known before. At the same time, he had to get used to Spanish football, which, especially back then, was very different from Serie A. The fact that the results were coming in did take a bit of pressure off, but if we're honest, for those first few months we were still adapting to the fact that he was so demanding of us. Looking back, years later, when I run into my teammates from that era, we talk about how Capello opened our eyes and it's certainly very true. He showed us the importance of daily work and discipline. At the time, we didn't all realize what was going on.'

There were times when Capello was still somewhat frustrated, feeling that his message wasn't getting through.

'When that happened, when he felt we or the players were a bit sceptical, he would say "¡Escucha a Fabio!" ['Listen to Fabio!'] which I think was his way of telling us to trust him, and that, even if they didn't they had to do what he said, because he was right,' says Grande. 'Fabio always had the last word. And he was almost always right.'

He also frequently employed sticks and carrots, much more than he had in Milan.

'I remember one game away to Zaragoza, where we played really badly but were still winning at half-time,' says Grande. 'Capello walked into the dressing room and wiped the smile off everyone's face. He kicked the kit men out, locking them in the bathroom so he could have a private word with the players. And then he let loose on one of the angriest tirades I had ever seen. He was absolutely furious. And then, when it was over, he kissed each and every player as they went back out for the second half. Needless to say, they got the message. We were much better after half-time.'

One particular phrase of Capello's certainly stuck in Grande's mind.

'Fabio used to tell me, "You need to put a razor blade up against the players' arses," ' he recalls. 'That's true. He did that. But he also knew when to give the players a little kiss, like that time in Zaragoza.'

Still, most pundits were convinced that Real's first place was just a blip, that they were benefiting from the fact that – unlike mighty Barcelona – they had no European obligations. And they were sure that, come 7 December, the date of the first *Clasico* between the two clubs, Barça would put Real back in their place.

They were wrong. Suker and Mijatovic, the latter after a brilliant one-two with Seedorf, sealed a 2–0 defeat which left Barcelona third, four points back (Deportivo La Coruña were second, two points behind).

'There was so much hype surrounding that game,' says

Amavisca. 'The press went on and on about how Ronaldo was coming, how the bogeyman was coming, how we would be found out. But what I remember most is the way he prepared us for that game. He simply convinced us we were going to win, end of story. They're playing well? So what? We're still going to beat them. Note that he didn't tell us we were wonderful, he never built us up,' he adds. 'He simply convinced us we would win and he did it with few words. In fact, he rarely spoke more than he had to. You see, for him, winning is normal. And he transmits that to the players. Thus, when you do win, it doesn't come as a surprise.'

A few weeks later, at the half-way mark, they were still in first place, still undefeated and with a three-point lead over Barcelona in second place. Capello felt the team were finally wrapping their heads around what he wanted them to do. And he and Laura had also made a home for themselves in Madrid. Whatever reservations they may initially have had about leaving Milan after nearly twenty years were wiped away. They both adored Madrid and delighted in discovering the city's art galleries and restaurants. Milan can more than hold its own culturally against any city (though I'm biased here, being Milanese myself . . .) but Capello knew its every cultural and gastronomic nook and cranny. Madrid was uncharted territory, although that soon changed.

'After three months or so, I started to ask myself: "How is it possible that this guy knows every fine restaurant in Madrid?" ' says Grande. 'He was just so curious and so eager to discover everything. He really loved it. I remember one day he told me: "Toni, this city has the very best quality of life in the whole world. The way you people live, nobody else comes close." And it's no coincidence that he comes back to Madrid any time he can.'

January also brought another piece to the puzzle: Christian Panucci. The defender had had his share of rows with Capello, but realized soon after the manager's departure that, in fact, his best performance had come under him. Things had started OK under Oscar Tabárez, but the Uruguayan was sacked on 1 December, after just eleven league games. Milan recalled Arrigo Sacchi, who had been relieved of his duties with Italy that summer, following the Azzurri's disappointing showing at Euro 96, but the relationship soon soured and Panucci was put up for sale. As soon as Capello saw he was available, he asked Real to swoop. Secretário, who had been playing right-back, was clearly out of his depth at the Bernabéu. Capello felt Panucci had the ability and tactical sophistication he would trust.

By this point, Real had perfected a scheme which the purists hated but which proved extremely effective. Hierro, playing in central defence, would pick up the ball and launch it forty or fifty yards for the streaking Roberto Carlos to run on to. Meanwhile, Mijatovic would ghost from his forward position to the left, providing an option for Roberto Carlos if he wanted to lay it off. And Raúl, starting from a left-wing position, would cut inside, eventually ending up in Mijatovic's place on the forward line, alongside Suker. When you explain it like that, it seems relatively simple, yet opponents struggled to defend against it.

'The press hated it,' Capello told me in 2005. 'But,

frankly, I would have been stupid not to do it. It worked perfectly well. And, in Hierro, I had a truly special player who could put the ball wherever he wanted to at a range of fifty metres. Why not use a guy who can do that?'

Note that this wasn't simply hit-and-hope long ball, at least according to Hierro. It was part of a design to restart quickly and stun the opponents before they could get set.

'[Capello] insisted that we central defenders never take more than two touches,' says Hierro. 'Indeed, if we ever took three, he would jump up off the bench and shout like a madman. So, I'd get the ball and quickly get it to Seedorf who would find Roberto Carlos racing down the wing. Or I'd hit it to Roberto Carlos myself. Because of where he received it, he'd have a wealth of options. He could play a one-two with Raúl or Mijatovic or go to the by-line and deliver a low cross or take it into the box himself.'

The whole dynamic worked because of the characteristics of the players. In that sense, it was a textbook case of good tactical management. Roberto Carlos went like a train up and down the wing, with the pace and energy to get behind opponents, starting from a deep position. Hierro had the accuracy to find him, Raúl the intelligence to cut inside at the right time, taking his man with him and clearing a path for Roberto Carlos.

Like all good tactical approaches, it also papered over some of the players' weaknesses. Suker was an exceptional finisher and a genuine penalty area predator, but he was neither quick nor mobile (the joke was that he ran around the pitch like a man with a washing machine strapped to his back); nor was he particularly good at holding the ball up. As for Mijatovic, he was not a genuine striker, but rather a man who liked to move around the pitch in a freer role, looking for space. The 'diagonal' allowed him to receive the ball in areas where he could hurt opponents, just as it enabled Suker to get the service he needed.

Even as it became a trademark of Capello's Real, the pundits crucified Capello for what they called 'long ball' tactics. 'An accurate long pass is a thing of beauty,' points out Amavisca. 'When Zidane or Beckham do it, it's OK. But when Hierro did it, the press couldn't accept that it was a defender doing it. In Spain, central defenders are supposed to defend and, at most, play it short to one of the so-called "good" players who can then do what they like. But we have this obsession with the short passing, this "tiki-taka", this pass, pass, pass . . . well, sometimes, you have to look for alternatives.

'In fact, there were times when we would retreat, inviting our opponents forward and then, once we had created the space behind them, hit them with Hierro's pass,' adds Amavisca. 'It was brilliant . . . and beautiful. But you see, in Spain, everything that comes from Italy is seen in a negative light. Because he's Italian, everything Capello does is seen as ugly, dirty, nasty or boring. But that's not right. If Capello had done everything exactly the same but had been Spanish, instead of Italian, without a doubt the pundits would have had a different image of him. He would have been a hero.'

Capello's other great 'crime' was relegating Raúl to the left wing. Raúl was Madrid's 'Golden Child', scoring nine goals after a mid-season call-up from Castilla, the club's feeder team, as a seventeen-year-old and then following up with nineteen in 1995–96. He had pace, technique, balance and an eye for goal and the club viewed him as a natural centre-forward. So when Capello shifted him to the left side of midfield, there was an insurrection among the pundits. Why was this strange Italian man taking this most gifted of goalscorers and relegating him to the wing, where he'd not only be further away from goal, but would also be burdened with defensive duties as well?

Indeed, Capello had originally considered deploying Mijatovic, who liked to start from deep, as his left midfielder. But the Serb was something of a lightweight defensively and his workrate wasn't what it should have been. Raúl, on the other hand, was still young and gladly soaked up Capello's instructions.

'Capello added a whole dimension to Raúl's game thanks to that year spent on the flank,' says Hierro. 'When he was out there, he was forced to think about the whole team, forced to help defensively, forced to better understand how his movement affected teammates. Raúl had the intelligence to take all that on board. Had he been playing up front, he would not have been faced with those issues. I think it made him a better player. I know it certainly helped Real.'

In fact, despite playing far deeper and out wide, Raúl scored twenty-one goals at the tender age of eighteen: to this day, it remains the third most prolific season of his career.

'That's because, despite putting him wide, Capello always encouraged him to come inside and get in the penalty area whenever he could,' says Amavisca. 'Raúl was given freedom and responsibility and he lived up to it. I lost count of the number of goals he scored with his late runs into the area.'

Capello's first defeat of the season came at the end of January in the Spanish Cup against Barcelona, a 3–2 defeat at the Camp Nou. A week later, a 1–1 draw at the Bernabéu in the return leg sent Real crashing out. Capello wasn't too bothered – the priority was the league and Real were flying – but he was concerned about his relationship with Sanz.

The two were growing increasingly distant. Sanz felt that Capello had demanded a lot from the club and they had bent over backwards to fulfil his request. And still, the president believed, Capello was complaining, talking about needing to strengthen the side over the summer, if they were to compete in the Champions League. Sanz felt Capello was asking for too much, especially since, while Real were doing well, they weren't winning many friends in the media. And, to Sanz, image mattered. There was a 'Real Madrid' way of doing things and Capello wasn't living up to it.

And, further complicating matters, in early February he received a telephone call from Milan. The *rossoneri* were a shambles. Sacchi's return had proved to be a failure on all fronts. Milan were twelfth in Serie A, and they were really missing Capello. Was there any chance that he might want to leave Madrid at the end of the season?

From Capello's perspective, he felt that everything was a struggle with Sanz. In later newspaper interviews he revealed that he felt he did not have the president's unconditional backing and that rankled with him. It had happened before, at Milan, when Galliani put those performance clauses in his contract. On that occasion, Capello saw out his contract and then walked away. This time, he was tempted to do the same, particularly since he had already proved his worth on the pitch.

Thus, on 17 February 1997, following a 2–2 home draw with Betis, Capello and his lawyer marched into Sanz's office. They asked for a 'release-clause', a document giving Capello the option of walking out at the end of the season.

The details of what was said at that meeting vary depending on who you talk to. According to reports in Spain, Capello had told Sanz that 'Milan had called him and, since Milan was his home, it was a bit like when your father calls you: you have to answer.' According to another source, Sanz was only too happy that Capello came to see him: many of the directors felt that his brand of football simply wasn't right for the club and this gave them the perfect opportunity for a parting of the ways, without acrimony or losing face. A third source maintains that Capello was simply looking for a vote of confidence from Sanz. And had Sanz refused to grant him the release, Capello would have taken it as a sign that the president was backing him fully and believed in him. But, when that didn't happen, he was glad he had his get-out clause.

Storm clouds were gathering overhead. Given that Capello's Real were still top and still undefeated in La Liga, it was an extraordinary development. And one which the players soon noticed.

'It was obvious that the relationship [between Capello and Sanz] was not ideal,' says Amavisca. 'With every day he seemed a bit more distant from the board. But he remained close to the players, in fact, he continued to demand that we think about football twenty-four hours a day and work our hardest, just like he did. We didn't let it affect us, also because we remembered how dreadful the previous season had been. None of us wanted to relive that, so we resolved that, come what may, we would hang in there and win the league. We obviously didn't take sides either, though, in hindsight, I'm sure that had Real stuck with Capello they would have achieved great things. After all, just a year later, Real won the European Cup and they did it with the team he had built.'

Amavisca may disagree, but the results suggest that it did affect the players on the pitch. On Wednesday, 19 February 1997, forty-eight hours after Capello's meeting with Sanz, Real Madrid suffered their first league defeat of the season, 0–1 away to little Rayo Vallecano.

Still, the club recovered and, by late April, the lead was up to ten points, with eight matches to go, a seemingly unassailable margin. A stunning comeback against Sevilla at the Bernabéu would prove to be decisive. Real found themselves 2–0 down, while Barcelona were a goal up at Valladolid.

'So, despite being two goals down, Capello takes off Suker . . . and brings on a midfielder in his place,' says Amavisca. 'The fans started whistling and booing. The hankies came out [known as a *panolada*, this Spanish footballing tradition signals the supporters' displeasure with their club]. But then we come back and win 4–2 [while Barcelona ends up losing 3–1]. To me, that's the perfect portrait of Capello. He has his methods and everything that goes on around him simply doesn't matter. He ruled. There was no asking "why?" The answer is: "Because Capello says so." He would tell you what to do, but he never told you why.'

And you learned not to ask him either. Because you knew that, more often than not, he'd be right.'

Still, things got a bit hairy in the next few weeks. Barcelona clawed back two points, setting up, on 10 May, a crucial *Clasico* at the Camp Nou, which could see them further cut the margin to just five points. Barcelona duly won, with a single Ronaldo goal deciding the match. The Catalan press chorused 'Game On!', while their colleagues in Madrid started an inquest over Capello's decisions that day. But, in fact, the dressing room remained calm. 'We wanted to win, of course, but we sort of budgeted for that loss,' says Amavisca. 'We knew it wouldn't be the end of the world at that stage of the season.'

Which, of course, is another sign of a good team: knowing when to take your knocks and knowing how to look at the bigger picture. How not to panic. Real had absorbed the loss, Barça were closing in, but they still had a mountain to climb.

Or did they? The following week, both clubs won, but the next weekend, Barcelona edged out Deportivo while Real fell at Athletic Bilbao, 0–1. The lead was now down to just two points.

And then came a spot of genuine good luck. Real Madrid rolled over Extremadura, 5–0, while Barcelona somehow contrived to lose away to relegation-threatened Hercules. The lead was back to five points. All Real needed was two points from the final two games – the Madrid derby against Atlético at the Bernabéu and a trip to struggling Celta Vigo – to be crowned champions.

They secured all three in one go, beating Atlético 3–1. The crowd soon forgot the hankies against Sevilla. The title was back at the Bernabéu where they felt it belonged.

'But there was no jubilation from Capello,' says Amavisca. 'Maybe he was too used to winning! He was happy, of course, but he wasn't going mad or anything. It was like he thought, Well, winning is my job; I haven't done anything particularly out of the ordinary here. It was normal for him. He just congratulated the players and that was it. Which was in keeping with his personality; he always maintained a bit of distance.'

It's hard to believe that, at least on the inside, Capello didn't have some degree of self-satisfaction. This was his fifth league title in six seasons. He had won at the first attempt, in a foreign country, with a foreign league. He had done it with six new players in his starting eleven. He had done it while giving playing time to a host of youngsters, from Amavisca to Victor, from Guti to Raúl. He had instilled confidence and a winning mentality in the squad: the statistic of which he was most proud was that in fourteen matches, Real had come from behind to win. And he had, once again, proved his employer wrong. He had triumphed with his bags already packed, knowing that his relationship with Sanz and Real was bound to end. In fact, the two sniped at each other via the media.

'The reason I'm leaving is that I don't believe I have the full confidence of the president,' Capello told *Gazzetta dello Sport*. 'That's the only reason.'

'Capello knew back in February, when he came to see me, that he was going to leave,' Sanz fired back. 'It's true, I did nothing to change his mind, because we are Real Madrid and that's our philosophy. If you don't want to be here, you can go. The same applies to Capello. We won twenty-seven league titles without him, we can win many more without him. He can say what he likes, but what I'm telling you is the truth.

'Fabio says Real Madrid didn't show him enough love? Well, he never fell in love with Real Madrid either,' Sanz added. 'If he had, he would never have behaved the way he did. I had further proof of this on the night we won the title. Rather than simply celebrating with the rest of us, he wanted to talk to me about who we were going to sign over the summer. That shows a lack of respect for the players on what should have been a night of joy and celebration and nothing else.'

The last part, of course, as we've seen, was more likely Capello being Capello rather than wanting to show a lack of respect. He'd just won the title, yet he was thinking forward to next season – even if both he and Sanz knew he wouldn't be around.

There was, of course, one last thing to do before he could jet off on his customary end-of-season holiday. Real had to face Celta on the final day of the season in what was essentially a meaningless game for Real. Capello went out with a bang, though not the kind he would have wanted. Real lost, 4–0, and he tore into the players after the match.

'You should have seen him!' says Amavisca. 'His re-action was incredible. We had won the league, we had been celebrating, we didn't much fancy playing and, in fact, we didn't really mind losing. But to Capello it was a question of honour. Because they were fighting to avoid relegation, he felt we had the duty to play hard and win. He said we owed it to the integrity of the league, we owed it to our fellow professionals. He was absolutely furious, telling us that he could not accept what we had done.'

In the event, it really didn't matter to anyone but Capello. Extremadura, who would have benefited from a Celta loss, were defeated and the issue became academic. He left Madrid with a knot in his stomach, partly for the Celta match, partly for the ugly end of his relationship with Sanz, partly because he knew he was leaving a city he had come to adore.

CHAPTER 11

Never Go Back: a Season of Discontent

The previous twelve months had been a massive blow to the *rossoneri* and the 'Milan way', as Silvio Berlusconi liked to call it. The 'perfect machine' they had created – the state-of-the-art training and medical facilities, the highly paid backroom staff, the top-notch scouting network – had broken down badly. They believed the club was so big and so well-organized that it could function seamlessly without Capello. They were wrong.

First Oscar Tabárez then – after three months – Arrigo Sacchi, struggled to get anything out of a first-team squad which had swelled to twenty-four. The core of the team was essentially the same (Roberto Donadoni and Paolo Di Canio were the only notable departures), but Milan had added pricey foreigners such as striker Christophe Dugarry and winger Jesper Blomqvist, as well as two of Ajax's brightest young stars, hardman Edgar Davids and defender Michael Reiziger. All four flopped badly.

The *rossoneri* tumbled down the table, finishing the

season in eleventh place. Only once in the past sixty-five years had Milan finished lower. It was a total humiliation and an indictment of the club's methods. Outwardly, Capello took no joy in Milan's distress. Privately, however, it's hard to believe that he did not see it as some kind of vindication. Especially since Berlusconi himself had asked him to return.

'After leaving Madrid, I could have gone to Lazio who made a very good offer and I probably would have gone if Berlusconi hadn't personally contacted me,' he said in a 1999 newspaper interview. 'The only reason I came back was because Berlusconi asked me.'

That may have been the case, but what was probably in the back of his mind was that this was an opportunity to truly overhaul the club and gain a greater say in Milan's affairs, with the kind of power enjoyed by managers in England. He had proved himself as a coach, yet both in his first stint at Milan and in the previous year at Real he had had to submit to sporting directors and presidents who thought they knew better, especially when it came to transfers, contracts and squad management. Now, he felt, he could ask for, and hope to receive, total control over the footballing side, including, crucially, ins and outs.

Except by the time he took over at Milan in late June 1997, chief executive Adriano Galliani and sporting director Ariedo Braida had already sealed most of the club's signings for the following season. The jewel in Milan's transfer crown was Patrick Kluivert, their 'executioner' in the Champions League final three seasons earlier, when they were defeated by Ajax. At twenty-one, the Dutchman was blessed with a rare cocktail of pace, size and skill, prompting some to call him Europe's answer to Ronaldo. Leonardo, the elegant, handsome Brazilian creative midfielder, joined from Paris Saint-Germain. At the back, the legendary Franco Baresi had retired, but, to bolster the defence, Milan had brought in no fewer than three internationals: Winston Bogarde from Ajax, the German leftback Christian Ziege (who had excelled at Euro 96 a year earlier) and the Brazilian sweeper André Cruz. There was also a new goalkeeper, Massimo Taibi, who controversially won the starting job from Sebastiano Rossi.

Though Baresi and Mauro Tassotti (a year earlier) were gone, much of Milan's 'old guard' were still around: Rossi in goal, Paolo Maldini and Billy Costacurta at the back, Demetrio Albertini and Marcel Desailly in midfield, plus Zvonimir Boban and Dejan Savicevic, as well as George Weah. On paper, it looked like a devastating side. But Capello felt there was one item missing, a world-class wide man to deliver the service for Weah and Kluivert.

Milan spent much of the summer chasing Barcelona's Luis Figo, the man Capello had earmarked for the job. As was the custom in Spain at the time, Figo, like most foot-ballers, had a buy-out clause in his contract: any club wanting to sign him had only to match it and he would be free to leave. Thus the *rossoneri* were confident they could do what their city rivals Inter had done that same summer with Ronaldo: pay his release clause and bring him on board. But Barcelona had already been deeply em-barrassed by the loss of Ronaldo. They simply could not afford to lose Figo in the same way. After weeks of back-and-forth, they persuaded the Portuguese to stay (an improved contract certainly helped make up his mind). When that deal fell through, Milan moved for Figo's team-mate Luis Enrique, but Barcelona were once again able to rebuff them. Finally, with the transfer window closing, the club opted for Capello's third choice, the French winger Ibrahim Ba.

The press hailed it as Milan's 'inevitable' comeback year. Upon his return to Milanello, it looked to many as if nothing had changed. A giant mural of Oscar Tabárez and the previous season's Milan squad, which loomed over the bar at Milanello, was promptly taken down. Capello and Italo Galbiati even got to move back into their old rooms, number 5 and 8 respectively. Everything went back to the way it was during the happy times.

In fact, everything was a little too much like before. Capello still did not feel like he had the control he wanted over footballing decisions. The club were scheduled to go on a pre-season tour of Brazil: Capello was opposed, but they went anyway. The Swedish striker Andreas Andersson, whom the coaching staff felt was wholly in-adequate, arrived from Göteborg, largely on the strength of a goal he had scored against Milan the previous year. Capello asked that he be moved on, but the club kept him around.

That said, while he still had a few reservations, Capello felt Milan were moving in the right direction. In fact, that August, the beaming manager announced that he felt his squad was stronger than ever and went on to praise his men effusively: 'I expect Blomqvist and Davids to have great seasons this year. Plus, I think we have a hidden gem in Bogarde. He's a special player, you'll see . . .'

Looking back, if you take his words at face value (and bear in mind that managers always praise their signings in pre-season), it's striking to note just how wrong he was. Blomqvist made just nineteen appearances (with one goal), while Bogarde featured just three times before being off-loaded to Barcelona in January, eventually becoming the punchline to many a footballing joke.

And then there was the issue of Davids. The Dutch pit-bull had missed much of the previous season through injury and many saw him as a stone-cold disappointment. Capello believed it was too early to write him off and wanted to wait until he had fully recovered before making a decision on his future.

Davids made a few substitute appearances early in the year, but the relationship soon soured. Capello felt he simply was not fit enough to be given a starting role and, besides, in Boban, Leonardo, Desailly and Albertini, it was hard to find space for him, especially since, with no European football, there simply wasn't enough playing time to parcel out.

'Fabio believed in Davids, he went out of his way to bring him back from injury,' Italo Galbiati said in a 1998 newspaper interview. 'But he wanted to play all the time and we couldn't do that. And then he grew very unsettled and asked for a move. We agreed, with the proviso that he be sold abroad. We did not want him to come back to haunt us.'

Instead, that winter, Milan sold him to, of all clubs, Juventus. Davids went on to become a stalwart at Juve under Marcello Lippi, leading them to three Italian titles. The fact that Milan had basically gift-wrapped him and handed him to one of their direct rivals proved very difficult for everyone to swallow and, to this day, must rank as one of the most humiliating and boneheaded moves in the history of football.

Capello's other big decision that summer was not renewing Roberto Baggio's contract, which had a year to run. The 'Divine Ponytail' had struggled under Tabárez and Sacchi the previous campaign, registering just five goals in twenty-three Serie A appearances. Some felt that Capello, who had managed to make him successfully coexist with Savicevic two seasons earlier, could find a way to revive his career. This time, however, Capello had a choice whether or not to keep him. And his mind was quickly made up.

'Baggio's contract is expiring at the end of the season,' Capello said in a July 1997 newspaper interview. 'We have other priorities right now. We are making other plans and those plans do not involve extending his contract. He is only going to stay if we don't find a club who will take him. It seems only fair to us that we find a home for him, a place where he can continue playing football. But it won't be at Milan.'

Thus, Baggio, just two and a half years after being named FIFA's Player of the Year and still just twenty-nine years of age, was shipped off on a free transfer to Bologna, a side who had only just returned to Serie A the previous season. Had he stayed, perhaps Baggio would not have been a success at Milan, as Capello suggests. We'll never know. But the fact remains that, far from being finished, he would go on to score a further seventy-five Serie A goals, including twenty-two that season at Bologna.

Savicevic was in a similar situation. *Il Genio* had also had a subpar season the previous year (seventeen appearances, one goal) and, at thirty-one, looked past it. Capello had enough clout – and enough alternatives – to do without him. He stayed on, but would start just six games all season, and failed to find the net. No longer would Capello have the headache of trying to accommodate him in his team.

The season began badly, with Milan winning just one of six and, by mid-October, they were thirteenth, just two points from relegation. The newcomers had largely failed to settle, the 'old guard' looked stale. The critics began to murmur, Capello asked for patience. He brought Donadoni back from his stint in Major League Soccer. Donadoni was thirty-four by then and had lost much of his pace, but Capello felt he needed some kind of a spark and, most of all, players he could trust. Sure enough, Milan embarked on a nine-match unbeaten run, which saw them go as high as sixth.

But cracks were starting to appear. Incredibly, Milan found themselves short-handed at the back. Cruz went down injured and missed most of the rest of the season. Bogarde turned out to be an absolute dud. Ziege proved that, while he may have been a competent wingback, he couldn't cut it as a leftback in Serie A, because his defending simply wasn't good enough. His pre-season pronouncement – 'I don't think we're going to allow a single headed goal this season, we're just too good at the back' – was widely lampooned.

Capello had to scramble, reinventing Desailly as a central defender alongside Costacurta and, on occasion, switching Maldini to rightback. When that didn't work, he was forced to turn to Giuseppe Cardone, a journeyman fullback. There were problems up front as well: Weah missed three months through injury, Kluivert too often looked like a deer in the headlights. Furthermore, a knee injury limited his mobility (he would later need surgery). Indeed, things got so bad that the club had to bring in two journeymen strikers, Maurizio Ganz and Pippo Maniero, just to have bodies up front. For those who don't know them, Ganz and Maniero would go on to play for twenty-five clubs between them in their careers, epitomizing the 'Have boots, will travel' rent-a-striker category. They were the Serie A equivalents of Marcus Bent and Dean Windass: solid pros who bounced around and did a job for whatever clubs needed them, but definitely not Milan-calibre strikers.

Problems emerged in goal as well. Taibi was the starter in the league, while Rossi played in the Coppa Italia. Taibi had decent skills, but seemed daunted by the San Siro and, more importantly, appeared to lack the confidence of the 'old guard', who preferred Rossi. Fans and the media clamoured for the big goalkeeper, but Capello, believing Taibi just needed games under his belt to regain his confidence, wouldn't budge. In fact, when told that Rossi was unhappy at being overlooked, he reportedly replied: 'Good. He can show me how talented he is in the Coppa Italia.'

By 1 February, the situation had become untenable. Rossi replaced Taibi between the sticks, though the goalkeeping hardly improved.

As Milan drifted closer to the bottom of the table, the

pundits ratcheted up the pressure on Capello. Ruud Gullit, his old nemesis, commented that Capello was so unpleasant that he 'would never want to go to dinner with him'. Capello shot back, saying: 'I'm the one who wouldn't want to eat with Gullit. He's so cheap, I'd probably end up being stuck with the bill and having to pay.'

For Capello it was definitely a difficult time. With these types of childish exchanges old scores were settled, the invincible Capello was being toppled and everyone wanted to get in a kick.

Another blow came on 28 March following a 4–1 drubbing away to Juventus. Luciano Moggi, Juve's general manager, commented: 'Capello is certainly stressed out and thin-skinned these days, isn't he?'

Moggi was a master of such barbs, engaging in the kind of mind games which tended to unsettle his adversaries. He was also a close friend of Capello's. But, as we will see in later chapters, both he and Capello put aside their relationship when it came to football and did whatever they could to get a psychological edge. Capello wasn't overly bothered by Moggi's words, but he did expect someone from the club, most likely Galliani, to come out and defend him. Instead, there was nothing but silence. And that's what bothered him. Because, if nobody was firing back on his behalf, it meant that the club had, once and for all, turned their back on him.

Still, as rumours of his demise intensified, Capello circled the wagons as much as he could.

'I don't know why I should leave,' he said in an interview in early April. 'Next year I'll still be here, I have a plan for restoring Milan to the usual levels of excellence. Next year will be the moment of truth and I'll be right here leading the club. I will have learned from the mistakes we made this season. And Milan will be great again. I'm not leaving this club until we've won more silverware.'

The media's response? Mockery and snide remarks. His enemies were loving it. One colleague of Capello's who witnessed it all told me: 'It's like the old saying, be nice to people on your way up, because they're the ones you'll meet on your way back down. Maybe Fabio wasn't so nice on the way up and now that he was on his way down, people weren't being nice to him. Plus, of course, the critics were also jealous. They had gleefully discovered that he was human and made mistakes, just like the rest of us.'

For the first time in his managerial career, Capello felt powerless, at least according to Galbiati.

'It's simple really, we all felt impotent,' he said in 1999. 'At the beginning of the season, everyone was enthusiastic, everyone listened to us and believed in what we were trying to do. Then, when things got tough, we lost them. Some of our most important players lost their motivation.'

While Milan were falling apart in the league, they enjoyed somewhat better success in the Coppa Italia, reaching the final against Sven-Göran Eriksson's Lazio. It was a very minor consolation, but at least, by winning, they would enjoy a route into Europe. A rash of injuries and pull-outs severely depleted his squad. Capello was forced to field Steinar Nielsen, a Norwegian mid-season pick-up, and Dario Smoje, a nineteen-year-old Croatian from the youth team, in his back four. Kluivert, Boban and Ziege were all sidelined, Leonardo could only make the bench, which meant Savicevic got a rare start. Weah's injury-time goal gave Milan a 1–0 win.

The return leg was played in Rome three weeks later. Savicevic again started, but came off after just half an hour, as Capello sent on Kluivert, who was not fully fit. Albertini gave Milan the lead early in the second half, before the *rossoneri* simply collapsed. Kluivert went down clutching his knee and had to be substituted. Lazio scored three times in the space of ten minutes. And, to add insult to injury, Desailly was sent off for a tussle with Diego Fuser ten minutes from time. Milan had let the trophy slip through their fingers in the worst possible way.

'If you go back through the history of Milan, I doubt you'll find the kind of blackout we witnessed against Lazio,' an angry Capello said after the game. 'I had a long talk with my players. But what could they say? They tell me I'm right, that they had a bad game. But so what? The result doesn't change. We just concede far too many goals. How many goals has our defence conceded in the past two seasons? There must be a reason, no? And I'll have you note that eight of the eleven players on the pitch were a part of the "old" Milan side.'

Whether he intended to or not, the media took this as an attack on the 'old guard': Maldini, Costacurta, Rossi, Albertini, Donadoni . . . these were legends and you don't mess with legends. Again, Capello was roundly criticized. The only support he got was from Weah, who agreed that maybe 'change was necessary'. This led to more tension in the dressing room and, within eighteen months, the Liberian was dispatched to Chelsea.

Perhaps the lowest point came four days later on 3 May,

again at the Stadio Olimpico. Milan faced Roma after winning just two of their last nine. It was a virtual blood-bath. Roma were 4–0 up by half-time before winning 5–0. A furious Capello stalked the sidelines screaming, 'You don't have any balls! You don't have any fucking balls!' at his own players, as the *giallorossi* toyed with Milan. On that day, you felt they could have scored eight or nine and that only courtesy limited them to five.

After the game, Capello fired back at the club who, in his view, had not given him enough latitude in decision-making.

'I can't believe some people say that I am a manager with full powers,' he said. 'That's the biggest lie you could imagine. The fact is that no manager of Milan has full powers.'

The reference to Galliani, Berlusconi, the unwanted summer signings and the influence of the 'old guard' was obvious. By then, everyone knew that Capello's time would come to an end that summer. Costacurta, speaking after defeat in the Coppa Italia final, put it most bluntly, telling one newspaper: 'The loss is painful, but at least it puts an end to a situation which most of us simply could not handle any longer.'

The message seemed clear. The 'old guard' wanted a new manager. Capello fired back: 'I'd love it if Costacurta could remember what he once was.' It was a reference to the defender's supposedly declining skills. And it was rather cruel.

On Saturday, 16 May, Milan closed out the season with a 2–0 defeat at Fiorentina, leaving them tenth, thirty points behind Juventus, the champions, and just nine points clear of the relegation zone. Sunday was a day of reflection; Monday brought the call from Berlusconi, summoning him to dinner that evening at the president's private residence, Villa San Martino, at Arcore, in the countryside north of Milan.

The media had been tipped off and, when he arrived, just after eight o'clock, he found an army of journalists and cameramen waiting for him. Among them was a television crew from *Striscia La Notizia*, a satirical programme which, ironically, airs on one of Berlusconi's networks. *Striscia* had a habit of door-stepping celebrities and, with cameras rolling, handing them a statuette known as the 'Golden Tapir', a spoof award given to those who had failed spectacularly. (For those not versed in zoology, a tapir is a pig-like animal from the forests of south and central America.) Capello nodded, jaw out, lips pursed, as he drove through the main gate to the grounds. I like to think that he thought to himself: 'Whatever happens, those bastards are not giving me that stupid Golden Tapir . . .'

Inside were Berlusconi, his son Piersilvio and Galliani. Over dinner, they told him that Capello would be free to leave the club. They were going 'in a different direction' (the standard phrase employers use when giving the bullet), but thanked him for all his hard work. Galliani would be out to brief the assembled press – it would be best if Capello did not speak to them that night.

And so Capello emerged at eleven-fifteen, driving straight past the media scrum. Whatever he chose to tell himself, this did not change the facts: he had failed, he had come up short. If you live by results, as he had, you die by results.

There was one more thing to do. Looking in his rearview mirror, he could see the camera crew from *Striscia* hot on his heels with their Golden Tapir. In these situations, he knew that the best thing to do was simply to pull over and get it over with. Let them have their fun and be on his way. After all, sooner or later, they were bound to find him.

That was the rational thing to do. But tonight was different. He made a sudden turn on to a side road, then another, and another, changing lanes and routes for a good half hour until he was sure he had lost them. They would have their moment of fun. But not that night. And it would be on his terms.

Theories abound as to just why Milan were so poor that season and how much of it was Capello's fault. His first public reaction was to accept responsibility, while noting that he wasn't the one who had assembled the side.

'When I arrived, most of the spending had already been done,' he said later that summer. 'I did not feel like it was my team, because I did not have a hand in assembling it. Still, what happened happened. And I'll accept that I'm not just the one who was responsible, I'm the one who was at fault.'

The openness with which he accepted blame – albeit while listing the mitigating factors – stunned me in writing this book. Think back and you'll see that very few managers are willing to hold their hands up and admit their mistakes. Admitting mistakes is seen as tantamount to admitting weakness: witness what happened to Kevin Keegan after he resigned the England job on live television, saying he 'could not take this team any further'.

Capello was the last man I expected to hold his hand up so openly. But he did.

Clearly though, the problem was not just with the new signings. In fact, with such a big squad, they had played a relatively small part. Kluivert was slowed by injuries, but he would prove at Barcelona (before going off the rails later) that he was a quality striker. Cruz's six-month enforced absence made him a non-factor. Ziege and, especially, Bogarde did turn out to be duds at this level, as did Blomqvist. Leonardo was a hit, though, and even Ba, the only hand-picked summer signing, had his only good season in Italy under Capello.

All told, the problem went deeper. The veterans of the 'old Milan' did not perform that year, just as they had not performed the year before. Were they demotivated? Were they burnt out? Were their professional careers on the wane?

The press suggested that Capello had blamed everything on the 'old guard' and that he had asked Berlusconi to have a clearout and start from scratch. Reportedly, he wanted Costacurta, Albertini, Rossi and Desailly axed, along with a fair few of the previous years' signings. Capello angrily denied those reports.

'I keep a small scrap of paper in my day planner,' he said in a January 2000 interview. 'On that bit of paper is the Milan XI I was planning to field in 1998–99, had I stayed at the club. And guess what? In that XI you will find the names of the entire old guard. All of them. So if people want to keep saying I was planning some kind of purge, they are free to say what they like. But I know the truth. And I carry that scrap of paper with me to this day.'

Maybe so. But it's undeniable that the relationship with the 'old guard' had soured once and for all. When Capello was appointed manager of Roma in June 1999, Maldini's response was icy: 'Am I going to wish him well? No. I only wish Milan well and nobody else.'

Six months later, Maldini's stance had softened. He told *Gazzetta dello Sport*: 'Capello did not leave us on good terms. But we all remember the many trophies we won together. Time is a great healer and, as far as I'm concerned, we hold no grudge. We would rather remember the good times.'

But there is little argument that Capello felt let down. The hungry, professional unit that he had left in 1996 showed all of its soft underbelly in 1997.

'I think it's a bit like eating cherries,' one Milan source told me. 'At first you're excited and you enjoy each and every one. After a while, it becomes automatic, you take it for granted. And then, eventually, you don't even really enjoy it any more. You can't be bothered to go on. Maybe in some ways that's what happened. That core of players was so used to success that, in those two seasons, when things started getting rough, they lost some of their motivation. It's not hard to be motivated when you're gunning for the title. It's harder to get motivated when you're trying to finish sixth rather than tenth. They were satiated. And maybe, once the losses started mounting up, it became unconsciously easier to write off the rest of the season.'

Capello has always recognized that returning to Milan was one of the biggest mistakes of his career.

'If you taste success somewhere, the biggest mistake you

can make is to go back,' he said that summer. 'It's never the same the second time around. I learned my lesson.' With hindsight, it's easy to say. And it's equally true that he did not, in fact, 'learn his lesson', as evidenced by the fact he returned to Real Madrid a decade later.

Now, however, he faced his first summer without club football in thirty-seven years. No pre-season training, no fixture lists, no worrying about his knee (and, later, the knees of others). He would take his usual holiday jaunt with Laura, perhaps trying to lose himself in some archae-ological ruins in a remote part of the world. And then what?

He received a number of offers that summer, but he decided to take a break from the everyday routine of foot-ball. Instead, he returned to something he had come to love: television punditry.

Throughout the 1980s he had worked as a football pundit, mostly for TeleMontecarlo, a small network based in Monaco which, due to the idiosyncrasies of European broadcasting regulations, was visible throughout Italy. It owned the broadcasting rights to a number of foreign leagues and, when he was working with Milan's youth academy, Capello would regularly drive the three and a half hours to Monaco to appear on TeleMontecarlo.

'He was a pioneer in many ways,' says Luigi Colombo, who worked with Capello at TeleMontecarlo. 'For example, I think we were the first in Europe, certainly the first in Italy, to introduce co-commentators during matches. Previously, it was just the commentator for ninety minutes. But we realized that by putting an ex-professional next to him, we could add another dimension to our coverage. Of course, it had to be somebody good. And Fabio was one of the very best.'

Capello found himself to be a natural in front of the camera, both as a co-commentator and later as a studio pundit.

'What made him good?' says Colombo. 'His timing, for a start. He knew exactly when to pipe up and when to stay silent. And he had this incredible ability to be concise, informative and entertaining, all at once. Unlike most ex-pros, he doesn't tell you what you just saw. He tells you what you didn't see and explains it to you.'

Jacopo Volpi, who works at RAI, Italy's state broadcaster, agrees: 'The thing about Capello is that his work could be enjoyed by anyone. My mother, who knows nothing about football, could sit and listen to him. And, equally, my father, who is a qualified coach, could listen to him just as happily. He's universal in that sense.'

He also proved to be unflappable and professional in front of the cameras. In March 1983, Juventus were playing Aston Villa in the European Cup. Capello and a presenter, Ettore Andenna, were supposed to provide pre- and post-match analysis from the studios in Monaco, while Colombo and his co-commentator, Giacomo Bulgarelli, were to do the live commentary from Villa Park.

Andenna was caught in traffic and never made it to the studio. Capello did the whole pre-game bit by himself, extemporaneous and unscripted, before handing over to the commentary team in Birmingham. They had just enough time to give out the starting lineups when their phone line went dead, leaving viewers with just the pictures. Capello did not miss a beat.

'He just took over,' says Colombo. 'He did the entire first-half commentary by himself, watching the monitor in the studio. It was unbelievable.'

TeleMontecarlo used him as much as they could. He was a regular on their flagship *QuasiGol* programme, persuading none other than Michel Platini to join him most weeks. And he covered the 1982 World Cup, the 1984 European Championships and the 1986 World Cup, for which he flew out to Mexico and provided daily reports.

And now, free of the daily stresses and strains of managing a football club, Capello could contemplate returning to the role of football pundit, with plenty of valuable experience behind him.

On 3 September 1998 RAI announced that Capello would join them for the upcoming season, working mainly on the Italian national team. Some were a bit sceptical: after all, the Azzurri were managed by Dino Zoff, who, along with Edy Reja, is Capello's closest friend in football. Would Capello give him an easy ride?

'Not at all,' says Volpi. 'In fact, Capello was brutal with Zoff, taking his team to task for every little mistake. It didn't matter that they were friends. In fact, when Capello left us to go to manage Roma, Zoff was so happy, he offered to take everyone out to dinner. His harshest critic was gone.'

Perhaps it's not surprising that Capello was so outspoken and tough in his commentary. He has said many times that, wherever he is employed, he puts everything he has into the job. Zoff may have been a friend, but Capello had a job to do, and he was going to do it, even if it meant putting his old mate through the wringer. That honest criticism made him extremely popular as a pundit, far more than he was as a manager.

Another thing people, especially in the media, noticed in his year of punditry, was that all of a sudden, he became immensely approachable. Previously, his relations with the media ranged from cold to frosty. But now that he had crossed over, he acted as if he were one of the gang. He travelled with the press, slept in the same hotels, mixed with them freely over dinner and at the bar, shared gossip and stories. For a man who had been distant from the media as a manager, it was a remarkable turnaround.

'I loved my television work,' Capello said in a newspaper interview years later. 'It allowed me to watch football from around the world in a different light. Because when you're playing or managing, you have an entirely different focus, you don't see the game in the same way.'

Capello always remained grateful to Colombo for introducing him to a world which he may not otherwise have known: television. And, years later, in the summer of 2003, he paid him back. Colombo was scheduled to commentate on the Confederations Cup final in Paris between France and Cameroon. Just before the final, his co-commentator dropped out.

'So I called Capello, who was on holiday in Marbella,' Colombo recalls. 'I was really just hoping he could recommend someone. After all, he was on holiday and, besides, he was managing Roma. Instead, he told me that he would do it. And, what's more, he paid his own way to Paris.'

Capello took the metro from central Paris to the Stade

de France, just like any other punter and even helped carry some of the equipment. After the match, he took Colombo and his producers out to dinner, staying up until four o'clock in the morning.

The anecdote reveals the other side of Capello, the one few get to see. Most know him as a man who seems to be in work mode twenty-four/seven, a man who can be gruff and dismissive, a man who disdains crowds and small talk. But, in the right setting, evidently the convivial Capello comes out to frolic. Paris was one of those times, as were many of the occasions when he was on the other side of the fence, looking in on football, rather than being a part of it.

CHAPTER 12

Worth Ten Titles at Milan or Juve

However much he enjoyed television work, Capello had given himself a schedule. He would take a year off and then get back into the game. There were a few options abroad, but Capello did not want to leave Serie A so soon after Madrid. In Italy, most of the big clubs were set. Carlo Ancelotti had taken over at Juventus in February 1999, while Sven-Göran Eriksson at Lazio and Giovanni Trapattoni at Fiorentina were both firmly entrenched. Going back to Milan was obviously not a possibility. And Inter had just signed Marcello Lippi, the man who had delivered three titles to Juventus. All of which left Roma, where Zdenek Zeman was completing the second of two turbulent seasons.

Zeman remains one of the most colourful and contro-versial figures in Italian football. Ironically, he is the nephew of Cestmir Vycpalek, Capello's manager at Juventus in the early 1970s, though the two are very different. Supporters loved Zeman's attacking, high-paced football, even though it often left the defence exposed. A strict disciplinarian, pre-season under Zeman was a kind of boot camp, replete with Victorian training methods.

Zeman could also be abrasive, confrontational and, on occasion, outspoken. In a 1998 interview with a weekly news magazine, he criticized what he described as the widespread misuse of legal drugs and supplements in football and the way the 'powers-that-be' (a phrase most interpreted as meaning Milan and Juventus) were allowed to get away with it.

These kinds of outbursts made him very popular among Roma supporters who traditionally – perhaps more than any other fan base in Italy – have a tendency to look for ready-made excuses and a penchant for conspiracy theories. They also provided a constant headache for Franco Sensi, the Roma president.

Sensi was a very wealthy man whose empire included petroleum refineries and construction. He was also the classic 'fan-owner' who too often thought like a supporter. He had come to believe the conspiracy theories circulating around Rome and became convinced that his club had very little power when it came to the 'Palazzo'. The 'Palazzo' is a purely Italian concept, which can be loosely translated as the 'corridors of power'. Italians are big believers in the notion that things are usually not what they seem. Behind the scenes, there is always someone or something pulling the strings. That 'something' was the 'Palazzo', the Establishment, the cabal of powerful figures who ran the game in Italy. As Milan and Juventus had, between them, won every league title since 1991, the 'Palazzo' clearly looked favourably on them. And, possibly because of Zeman and his outbursts, they did not look kindly on Roma.

In Sensi's eyes, Capello was the best antidote to all this. Not only was he one of the top managers around, he was Mr Establishment, having spent most of his career at Juventus and Milan. He was at home with the very powerful, and would not be intimidated by them, but would, in fact, guarantee that Roma got a fair shake. Indeed, a few days after Capello's appointment, he told *Gazzetta dello Sport*: 'One of the reasons we got Capello is that, with him on board, the "Palazzo" has no choice but to treat us with respect.'

On 30 May 1999 Capello flew from Malpensa to Rome to meet Sensi. They spent the day at Villa Pacelli, the Sensi family's headquarters, and ended up dining in the Testaccio neighbourhood. Capello liked the fact that Sensi was giving him carte blanche. And he loved the idea of rediscovering Rome after nearly thirty years. He flew back to Milan with a smile on his face. Yes, the vibe felt right.

He returned a few days later to sign his contract. Naturally, he would be bringing Galbiati with him. While Capello had been spending his year off on television, Galbiati was back in Milan, working with the Under 11s at Cimiano, an amateur club. Going from George Weah and Paolo Maldini to a bunch of stumbling ten-year-olds was not a difficult transition for him: he just loved coaching and needed something to do.

When his phone rang, Capello was curt as always, despite the fact that they had not spoken in a while: 'I'm at Franco Sensi's house. We're going to Roma. Pack your bags.' That was about it.

Some supporters were sad to see the combative Zeman go. But Capello soon won them over, starting with his very first press conference, where he said all the right things.

'I don't have a minimum target for next season, I only have one objective: winning it all,' he said. Nils Liedholm, the old master and his former manager at Milan, was sitting next to him. 'The man to my right is the last manager to win the *scudetto* at Roma. He's right when he says that a *scudetto* at Roma is worth ten in other cities. I am going to touch him in the hope that he will bring me good luck.'

And, with that, Capello reached out and brushed Liedholm's arm, while the Swede grinned from ear to ear. The local press lapped it up. Capello was proving himself to be not just a man of the Establishment, but a man of the people as well.

He soon realized just how big the task before him was going to be. Rome was a big city with a small-town mentality, a metropolis with all the insecurities of a provincial city. He already knew this of course, but the point was driven home at one of the very first meetings with club officials. For around forty minutes the only talk was of Lazio, their crosstown rivals. How much better were they going to be this year? What did everyone think of the new signings? Did Eriksson have what it took to deliver the title? Was Roma going to win the derby? 'Enough!' Capello roared at one point. A stunned silence descended on the room. 'Why are we talking about this? We are Roma. Let's worry about us and our issues. The rest should not concern us.'

Again, the press loved it. Roma had themselves a winner, a kick-ass-and-take-names kind of guy. For years it had been said that Roma fans would rather win the derby against Lazio and finish in mid-table, than win the league but lose the derby. It wasn't quite that bad, but almost. But now, with Capello, the underachievement would end and Roma would go from being a big club to being a Big Club.

Capello fitted the image of the man who could tell Roma what they needed to hear, rather than what they wanted to hear. He talked about how the 'culture of winning' was lacking in the nation's capital.

'We've been underachieving for years, not just Roma, but Lazio too,' he said in early August. 'It's something which concerns the whole city. Look at Lazio last season, they were easily the best team in Serie A but they didn't win. Why? I'd hate to think it was the usual things, the fear of success, the Roman spring, mental block . . . whatever you want to call it. We have to move beyond that.'

What he was saying wasn't necessarily new. There had to be a reason why the city of Rome, at that point, had won just three titles in the history of Italian football and many had raised the issue of the 'culture of winning'. But the difference was Capello's vantage point. He had been a Roma hero in the late 1960s and the old-timers still remembered him, which in some ways made him a local. This made his words easier to accept, much more so than when the same verdicts came from pundits or managers from the north of Italy, with no links to Rome. Equally, compared to Romans making the very same argument, Capello's words had gravitas: after all, he had the track record to back it up.

His pronouncements became increasingly reminiscent of Helenio Herrera, some thirty years earlier: 'I think I now know why Roma hasn't won anything in a long, long time . . . but I'm not going to go over the mistakes of the past, I'm going to focus on the future.'

He even traded barbs with Moggi, who had expressed scepticism over Roma's chances of success. In the past, Roma – either through Sensi or Zeman – would have replied with a volley of invective, much of which would only have served to plant the seed in people's minds that Moggi may well be right. Capello took a different approach.

'Look, I've known Moggi for many, many years,' he told *Gazzetta dello Sport* in July. 'He doesn't just play mind games with us, he does it with everyone. And he does it because he works for Juventus and wants what's best for Juventus. Don't worry. I work for Roma and I'll do what's best for Roma.'

Pledging that he was not distracted by barbs from the likes of Moggi, he got down to work with Franco Baldini, the club's sporting director. Baldini was somewhat apprehensive upon meeting Capello for the first time. He was a former professional footballer who went on to become Italy's first licenced FIFA agent. After concluding a number of deals on behalf of Roma, Sensi had asked him to join Zeman and take over as sporting director with a brief to buy and sell players and deal with contracts, and to work to break the stranglehold of Milan and Juventus over the Italian game. But now Zeman was gone and, in his place, Baldini found himself dealing with Capello who, from his perspective, was an unknown quantity. After being at Juventus, Milan and Real Madrid, would he buy into the underdog ethos Baldini and Zeman had created?

Capello had asked for wide-ranging powers, the kind he did not have at his previous clubs: would that mean replacing Baldini with someone more to his liking?

For his part, Capello was curious about Baldini. He had a growing reputation as a talent-spotter and was generally well regarded on the transfer market, but he also didn't fit the traditional image of a football man. With his boyish looks and wide-eyed demeanour, Baldini at times seemed almost child-like in the way he spoke. There were two ways you rose to power in Italian football, particularly in agent circles: you either paid your dues by fighting and scrapping your way to the top over several decades or you had someone rich and powerful behind you. Baldini was thirty-seven so his rise had been meteoric, particularly since he was a relatively obscure second division footballer for much of his career. And yet, in Capello's eyes, he had no patron saint, he was nobody's man. He was, in fact, something of a loner, operating outside 'the system', much like Zeman.

Still, Capello found that they were on the same wavelength, from their first meeting. It was obvious that Roma needed some sweeping changes. The side had been built to operate in Zeman's frenetic 4-3-3, and Capello made it clear that would have to change. For a start, it did not suit Francesco Totti, Roma's best player, who often found himself pushed out on the wing.

Capello believed that one of the key principles of football was to put your best players in a position where they could contribute the most. Totti may be productive out wide, but clearly he was more effective closer to goal, not least because he had an uncanny ability to find the target.

That's why his best position was in the middle and, prefer-ably, up front.

The club had spent big to acquire the prolific Vincenzo Montella from Sampdoria. Quick, gifted and with a natural eye for goal, he had scored ninety-two goals in the previous five years. He was pencilled in to star up front, alongside Marco Delvecchio, the club's returning top goalscorer, with Totti just behind.

It added up to an explosive frontline. But to accom-modate three such players, adjustments had to be made at the back. Roma had two outstanding fullbacks in Vincent Candela and Cafu, both of whom excelled at going for-ward under Zeman's system. Capello wanted to preserve that attacking freedom, particularly since, unlike the previous year, Roma would not be playing with genuine wingers. At the same time, he felt Roma needed solidity at the back, certainly more than under Zeman.

And so he decided to change the system, turning Candela and Cafu into wingbacks and switching to a three-man defence. It was something he had toyed with at Milan in 1997–98, largely to accommodate the attacking instinct of Christian Ziege, but soon abandoned the plan when he realized the rest of his squad, particularly in mid-field, were not suited to the formation. Plus, he was told, Berlusconi did not like the 3-5-2. Here, however, he had free rein.

Amedeo Mangone – a fan favourite nicknamed the 'white Thuram' in homage to the French international – arrived from Bologna. Capello had worked with him when he was in Milan's youth academy back in the 1980s and knew that he was athletic and hard-working, though not exactly Franz Beckenbauer on the ball. Which suited him just fine, given that his other two central defenders – Zago and Aldair – were both Brazilian and both could play.

There was one more cog to add to his machine. Capello wanted a deep-lying playmaker, an Albertini-type figure who could take some of the creative pressure off Totti (who, on occasion, tended to try to do too much). Baldini delivered the Brazilian Marcos Assunção, star of Flamengo's midfield. Assunção was a talented passer and an inventive creator, whose only obvious flaw was a lack of pace. But, with the combative Damiano Tommasi at his side, Roma felt confident that he could get the job done.

After two draws in the first two outings, Roma went on a tear, winning three straight each by 3–1. It was mid-October, Juventus were up next, after an international break. Capello was worried that the players would return from national team duty distracted – many of them faced important World Cup qualifiers. He wasn't going to take any chances. On Tuesday, 12 October, in full view of journalists and supporters (the latter often were allowed to watch at least part of the session at Trigoria, Roma's training ground), he tore into his players.

'That's it!' he shouted. 'Get off my pitch! You can all go to the gym or wherever it is that you go . . . And you can all do whatever the hell you like! Obviously, you're all too tired to train properly!'

With that, he stormed off the pitch. Everyone was stunned. It was Capello's first major public blow-up. True, some players might have been still thinking about the international break, but surely there was no need for Capello to react that way. After all, there were five days to go until the clash with Juventus. The media were a bit nonplussed; some called it a 'calculated' row, meaning Capello had chosen that moment to rattle the players in front of everyone.

'Yes, you could call it that, it was a surgical outburst,' Capello said later in a newspaper interview. 'I know it's hard when you come back from internationals to focus on your club. But some of them were going through the motions. And I wanted to send them a very clear message.'

Capello had, to put it in Madrid parlance, put the *cuchinillo* – the razor blade – up against Roma's rear end. Unfortunately, it didn't work, at least not that Sunday. Zinedine Zidane scored the only goal as Juventus condemned Roma to a home defeat. The *giallorossi* had been without both Totti and Delvecchio, while Mangone was also missing at the back. It was a mitigating circumstance, but it also showed that Roma's squad was rather thin. Without Totti, the side lacked the character to hold their own against the bigger clubs. That would need to change.

Over the first half of the season, he began laying down some clear boundaries. It began at Trigoria. The Sensi family – Franco, the patriarch and president, plus his daughters and in-laws – tended to come and go as they pleased, to the point that, as the joke went, Trigoria was a branch of Villa Pacelli, the Sensi family home. Roma were obviously a family-run club – Sensi's daughters held administrative roles, as did his sister-in-law – but Capello made it clear that they were not to distract the players. Trigoria had to become a bubble, a sanctuary where they could work on football and nothing else.

Like he did at Real, he banished agents and 'friends-of-friends' and limited media access. He knew he couldn't ban the supporters from the training ground, so he set very clear ground rules on what was and was not acceptable. And, when they were around, he tried to use it to his advantage, like he did with his outburst before the Juve match.

'The way he managed the club, the media and the fans was quite impressive,' says Candela. 'He protected us by drawing clear boundaries around us, which, in turn helped give us confidence, which many of us desperately needed. He knew that, when things went badly, especially in Rome, somebody had to answer for it and he went out and faced up to the criticism when things went wrong . . . He knows how to make a player better by making him truly believe that he is trusted and loved.'

Still, the results were hit-or-miss. Roma enjoyed another run of four straight wins, before going down at Bologna, 0–1, on 12 December. Then came an incident which solidified his relationship with Roma supporters and, once and for all, signalled the end of his rapport with Milan.

On 16 December 1999 Milan celebrated their centenary with a gala evening and a huge party in the city centre. Capello, naturally, was among the guests of honour. However, when he showed up wearing a suit emblazoned with the Roma club badge, many were annoyed.

'When I saw what he was wearing, I thought to myself, "What a dickhead,"' one Milan player told me. Some Milan fans booed him, others watched with indifference. Whatever relationship he had built with the *rossoneri* supporters – and, to be fair, it was never outright love – was now gone, once and for all.

Looking back, Silvano Ramaccioni is somewhat understanding of what Capello went through that night. 'I know it wasn't easy for him, he was torn about what to do,' he says. 'Obviously he wanted to be a part of our centenary, he was a big part of the history of our club. At the same time, it was his first season with Roma, he was committed to them. So he chose to do it this way. I thought the reaction in some quarters was, frankly, excessive.'

At the same time, whatever he lost in terms of love from Milan, he gained back tenfold in Rome. Fans and local media alike were delighted with what he had done. Displaying their badge and their colours under the noses of Berlusconi, Galliani and the rest of the *rossoneri* was a PR masterstroke, regardless of whether Capello had intended it that way.

By the winter transfer window, Roma were out of the title hunt, but there was a general sense that the side were finally moving in the right direction. Totti was linking well with Montella, while Delvecchio was impressing Capello with his work off the ball. The big striker's workrate was phenomenal and his ability to help out the midfield was crucial. And, indeed, it was the midfield that needed help. Cristiano Zanetti, a player Capello adored, racked up one injury after the other, Tommasi and Eusebio Di Francesco were struggling too, and, furthermore, Assunção had just gone down injured and would miss the next three months.

Capello and Baldini knew they needed more quality, but also a guy who could, occasionally, take some pressure off Totti in the final third. Sensi was loath to spend more money. While he believed in Capello's project, the fact was that, even after spending big on Montella, the side were doing no better than they had under Zeman.

Baldini came up with the answer: Hidetoshi Nakata. The Japanese star had been a revelation at Perugia the previous season, playing just off the main striker. He was quick, athletic and technically sublime and had settled brilliantly in Serie A. Best of all, Baldini made Sensi realize that he was, effectively, a self-financing player. Such was his popularity back in Japan, that Perugia earned back their £3.5m outlay in the space of a few months, with a combination of sponsorship deals, shirt sales and package tours to see him play.

Other clubs had, of course, taken the shortcut of signing Japanese players to increase their popularity in the Far East. The reasoning was simple: put a Japanese guy in the club kit and then sit back and watch the shirt sales and sponsorship offers go through the roof. Pre-season tours and further commercial opportunities in Asia were sure to follow. At least, that's how the thinking went. What those clubs had failed to realize was that the Japanese public were not stupid. They weren't going to pay through the nose to watch somebody if the player obviously could not cut it or if his signing was clearly nothing more than a craven marketing move.

Nakata, however, was different. He really could play, as evidenced by his ten Serie A goals the previous year. That was what made him popular in Japan, his 'bad-boy' image (well, he did dye his hair) only serving to have a multiplier effect. Sensi was initially sceptical, but when he found out just how much Perugia had benefited from his presence – 150,000 shirt sales in the first twelve months – he agreed to part with £15m to bring him on board. They didn't know it at the time, but it was to be a signing that would bring serious dividends – and not just financially.

Still, Capello was under no illusions. Roma had a way to go. He knew he had a hard core of players on whom he could count, but equally he was only just beginning to understand how much the mentality of the club, supporters and local media had to change. Every win was dissected endlessly and taken as evidence that Roma were on the verge of turning into an all-conquering force. Every defeat was seen as a sign that the players were heartless duds. It was feast-or-famine. And it was all magnified by the fact that Roma measured themselves against Lazio, who happened to be contending for the *scudetto*.

'This is a city which suffers its football, rather than celebrating it,' he said in a magazine interview in 2000. 'I think there are few places in the world like it. Madrid perhaps is a bit similar in terms of media pressure and demands. But the difference is that in Madrid they have a world view, they look outwards and measure themselves against the whole footballing universe. But here, everything begins and ends in Rome. We're a big fish in our little pond, but we don't think about the wider ocean out there. We need to break that psychological block and compete in the wider world.'

He had seen it in the UEFA Cup. In the first round, Roma had beaten Vitória Setúbal with a resounding 7–0. But in the return leg they looked terrified and eventually fell 1–0 to a vastly inferior team. It was a similar story against Newcastle United in the third round. Roma won 1–0 at the Stadio Olimpico and probably should have scored more. At St James' Park, however, they were battered and were fortunate to escape with a scoreless draw which saw them through.

That February he spoke for the first time about the 'Palazzo', the powers-that-be of Italian football. Juventus and Milan had agreed a deal whereby they would work together to maximize their marketing, commercial revenues and television rights. The latter was especially important as, under Italian law, clubs could sell their TV rights individually, which basically meant that the bigger the club, the more they earned from their TV contract. By pooling their resources, Milan and Juve were getting a tremendous amount of leverage. And, as the conspiracy theorists in Rome saw it, it effectively gave them leverage over match officials as well.

Italians call it *sudditanza psicologica*, literally 'psychological subjection'. The theory goes that if a referee makes a mistake which damages a big club, he will attract lots of media attention and end up all over the back pages. Lots of supporters will be angry and his reputation will suffer which, in turn, could hurt his image and his career. Whereas if that same referee were to make the same mistake and end up hurting a smaller club, it would be much less of an issue. That's why – as the theory goes – when match officials are unsure of themselves, they tend to err on the side of caution.

Milan and, especially, Juventus were the prime beneficiaries of this 'psychological subjection', according to Sensi. And, through their increasing commercial links, they were strengthening their stranglehold on the game. That's why Sensi was leading a rival faction of clubs who were trying to wrest control from Milan and Juventus by getting him elected to the presidency of the Italian league.

'Sensi knows what he's doing,' Capello told *Gazzetta dello Sport* in February 2000. 'They are trying to change football. The Milan–Juve axis is right there under all our noses. It's a power base which extends from merchandising to transfers, from television rights to sponsorship and, obviously, other things as well [*note*: a reference many took to mean influencing match officials]. And I notice that when Sensi says certain things, [Juve and Milan] get really uncomfortable. Evidently he's not wide of the mark. And, evidently, he's getting under their skin. If it were otherwise, they wouldn't be getting so angry.'

The Rubicon had been crossed. Anybody who had wondered whether Capello would shed his institutional demeanour and embrace Roma was getting his answer. The doubts, the mindgames, the veiled allusions to referees, the complaints over certain transfer dealings . . . Capello waded right in and joined the attack on Juve and Milan. Which, effectively, meant taking on Luciano Moggi and Adriano Galliani. Both men he considers friends, but both, at the time, enemies.

Four days later, speaking on a radio programme, Capello kicked it up another notch, this time focusing on the way referees treated big clubs.

'It may be unconscious, but psychological subjection exists, it's very real,' he said. 'If we just analyse incidents, for and against, it's obvious that something is going on. Juventus are favoured because they are a big club and they have been successful for many years. This kind of thing doesn't just happen in football, you can see it in all walks of life. It's clear that many years of power, their history, their titles, all of that tips the balance in their favour.'

'We at Roma have to be clever and make sure that referees respect us too,' he added. 'In fact, referees should respect all clubs. We talk about the need for dialogue and transparency. But that doesn't always happen . . .'

Shortly thereafter, referring to his time as a player at Juventus, he went even further: 'History is there for all to see,' he told SportWeek, *Gazzetta dello Sport*'s weekly magazine. 'The problem is that, when you're in the middle of it and you're a part of it, as I was, you don't always realize what's going on.'

Juventus and Milan were not amused. Galliani fired back, reminding him that, when they were together at Milan, they were on the receiving end of a notable refereeing error in the Champions League final: 'Capello may want to remember that we lost to Marseille because of a corner kick that should never have been given . . .'

'Yes, I remember that,' Capello retorted. 'And I also remind Galliani that the very same referee who awarded that corner kick was later banned. The authorities opened up an inquiry and he paid the consequences. I hope he catches my drift . . .'

He may not have intended it this way, but his back-and-forth with Milan and Juve helped buy Capello precious time. The supporters and Roman media figured that if someone like Capello – who had been, as Milan coach, part of the Establishment – made the very same accusations they had been making for years, there had to be some merit to them. And they loved the fact that he was now on their side, to the point that they were happy to overlook the fact that Roma were floundering.

They were knocked out by Leeds United in the UEFA Cup in a tie which laid bare all their limitations. And they slipped further down the table as the season went on, missing out on a Champions League spot, which, at one stage, seemed certain. With ten matches to go, they were fourth, one point behind Inter in third, one point ahead of Milan and a full eight ahead of Parma.

From there on out, they won just once, drawing six of their last seven games. Milan and Parma both passed them and they finished in sixth place. Especially upsetting was the fact that in four of those last ten matches they scored first, only to let their opponents back into it – a worrying lack of character. This also occurred, most notably, in the derby in late March: Montella had given them an early lead, but Juan Sebastián Veron and Pavel Nedved turned it around for the opposition.

Just as he had done at Milan, Capello took responsibility, albeit with a few provisos. 'I blame myself for not having the courage to make decisions which would have been unpopular at the time, but which were necessary,' he said in May 2000. 'I should have rotated the squad more, it would have allowed us to be fresher late in the season. But, partly because of injuries, partly because of my choices, this did not happen.'

To make matters much worse as far as the Roma faithful were concerned, Lazio incredibly won the title on the final day of the season. They went into the last game two points behind table-topping Juventus. Lazio duly beat Reggina, and patiently waited for news from Perugia, where the local side were hosting the *bianconeri*. That day, however, the heavens opened and a violent thunderstorm forced referee Pierluigi Collina to suspend the game for a seemingly interminable eighty-two minutes. When the teams finally came back out, defender Alessandro Calori scored an improbable winner, condemning Juventus to a 1–0 defeat and handing Eriksson's Lazio their second-ever *scudetto* – equalling Roma's total.

By that point, Capello had a clearer picture of what needed to be done. Changing the team's mentality – teaching them how to win – was an important first step. But he also needed new players in every department. Mangone had done a job for him, but obviously wasn't international calibre. In midfield, Assunção was clearly unsuited to Serie A. Up front, Montella and Delvecchio had combined for thirty league goals, but something was missing. Montella was a predator, Delvecchio a worker bee. What was needed was an upgrade, a genuine centre-forward who combined the attributes of Montella's goalscoring and Delvecchio's workrate.

Baldini had been working on just such a player: Gabriel Batistuta. Fiorentina's Argentine striker was a folk hero who had scored more than 200 goals in nine seasons with the Tuscan club. The Fiorentina fans had even put up a statue to him outside the stadium. He had made it clear that he loved Florence and never wanted to play for another European club, despite the fact that Fiorentina did not have the means to compete with Serie A's big boys.

Yet Baldini knew that Fiorentina's financial situation was far from solid and that everyone, even Batistuta, had his price. He also knew that, while the Argentine was fiercely loyal to the club and its fans, in the right circumstances he could be persuaded to move. Especially if he could be convinced that, by moving, he could generate enough money to keep Fiorentina afloat.

The problem was agreeing the kind of fee that would persuade Fiorentina to sell. An early approach was made with Sensi, whose attitude was far from encouraging: he suggested that maybe Roma could go up to £8m or £10m, but no more. Baldini knew that Fiorentina would laugh in his face at such an offer. Even at thirty-one, Batistuta was as close to a sure thing as there was in the modern game. Furthermore, given his relationship with the Fiorentina supporters, the only way to work a deal was to pay over market value. Way over market value.

Baldini and Capello hatched a plan. Sensi would need to be persuaded, but the pair could not do it alone. So they called Mario Sconcerti, editor of *Corriere dello Sport* and invited him round to dinner, along with his deputy Enrico Maida. They knew Sconcerti had a big problem: his readership had plummeted since Lazio had won the title. When Lazio do well, a big chunk of Roma supporters don't buy the newspaper. They don't want their noses rubbed in Lazio's success. Therefore *Corriere dello Sport* needed something to fix the situation; they needed to give Roma supporters some reason to go out and buy the newspaper.

That's precisely what Baldini and Capello were offering – but Sconcerti would have to play along. Baldini revealed that he had been sounding Fiorentina out about the possibility of bringing in Batistuta, but that Sensi was very reticent, not wanting to spend the necessary money. Maybe, just maybe, if *Corriere* ran with the story, it would gather steam, fans would get excited and a whole campaign to bring Batistuta to the capital would spring into action more or less spontaneously. Roma would get their man and the paper would sell a shedload of copies that summer, narrating the ins and outs of the deal.

The plan worked perfectly. Two days later, *Corriere* broke the story. Sconcerti remembers going to work that morning and seeing mothers dropping off their kids at school clutching a copy of the newspaper and animatedly discussing how Batistuta would link with Montella and Totti. Rome's famous local radio stations were abuzz around the clock with Batistuta chatter. As for Sensi, every time he appeared in public he was greeted with applause and backslapping, as people thanked him for delivering Batistuta to Roma.

Sensi loved the attention he was getting, but he was also somewhat nonplussed. Batistuta was still, in every sense, a Fiorentina player. As far as he knew, Baldini had made an initial approach, but that was it: Batistuta was bound to be far too expensive anyway.

Yet the 'Bati's coming!' phenomenon snowballed. People took it for granted. And, as the days passed and Batistuta failed to materialize, Sensi began to feel the pressure. *Corriere*'s coverage, which began with triumphalism, soon began asking: 'Where's Batistuta? Why isn't he here yet?'

The unwitting popularity Sensi had been enjoying risked turning into disappointment and disillusionment. And that made him very uncomfortable. He eventually asked Baldini what it would take, realistically, to get Batistuta. Baldini said it would be very expensive. Sensi sighed and commented that they had better move quickly, otherwise he'd never hear the end of it from the Roma fans, *Corriere dello Sport* and the rest of the local media.

And so a deal was done for £23.5 million, still a world record for a player over the age of thirty. Everyone was happy. Fiorentina got some much needed cash. Batistuta got a legitimate chance to win the *scudetto*. *Corriere dello Sport*'s sales went through the roof. Sensi basked in his newfound popularity as the club's generous benefactor. And Capello got the striker he craved. But it didn't end there. Baldini and Capello persuaded Sensi to spend heavily that summer. It was the only way to keep up with Lazio, they told him. Sensi, always more of a fan than a businessman, got out his chequebook and didn't put it away until the transfer window had closed.

The defence was strengthened with the arrival of Walter Samuel, a tough-as-nails Argentine hardman who cost £14m, and Jonathan Zebina, a big, mobile Frenchman. In midfield, Capello stuck with Brazilians, except this time he went for a proven quantity: Emerson. Unlike Assunção, who was straight off the boat from Brazil, Emerson had spent three seasons at Bayer Leverkusen, in the German Bundesliga, and was well versed in European football. He combined the skill and vision of Assunção with the dynamism and workrate of his European brethren. Capello felt he could hand him the keys of the midfield and stop worrying.

On paper, it really did look a formidable side, a team built to win here and now. Even Capello got caught up in the enthusiasm, telling the Rome daily *Il Messaggero* on 15 July: 'Batistuta is the best striker I have ever worked with.' Better than Marco Van Basten?

'Let's just say they're different,' Capello corrected himself, perhaps realizing that he had gone a bit too far. 'But this team is complete from top to bottom. With the squad we have put together, we simply cannot fail.'

However, the end of pre-season training was not quite as smooth as Capello would have liked. For a start, Emerson got injured, robbing Roma of their midfield general. The 'Puma' would not return until January. His Brazilian teammate Aldair, who was expected to anchor the three-man defence with Zago and Samuel, also went down injured. Here, Capello was a little less concerned: Aldair was a fan favourite who was in his eleventh season at the club, but he also turned thirty-five in November and was showing signs of slowing down. In some ways, it might even have been a blessing in disguise because it allowed him to give Zebina, whom the media initially viewed with some suspicion, a chance.

Also, that year, because of Italian football's Olympic commitments in Sydney, the season did not begin until 1 October and September was marked by the early stages of a simmering controversy. On paper, everyone had Montella pencilled in as the starter alongside Batistuta and Totti, with Delvecchio coming off the bench. But it soon became obvious to Capello that playing Montella and Batistuta together was a tricky proposition. Both were penalty box strikers who rarely tracked back, which had a variety of knock-on effects on the squad. For a start, their presence created congestion in front of Totti, who often had to retreat to find space, something which, as we've seen, Capello wanted to avoid, believing that Totti was most effective when he was within striking distance of the goal. Second, because both tended to operate centrally, the flanks were often undermanned, with Candela and Cafu often finding themselves isolated out wide. And this was problematic, not just defensively, but going forward as well.

He solved the problem by developing – with Galbiati's help – a somewhat unorthodox tactical system which worked exceptionally well. Indeed, it may well have been his finest tactical work as a manager. The key, in some ways, was Cafu. The Brazilian was a wingback in name only: he was encouraged to attack at every opportunity and, for long stretches, was the furthest forward Roma player apart from Batistuta.

'Cafu was playing almost as a striker,' says Candela. 'He was always forward. We could afford this partly because he had so much energy, partly because of the character-istics of the players behind him. Tommasi, who sat just in front of the defence alongside Zanetti, was outstanding at reading the game and, when necessary, would come across and cover for Cafu. Or, Zebina, who was on the right side of the three-man defence and was probably our fastest player, would advance to plug the gap. It was a delicate balance, but we had the players to make it work.'

Emerson was missed, of course, but, luckily for Capello, Zanetti was actually fit for a long stretch. He was a player with solid technical gifts, strength and stamina, the kind Capello loved, but he was also about as durable as a Fabergé egg. That season, however, he avoided injury and played a crucial role while Roma waited for Emerson's return.

On the left, Candela was not quite as marauding as

Cafu, but still had licence to get forward, where he linked very well with Delvecchio. Yes, Delvecchio, the man whom Capello preferred to Montella – the Italian international and darling of the Roma supporters – ended up being the man who made the system work.

'When we had possession I would come into the box as an additional target or move wide almost as a traditional winger,' he said. 'But when we lost possession, I would retreat to the point where I would be in a line with Cafu on the opposite flank and, many times, even deeper.'

Delvecchio had an unorthodox skill set: he was good in the air, without being powerful, he was mobile, without being quick, he came up with key goals at key moments without being a particularly outstanding finisher. He was the kind of player whose contribution to a side was not immediately obvious, particularly since his movement bordered on the ungainly. Yet he was unselfish, hardworking and had plenty of tactical sense, with a keen awareness for anticipating how play would develop.

Prior to the campaign, Capello took him to a small room in Trigoria where he laid out Roma's formation for the season. 'If you do exactly what I'm asking for, we're going to win the title,' Capello told him. 'I was just happy to play,' said Delvecchio. 'With Totti, Batistuta and Montella on board, I felt I had to find other ways to contribute. So I tried to understand and put into practice exactly what was asked of me.'

The odd man out in all this was, of course, Montella. Capello knew that he had a potentially explosive situation on his hands when, in pre-season, Batistuta asked for the number nine jersey. He had worn it his entire career, he was the star striker – after paying £23.5m for him, surely Roma were not going to deny him 'his' number. The problem was that the number nine had belonged to Montella, who was reluctant to give it up.

For all Capello cared, they could go out and play with the letter 'X' on their backs. But he knew that it was important to both players. And he also knew that stripping Montella of the number nine was akin to telling him he wasn't wanted, an impression which the Neapolitan striker was already getting following the arrival of Batistuta. A compromise was reached. Montella could retain the number nine, but Capello made it clear that he would have to adapt to the needs of the team. Batistuta would settle for 18: '1 + 8 = 9'.

But the Montella/Batistuta shirt controversy was nothing compared to what Roma experienced on 26 September, after their shock exit from the Coppa Italia at the hands of Atalanta. They had been somewhat unlucky to draw the first leg in Rome but were ripped apart in Bergamo, losing 4–2. To make matters worse, some of Capello's post-match comments – which appeared to question the players' efforts – infuriated the squad.

'We're disappointed that the manager should choose to shift all the blame on us, the players,' Totti said. 'He's in charge, he makes the decisions. We need to accept responsibility, but I think it should be evenly split, fifty-fifty, between us and him to fire up the players.' It backfired badly. Public criticism can be a motivational tool, but, in this case, many found his comments well out of line. Galbiati and Baldini stepped in to try and calm the situation on the trip back from Bergamo, but it was nothing compared to what was awaiting them at Trigoria.

More than a thousand angry supporters showed up at the training ground the next day. They disrupted training with slogans and insults. Everyone – except for Totti (naturally), Batistuta and two seldom used reserves, Gianni Guigou and the ageing Abel Balbo – was roundly insulted, including Capello and Sensi. Aldair, a fan favourite until a few weeks earlier, had to be escorted by police. It was a very ugly scene: Cafu, who had taken his two young sons to training, was so upset that he broke down crying and had to be consoled by teammates. Many of the players' cars were vandalized. Totti went out to meet the fans in an attempt to mediate, but was shouted down.

Capello looked unperturbed to his staff and players. Inwardly though, he reflected upon the absurdity of it all. Roma had lost one game and had been knocked out of a competition which many of the fans themselves regularly snubbed. And this was their reaction? What kind of people were these?

Then again, he knew this was Roma. And these were the hardcore of Roma fans. They were the ones who travelled up and down the Italian boot, who sang their hearts out for ninety minutes every Sunday. He had committed himself to the club, which meant he had to take the bad with the good. He didn't care what they said about him or even if they destroyed his car (heck, he was insured . . .) But he did care to the extent that it would affect his players. Days like these were the reason why he had said that a single *scudetto* in Rome was worth ten in Turin or Milan.

The fans had put the fear of God into his squad; maybe

there was a silver lining. He saw that each player reacted differently. Cafu was completely shaken up, someone would need to talk to him. Some of the younger players, like Zebina, also needed a word. He looked at Samuel, the hardman with the icy stare. Nope, he'd be fine. Heck, he had played for Boca Juniors, where some supporters carry guns: if anything it was a miracle he did not choose to go out and single-handedly take on all those irate supporters.

Totti was angry: he was, after all, Roma born and bred, he, better than anyone, understood the fans' anger. As captain, he would need to step up, something he had already attempted to do by going out there and trying to speak to the fans. Now he needed to make himself heard with his teammates.

Capello took a step back and, apart from dispatching some of his assistants to console the more sensitive players, watched how the situation evolved. After his public criticism in Bergamo, had he stepped in now he might have made the situation worse. He trusted in his veterans – Totti and Tommasi above all – to take charge. And they did. Totti called a players-only meeting where the situation was discussed. The Serie A season had yet to kick off, they weren't going to give up before the opening bell. Although he never admitted it, Capello was proud of Totti that day. He had shown the kind of leadership which was expected of a captain, he had grabbed hold of a situation which was in danger of spinning out of control. He probably knew, even then, that the pair of them would never be close. But that did not mean they could not reach great heights together.

The league season began with three consecutive wins

and the pendulum of enthusiasm swung back to 'sky-high'. Perhaps even higher than Capello would have liked. Sure enough, it was followed by a 2–0 defeat at Inter, which served to highlight the usual insecurities. The inquest began: Why do we always flatter to deceive? Why isn't Montella playing more? Isn't Capello no different from all the other managers we've had before?

Capello, however, was unflappable. He told his players that he firmly believed they were going to win the title. And he fired back at the sniping from fans and media alike. These were his players and he was going to protect them.

Roma responded with four consecutive wins and some of the best football they would play that season. Batistuta was proving to be an instant hit (he had nine goals in his first seven outings), Cafu was loving his new freedom, and Totti benefited tremendously from having a big, strong reference point in front of him. One player who did get occasional stick was Zebina. At twenty-two, this was his first season on the big stage and while his effort and athletic skills were never in doubt, he was prone to lapses in concentration. Local radio stations coined the term *Zebinate* which, loosely translated, means 'pulling a Zebina' or screwing up royally.

'I was criticized a fair bit,' Zebina recalls. 'Partly it was because I made some mistakes, partly because I was seen as the guy who had replaced Aldair and Aldair ranks just below Totti in the hearts of Roma supporters. [But] Capello always supported me and believed in me, even when it would have been natural, even normal, for me to get depressed. He made me feel special and I will forever be grateful for that. Of course, it also meant that, in the eyes of the press, I was seen as "Capello's favourite" or "Capello's baby".'

Meanwhile, on 7 October 2000, following a 0–1 loss to Germany in the last-ever international at Wembley Stadium, Kevin Keegan resigned his post as England manager – on live television. The Football Association, led by Adam Crozier, scrambled to find a replacement, much as they would do seven years later under Brian Barwick. Crozier made the courageous and unprecedented choice of compiling a short-list that included foreign managers. Capello was approached, as was Sven-Göran Eriksson, the Lazio boss.

Capello was not about to walk out on Roma, but the violent scenes at Trigoria just the previous month had made him wary. It certainly did not hurt to see what was out there and, even then, the England job fascinated him.

On 29 October he found himself standing alongside Eriksson, whom, he knew, was the frontrunner for the job. The occasion was something called the 'Sportsman's Jubilee', a football match organized by the Catholic church to help celebrate the Millennium which Pope John Paul II had designated as a Jubilee year. That night, Capello and Eriksson were co-managers of a Serie A all-star team made up of foreign players which was to take on Giovanni Trapattoni's Italy side.

It was a rare occurrence for the managers of Roma and Lazio to be standing next to each other, rarer still for them to be on the same side. Eriksson and Capello made small talk until the issue of the England job came up. Eriksson wondered aloud who, between them, was going to be awarded the job. 'I think you will,' Capello replied with a smile. And he was right. Two days later, the Football Association appointed Eriksson to succeed Keegan. Capello was left wondering what might have been. But he wasn't too bothered. His job was here with Roma. At least for now.

And, indeed, Roma rumbled on. The fear and insecurity in the back of people's minds was still there, the sense that one bad defeat would open the floodgates. But, unlike previous seasons, Capello was able to bury it. Indeed, after a 3–2 defeat to Milan at the San Siro in January, the side stormed back with seven consecutive victories.

There was also a sense that something had changed. Many Roma supporters historically lived in fear of the 'Palazzo', a sense that the powers-that-be would emerge at crucial moments to derail the team. With hindsight, it's not always easy to determine to what degree those fears were valid. The 'Calciopoli' scandal which engulfed Juventus in 2006 was seen by many as vindication of the claim that the *bianconeri* – and, perhaps to a lesser degree, Milan – had been manipulating the league and the referees to their advantage for decades. In fact, to this day, you'll still hear Roma supporters complaining about 'Er gol de Turone', a headed goal against Juventus by sweeper Maurizio Turone back in the 1980–81 season which could have sent the *giallorossi* on their way to the title but was disallowed for a disputed offside. Now, however, the tables were turned. There was a sense, at least among supporters and local media, that Roma were respected by the 'Palazzo' and by match officials. Which, incidentally, as Sensi had said initially, was part of the reason why Capello had been hired in the first place.

Moggi, at Juventus, was not shy about fuelling this notion that Roma had, somehow, broken into the 'boys' club' of those who mattered in Italian football.

'Capello is right,' Moggi said in a 22 February 2001 interview with the newspaper *Il Giornale*. 'He played for Juventus and Milan, he managed Milan and Real. So I think he knows exactly what he's doing because he knows exactly how certain things work.'

It was the kind of coded language of which Moggi was a master. At first glance, it seemed like a compliment to Capello. Read a little closer and it can be interpreted many different ways. Was Moggi saying that referees were now favouring Roma (and, by extension, penalizing Juventus)? Was he suggesting that Capello's own success as a manager and a player had been 'helped' by being at big clubs? Was he sending a message that Roma needed to be put back into their place?

Moggi's words were like tea leaves. You could read them any way you liked. Except, unlike tea leaves, there really was a message there. And they did have an effect.

In the meantime, Roma crashed out of the UEFA Cup against Liverpool, though Capello had made it clear that it was hardly a priority. Indeed, in the first leg, which they lost 2–0 to Michael Owen's brace at the Stadio Olimpico, they rested Zago and Totti, while Batistuta only made the bench. In the return leg, Capello again rested his troops, leaving out Cafu, Emerson and Totti. Batistuta only came on after an hour. With Roma leading 1–0 thanks to Gianni Guigou's long-range strike, referee Manuel Garcia Aranda appeared to give a penalty after the ball struck Markus Babbel's elbow. The Kop groaned its disappointment, Montella prepared to take it, but, just then, Garcia Aranda signalled for a corner kick, prompting furious protests from the Roma players. Liverpool hung on to win 2–1 on aggregate.

An angry Capello had a pop at the match official for changing his mind. Roma's enemies joked that, whatever hold over the 'Palazzo' the club had obtained that season, it clearly did not extend to Europe.

Still, by April Fools' Day, the Serie A lead had ballooned to nine points over Juventus and twelve points over Lazio. And then came the moment Capello feared. He called it '*il vento di ponentino*'. Literally, it means 'westerly wind' and it's a typically Roman phenomenon which manifests itself in spring and early summer, when a light, pleasant seabreeze wafts in from the Mediterranean. Romans say 'it warms the heart and dulls the mind'. It's the wind of films like *Roman Holiday*, the breeze which signals the beginning of summer and, with it, summer customs, including lazy afternoons and long bacchanalian dinners under moonlight. It's basically a mindset which, at that time of year, makes Rome a more laid back and pleasant place to be. Capello, of course, wanted his team to be neither laid back nor pleasant. He wanted them hungry and focused on capturing the title. But there was another 'wind' whistling down on Rome in the collective imagination of the supporters. A wind which, they believed, had been blowing for a long time: '*Il Vento del Nord*', the 'Northern Wind'. By this they meant the inevitability which enveloped previous title wins for Milan and Juventus.

The long-held fears about the 'Palazzo', about referees

favouring clubs from the north was only part of it. There was also a certain fatalism, a certain sense that Roman clubs were going to crumble and fall down the stretch, blown over by the *'Vento del Nord'*. As I said, it wasn't just the officiating, it was the confidence and mentality with which Milan and Juventus took to the field.

Capello had spoken many times of the decades-long 'culture of success' which Roma seemed to lack. And it was the main reason he was at the club. He had to provide the psychological breakthrough which would help his men believe in the title and act like winners.

It began on 9 April with a defeat at Fiorentina in which Roma went a goal down, equalized and then conceded two in the last half hour. Then came arguably one of Roma's most disappointing performances of the season: despite dominating and creating countless chances at the Stadio Olimpico, they twice had to come from behind to grab a 2–2 draw with Perugia, their final equalizer coming with an own goal in injury-time. In two games Juventus had made up five points and were now just four back with eight games to go.

Fear seemed to be affecting every Roma supporter, starting with Sensi. 'I guess everyone is happy now, they managed to stop Roma,' he said, after the Fiorentina defeat, not specifying who 'they' were, but leaving it to everyone to fill in the blanks. 'We can win the title, but only if they let us win it.'

Capello was seething. 'They' may very well have existed (or 'they' may just as easily be the bogeyman under your bed who kept you up all night as a child). But by playing the victim card, Sensi was giving the Roma players an excuse, a reason to doubt. After all, if Roma could only win if 'they' allowed it, what was the point in trying?

'We deserve the title,' Capello said after the Perugia draw. 'And we will win the title.' His certainty seemed to be well founded when Roma went to Udinese and won 3–1 while Juventus could only draw at Parma. Now the gap was six points coming into two tricky fixtures: Lazio in the derby were next, followed by Juve away.

On the afternoon of 29 April, Derby Day, Capello got a great boost. Juventus were held 1–1 at home by relegation-threatened Lecce, which meant that, by winning the derby, Roma could go eight points ahead. After a tense first half, Batistuta and Delvecchio scored to give Roma a 2–0 lead. Then, twelve minutes from time, Pavel Nedved pulled one back. And, deep into injury time, the unheralded Lucas Castroman found the equalizer with a vicious right-footed volley which sealed the draw. Lazio supporters celebrated as if they had won the Champions League. Roma fans felt the title slipping away: a loss to Juve the following week would reduce the margin to just three points.

But now, even as Roma were doubting themselves again some good news came from the 'Palazzo'. A lawsuit filed earlier that year by players and clubs forced the lifting of restrictions on non-European Union passport holders with immediate effect. It struck down the Italian league's rule which maintained that, while clubs could have as many as five non-EU players on their books, only three could be included in the matchday squad. This was crucial to Roma, whose non-EU players were Batistuta, Cafu, Samuel, Nakata and Assunção. Because the first three were certain starters, Nakata rarely, if ever, made the bench. The Japanese star had originally been signed as a utility player who could fill any of the central midfield positions or, on occasion, come in up front, but Capello had not been able to use him because of the rule, much to his chagrin. Now, however, the playing field was level.

Juventus were absolutely furious. Though they also had five non-EU players, the difference was that their fourth- and fifth-choice non-EU guys were squad players who contributed very little. They got no real benefit from the rule change, unlike Roma. Furthermore, as Moggi pointed out (and, in this case, it's hard to argue with him), you can't change the rules in mid-season. The problem was, this wasn't a footballing rule, it was civil employment law. The courts had spoken. There was nothing Juventus could do.

Forty-eight hours later Nakata took his place on the bench at the Stadio delle Alpi against Juventus. Capello felt he had an ace up his sleeve. And he certainly needed it. Roma were 2–0 down inside six minutes as Del Piero and Zidane found the back of the net. Capello considered making a first-half substitution just to shake his team up, but held back: the players got themselves into this, let's see if they can get themselves out of it.

Montella came on at half-time for Delvecchio. Juve seemed content just to protect their two-goal margin and hit on the break. Montella was better at feeding off scraps. With half an hour to go and nothing left to lose, Capello sent on Assunção and Nakata, the two players who, just two days earlier, would not have even been on the bench because of their non-EU status. What's more, Nakata replaced Totti, much to everyone's surprise. Totti had been marked out of the game, but for Capello to remove Roma's star player at such a crucial moment had to be the boldest of moves.

'If this doesn't work out, we're not making it back to Rome alive,' one member of Capello's staff thought to himself. Totti was the magic man, the guy who could generate something out of nothing, even when he was playing badly, whether it be a free kick or a moment of skill. Roma players looked dumbfounded as Totti's number came up on the fourth official's board. Capello was either a genius or the most dangerous kind of fool, one who believed in his own infallibility. Was he really just about to take off Roma's best player with the title slipping away and replace him with a guy from Japan who had made just four league starts all season?

Indeed he was. And there was a method behind his madness. Capello wanted Nakata on the pitch and Totti was really the only man who could make way. Montella had just come on and was proving a handful, Batistuta needed to stay in there because Roma were chasing the game. Putting Nakata on for one of the wingbacks didn't make sense. And, with Assunção already coming on for Zanetti, Capello wasn't about to take off Tommasi and sacrifice both his central midfielders in one go.

Totti saw his number come up and stopped for a beat or two. He quickly removed the captain's armband, tossed it to Tommasi and began walking off the pitch, taking unusually long strides. His face was set, his eyes steely; years later he would sport the very same expression before taking the injury-time match-winning penalty against Australia at the 2006 World Cup. He slapped Nakata's hand as he came off the pitch, twisted to avoid the embrace of an assistant and took his seat on the bench, without saying a word. Capello, staring out over the pitch, ignored him completely. Both knew there would be hell to pay if the manager got this one wrong.

But Capello got it right. Dead right. With eleven minutes to go, Nakata won the ball off Alessio Tacchinardi just inside the Juve half. Taking two quick strides towards the goal he unleashed a swerving right-foot shot which left Edwin Van der Sar in the Juve goal no chance. Half-way there, ten minutes to go. Then, deep into injury time, Nakata tried his luck again. His thirty-yard strike bounced in front of Van der Sar, who failed to control the ball and deflected it right into Montella's path. The 'Little Airplane' threw his body to meet it and beat the big Dutchman, clinching Roma's last-gasp equalizer.

For once, even Capello, Mr Confidence, had to concede how improbable it all was. 'I would have never ever dreamed that we could be two goals down with ten minutes to go at Juventus and come away with a point. Ever.'

Both clubs won their next two games. Roma had a six-point margin with three matches to go, but it was bound to be a tricky finale. They hosted Milan at the Stadio Olimpico, followed by a trip to Napoli, with whom they had a fierce historic rivalry. Milan were having a poor season but they were still Milan, and there was always the chance of Roma suffering stage fright. Which is pretty much what happened as they went a goal down just before half-time. Capello again called upon his super-sub, Montella. Half-way through the second half, Montella cut in from the right, skinned a defender and from the edge of the 'D' beat the goalkeeper with an exquisite chip.

Juventus, however, defeated Perugia, cutting the lead to four points. And the Roman airwaves were abuzz with chatter: given Montella's form, why wasn't he starting? The question bounced from radio station to TV programme to the newspapers. Why had Capello grounded the 'Little Airplane' at a time like this?

Montella himself voiced his displeasure after the game. 'Yes, on the one hand, I'm very happy for the goal, but on the other hand I'm bitter and angry because for the umpteenth time, the manager left me on the bench,' he said. 'Frankly, this situation is unsustainable. With me on the pitch, Roma have never lost this season. Let's focus on winning the title, but, afterwards I'm going to have to sit down and have a long chat with the manager. As I said, we can't go on like this.'

Capello held firm. He wasn't about to engage the press or the fans and, least of all, Montella in his decisions. 'In some games I think it's best to start with Delvecchio, in others Montella,' he said dismissively. 'Sometimes he's more effective when he comes on as a sub. I make my choices for the good of Roma and nobody else.'

On to Napoli, with Roma knowing that a win would guarantee the title. All week long the talk was of Montella, who, for his part, only seemed to get more and more wound up. Galbiati, as ever, tried to play the part of 'good cop'. Capello kept his distance. There wasn't much he could say. All season he had explained to Montella just how important he was and the two had come to an uneasy truce. But now Roma's lead was being whittled away.

Batistuta, Totti and Delvecchio had scored just six goals between them in the previous four months. Montella had scored ten on his own in those four months, despite coming off the bench half the time. He was on fire and yet he could not get a place in the starting lineup. This had become personal.

Capello, undeterred, left him out again against Napoli. Montella, a Neapolitan, seethed silently on the bench. Napoli scored first, but Batistuta pulled one back just before half-time. Capello sent Montella to warm up, everyone figured he'd be coming on – again – after the interval. Instead, nothing. Capello waited a full six minutes before calling on him. By this point, Montella was so wound up he was ready to explode. Just before announcing the substitution, Totti scored, giving Roma a 2–1 lead. Capello told Montella to sit down. With Roma ahead, Delvecchio's workrate was more useful to the side.

Montella was furious. He kicked a water bottle in Capello's direction and, for the next fifteen minutes or so, kept up an incessant chatter directed at the manager, who summarily ignored him. Capello didn't care. Juventus were winning 3–0 in Vicenza, but it didn't matter: if Roma could just hang on, the title would be theirs and Montella's tantrum would be quickly forgotten. He even tightened up the midfield by replacing Delvecchio with a holding midfielder, Zanetti. Nine minutes from time, Fabio Pecchia found the equalizer for Napoli, sending 80,000 Neapolitans wild. Capello motioned to Montella, 'You're in.' But the striker was still furious and launched another barrage of abuse. It was so bad that it took a full three minutes for him to actually get on the pitch, eating up valuable time. To make matters worse, in the dying minutes Montella missed a sitter, the goal which would have given Roma the title.

After the game, Montella sought out Capello and the two had a heated argument. According to reports, Totti had to step in to separate the two. Each blamed the other. Montella felt Capello had wilfully disrespected him by making him warm up for so long before bringing him on. Capello thought Montella's outburst had been very unprofessional. And, of course, the fact that he had fluffed his sitter at the end did him no favours either. Public opinion was divided. Yes, Montella's outburst was out of line, but, deep down, understandable: he had carried the side over the past few weeks, he should have come on at half-time, in fact, he probably should have started. As for Capello, some questioned whether it was wise to even send Montella on for the final few minutes, given his state of mind. But he believed that the striker could channel his rage into something positive. Had Montella scored the winner, he would have been the hero of the day, if not the season. Sure, Capello would have come across as the 'bad guy'. But what did he care? Roma would have won the title.

Instead, it all came down to the final ninety minutes. Roma at home to Parma, with Juventus, two points behind, home to Atalanta. Neither opponent had anything left to play for, and, in normal circumstances, everything looked to be in Roma's favour. But nothing was ever quite normal with Roma.

Capello pulled a rabbit out of his hat when, given events the previous week, he named Montella in his starting eleven. The striker was surprised, but grateful. Relations had remained frosty all week, and he had expected a fine and a tongue-lashing, not a place in the side. But Capello felt it was a good way to defuse the tension. And, frankly, Montella remained a very good player. He didn't want the season ending with him sulking his way through the summer and, perhaps, forcing Sensi to sell him, most likely at less than market value. More vintage Capello: the row had come and gone, it was time to look ahead. Plus, of course, if Montella was on the pitch, he wouldn't be chattering in Capello's ear, demanding to be sent on.

The game went according to plan. Totti and Montella scored in the first half, and in the dressing room the champagne was put on ice, ready to be uncorked. With twelve minutes to go, Batistuta scored to make it 3–0. Capello took Montella and Batistuta off so they could enjoy the standing ovation. As they walked off, he noticed the crowd – officially 74,780, but there were probably many more who had sneaked in ticketless – had surged forward and now were virtually pitchside. Di Vaio pulled one back for the visitors, an entirely meaningless goal. The crowd loomed over the pitch, a mass of humanity. And that's when panic set in. It was obvious to everyone there was going to be a pitch invasion. The police clearly were not going to be able to hold anyone back. Many of them were watching the game and cheering like fans anyway.

Rumours spread like wildfire along the Roma bench. What if Moggi had deployed some people in the crowd to cause havoc? What if the referee was assaulted or the goalposts torn down? In Italy, clubs are directly responsible for the crowd's behaviour. Should they invade the pitch and cause damage or, worse, attack the match officials, Roma would likely forfeit the match and Juventus would be crowned champions.

With hindsight, it seems like paranoia of the highest order. Surely not even Moggi would think of hiring some goons to infiltrate the Roma fans, provoke the crowd and cause the club to forfeit the game? Or would he? Such was the mystique of Moggi that, many Roma supporters felt, you couldn't put anything past him.

And then it happened. About two hundred Roma supporters surged on to the pitch with a good five minutes left to play. Capello jumped out of his seat and began screaming at the top of his lungs, while waving his arms. 'You dickheads, get off the pitch! Off the pitch!' he roared. It was useless. A number of players had their jerseys literally ripped from their bodies. They all seemed peaceful enough, but Capello and his staff frantically searched for referee Stefano Braschi and his assistants. All it took was one moron (or, more likely, a hired thug) to ruin everything. No, they were safe, if a bit bemused. The goalposts, what about the goalposts? Nobody was climbing up them, nobody was trying to rip them down, nobody had thought to take a chainsaw to them. Good . . . good . . . but the game wasn't over yet.

Somehow, Braschi and the players – with a fair amount of help from a none-too-gentle Capello – managed to get the fans off the pitch. Amidst the confusion, they explained that if the game wasn't allowed to finish, Roma would not be crowned champions. It was no joke, they just had to hold out another five minutes or so. It took nearly a quarter of an hour to clear the playing field. Braschi whistled the restart and, five minutes later, the game was over. Roma were champions.

'This title makes me especially happy,' Capello said after the match. 'This season went on for ever, we had to break records to win it. The reality is that winning in Rome is far from easy. Everybody gets too excited or too depressed, there is a constant stream of controversy, there's always something going on. I'm just glad we were able to isolate ourselves to some degree and let our ability shine through.'

That night, one and a half million people spilled out into the streets. Rome had sweated and suffered this title like no other. Roma supporters didn't have too many occasions to celebrate, but, when they did, they made them count. Capello wasn't going to miss out. After an intimate dinner at Il Pescatore, one of his favourite restaurants, he and Laura set out into the Rome night, going by Batistuta's house, where many of the players had gathered. It was very late when they left, but Capello had one more stop to make.

'There were four or five us at Montella's house that night,' recalls Candela. 'I guess you could call it the after-party. And then, suddenly, Capello shows up with a bottle. We were shocked, but it was his way of showing Montella that there were no hard feelings, that they had their rows, but now it was over and it was time to celebrate together.'

Somehow Montella and Capello, who until a few weeks before had come within inches of tearing into each other, found it in themselves to wish each other happy birthday. It was well past midnight and a strange quirk of fate had determined that they were born the same day, 18 June.

With the partying done, Capello set off the next day for his holiday in Belize. He was worn out, he needed a break, this was his time with Laura. Diplomatically, it was, however, a mistake (not that Capello cares particularly about such things). The Sensi family had organized a lavish do at La Leprignana, the family's estate in the seaside town of Fregene, half an hour outside Rome. Around a thousand people attended, but not the Capellos. The absence was duly noted, as was his absence a week later at a concert featuring the popstar Antonello Venditti, who had written the Roma anthem 'Grazie, Roma'. It was held at the Circus Maximus and attended by a number of players, including Totti, Montella and Candela. But Capello was somewhere in Belize, probably immersed in pre-Colombian archaeological sites.

Capello has never played the 'man-of-the-people' card and he wasn't about to now. He had delivered the title as promised, he had celebrated with his players and staff, now he was on holiday. He saw no reason to delay his vacation to attend some lavish catered affair with the Sensi family and a thousand of their closest friends (read: politicians, B-list celebs, hangers on, etc.). The concert was a nice touch and, had he been around, he might have attended, but he wasn't about to disrupt his holiday to stand around in front of one and a half million people. This was the fans' celebration, they wouldn't care if he was there or not.

Except they did. It mattered to them. You can't just be *in* the Roma world, you have to be *of* the Roma world. You have to let yourself be swallowed up by the Roma supporters' passion. Capello did not do that. And it would create problems for him later on.

'I don't do things to be seen, I don't genuflect in front of people so they'll like me,' Capello told *Il Giornale* that year. 'I'm no arse-kisser, not with the fans, not with my colleagues, not with presidents, not with anyone. My real friends are from outside this world of football.'

Even as he flew to Belize, Capello began thinking about next season. The main risk was going to be the hangover from the inevitable partying that followed the *scudetto*. He decided he would rather have a shorter pre-season training camp, than coming back at the usual time and finding the players still mentally on holiday or, worse, exhausted from all the celebrations.

'So he gave us all two full months off,' says Candela. 'Two months! It was unprecedented, but also very smart. He made it very clear that we had earned it and that we should enjoy it and get everything out of our system, because, when we returned, we would have to get straight to work. It was a very clever thing to do and a nice surprise for us.'

CHAPTER 13

Roman Heartbreak

The players may have been enjoying a long break, but Capello and Franco Baldini were hard at work. The squad was already, obviously, competitive, but it needed some tweaks. One man controlled Roma's pursestrings – the president, Franco Sensi – and they knew very well that it was best to strike while the iron was hot. It would be far easier for Sensi to get his chequebook out now that he was riding the wave of enthusiasm than at a time when the club were struggling and needed help, as it had been the previous summer at the time of the Batistuta saga. 'It's a lot easier to address weaknesses when things are going well than when you're in trouble,' Capello liked to say. And, in his eyes, there were a number of things to fix.

Francesco Antonioli had done a fair job in goal, but his relationship with the supporters, who pounced on his every error, had become strained. At thirty-two years of age he was never going to become a superstar, the kind of dominant goalkeeper Capello craved. And so he asked for Parma's Gigi Buffon, who was already regarded by many as the best in the business. The immense debt and accounting fraud which would ultimately bring down Parmalat, Parma's parent company, were still a few years away, but Capello and Baldini knew that, if faced with the right offer, Buffon was available.

Thus began a virtual auction pitting Roma against Juventus, where Edwin Van der Sar, the scapegoat for the lost *scudetto* the previous year had been shown the door. It wouldn't be the last time Baldini and Juve sporting director Luciano Moggi crossed swords. Sensi had agreed to break the then world record £8m for a goalkeeper; what he didn't know was just how much the Buffon auction would force up his price. According to a source, Roma were never prepared to spend more than £20m, but Juventus ended up shelling out around £32m, which, to this day, is far and away a world record and which makes Buffon one of the five most expensive players of all time. More than a few praised Baldini's handling of the affair: his aggressive stance drove up Parma's demands and probably forced Juve to spend more than they needed.

Having missed out on Buffon, Baldini went for a 21-year-old giant of a goalkeeper named Ivan Pelizzoli. He had come out of nowhere the previous season at Atalanta, winning the job after the regular keeper got injured and wowing the critics with his size, athleticism and totally unflappable demeanour – hence his nickname, the 'Iceberg'. Pelizzoli was expensive at £10m but it was felt that he could be the long-term answer to Roma's goal-keeping issues.

Capello felt they needed strengthening in defence as well. Samuel was a rock, but Zago wasn't always comfortable on the ball, while Zebina still hadn't entirely banished his defensive lapses. Aldair, close to his thirty-sixth birthday, was a sub at best. For much of the summer, Baldini chased Fabio Cannavaro, the Parma stalwart and Italian international. As with Buffon, Cannavaro was formally not for sale, but Baldini knew that, at the right price, nothing was impossible. It went right down to the wire. Parma were quoting an outrageous £30m, Baldini knew he had to get them down, way down. Then, just hours before the transfer window closed, Parma pulled out. Having already sold Buffon and Lilian Thuram that summer, they simply could not afford to let Cannavaro go as well. Baldini quickly turned to Plan 'B', an old acquaintance of Capello's: Christian Panucci.

Panucci's career had stalled after winning the title with Capello at Real Madrid. He stuck around another season, before a disastrous move to Inter which saw him embroiled in a nasty row with Marcello Lippi. From there, he was called to Chelsea by Gianluca Vialli, but he was replaced after just six league matches by Claudio Ranieri, a man Panucci simply did not get along with. He was sent to Monaco in January of 2001, but still failed to find his feet. By this point he was twenty-eight and his career was at a crossroads. His critics saw him as someone who was arrogant, a troublemaker, and prone to unsettling the balance of a dressing room. Baldini was aware of his reputation. But he also knew that Panucci had played the best football of his career under Capello. And if anyone could bring him back close to his potential, it was Fabio. Thus, amidst much scepticism (Roma supporters felt short-changed: they had been promised Cannavaro, they ended up with Panucci), Capello and his prodigal son were reunited.

In midfield, Capello suffered a setback when Cristiano Zanetti was allowed to leave. Zanetti – tough, hard-working and gladiatorial – was the kind of player Capello hoped to build his team around. Roma's problem was that he was half-owned by Inter, which meant that, under Serie A rules, each year the clubs would have to agree which one would get his services. If they failed to do so, one club could buy out the other by agreeing a fee for their 'half'. And, if no agreement was reached, the player's future would be determined by sealed bids for the other party's half.

Zanetti wanted to stay, though it was clear that with Tommasi and a now-fit Emerson, he would not be a starter. Plus, Assunção – a favourite of the supporters and, crucially, President Sensi – was still around. Capello lost that battle: Sensi sold Inter his half of Zanetti for around £5m. From his perspective it was a great bit of business for an oft-injured player who had made more than twenty league starts in a season just once in his career. To replace him, Baldini signed Francisco Lima, an understated workmanlike Brazilian from Brescia.

Up front, of course, Roma had already made their big transfer pick-up: Antonio Cassano, the eighteen-year-old wonder-kid from Bari. Indeed, the Cassano deal had been inked way back in March 2001, in the midst of Roma's title chase, when Baldini persuaded Sensi to part with £18m, until very recently a world-record transfer fee for a teenager. It was a very steep price for a kid who had made only forty-eight professional appearances and scored just six goals.

But Cassano was drawing comparisons with Diego Maradona. And he had the kind of background which was, at once, both straight out of a Hollywood film and a massive warning sign. His mother raised him on her own (his father was married to another woman at the time) in the back alleys of Bari Vecchia, one of the most crime-infested neighbourhoods in Italy. Giovanna, his mum, worked as a cleaner and sold candy door-to-door. On more than one occasion, she fell foul of the law. But as the boy wonder began making headlines (as early as the age of eight) the entire neighbourhood – from drug dealers to the local priest, from mob hit men to single mothers whose husbands were in prison – closed ranks around him.

Capello knew that Cassano was, potentially, a walking, talking headache. He was hotheaded, immature, instinctive and childish (he regularly replaced the sugar with salt in Trigoria's cafeteria, creating serious rows at cappuccino-time). Few people with his background and baggage made it in life, least of all in the disciplined world Capello was trying to create at Roma. Then again, a talent like his came along once every thirty years: pace, creativity, strength, balance, a familiarity with the ball which seemed almost unnatural.

Capello was getting Cassano young enough that he believed he could mould him, protect him, isolate him from the inevitable temptation that was to follow. Temptation which was bound to be even greater for a kid like him, who had grown up surrounded by people who felt life was cheap, selling drugs was as legitimate a business as peddling fruit or flowers, and money was the measure of everything.

The press were full of praise for Roma's summer transfer campaign. Indeed, Capello was given the back-handed compliment of being the best at persuading clubs to buy him the very best players available.

'That too is a skill,' says Luciano Spinosi, his old team-mate at Roma and Juventus, who was now across the barricades, working as an assistant coach at Lazio. 'Capello is very good at getting his presidents to open their wallets and buy him outstanding players. He knows exactly what he needs and he has the gravitas and personality to ask for them and to convince the clubs to pay for them.'

When I met with Capello in writing *The Italian Job* in 2005 he bristled at that characterization. He had heard it many times before.

'People say Capello is good because his clubs buy him whatever he wants,' he told me, speaking in the third person. 'No, Capello is good because he knows what he wants and chooses the right players. It's easy after the fact to say: "Oh, look, so-and-so is a great player and Capello won because of him." Well, Capello chose that great player, he could have chosen dozens of others. It's not a self-fulfilling prophecy.'

It's true that Capello excelled at big clubs, and, obviously, coaching a big club means you will by definition benefit from having great players at your disposal. But, in fact, for much of his career, Capello did not exactly have blank cheques in the transfer market. Milan, for example, spent big in just three of his six years at the helm. And the amount of input he had in those signings is highly debatable. Leaving aside the 1997–98 season (when most of the players were bought before his arrival), he often found himself saddled with guys who were bought at the president's whim (Roberto Baggio being the most obvious case). At Real, the first time around, the team had already been assembled when he arrived. At Roma, they spent big for two summers out of five (though, even then, he missed out on his top targets like Buffon and Cannavaro). He did get his way at Juventus and in his second stint at Madrid, but Capello would probably say that by that point his CV had earned him the right to make certain demands of his clubs.

Back to 2001. If Capello's 'long summer holiday' was supposed to let the players sleep off their *scudetto* hangovers and bring them back recharged and ready to go, it didn't quite work out that way.

After their first five outings in Serie A and the Champions League they were still winless and, apart from a battling 2–1 loss to Real Madrid at the Stadio Olimpico (a match which should never have gone ahead: it kicked off six hours after the 9/11 attacks on the World Trade Center), had shown very little. Rock bottom came in a 2–0 loss at Piacenza in which the 2,000 visiting Roma supporters cheered for fifteen minutes and then remained mute, a 'silent protest' directed at the team. Capello said after the match that he feared that the players had lost their hunger after the *scudetto*. 'Evidently success has made them weaker psychologically,' he observed.

And then, suddenly, things began to click into place. Roma would not lose a game in the league or in Europe for another six months. Typically, Capello built from the back. Pelizzoli, crucified by the fans for some early blunders, was relegated to the bench: Capello wasn't about to let the supporters destroy a youngster's confidence, not when he had Antonioli, a guy who took abuse like water off a duck's back. Panucci helped settle the defence, Emerson did the same in midfield. On many occasions he pushed Totti up front alongside Batistuta, adding an extra body in midfield. Cassano, whom the coaching staff felt was still extremely raw, was used primarily as a substitute. The fact that Montella missed three months through injury spared Capello the usual ticking timebomb on the bench. The previous year's 3-4-3 formation had now become 3-5-2. Roma were clearly becoming more defensive.

'I don't see why we have to be the only team in Europe playing with three central strikers!' Capello shot back, visibly annoyed, at those who accused him of being too defensive. 'Why do we have to be the mugs who go out there and attack more than anybody else in the world? I can't believe nobody is noticing that we're the most attack-minded side in Europe already . . .'

When Capello made such statements, reaction was mixed to say the least. Did he really believe what he was saying? Was he trying to manipulate the fans? Did he think that, by saying something, it would become true?

The evidence was there for all to see. To suggest that Roma were the most attacking side in Europe was clearly a provocation. But then, on occasion, throughout his career Capello had come out with statements which seemed to defy reality. One pundit compared him to Saddam Hussein's spokesman who told the cameras that there was no invasion, that the American forces had been repelled, even as you could clearly see US tanks rolling past behind him.

'That season was the year we all began to see through Capello,' says Mario Corsi, aka Marione, a leading figure among Roma's Ultras and the host of a popular local radio phone-in. 'The fact was that the supporters were angry because the football was bad. They started re-evaluating everything. Some even began to see the year before, the *scudetto* season, in a different light. We came to realize that we won and were entertained because we had outstanding players at the peak of their careers, not because Capello was this brilliant tactician.'

And yet Roma, while less impressive than the previous season, found themselves top of the table at the half-way point. What's more, they were through to the second group phase of the Champions League.

'We began so badly and yet here we are, top of the table, on track for the title and with plenty to play for in Europe,' Capello said on 6 January 2002. 'I'm proud of my players. They are beginning to understand that, even playing in a slightly different way, a way which you call more defensive, but I don't, we can get results.'

Roma continued undefeated in the new year, but, perhaps precisely because of their more measured approach, failed to pick up wins, particularly away from home. Thus, by late February, Inter and Juventus had joined them at the top of the table.

'We shouldn't have been dropping points away from home against smaller clubs,' says Francisco Lima. 'Capello would get furious when it happened, he knew how important it was.' The supporters greeted a 1–0 victory over

Perugia with a chorus of resounding boos directed at Capello. As always, he defended their right to criticize him: 'The fans are emotional and when they are at the game, they need to feel free to express themselves,' he said. 'I don't like to be criticized, but I accept it from them.'

He was a little less tolerant of criticism from the press. Now that Montella was fit again, he felt he was in a no-win situation. Play Montella and he'd be asked about dropping Batistuta. Play Batistuta and there would be an inquest into why Montella wasn't starting. Play them both and the fans of Delvecchio or Cassano would come out of the woodwork to give him grief.

Batistuta, however, was a slightly different issue. He had turned thirty-three and had clearly lost a step. He appeared more comfortable in the previous year's system, with the additional support of Delvecchio, rather than the current one, which often left him alone to lead the line. An old knee injury had also resurfaced, doing him no favours. Capello defended him in public, putting his lack of goals down to bad luck, yet in the back of their minds, several of his staff felt that Bati-Gol had entered the downward phase of his career.

A resounding 3–0 victory over Barcelona in the Champions League stoked some enthusiasm among the fans ahead of the derby on 10 March. In the build-up to that game Capello granted an interview which would have far-reaching implications. It appeared on 7 March 2002. Capello was asked about the old rumours of conspiracies and the powers-that-be which, as always, rumbled on in Rome. The previous month, during Roma v

Juventus, Moggi and Antonio Giraudo, Juve's chief executive, had gone to speak to the referee at half-time. They were angry about the fact that defender Mark Iuliano had been sent off with just thirty minutes gone. Was this an example of an 'exercise of power'?

'I'd say so,' Capello replied. 'It's a question of personality and respect. I really don't think I would do something like that. If there are rules, they need to be respected. But yes, you can win leagues by exercising your power. Though, in the end, matters are mostly decided on the pitch.'

But Capello did not stop there.

'There are conflicts of interest everywhere and, in ethical terms, it's not ideal,' he added. 'I'm not just talking about Moggi here . . . we have a company like GEA which is operating almost in a monopoly situation. They control six managers and a hundred or so players. It's an obvious conflict of interest. And there could be obvious repercussions. But I'm not the one who should be thinking about this. The people who run football should be looking at this.'

His words echoed around the game. Capello had said what many believed, but, until then, nobody of his stature had expressed. It wasn't just about the 'Palazzo' and the 'psychological subjection' of referees. This went much further.

GEA was a football agency founded the previous year and run by Alessandro Moggi (son of Luciano) with the help of a number of influential shareholders, all of them scions of powerful figures in the Italian game: Chiara Geronzi (daughter of Cesare, the head of Capitalia, Italy's second biggest bank, which provides lines of credit to a number of Italian clubs), Francesca Tanzi (daughter of Calisto, the Parmalat supremo and then Parma owner), Davide Lippi (son of Marcello), Gianmarco Calleri (son of Riccardo, the former Torino owner), Andrea Cragnotti (son of Sergio, the Lazio owner) and Giuseppe De Mita (a former Lazio executive and son of Ciriaco, a former Italian prime minster).

The fact that, at the tender age of twenty-eight, Moggi Jr found himself controlling hundreds of footballers did not sit well with many, particularly in Rome. It wasn't just the blatant appearance of nepotism, it was, as Capello pointed out, an obvious conflict of interest. GEA was linked to a whole galaxy of clubs and managers, its chief executive was the son of the sporting director of Italy's biggest and most powerful club.

Four years later, in the aftermath of the Calciopoli scandal, GEA would come under attack and, at the time of writing, some of its former directors (the agency has since shut down) and some of its prominent allies, including Moggi Sr, would be put on trial, charged with using intimidation and threats to secure player mandates and push through deals. Both Baldini and Capello would be called as witnesses, with the former testifying against Moggi and the latter, who has always described Moggi as a 'dear friend', claiming in court that he was 'unfamiliar' with GEA's activities. A statement which would appear to directly contradict the above interview, which is why the prosecutors asked that Capello be charged with contempt of court. But more of this later.

The Capello interview sent shockwaves. It wasn't just

Juventus, in the shape of Giraudo and Moggi, who were upset. Behind the scenes, some members of the Agnelli family were embarrassed. And the media started demanding answers of the Italian FA and the Italian league: why were certain things allowed to go on unchecked?

It was music to the ears of Sensi, but also for many Roma supporters, who on local radio airwaves and in internet chatrooms had been voicing the same concerns. They had been laughed off, called 'professional victims', ridiculed as losers who could not accept their own shortcomings. Now, however, Capello was in their camp. He may not have been the most effusive character, his football may not always have been pleasant, but they knew that, like them, he was fighting the 'good fight'.

'Capello does not openly suck up to the supporters, he's much more subtle,' says Marione, who clearly does not have Capello at the top of his Christmas card list. 'He ignores them, at most he'll defend their right to say what they like. But then he comes up with certain buzzwords or themes in his press interviews which resonate with the fans. He knows what to say to muddy the waters and be hailed as a hero, while distracting the supporters from his own failings. He's a very intelligent man that way.'

It may have been Capello's comments and the 'Us v Them' ethos it generated which lifted the whole squad and their supporters. Or, maybe it was just the fact that Lazio were in free-fall. Either way, Roma proceeded to demolish them 5–1 in a memorable derby. Capello abandoned the 3-5-2, deploying Totti, Delvecchio and Montella up front. The 'Little Airplane' scored a hat-trick in the first half and added a fourth after the break. With

Inter and Juventus drawing 2–2 at the San Siro, Roma soared back into joint first.

Next up were Galatasaray in the Champions League. Roma led the group and a win would have put them through. Instead, they struggled to a 1–1 draw. The derby had left them physically and mentally drained. But headlines were made at the final whistle. The last few minutes had been tense, with referee Anders Frisk appearing to lose control. As the two sets of players walked off the pitch, Lima appeared to lose it completely.

'A few Galatasaray players called me a "nigger piece of shit",' Lima told me. 'I understood exactly what they said because I had played several seasons in Turkey. I wasn't going to put up with it.'

Lima responded with a shove which soon turned into a full-fledged mêlée. Indiscriminate kicks and punches flew (you can relive the moment on YouTube), Rome's riot police, not known for their subtlety, waded in with their truncheons. But the man who forced his way through the bodies and practically tackled Lima was none other than Capello.

'He came up behind me and just smothered me in a bear hug, all the while repeating "Enough! Enough! Calm down . . . let's go to the dressing room!"' Lima recalls. 'Had he not stopped me, things could have got really out of hand.'

Lima and Batistuta were both banned, as was Capello, although that was later reduced when it emerged that he had, in fact, acted as a peacemaker (albeit a very forceful one). Still, Capello was angry: after two and a half years he would have expected Roma to be able to maintain their cool and not waste what in tennis terms was effectively a matchpoint. Instead, what he got was the same old Roma.

That said, they still controlled their own destiny. To qualify for the quarter-finals, all they had to do the following week was avoid defeat at Anfield against Liverpool. Having won there the year before, everyone felt confident. Liverpool had scored just two goals in the group stage and had not won a single game.

After just six minutes, Liverpool were ahead as Jari Litmanen converted a somewhat dubious penalty. Capello had reverted to the 3-5-2, with Batistuta, clearly off-form, up front. Chasing the game, he sent on Delvecchio and Montella at the interval plus Cassano in the second half. But it was to no avail. Emile Heskey added a second and Roma, again, went crashing out of Europe.

There wasn't much time to think about it. That Sunday Inter lay in wait at the San Siro in a top-of-the-table clash. He changed it around again: three strikers, Totti with Delvecchio and Montella. When Delvecchio hit the post and Montella fluffed two early chances, Capello knew it wasn't going to be his night. Inter won 3–1, but Roma's performance was, nonetheless, encouraging. If they weren't going to be consistent, at least Capello wanted his Roma side to play well when it mattered. And, that night, they did. It's just that Inter were better.

The following week, Sensi met Italian FA officials to discuss the officiating. As ever, he felt Roma were 'not respected' by referees. Several members of Capello's staff felt it was a risky thing to do. Their fears were borne out some ten days later.

Inter, who were top of the table, contrived to lose at

home to Atalanta, in a game marred by several controversial decisions. Roma, playing away to bottom club Venezia, found themselves two goals down with four minutes to go. Referee Pierluigi Collina awarded two late, late penalties which were duly converted by Montella.

It was all Moggi needed. He cast doubt on the officiating, congratulating Sensi on his 'diplomacy' in meeting with the FA earlier that week. And he also mocked Collina. 'Clearly he's shown once again that he's the best referee in the world.' Moggi had spun the situation to his advantage. By tying Sensi's visit (which, lest we forget, was a very public event) to the officiating that weekend, he was giving the impression that the referees were now favouring Roma over Inter and Juventus. It was a brilliant tactical move: in one fell swoop he deflected attention from the accusations against Juventus and cast Roma as the villains.

Candela subsequently commented that 'this game proves Italian football is not rigged', but his words had a boomerang effect. Many Juve faithful responded by saying: 'Yes, it's not rigged when things go in your favour.'

Capello tried to ignore him, saying: 'I don't listen to Moggi, I don't know what he said and I don't care.' But the damage had been done. And it wasn't just about perception: those were two points lost for Roma, who could have been level at the top.

Inter again dropped points with two matches to go, but again Roma weren't able to capitalize, settling for a scoreless draw in Milan. Meanwhile Juventus kept on winning. Inter were still top, with a one-point margin over Juve and two over Roma. On the penultimate day of the season everyone won, setting up a dramatic final day. Inter's fate lay in their own hands. They were away to Lazio, but it looked like a foregone conclusion. Not only did Lazio have nothing left to play for, they clearly preferred to see Inter crowned champions, compared to Juventus (with whom they had rowed bitterly two seasons earlier) or Roma (for obvious reasons). Instead, the unthinkable happened. Lazio rolled to a 4–2 win, in a dramatic match which would be remembered for Ronaldo's tears and Marco Materazzi's tantrum. Juventus won 2–0 at Udinese to win their twenty-sixth *scudetto*. Cassano, the forgotten man at Roma, scored the only goal in their 1–0 victory at Torino. Roma finished second behind Juve, who lost one more game than the runners-up.

Disappointment was rife. Roma had lost the title by just one point, having drawn too many games against inferior opponents, most recently at Venezia. Take away the horrible start – seven points dropped in the first three games – and Capello would have retained the championship.

'The fact is, we threw the title away,' he said. 'I was right all along about Juve. But we still threw it away with all those draws against little clubs.'

The supporters felt the same way. Second place was not good enough. Not with this team. They needed a scapegoat. 'Capello cost us that title, we simply threw it away,' says Marione. 'Just as we threw away the Champions League.'

Capello would no doubt dispute this. But Marione and the other Roma fans had a valid point. Roma were the best team in Italy that season. As for the Champions League, we'll obviously never know. But what was becoming clear was that Roma had become as demanding as anything Capello had experienced at Milan or Real Madrid. With one major difference: Milan and Real had a culture of success. Roma's was only just beginning.

For his part, early that summer, Sensi was on a similar wavelength. He began to feel that he had done his part, matching the traditional powers pound for pound and delivering a top-notch squad, top-to-bottom. Now it was up to Capello to make it work. Especially because, Sensi felt, Capello had nothing to complain about. He had the staff he wanted, he had the best players that Baldini could realistically get him and he had a fat long-term contract, signed the previous season. Sources vary about how much Capello was actually getting paid at this stage, but estimates range from £2.5m to £4m, which easily made him one of the highest paid managers in the world.

Capello's financial dealings were coming under increasing scrutiny and not just because of his colossal salary. That year, he negotiated a settlement with the Italian tax authorities after magistrates initially requested a three-month custodial term. It all stemmed from a deal which looked too good to be true.

In the mid-1990s Capello had befriended a man named Roberto Salmoiraghi, mayor of Campione d'Italia, a tiny hamlet in Switzerland, not far from the border. Campione d'Italia was something of a bizarre legal and diplomatic aberration. The village of 2,500 people – many of whom worked at the casino, Campione's main employer – was fully in Swiss territory, but was technically a part of Italy. The local currency, however, was the Swiss franc, although residents paid their taxes to the Italian government. However, there was an incredible fiscal wrinkle in all this, which allowed for a remarkable tax loophole. Residents were paid in Swiss francs and then had to convert their earnings into Italian lire. But, rather than using the official exchange rate (which, at the time, was around 1,200 lire to the franc), the Italian taxman allowed them to use a special exchange rate of just 250 lire to the franc.

What this meant was that Campione d'Italia residents could effectively reduce their taxable income by nearly 80 per cent. For example, if you earned 100,000 francs a year, it would be equivalent to around 120m lire based on the going exchange rate. But, if you were a Campione d'Italia resident, when you filled out your tax return, you got to use the 'special exchange rate' of 250 lire to the franc, which set your income at just 25m lire. Put another way, if you had to pay, say, 40 per cent in taxes on your 120m lire income, you'd be shelling out around 48m. But if your income, thanks to the 'special exchange rate', shrank to 25m, you'd be liable for just 10m. A nice little saver, no?

Of course, to do this, you have to be resident in Campione d'Italia. And, establishing residency there is far from easy. You can't just buy property there, you have to physically live there. And, more importantly, you need to get the local authorities to confirm that you are, in fact, one of them. Which is basically what happened to Capello. Salmoiraghi, who, as mayor, enjoyed wide-ranging powers, helped push through the paperwork that established Capello as a bona fide resident of Campione d'Italia, thereby potentially saving him millions in taxes.

Salmoiraghi was later found guilty and given a

twenty-month suspended sentence. Capello, who collaborated with investigators and never actually benefited from the bogus residency – the scam was exposed almost straight away – settled out of court and paid only a small fine. With hindsight, it seems extraordinary that he would be tempted to fall for such a simple and transparent scam. Did he really believe the Italian tax authorities – who are notoriously meticulous, especially when it comes to high-profile taxpayers – would swallow the fact that, while he was managing Roma, he was actually residing some six-hundred miles away in Campione d'Italia?

Accepting Salmoiraghi's deal was one of the most foolish choices he made in his career. True, Capello wasn't the only person to benefit from Salmoiraghi's largesse in establishing bogus residencies. It seemed that the mayor liked hanging out with celebrities and others were tempted by his offer of a vastly reduced tax bill. Not surprisingly, around this time, Capello's sons Pierfilippo and Edoardo took over much of his business dealings.

Sensi had told Baldini and Capello that the squad was complete and he wasn't going to be spending big. On the contrary, Roma ended up with a small transfer surplus. Panucci's move from Monaco was made permanent for a small fee and the hulking defender Traianos Dellas was signed from Perugia. The departures of Assunção and Zago brought in some cash, for which Sensi was grateful.

For his part, Capello's feelings were mixed. Like the previous season, he tried to get his hands on Cannavaro: Parma's financial situation had deteriorated and they were willing to do business. But Inter and Juventus were both on his trail and the last thing Sensi wanted to do was join a bidding war for a defender who was about to turn 29. Cannavaro joined Inter for £17m, a fee Capello knew Sensi was never going to be able to match. Another player they chased all summer was Edgar Davids. Capello had rued the day he let him leave Milan six years earlier and was desperate to have him on board. The Dutchman, who had a bumpy relationship with Juve manager Marcello Lippi, was equally willing to reunite with Capello. Negotiations went on all summer, before Moggi vetoed the deal: he was too clever to sell Davids to a direct opponent, thereby repeating the mistake that Milan had made back in 1997, when they let him join Juve.

So much for Capello's dream of strengthening the squad year after year. He was clearly apprehensive going into the 2002–03 season. The supporters were expecting more and more, the competition had splashed the cash (Inter picked up Matias Almeyda, Hernán Crespo and Cannavaro, Milan added Alessandro Nesta, Clarence Seedorf and Rivaldo) and yet the only meaningful new face around Trigoria was – with all due respect – Dellas.

A dispute over television rights delayed the start of the season until 14 September and, from the very first match, a 2–1 loss to Bologna, Capello could tell something wasn't right. Three days later they were hammered 3–0 at home by Real Madrid in the Champions League. To make matters worse, later that night, two players borrowed Vincent Candela's Ferrari and crashed it on the outskirts of Rome. The idea that Roma players, after such a humiliating loss, would be out partying and joyriding around town only served to infuriate the local media and fans. The press reported that Zebina had been at the wheel (Candela was not involved) and, while he got the brunt of the abuse, Capello wasn't spared either: after all, wasn't he supposed to be the big disciplinarian? And wasn't Zebina 'his guy'?

'I took the blame that night,' Zebina told me. 'After the match, a bunch of us got together. We didn't party, we just played cards and chatted into the night. When it came to leave, one of my teammates, who maybe had had a few drinks, got behind the wheel. It was a foolish thing to do and we crashed into some dumpsters.'

The Ferrari was ruined, the players were unscathed. Zebina, who had not been drinking, took the blame, saying he had been at the wheel, possibly to protect his teammate (whose identity remains a mystery). It was the last thing Capello needed. But he appreciated Zebina's loyalty to the team, taking it on the chin when he was largely blameless, even if it meant more torrents of abuse from fans and media alike. Rather than punishing Zebina, he told the squad to rally around him.

'He was very fair that day,' says Zebina. 'He could have just turned me into a scapegoat, not least because I wasn't playing well at the time. But, instead, he protected me. I will always appreciate that.'

After another home defeat, this time against little Modena, the fans were furious, insulting the players and calling them mercenaries. When Totti and a few others went over to them and, as per tradition, threw their jerseys into the crowd, they were thrown back on to the pitch. The fans didn't want them. Capello vented his rage at the match officials, who had awarded Modena a disputed penalty and sent off Panucci: 'Clearly the referees still have it in for us.' If it was meant to deflect attention from Roma's performance, it didn't work. An angry Sensi demanded a face-to-face meeting and Capello, along with Baldini, spent an hour locked in the bowels of the Stadio Olimpico with their president.

Roma recovered and slowly crept back up the table. The fans were still demoralized and cracks were beginning to appear, but the results rolled in. Part of it was a tactical shift: Capello alternated between the 3-4-1-2, the 3-5-2 and an orthodox 4-4-2. The latter was used with tremendous success at the Bernabéu against Real Madrid's 'Galacticos', the defending Champions League champions. Zinedine Zidane, Raúl, Ronaldo, Luis Figo . . . they all watched powerless as Roma, spurred on by a magnificent Totti, came away with a one-goal victory.

The side, however, lacked any kind of consistency. Brilliant one week, anonymous the next. Up front, Batistuta, partly because of a niggly knee injury, was showing his age. Capello often opted for pace over power, turning to Montella and Cassano. The latter, still just twenty-one, clearly had a lot of growing up to do, but was slowly harnessing his potential. Capello showed a patience with him that few would have expected. Relations with Totti were frosty, but professional, as they remained throughout his time at Roma.

Capello felt the side needed a big win against one of the contenders to fire up the side and the fans and send the team on some kind of run. On 16 November they played top-of-the-table Inter at the Stadio Olimpico. It finished 2–2, with Okan Buruk scoring a late goal to deny a Totti-less Roma the three points, but the match will be remembered for the scuffles which broke out at the final whistle and for some controversial refereeing.

'They don't want us to win the title, at best they'll let us into the UEFA Cup,' a furious Capello said after the match. 'If this continues, I'm going abroad.'

Two weeks later, against Juventus, Roma had another chance to kickstart their season: high-profile opponent, high-intensity game, same result. This time, they were actually two goals up thanks to Totti and Cassano (who found time to insult Capello when he was substituted). But Juve stormed back, snatching a late equalizer with Nedved, before Totti and Candela were sent off.

Again, Capello pointed the finger at the match officials. 'There are very strange things happening to us, I think we can all see it.' By this point, however, the fans' attitude had changed somewhat. Sure, they thought, Capello had a point in blaming referees. And sure, there probably was a vast northern conspiracy against them. But he knew that before coming here. And, what's more, his football was decidedly uninspiring. Against Juventus, he played two defenders – Cafu and Candela – wide in midfield in a 4–4–2. What had happened to the brilliant and entertaining Roma seen two years earlier?

The New Year came and went and Roma were stuck in eighth place. They were through to the second group stage of the Champions League, but they had already lost twice, at home to Arsenal and away to Ajax.

Batistuta was sent to Inter on loan. Given that his contract was expiring that June, it effectively meant he was being released on a free. It wasn't exactly a fitting farewell to the man who had proved so instrumental in delivering Roma the title. But, in fact, the club had been trying to get rid of him since the end of the previous season. The Argentine wanted to extend his contract and, when he approached Baldini and Sensi about it, they went straight to Capello for an opinion. He told them that, at thirty-three and with a bum knee, Batistuta was on the decline. If he stuck around, he could still contribute, but a long-term deal which would tie up lots of money (and cash was scarce in the Sensi coffers) did not seem like a good idea. Sensi asked Baldini to quietly see if there were any interested buyers. But Roma's asking price – reportedly in the region of £6m – scared everybody off, given his wages and the fact that he was a year away from going out of contract. And so Roma lost him for nothing, though Sensi did save six months' worth of his wages.

The situation could and should have been handled better. But Capello wasn't sorry to see Batistuta go. He had been a great player, but he was becoming a bit of a problem in the dressing room ever since Capello stopped including him in his private chats with the team's veterans (a group which included Totti, Emerson and Cafu). When the club picked up another holding midfielder, Olivier Dacourt, on loan from Leeds United, it was obvious to all which way Capello was heading tactically.

The Dacourt deal also represented a sign of the times for Roma. The Frenchman had fallen out badly with Leeds and manager Terry Venables. He had plenty of offers, but chose Roma. 'I signed for just one reason: Capello,' Dacourt told me. 'I could have gone elsewhere, but I was desperate to work with the best. I'm not ashamed to say it, I signed because of him, not the club.'

Baldini pulled off some transfer magic with Dacourt. Not only did he convince Leeds to loan him for free, he also got the Yorkshire club to pay the bulk of his wages. Sensi was delighted: Baldini had saved him a lot of money. The fans less so. It was nothing against Dacourt, it's just that it showed once again that Roma could no longer compete with the big boys financially and had to feed off scraps.

Dacourt did settle the midfield, but, even with a more cautious stance, Roma continued to be hit-or-miss. Capello was at his wits' end, he had tried everything but to no avail. They were knocked out of the second group stage of the Champions League, and remained anchored to the middle of the table.

Only the Coppa Italia offered some joy. They beat Lazio in both legs of the semi-final, advancing to face Milan for the cup. In ordinary circumstances, the Coppa Italia was treated as an annoyance and nothing more, but, given the way the season was going, it was something to cling to. And even the fans got excited. Beating Lazio in both legs made it all the sweeter.

As the season petered out towards a disappointing eighth place finish, Capello prepared for the Coppa Italia final. It did not take a genius to figure out how much more the game meant to Roma. Milan had reached the Champions League final and their manager, Carlo Ancelotti, rested a whole bunch of players: Paolo Maldini, Billy Costacurta, Clarence Seedorf, Manuel Rui Costa, Andrea Pirlo and Dida all missed out, while Kakha

Kaladze and Andriy Shevchenko only made the bench. It was all set up for Roma to capture the second major trophy of the Capello era.

Sure enough, Totti put them ahead inside half an hour. But in the second half Roma fell apart. Milan scored four in the final twenty-eight minutes, leaving the fans in the Stadio Olimpico unsure of whether to sit in stunned silence or vent their anger on the players (most chose the latter option).

Corriere dello Sport had a succinct headline title the next day: 'Shame'. Capello ranted about the officiating: 'The referee gave them a highly dubious penalty, we were unlucky and then, as always, we failed to capitalize on the many chances we created. This is the season from hell.'

But, to most supporters, his excuses had started to wear thin. Once again, it wasn't his fault, it was the referees, or his own players, or the 'season from hell'. Capello's attempts to engender a siege mentality in his squad, or a show of pride, were clearly not working.

The return leg was if anything even more humiliating. Capello had managed to convince the players that they could turn it around. Milan had won the Champions League on penalties three days earlier, and were clearly hung over from the celebrations. Plus, Ancelotti had already announced that he was going to give most of his regulars the night off. Surely – and now Capello was appealing to the players' pride – it was within them to pull off one of the greatest comebacks in history, even if it did mean winning 4–0 at the San Siro?

Ancelotti was true to his word: just five of the starters who had won the Champions League at Old Trafford were on the pitch. And, initially at least, Roma followed the script. Totti gave them the lead after eleven minutes and then, twenty minutes into the second half, made it 2–0. Rivaldo pulled one back immediately, but it didn't matter: Roma were dominating, they just needed to score two more to take it into extra-time.

Capello was fired up, as were the players. Too fired up, evidently. Cassano, angry at not being awarded a free kick, lost it completely. TV images clearly show him first telling the referee to 'fuck off' and then running thirty yards to jab a finger in his face. Totti was also sent off after receiving his second yellow four minutes from time. And, to cap Capello's season from hell, Pippo Inzaghi equalized in the final minute. At least 2002–03 was over.

Relations with the local press, which had always been strained, only got worse as the calls for his head intensified. Rumours began circulating that Sensi wanted rid of Capello as well, but did not want to (or could not afford to) pay out the millions in compensation which would be due to him if he were sacked. Whether true or not, the local press and radio stations did little to suppress it.

Capello has rarely enjoyed a good relationship with the media. His modus operandi is to identify no more than a couple of influential journalists and, occasionally, deal with them when he had a message to send, but always being careful not to give the illusion of anything other than a professional relationship.

In Rome, this was a tricky thing to do, because of the tremendous reach and audience of the local radio stations. From early morning till late at night the airwaves are abuzz with phone-ins and chatshows involving journalists, ex-professionals and high-profile fans. There is usually only one topic: Roma. It's nearly impossible for the players and club staff not to get drawn into this. Declining an invitation to come on air can be dangerous as it could lead to days of criticism. Capello, never one to curry favour, regularly snubbed the radio stations, much to their annoyance.

'One day we had a journalists' round-table with some of the most influential reporters in Italy,' one radio producer recalls. 'Capello, as usual, was being criticized and we felt we should give him a right to reply. So I rang him up. His answer? "No, and I say it in the strongest terms possible. I don't speak to local media." Of course, we weren't happy about it. Especially since, during his time in Rome, he happily went on whenever the Spanish radio stations called him.'

But that too was part of Capello's approach. When he was in Madrid, he was far more available to the Italian media than he had ever been in Italy. And now, the tables were turned.

It was clear Capello was nearing the end of his Roman experience. Sensi was now seventy-seven, not in the best of health and no longer went out of his way to defend his manager publicly. Furthermore, the club was in financial trouble, as was Sensi's vast business empire. He wasn't going to give the financial backing Capello enjoyed in the first few seasons.

In fact, Sensi's behaviour appeared to become increasingly erratic. On 24 June 2003 he gave a bizarre interview which appeared to underscore just how bad his relationship with Capello had become. Real Madrid had sacked manager Vicente del Bosque the previous day and Capello was rumoured to be on Real's shortlist.

'If only that were true,' Sensi said when asked about it. 'If Real took him off our hands, I'd be so happy, I'd be doing back-flips! The fact is, Capello screwed me when I gave him that contract extension. He needs to go. And if he doesn't get the message, I'll just have to pay off the remainder of his contract and send him on his way.'

It was extraordinary stuff. A few hours later, Roma issued a statement 'clarifying' Sensi's comments. Sensi claimed that he had been misinterpreted, that his words were meant to be 'sarcastic' and that he was speaking 'in paradoxes'. And, he said, Capello would see out his contract.

Capello was stunned, but not entirely surprised. He knew what the situation was. He knew how Sensi felt, he knew how many of the supporters felt, he knew how some of his players felt. But most of all, it seemed obvious that Sensi's statement – and his immediate climbdown – was, above all, sad. How could somebody like that be taken seriously?

Capello could have walked away, but he felt his job was not done. Yes, he had delivered a title, but he wasn't going to resign after a bad season. That would have been an admission of failure. Moreover, his relationship with Baldini was reason enough to stay. Capello had found the perfect sounding board in the boyish, self-effacing Tuscan. Unlike many, he wasn't the slightest bit intimidated when Capello was angry and gave as good as he got. There was plenty of mutual respect there and, in fact, Capello now trusted Baldini's footballing judgement as much as he trusted anyone's, with the possible exception of Galbiati.

Capello seemed fascinated by Baldini. Unlike most men in football, Baldini did not bore him. He could more than hold his own in a non-footballing conversation. Baldini slowly introduced Capello to another side of Rome and, by extension, of life. He had a wide circle of friends – musicians, artists, entrepreneurs, writers – and Capello began frequenting them regularly. Most of them had virtually no interest in football: they might have known who Capello was, but, frankly, they couldn't care less. They did not hang on his every word, they were neither obsequious nor sycophantic and they most definitely did not ask him why Montella was on the bench the previous Sunday. Corny as it may sound, Capello got the impression that they spent time with him because they actually found him interesting for reasons which had nothing to do with football or with his celebrity status.

He had cultivated an interest in the arts, fine dining and travel for many years. But something changed in Rome. One acquaintance who has known him since the early 1990s put it like this: 'Prior to moving to Rome, he was almost competitive in his approach to art. He decided what he liked, studied up on a particular movement or artist or whatever and then proceeded to tell you everything he knew. It was the same with food or wine. He would go to a restaurant or sample some wine and then tell you everything in excruciating detail. He was enthusiastic, but also a bit preachy.'

'In Rome, it all changed. It became more about dialogue, more about discovery. You could say he became a little more humble. And his tastes changed as well. He became more bohemian. Of course, he still tried to explain why he was right and you were wrong. But, at least he heard you out.'

Capello's favourite restaurant in Rome was a place called Pommidoro in the Piazza dei Sanniti, the hub of San Lorenzo, a working-class area whose low rents made it popular with students, artists and out-of-work intellectuals. It's the kind of place where people drop in for lunch and stay all afternoon, largely because many of the patrons don't have day jobs to return to. Artists such as Giorgio De Chirico and Renato Guttuso were regulars in their day, as was the writer and filmmaker Pier Paolo Pasolini. Now, years later, Capello and Baldini held court there, with a rotating cast of characters from all walks of life (except football). It served as a kind of bubble, insulating him from the city's footballing passions.

Even in his mid-fifties, Capello was changing, some might say evolving. Part of it had more to do with others than himself. Luciano Spinosi, his old buddy from his days at both Roma and Juventus, lived nearby, but they hardly saw each other. 'But that was my fault, not his,' says Spinosi. 'He was managing Roma, I was the assistant coach at Lazio. And I let the rivalry get to me. I worried about what people would say if we were ever seen together. Rome is a big city, but it's really like a big village. And people talk. It's one of my biggest regrets. I let . . . the rivalry between the clubs get in the way of what had been a very special friendship.'

Capello was apparently less bothered by what people would have thought if he'd been seen out with Spinosi. But he nevertheless kept a separation with much of the football world in his private life. As for his players, the distance remained on a professional level, but, at least with some, he found common ground off the pitch. Dacourt remembers an away trip to Reggina towards the end of the 2002–03 season. The players had some time to kill the day before the game and Capello approached Dacourt, whom he knew had an interest in art, and asked him if he wanted to go with him to the local museum. The star attractions were the *Bronzi di Riace*, two life-size bronze statues of Greek warriors, dating back to the fifth century BCE. They were found in pristine condition buried at the bottom of the sea just off the Calabrian coast, back in 1972. How they got there remains a mystery.

'At the beginning, I was a bit scared of him,' Dacourt says. 'And when he asked me to come with him that day, I wasn't quite sure what to expect. But we had a delightful time . . . he chatted amiably and was relaxed and warm. It was completely different from what I had seen of him on the training ground.'

Money remained tight and, as ever, Baldini had to get creative that summer. Aldair and Cafu, at thirty-seven and thirty-three respectively, were let go, lopping a decent amount off the wage bill. Antonioli, who had lost the starting job to Pelizzoli half-way through the previous season, also moved on. Dacourt's loan was made permanent and they brought in the Norwegian John Carew, a lanky, mobile striker to add some muscle up front. But it was Cafu's replacement, Amantino Mancini, who earned Baldini the biggest plaudits.

Mancini had actually been acquired the previous January from Brazil's Atlético Mineiro, where he had established himself as a goalscoring full-back. Roma managed to pick him up on the cheap, loaning him to Venezia in Serie B for the second half of the 2002–03 season. He looked to everyone like an absolute dud, making just four starts and being described as a 'circus act' by his own manager. But Baldini trusted his instincts and, just as importantly, Capello trusted Baldini. Mancini was recalled to Roma in July, with hardly anyone noticing. He would go on to become one of the best wide men in Serie A.

Capello had to sweat on his final – and most important – reinforcement: the Romanian international Cristian Chivu. Dacourt, Mancini and Carew were all well and good, but Roma needed at least one marquee signing, if only to appease the disgruntled supporters. While many of them now had no love for Capello, they were just as frustrated with Sensi, partly for the club's financial woes and partly for not sacking Capello.

Again, Baldini found himself operating on the cheap. Two other deals having fallen through as clubs became wary of Roma's precarious financial situation, he moved on to Chivu, a player whom he originally felt was out of the club's budget. But at this point, there was no harm in trying. He discovered that Chivu was delighted to be linked to Roma and would do whatever he could to facilitate a deal. Chivu's club Ajax had originally been quoting a fee of around £20m, but using the Romanian defender's desire for a switch as leverage, Baldini was able to get them down to the £12m region and, in early July, the deal was done. Baldini agreed to pay the fee in three instalments, with the first due in a few weeks' time.

On 9 July 2003 Chivu was unveiled as Roma's newest signing. The press were ecstatic, saying he would team up with Walter Samuel to form one of the finest defensive partnerships in the world. Sensi basked in the adulation of the fans. Capello had his man.

Except he didn't. The following day, FIFA froze Chivu's transfer and banned Roma from making any cross-border signings of any kind. It emerged that the club had an outstanding debt of around £250,000 towards Peruvian club Sporting Cristal over the signing of Gustavo Vassallo. Gustavo who? Exactly.

As it turned out, Vassallo was a striker that Sensi had bought for the French club Nice, in which he also had a controlling share, back in 2000. However, technically it was Roma who acquired Vassallo, before immediately loaning him out to Nice. Just why Sensi had arranged the deal this way is not clear. The fact remained that nobody had paid the second instalment in Vassallo's transfer fee. Even though he had never played a single minute for Roma, the club were on the hook for him. And, what's more, it risked jeopardizing the Chivu transfer.

Capello was furious that the club should risk losing their prime transfer target in these circumstances. However, after a few days Sensi eventually reached a deal with Sporting Cristal, who withdrew their complaint to FIFA and the Chivu transfer was unfrozen.

Or so Roma thought. A few weeks later, when Capello was already planning Roma's season opener, the club secretary informed him that he would not be able to use Chivu because 'the player's registration had not arrived yet and thus had not been lodged with the Italian FA'.

How was this possible? They had signed Chivu back at the beginning of July. He had been paraded in a Roma shirt, he'd been training with his new teammates. How could it be that Roma did not have his registration?

Later that day, everything became clear. Ajax issued a statement ordering Chivu back to Amsterdam for training. Because Roma had not paid the first instalment of his transfer fee, they were withholding his registration. More embarrassment.

This was beyond a joke. Baldini was gutted: he was made to look like a charlatan, buying players with the footballing equivalent of bouncing cheques. The problem was that Sensi, already stretched to the limit financially, had been unable to find the necessary lines of credit and bank guarantees. In other words, nobody would lend Roma the money to sign Chivu.

Baldini was dispatched to Amsterdam tasked with finding some way to get his hands on Chivu's registration. The club's credibility was close to zero. The only thing they had going for them was that Chivu wanted to be at Roma. With the clock ticking down, Baldini conjured up a miracle of diplomacy and negotiation. Ajax agreed to release his registration, but the deal was scrapped and restructured. Now, rather than a transfer, it was a four-month loan. Roma had until the end of January to pay the first instalment of the agreed fee. If they failed to do so, Ajax would recall Chivu and there would be nothing they could do. Baldini sighed in relief. Of course, all this came at a price. Ajax added another £1.2m to Chivu's transfer fee.

The sheer absurdity of the Chivu situation led many to

believe that there would be no way that Capello and Baldini would stick around Roma much longer. They did not deserve a club perennially fighting off the debt collectors, nor, especially in Capello's case, a club where the vast majority of the supporters did not want him.

Still, the campaign kicked off with a string of excellent results, including a 2–2 draw away to Juventus, the defending champions, a match which Roma dominated for long stretches. By Christmas, they had opened up a six-point lead at the top of the table. What's more, there were shades of the Roma of old, with Totti, Cassano and Montella (or, after the latter's injury in November, Carew) up front. Mancini did his best Cafu impersonation on the right, Emerson and Dacourt dominated the midfield and Chivu formed a natural partnership with Samuel and Panucci at the back.

In January a group linked to Nafta, a Russian oil conglomerate, made contact with the club. They approached Baldini and Capello directly, as well as Sensi. They had a plan to buy out Roma, leaving Sensi as honorary president, while also taking over some of his oil refining interests. And they made it clear that both Baldini and Capello would stay on: they considered them a crucial part of Roma's rebuilding plan.

Baldini (and to a lesser degree Capello) pushed hard for the deal. It would have given Roma a financial lifeline, it would have kept Sensi involved (albeit in a position in which he could do little 'damage'), it would have laid the foundations for Roma to finally fulfil their potential as a club. Roman Abramovich had bought Chelsea some six months earlier and results were there for all to see. He had injected more than £120m into the club and seemed determined to turn them into a global force. Roma's potential was even greater: they had a far larger catchment area, an 80,000 seat stadium (which, when things were going right, they had no trouble filling) plus one of the best youth academies in Europe.

But by late February, whatever hopes they may have had had evaporated. Due diligence showed that Roma's books were in a far worse financial state than had been anticipated. There were doubts over whether they would even obtain a licence for the 2004–05 season. In fact, bankruptcy loomed. Nafta would have had to take over the club's enormous debts and there was no guarantee that they could pump in enough money in time to sort out the licence for next season.

Sensi, who had never been too thrilled by Nafta's offer, went in a very different direction. In exchange for new lines of credit, he ceded control of 49 per cent of ItalPetroli, the holding company which controlled all of his assets (including Roma), to Capitalia, the Roman bank run by Cesare Geronzi.

Around the same time, Rosella, Sensi's daughter, had begun taking on a far greater role within the club. While her father had led the fight to sell Serie A's television rights collectively, she was happy to carve out a deal with Juventus, Milan and Inter to maintain the individual rights sale. Selling the rights individually, of course, meant that Roma could earn more TV money in the short term, although in the long run it undermined the financial stability of the rest of the league.

Baldini was gutted. He had long believed that TV rights

ought to be sold collectively and that the allocation of revenues should be based on performance, as was the case in the English Premier League. Individual negotiation ultimately benefited Milan and Juventus far more than Roma. Far from shrinking the gap, they only served to increase it.

It was hard not to view it as a sell-out. Sensi had many faults, but at least he stuck to his guns. He viewed himself as the man who would lead the smaller teams to rise up and ensure a more equitable distribution of footballing wealth. His daughter Rosella had crossed to the other side. She no doubt would argue that she did it to save Roma. And maybe she was right (though Baldini felt that Nafta could have saved Roma without giving up the fight). One thing was certain, however: nothing would ever be the same again.

Capello shared some of Baldini's views, though he was a bit less passionate about it. He had been around for much longer, of course, and knew that some things weren't going to change. Or, if they did, it would take years of battle and the battle wasn't his to fight. His job was to focus on the football, at least until the end of the season.

The attitude of the press had shifted somewhat the previous summer and Capello was getting credit for Roma's overachievement. On a pre-season tour to Mexico, he had talked at length off the record about all of football's hot issues: Moggi, GEA, referees, young players, fans, performance-enhancing drugs, bogus accounting, agents, bungs. The press saw another side of him, that of a man who seemed genuinely concerned with the way the game was going. And, just as important, a man who would not give up. This, coupled with the fact that Baldini, who was wildly popular with the press, continued to be loyal to Capello led many to review some of their preconceptions about him. Yes, he could be arrogant, unpleasant and distant, and, yes, he sometimes didn't own up to his responsibilities in public. But, behind the façade, they discovered a man who seemed to genuinely care about many of the things they cared about. And given Sensi's erratic behaviour that summer (witness his comments about doing 'backflips' if Real took Capello off his hands), they began to see things from his point of view.

A month earlier, on the eve of their clash with Juventus at the Stadio Olimpico (a game which Roma dominated, winning 4–0), Capello had made a statement which would be held against him for years to come. Massimo Cecchini, from *Gazzetta dello Sport*, asked him flat out: 'Would you ever manage Juventus?'

'[Juventus] are one of the top five clubs in the world,' Capello replied. 'Everybody would want to go there. But I am not interested. It's a lifestyle choice . . .'

Those words would come back to haunt him. But more of this later. By March, Capello's disillusionment had reached peak levels. He didn't like the direction the Sensi family had taken the club and he didn't appreciate the president's occasional little jibes. He was performing a minor miracle in keeping Roma in second place, but he knew the glory days of 2000–01 were unlikely to return. He was also growing weary of the attitude of some of the supporters. He had always defended their right to voice their opinions, while insulating himself from them: the 'folk hero' role clearly did not suit him. But now things were spinning out of control.

On 21 March 2004 the Rome derby was abandoned early in the second half in bizarre circumstances. There had been some trouble outside the ground, but it was nothing out of the ordinary and the game kicked off as normal. Then, towards the end of the first half, both sets of supporters seemed to go silent, before a raucous chorus of anti-police slogans and pleas to stop the game rose from both ends of the ground. A totally unfounded rumour was circulating among both Lazio and Roma fans that a police van had run over and killed a ten-year-old boy.

Three Roma Ultras jumped the fence, crossed the running track and made their way towards Pelizzoli's goal. Totti, who knew them personally, went over to speak to them. They told him about the dead child and that the game had to be halted. Otherwise, things would get worse, far worse: they had been in touch with Lazio's Ultras and both were prepared to storm the pitch and take out their anger on the police.

Totti, with no time to think, told referee Roberto Rosetti that if it was true that somebody had died, he would refuse to play on and he was confident most of his teammates and opponents would do the same. Moments of confusion followed. Rome's chief of police got on the tannoy and, after the usual appeals for calm, denied the rumour. Given the circumstances and the mistrust towards the police, nobody believed him.

Capello spoke on the phone with – of all people – Adriano Galliani, his old chief executive at Milan who was now head of the Italian league. It was Galliani who instructed referee Rosetti to take the teams off the pitch. Fighting between the police and supporters continued late into the night. Capello returned home, confused and disgusted.

What kind of a place had this become? How could a handful of morons armed with a stupid rumour and an inflated sense of their importance walk on to the pitch with impunity and speak to the Roma captain like that? Football was spinning out of control. Roma deserved better. Its players deserved better. The city deserved better. The civilized majority of the club's support deserved better. And, yes, Capello himself deserved better.

It was time to move on. Roma ended the season in second place, eleven points behind Milan. After a highly eventful season there were reasons to be proud. He had got the best out of the mercurial Cassano, who scored fourteen Serie A goals and earned himself a place in the Euro 2004 side. The youngster from Bari Vecchia, still not twenty-two, had not been easy to handle. Capello had come to know which tantrums to ignore and which ones to crack down on. The joke about Capello among some Roma players was that he had selective hearing. If a squad player like Dellas told him to 'fuck off' there would be hell to pay. If Cassano did it, sometimes Capello simply wouldn't hear it.

'He had a special relationship with Cassano,' says Dacourt. 'It was one of those tough-love father-son relationships, where they are always rowing and then making up. And, yes, like a son, Cassano got away with certain things that other players might not.'

Capello himself admitted as much in an October 2005 interview with *Gazzetta dello Sport*: 'Yes, there were occasions when Cassano would provoke me and I wouldn't react. But that was because I wanted his teammates to step in and sort him out. I wanted them to set the internal discipline. Psychologically, I thought it was important.'

Capello's football is not a democracy. Some are more equal than others.

'I can't say Capello treats everyone equal,' says Candela. 'I don't know that I would be like that, but it is a formula which has worked for him over the years. It is hard to treat everyone the same when you have players like Batistuta and Totti who are stars in your team. He treats players differently at different times depending on what is good for the team. You have to accept it. The only thing is that, over time, it wears you down.'

Candela is a prime example. In his final season, as he puts it, he had 'lost the will to play'. He was weary and demotivated and his performances dipped badly. Had Candela been younger, had Capello believed that he still had a lot to give, he might have reacted differently. In this case, he was a soft touch.

'He was very understanding and supportive,' says Candela. 'I told him I wasn't motivated and asked for some time off. He understood me. Maybe he wouldn't have done it with another player, but he showed his human side that day.'

Capello's main feat, however, was the successful co-existence he developed with Totti over those five seasons. Oceans of ink have been devoted to exploring the psyche of the Roma captain. The fact that he was Roma born and bred and turned down the opportunity to chase fortune and silverware elsewhere; the fact that he was hailed as a Messiah from the time he first made his debut ('At sixteen it was obvious to all that had eyes and a brain that he was wasted in youth football,' says Spinosi, who coached Totti at Roma's academy); the fact that he was at once idolized and bore the weight of an entire city on his shoulders . . . few players in the modern game have coped better with the pressures placed on him.

Capello respected Totti's role as captain and resident icon, assigning him responsibility, but always maintaining his distance. He didn't try to be his friend, to build a relationship with him the way others had tried to do. The message was clear: do what I say and, together, we'll win things.

He also pushed the right buttons at the right time, especially when it came to Totti and Cassano. 'Looking back, I don't know if it was great man-management or just cold, cynical manipulation,' one Roman radio journalist told me. 'The fact is that the Totti–Cassano–Capello triangle was one which could explode at any time. The fact that it didn't, I guess, is down to him and to Totti, who showed tremendous spirit and leadership. But Capello would say things to the press at certain times which I'm certain were meant to get a response. For example, he would praise Cassano to high heaven and talk about him winning the Ballon d'Or [European Footballer of the Year Award], while describing him as the team's true leader. Well, obviously, Totti wouldn't like that. But he reacted not by having a go at Capello, but by working even harder on the pitch.'

Shortly before the end of the season, Capello was contacted by Inter. Vice-president Giacinto Facchetti asked him to come on board and suggested he could bring Baldini with him. It wasn't the first time he had been approached by Inter and he knew the club could provide the kind of transfer budget and control that he no longer had at Roma. But somehow it didn't feel right and not just because of his Milan past. On the eve of the final day of the season, he received a call from Giorgio Tosatti, a journalist at *Corriere della Sera*. The late Tosatti was something of a legend in Italian journalism. He was known for his balanced views and tendency to remain above the fray. Tosatti had a surprise for him: Luciano Moggi and Antonio Giraudo, the Juventus chief executive, wanted to meet him, with a view towards offering him the manager's job. What should he tell them?

The fact that Moggi should go via Tosatti struck him as strange. Then again, Moggi moved in mysterious ways. Or maybe it wasn't so strange. Capello knew that Juve needed a new manager. Marcello Lippi, in his second stint at the club, was leaving. Moggi had lined up Didier Deschamps, the Monaco boss and former Juve star, and Claudio Prandelli, another Juventus alumnus, to take over. Both were promising young managers. But Capello, of course, was on a different level. Before committing the club's future to Prandelli or Deschamps, Moggi felt he needed to take one last crack at Capello. But he wasn't sure how Capello would react. And, if he turned Juve down, Moggi didn't want news of it getting out. You never know, it was something that Capello could use against him in the future. Tosatti, on the other hand, could be relied on to keep his mouth shut. And, if word ever got out, Moggi could always deny it.

For the previous five years, they had been engaged in a virtually continuous row which alternated between the simmering and the raging. Both have since said it was all part of the game and that, regardless of what they said (or did) to each other in public, they remained friends beneath it all. After all, they had known each other for some thirty years and both admired what the other had achieved. Capello agreed to meet Moggi and Giraudo the following week, after the final game of the season.

What happened next is a matter of whom you choose to believe. Capello maintains that he told Baldini about his meeting and even suggested a way to bring him with him to Juve. Baldini has said for the record that Capello may have mentioned it in passing, but not in such a way that Baldini took seriously. And, indeed, you can see why Baldini would not have taken him seriously. It seemed outrageous. After all, Capello had stood side-by-side with Baldini for the previous five years, railing against much of what Moggi and the 'Palazzo' stood for. And Capello himself had stated four months earlier to Massimo Cecchini of *Gazzetta dello Sport* that he would 'never' join Juventus, although he did acknowledge that the Turin club was one of the top five in the world.

On 26 May, Roma's last day at Trigoria before everything broke up for the summer, Baldini and Capello met with Philippe Mexès, a defender they had just signed from Auxerre. Capello used glasses from the cafeteria to outline where the Frenchman would play and what defensive movements were expected of him. He also had a private meeting with Baldini, in which they laid out their plans for the following season: which players to keep, which ones to sell, which ones to try and bring in. At around half past two, it was time for Capello to leave. Baldini was sitting at his desk taking some notes, when Capello again reminded him of the meeting with Moggi and Giraudo. Baldini nodded absent-mindedly. He either didn't hear him or it didn't register or maybe he found the whole thing so far-fetched that he figured Capello was joking. After all, they had just spent over an hour planning next season's campaign with Roma.

It was a torrid day, summer had arrived early. Fabrizio Aspri, a Roma beat reporter for a local radio station, remembers approaching Capello as he drove out of the gate.

'Take care, gaffer, we'll see you in pre-season training!' he said.

Capello stopped for a moment, looked him in the eye, half-smiled and said: 'Good-bye.' And then he drove off.

'Looking back, it strikes me as very strange,' says Aspri. 'Normally he would have cracked a joke or said yes, see you in July or whatever. This time it was just one word and he was off. And he had that look in his face . . .'

The next day was the calm before the storm. Baldini went out to dinner with friends. Afterwards, he noticed that his mobile phone showed a missed call from Capello. But it was very late and he did not think to call him back.

Baldini usually sleeps with his mobile off when he is at home. That day, it remained on. At half past seven he was woken up by a call from a TV journalist who did the morning paper review for Sky Italia. According to a front-page article in *Corriere della Sera*, Capello had signed for Juventus the previous night. No other paper had the story. Baldini was stunned. He had nothing to say, he knew nothing. Or, rather, he knew that he would have a busy day ahead. He jumped under the shower and, as the water came trickling down, he tried to piece together little fragments of the last few days. Was that what Capello was talking about when he mentioned Giraudo and Moggi? What exactly had he said? It was a little bit like that scene in *The Usual Suspects*, when Chazz Palminteri sees all the pieces falling into place.

At around the same time, Aspri was getting the morning papers at the news-stand. When he saw the front-page story in *Corriere*, he stopped dead in his tracks. He immediately started ringing around to his colleagues, most of whom thought it was some kind of stupid sick joke.

Capello had pulled off one of the biggest shocks in the history of Italian football. To some, he had moved to the dark side. To others, he had returned home.

CHAPTER 14

The Old Lady

Just as everyone remembers where they were when they found out John Fitzgerald Kennedy had been shot, most people with even a passing interest in Italian football can tell you exactly what they were doing when the news of Capello's move to Juventus emerged. (I was actually very late to the story. I was getting married the next day, my work mobile was off, I didn't buy the newspaper and only found out at the rehearsal dinner that evening when one of the waiters told me the news.)

Fabio Cannavaro was training with the Italian squad ahead of Euro 2004.

'It was in the papers one day, a normal day,' he says. 'There had been nothing before and then, suddenly, "Capello has signed for Juve." Everyone was asking how it could be? I personally didn't think anything of it, really; that's football. We have to respect fans but this is a normal job like any other. If some boss somewhere in any job says, "Come with me, I'll give you more money and better prospects," you'd go, wouldn't you? Football is the same.

And Capello recognized that. Of course, in Italy, we had many people taking the moral high ground. But I don't think they had a case.'

Cannavaro is in the minority here. Yes, Capello's departure from Roma was on the cards. But to Juventus? The press helpfully went back into their archives and found what Capello had said about a possible move:

8 April 2003: 'I already said many times that I am not interested in joining Juventus, I have my own personal reasons for saying this.'
7 February 2004: 'I am not going to Juve. It's a lifestyle choice.'
19 February 2004: 'What do I have to say to convince you? Juve do not interest me. I don't find it a stimulating club. I am simply not interested. I respect their players and the Agnelli family, but, at my age, I need to find something intriguing.'

Capello knew that he had a lot of questions to answer. And, while he would have liked to avoid them and simply take some time off and then focus on his new club, he knew he had to face the press. Better to get it out of the way now than have it hanging over him when he joined up with Juventus for pre-season training. He had flown to his retreat in Marbella for a few days off and, from there, called a press conference in Madrid.

Why Madrid? To Capello it was purely a matter of convenience. Doing it in Rome would have been courting trouble. There were no direct flights between Marbella and Turin. And he definitely didn't want the world's media on his doorstep in Marbella. Madrid, an hour's flight away, was a neat choice. Alas, the press, especially in Rome, saw it as an act of cowardice. Capello was evidently too scared to own up to his decisions in his own country, he had to do it from Spain. Thus, on 5 June 2004 in the ballroom of a Madrid hotel, he gave his version of events. Outside, half a dozen Roma Ultras paraded around with a sign that read: 'Capello: Moggi's Whore.'

'I am not running away and I am not a traitor,' he said. 'Roma knew I was leaving. Why else would they have given me the fifteen-day window in which to talk to other clubs?'

Then he tried to explain how Juventus was not a challenge in February but suddenly became one in late May.

'It's true, I had said I wouldn't join Juventus because, at the time, they were doing well and leading them would not have been a challenge for me,' he went on. 'Now, however, it's different. Now it's a challenge for me. The fact is that, if instead of going to Juventus I had joined another club, I wouldn't need to be here to explain myself.'

When asked about Baldini and Moggi and being caught in the middle of a tempestuous relationship, he simply replied: 'Everybody looks out for themselves and their tribe. It's only normal.' Maybe so. Except people don't usually swap one tribe for another.

Capello was slaughtered via the airwaves for much of that summer. He was the ultimate Judas. Rumours circulated with abandon, the most popular one concerning a company car. He had just obtained a minivan from the club sponsor, Mazda (which he was planning to keep in Marbella, to ferry his grandchildren around) and it was rumoured that he'd never paid for it. Capello disputes the story and, in fact, some checking reveals that he did, in fact, pay for it. But the story took on a life of its own and, when he returned to Rome with Juventus, he was greeted by banners which read: 'Give us back the Mazda!'

For his part, Sensi was entirely nonchalant. 'Good riddance' was his attitude. Capello's departure had saved him a chunk of money. His daughter Rosella said she was upset only because Capello 'left without saying good-bye'.

Baldini was a different story. He felt hurt. You don't walk out after five years without fair warning. Not after what they had been through, the *scudetto* and the two second-place finishes, the roller-coaster relationship with Sensi, the battles to keep Cassano, Totti and the rest of the squad happy in the daily insanity that had been Roma. And, most of all, what did it mean that he was joining Juventus? Especially the Juventus of Moggi and Giraudo. Didn't they stand for what was wrong in the game?

On the very same day that Capello signed for Juventus, Umberto Agnelli passed away. He was the younger brother of Gianni, who had died the previous year. The Agnelli family are the closest Italy have to a functioning aristocracy. They embodied the Establishment, but it was a certain kind of Establishment, one based on industrial power and capitalism, rather than political cronyism. Italy was fascinated with them, especially Gianni, whose bons mots, sharp wit and ability to remain above the fray made him appear regal and statesmanlike. Even Juve's enemies had a weak spot for him. One anecdote illustrates the extent of Gianni's hold on the Italian psyche. The late 1970s were a turbulent time in Italy, with powerful unions, many with ties to the far left, lobbying hard for additional worker benefits. As Italy's leading industrialist, Gianni was naturally on the opposite side of the barricade and FIAT, Italy's largest company, was the natural theatre for such conflict. In the autumn of 1980 the unions called a general strike, shutting down FIAT's production plant for thirty-five days. It was broken neither by Thatcherite aggression, nor by police action. Instead, 40,000 FIAT employees took to the streets of Turin in a stunning 'counter-demonstration' which called for an end to the strike and a limit on the powers of the unions. It's unlikely that, had FIAT been led by anyone other than Gianni, such a counter-demonstration would have ever taken place. Umberto, while keeping a somewhat lower profile, was a continuation of that same line.

Alas, they had no natural successors. Gianni's son, Edoardo, showed no interest in the family business (including the football side), pursuing more esoteric fields like astrology and eastern religions, before committing suicide in 2000. Umberto's eldest son, Giovannino, did plan to take over FIAT, but he died of a rare form of cancer at the age of thirty-three in 1997.

By the late 1990s, both Umberto and Gianni had limited their involvement with the club. They were both ageing and in poor health. The next generation down of Agnellis – Umberto's grandson Andrea and Gianni's grandsons John and Lapo Elkann – were too young to take over and so, by the year 2000, Juventus was governed in every sense by what came to be known as 'La Triade' (the Triad): chief executive Antonio Giraudo, vice-president Roberto Bettega (Capello's old teammate from the Juve days) and Luciano Moggi, the sporting director.

Juve's critics took an instant dislike to them. The long-running conspiracy theories about the club's supposed hold on the 'Palazzo' had been around for several decades, but, without Gianni Agnelli as the public face of the club, they had intensified from the late 1990s. Juventus' image took a hit. There was a long inquiry into the club's use of legal pharmaceuticals to improve player performance. Juventus were ultimately cleared – and no Juve player ever failed a doping test – though the court found that prescription medication had been administered in large quantities.

Accusations of pro-Juventus bias on the part of referees became increasingly hysterical – some of them coming from none other than Capello. Moggi, always controversial, was accused of exercising undue and improper influence over the transfer market, not just at his own club, but at others as well.

Juve, like most successful clubs, were never liked by neutrals and fans of rival clubs. But, by that point, it had developed into full-blown hatred. Part of it had to do with the Triade themselves. Bettega was seen by many as arrogant and needlessly aggressive. Giraudo, always serious and unsmiling, looked like the apparatchik from hell. As for Moggi, well, to his enemies he was the devil incarnate.

The younger Agnellis were split on this point. Andrea was very close to the Triade, John and Lapo kept their distance. In fact, it was the outspoken Lapo who famously declared: 'We have an image problem. The Triade would do well to occasionally smile and show some grace. The fact that, of the three of them, Moggi is the most likeable, pretty much says it all.'

The obvious tension between Lapo (and to a lesser

degree John) and the Triade would ultimately play a huge part in the club's future. Perhaps sensing this, Capello inserted a very specific clause in his contract when he signed with Juventus: should any of the three members of the Triade leave the club for whatever reason, he too would be free to walk away. As they grew older Lapo and John would exert ever-greater power over the club. He had nothing against them, he just wanted to make sure he did not find himself in a situation he could not control.

To his enemies, Capello had found his perfect dimension at Juventus with the Triade. In the highly polarized world of Italian football, Juve's fiercest critics depicted the three as amoral bullies, arrogant and disdainful towards the weak, manipulative and secretive with the powerful, obsessed with just one thing: winning at all costs. Just like Capello. The difference, they felt, was that Moggi, Giraudo and Bettega were honest about their role as villains. At least they chose a path and stuck to it. Capello, on the other hand, was a turncoat, pretending to fight the good fight at Roma, then sneaking off to join the Evil Empire at the first opportunity.

It's hard to imagine exactly what was going on in Capello's mind. But a few things seem obvious. The first is that the situation at Roma had been unsustainable for several seasons, the working conditions were unacceptable. He stuck around because of his love of the city itself, his relationship with Baldini, a degree of affection for certain players, a desire to prove the critics wrong in his final season – and the fact that he had a highly lucrative contract. Those cynics who say that the last reason was the most important one miss one key point:

Capello took a hefty pay cut when he moved to Juventus.

So Capello was quite sure he did not betray Roma. Roma did not want him any longer. In fact, when he went to see Sensi just before the end of the season, and obtained the fifteen-day window in which he could leave the club without penalty, the Roma president was only too happy to grant it.

That part is easy enough. But what about the move to Juventus and joining forces with Moggi, Giraudo and Bettega? Weren't they his enemies? Hadn't he attacked Juventus and the 'Palazzo' at every opportunity while at Roma? Capello has explained that he has always defended the interests of whichever club employed him at the time. 'If I said certain things when I was at Roma it was because they served Roma's interests.'

Does this mean that he didn't believe the accusations and was simply making things up because it suited Roma's interests at the time? Or is it that he believed the accusations but, now that he has another employer, he has no reason to make them?

It's hard to determine what his real stance is. You'll just have to make up your own minds. The best hypothesis I could come up with is this: Capello truly believed that 'something' was going on with the powers-that-be and referees. But he did not know exactly what and, in many ways, it didn't matter. By taking on Juventus, he was serving Roma (and, in the process, himself: if Roma were getting a raw deal from officials, it obviously meant that any under-achievement was not entirely his fault). At the same time he viewed these mindgames as an essential part of football. And, because this is the way football is, there is nothing wrong in engaging in them and using every element you can find to gain an advantage. Nearly everybody tried to find an edge using those tactics, but Moggi was the master at it. That's all it was. So, if Capello believed these mindgames, that this 'exercise of power' was something everyone tried to do, what was the problem with joining forces with Moggi? Certainly, what emerges in all this is that he believed that the one true measure of a football man is silverware. Everything passes, trophies remain. How you get there – barring outright cheating – is irrelevant.

His behaviour towards Baldini when he left the club is even more difficult to explain, let alone justify. The pair had worked side by side for five years, they spent time together outside football, they created one of the most respected partnerships in the game. And then, all of a sudden, Capello ended it, without warning. If you buy Capello's version of events, he did tell Baldini – on two occasions – that he had been contacted by Juventus and that, seeing Baldini's lack of interest or reaction, he felt free to move ahead on his own.

That may be true and, strictly speaking, Capello may have been justified. But on a human level, it's hard to accept. What kind of person would behave like that? There are two theories. The first is that Capello is simply cold and heartless. He wanted to leave Roma (for, admittedly, legitimate reasons), he liked Baldini a lot, but Baldini was not as good at his job as Moggi was at his. So he swapped one for the other. And, in the process, exchanged Roma, with all their troubles, for a far more solid club like Juventus. Simple as that.

The other, put forth in *Corriere della Sera*, is that, in

reality, it was all a sham. Capello wanted to leave and told Baldini. Baldini accepted this, realized he wasn't going to change Capello's mind and made the best of it. Baldini would end up looking like the good guy (an image he has been keen to cultivate) and, in the process, would enjoy greater powers at the club, because whatever manager replaced Capello was going to be far more subordinated to Baldini.

Both are very cynical views, both paint one or the other in a very negative light. Both are, I suppose, plausible. My research, however, leads me to discount both. In writing this book I spoke to a lot of people who know both Capello and Baldini well, including some of their worst enemies. Not one believed the theory proposed by *Corriere*. Baldini simply isn't like that, they told me. Many more people, on the other hand, subscribe to the first version of events.

My guess is that Capello felt he had to tell Baldini, maybe even give him the opportunity to come along to Juve in some capacity. But it was not an easy conversation. And when Baldini barely registered his words, he did not press the issue further. Why force himself into that position? He had done his ethical duty in telling him. If Baldini didn't fully comprehend what he was saying, that was his problem. As for the meeting with Philippe Mexès and the plans for the following season, Capello was simply doing his job as a Roma employee until the very last minute. Just like any good professional.

Marcello Lippi – who, later that summer, would go on to manage the national side – had left behind a strong squad, albeit one which needed some tweaking. Juventus

Berlusconi and Capello: a formidable partnership. Milan won four championships in five years between 1991 and 1996, as well as the Champions League in 1994.

Capello was handed a selection headache in the summer of 1995. New signings (*from left*) Paulo Futre, Tomas Locatelli, George Weah and Roberto Baggio pose with Capello and Baresi.

28 April 1996. Milan stalwarts Billy Costacurta and Paolo Maldini (in vests) join in the celebrations of a fifteenth *scudetto*.

Left: All smiles at Real Madrid in the summer of 1996.

Below: He was sad to leave the Spanish capital and the return to the San Siro did not improve Capello's mood.

Bottom: Fans protest during the last home game of the 1997–98 season. Milan finished tenth. The banner translates as: 'And now may you remain alone with your shame'.

E ADESSO RIMANETE SOLI CON LA VOSTRA VERGOGNA

Roma president Francesco Sensi welcomes Capello back to the club in June 1999.

17 June 2001. Helping to get the fans off the pitch so Roma can win the title.

Right: Offering instructions during a 4–1 derby win.

Below: Capello didn't try to become friends with Totti but made him a champion.

Left and below: Adriano Galliani congratulates Capello, and the players celebrate as Juventus win two more championships in 2005 and 2006.

Below: It all ended badly, though. *(Left to right)*: Antonio Giraudo, Luciano Moggi, Capello and Andrea Agnelli.

Above and top right:
Returning to Madrid
in July 2006 and a
first encounter with
David Beckham.

Right and below:
Winning La Liga
again was 'a miracle',
according to Fabio
Cannavaro, and
Beckham joined
in the celebrations.

Above: 17 December 2007: FA chief executive Brian Barwick presents the new England manager. There was some predictable protest (*right*).

Below: The fans get on-message as a 2–1 win over Switzerland kicks off Capello's reign.

Above: The new team (*left to right*): Franco Baldini, Capello, Italo Galbiati and Stuart Pearce.

Michael Owen (*below*), Wayne Rooney (*right*) and match-winner Shaun Wright-Phillips (*bottom*) were just some of the attacking options open to Capello.

had finished third in 2003–04, after winning consecutive titles in the previous two seasons. The backbone of the team was replete with players who had been together for years: Gigi Buffon, Pavel Nedved and Lilian Thuram were entering their fourth season at the club, David Trezeguet his fifth, Gianluca Zambrotta his sixth and Alessandro Del Piero his eleventh season at the club. Plenty to work with there, but still room for improvement.

Typically, Capello began with the defence. Juventus had picked up Jonathan Zebina on a Bosman transfer (well before Capello signed), so there was one familiar face already in camp. But the defence needed stiffening up. And so he turned to Cannavaro, the man he had chased for so long while at Roma. Cannavaro had been through a very rough two years at Inter. Injuries and the fact that the club had tried to turn him into a rightback (a position to which he was clearly entirely unsuited) had turned his time at the San Siro into a nightmare. He kept his place with the national team (only just), but his stock was falling rapidly. Moggi leveraged this, together with the fact that Cannavaro wanted to leave and that Inter wanted to get rid of his wages to engineer an absolute sweetheart deal. He was traded, in a straight swap, for Fabian Carini, a 24-year-old backup goalkeeper. Carini had spent two years at Juve, without making a Serie A appearance, followed by another two years on loan in Belgium. And yet Moggi had persuaded Inter to rate him as highly as the Italy captain. Was there any wonder that Moggi was known as the 'king of the transfer market'?

In midfield, Capello asked for Emerson, his safest pair of hands, and Moggi duly delivered, acquiring him for

£11.5m plus midfielder Matteo Brighi. Capello was loath to raid his former club, but then he knew that Roma needed to raise some cash and – Totti and Cassano aside – Emerson and Walter Samuel (who was sold to Real Madrid) were the most saleable assets.

Up front, Capello got another player he had chased before and who had become something of a 'forbidden fruit': Zlatan Ibrahimovic. He had to wait until the very last minutes of the transfer window to get him – negotiations went on throughout the night – but the big Swede was now a Roma player.

'Capello asked for specific players to fill specific needs,' says Cannavaro. 'He is one of the best managers I have ever had, but, above all, he is very intelligent at reading the situation. At Juventus, he already had a strong bloc of players, he simply added one each to the defence, midfield and attack: me, Emerson and Ibrahimovic. And he did it while respecting the integrity of the side and the players who were already there.'

Indeed, Capello was very mindful that this job was different from the situation he faced at Roma or Real Madrid, having to overhaul an underachieving side; he was there to lead a team which had won its second straight title just a year earlier. Rather than effecting massive change it made more sense to work on what his predecessor, Lippi, had already built. In that sense, it was a similar situation to the one he found when he arrived at Milan back in 1991.

He did, however, fix a few things. Thuram, whom Lippi had switched to rightback, returned to central defence alongside Cannavaro. The Frenchman was an outstanding defender, but was clearly not a natural fullback: yes, he was fast, but he was neither a great crosser nor a gifted dribbler.

He knew he would face a tricky situation in attack, where he had three top-drawer strikers for just two slots. Playing all three was really not an option. Any kind of 3-4-3 or 4-3-3 formation would have forced him to leave out one or both of his gifted wingers, Pavel Nedved and Mauro Camoranesi, and he was not about to do that. Someone would have to miss out. But who? Trezeguet had scored 63 goals in 101 Serie A appearances, a total made all the more impressive when you consider that twenty of them were off the bench and he did not take free kicks or penalties. Tall and angular, he was the kind of striker who you might not see for long stretches, but who regularly popped up in the box to finish off chances.

Ibrahimovic was a player who fascinated Capello because of his unusual mix of skills. He was tall, strong and heavy, but had the talent, creativity and flair of a much smaller man. That summer, he had effectively knocked Italy out of the Euros with an outrageous goal, a flicked backheel from the edge of the box. Not many players would have even thought of such a finish, fewer would have attempted it and fewer still could have pulled it off. There were question marks about his attitude and his workrate, but Capello believed he had the makings of a superstar and that, if he could harness his talent, he would be unbeatable.

And then there was Del Piero, Juve's resident icon. He had been at the club since 1993 and the supporters adored him. He was quick and strong, but also blessed with subtle, creative skills, a selfless attitude and a sharp tactical mind. For a spell, he was arguably among the very best players in the world, but that was six years ago, before several serious injuries had slowed him down. Still, he was a living legend, and leaving him out seemed unthinkable. In some ways, he was Juventus' version of Totti, with one major difference: Totti was far and away the best player at the club, Del Piero wasn't.

Luckily for Capello, there was another difference. Juventus were not Roma. And Del Piero was not Totti. Taking on Totti in Rome meant taking on the local media and the club itself. Leave him out and you would face a battering from the press, plus the risk that Totti would turn the dressing room against you or, worse, seek solace from the president. And, at that point, you would be severely undermined. Leaving out Del Piero was a different proposition. Yes, the fans would still be angry. But Del Piero himself was quieter, more laid back, more prone to sulk silently than start a war. And, crucially, Capello knew he had the backing of Moggi and Giraudo, which meant that, unlike in Roma, he would not be getting flak from the club if he made an unpopular decision.

Capello rotated his strikers in the early part of the season, parcelling out playing time more or less equally. But an injury to Trezeguet in early October made his mind up for him: the French striker would be out until January, clearing the way for a Del Piero–Ibrahimovic partnership.

Juve went on a run of eight wins and one draw in their first nine games. Then came a setback at Reggina, in a game that would later surface in the Calciopoli inquiry, because Moggi stormed into the referee's dressing-room after the match and berated the referee. Still, Juve had played well, they had a four-point lead over Milan and things were looking up.

That January, Moggi and Capello pulled another rabbit out of the transfer hat, when they signed Adrian Mutu. The Romanian was a very gifted striker whom Chelsea had signed for £16.5m in the summer of 2003. After a dis-appointing first season at Stamford Bridge, he had grown depressed – an acrimonious split from the mother of his child didn't help – and in October of 2004 tested positive for cocaine. Chelsea voided his contract and he received a seven-month ban. Nobody would touch him. Capello realized that Mutu, at twenty-five, had plenty of football left in him. Moggi, who knew how to do his research, also understood that, far from having a drug habit, Mutu was an intelligent kid who had suffered a serious personal crisis (at one point he was referred to a psychiatrist) and had made some serious mistakes. Both agreed that he was worth taking a gamble on, particularly because he was a free agent. His ban would be in place until the end of the season, but it didn't matter: he was one for the future, a calculated risk with almost no downside.

Juve had been knocked out of the Coppa Italia by Atalanta, but, frankly, nobody cared. There were only two real objectives, the *scudetto* and the Champions League and they were on track for both.

They did not lose a game until a blip in early February, when they fell in consecutive matches to Sampdoria and Palermo. This allowed Milan to catch up and the two sides would remain neck-and-neck for most of the rest of the season. Trezeguet returned from injury and, because Nedved had in the meantime gone down, Capello experimented with a three-striker formation, putting Del Piero out on the left flank, with Trezeguet and Ibrahimovic up front. It lasted a few games, until Trezeguet went down again, but – while it had yet to be perfected – it did offer Capello a useful alternative should he ever need it.

They were flying in the Champions League, winning their group hands down with five wins (including two over Bayern Munich) and a draw, before eliminating Real Madrid in the first round of the knock-out stage (0–1 at the Bernabéu, 2–0 at home, with a goal from Marcelo Zalayeta in extra-time).

On 19 March 2005 Baldini reopened old wounds, citing Capello in a television interview. Baldini evidently felt there were things which needed to be said about Juventus, about Italian football and about Capello. He may have been on his own now, but he was not about to give up the struggle.

'The best clubs in Italy have, in recent years, scientifically put together a system designed to keep them on top for as long as possible,' he said. 'If you look at all the recent hot-button issues, from drugs, to referees, to TV rights, these are all just parts of a larger mosaic, a bigger system of power and control. In the last twelve years, Juventus and Milan have won five times each. Roma and Lazio just once and, to do it, they have had to go to the edge of bankruptcy.'

And then, he turned to Capello.

'Ours was a very important friendship, not just for our common interests outside football, such as theatre and art,' he said. 'We had the same thoughts on many issues, from referees, to doping, to GEA. In fact, he's the one who opened my eyes to a lot of things. Now, of course, we rarely speak. So much so that I have yet to ask him why he chose to go to Juventus.'

Baldini was fined for bringing the Italian league into disrepute, but his words found their mark. If what he was saying was true – and most neutrals tended to believe him – Capello's argument that he said things because they were 'in Roma's interest' looked weaker. It meant that either Baldini was incredibly gullible or that Capello had put his ethical concerns to one side when he joined Juventus.

Capello did not respond. Five days later, Baldini resigned his post at Roma and flew to South Africa for an extended break. God knew, he needed it.

The Champions League draw had served up the worst possible opponent for Juventus (and for UEFA): Liverpool. It wasn't so much that the Reds were some kind of powerhouse, it was the fact that this was to be the first time the two sides had faced each other since the Heysel disaster of 1985. And, to make matters worse, it was the twentieth anniversary of one of the darkest days in the history of European football.

On 29 May 1985, Juventus and Liverpool had squared off in the European Cup final at the antiquated Heysel Stadium in Brussels. It was a wholly inadequate venue, with poor policing, segregation and organization. Fighting broke out between the two sets of supporters, one group of Liverpool fans charging a neighbouring section, largely filled with Juventus supporters. As they retreated, they were crushed against a wall and a fence, both of which collapsed. Thirty-nine people, most of them Juve fans, lost their lives. Liverpool were exiled from European competition for six years.

Twenty years on, the tie was inevitably played in a highly charged atmosphere, both at Anfield (where the Liverpool supporters formed a mosaic of placards spelling out the word 'friendship') and at the Delle Alpi (where some Juve Ultras tried to attack the visiting supporters). Capello had done his best to insulate his squad from the surrounding controversy, but to no avail. This was just too big an occasion, one which was too emotional and volatile, especially since both clubs, as well as UEFA, had largely ignored it until then.

Juventus lost 2–1 at Anfield against an injury-riddled Liverpool. They hadn't played well and Capello felt that Del Piero had a goal unjustly disallowed for an imaginary offside. But it was a manageable result. Trezeguet was unavailable for the return leg, which made things simple: Ibrahimovic and Del Piero up front. At the back, because of the injury Zebina had picked up in the first leg, Thuram moved to rightback with the ageing Paulo Montero slotting in alongside Cannavaro. But it was in central midfield that Capello gambled, calling upon the 21-year-old Uruguayan Ruben Olivera (normally a winger) to partner Emerson.

Capello will, no doubt, point to the fact that Cannavaro hit the post, that Ibrahimovic fluffed an easy chance and that Juventus deserved more than the 0–0 which ultimately sent them out of the competition. Maybe so, but there is no question he got his tactics wrong on the night. Emerson, without a natural holding midfielder alongside him, was overrun. Liverpool's men out-thought and out-fought Juve. On nights like these only a moment of magic from one of the big guns – Ibrahimovic, Del Piero, Nedved – could have saved them: as it happened, all three had off nights.

'I think Capello got it wrong that day,' says Cannavaro. 'Emerson wasn't right physically. But when Capello is on a player's side, he backs them until his last dying breath. That's just the way he is. That season, at crucial moments, we lacked something, we always seemed to arrive at key matches with players injured or fatigued. That said, against Liverpool we were also unlucky.'

Capello was looking to bounce back in the league, but instead they fell 1–0 at home to Inter in an incredible game which Juve dominated but which saw Francesco Toldo, in the visitors' goal, pull off a string of outrageous saves. Milan won that day, pulling level on seventy points. Both sides won their next two outings, setting up a crucial head-to-head on 8 May at the San Siro. The season was to be decided right there.

The build-up, as ever, had been marked by controversy. Ibrahimovic had been banned for three games for head-butting an opponent against Inter. The referee had not seen the incident, but the TV cameras had and it was replayed endlessly, particularly on the Mediaset networks, owned by Silvio Berlusconi, Milan's owner. This annoyed Moggi no end. He felt that it was the insistent replays of the incident which had led to the three-match ban. And the paranoia continued a few weeks later, when the cameras tracked Del Piero after a substitution and showed him having angry words with someone out of view on the

Juve bench. On Berlusconi's networks they wondered if Capello himself was the target of Del Piero's bile. Moggi ordered a media blackout and Juventus issued a statement, alluding to the suspicious television coverage and pointing out that, unlike Milan, they did not own any TV networks. The implication was clear: Milan were using their media muscle to hurt Juve. 'We can't let some TV producer in an editing suite decide the title,' Moggi complained. In Rome, they chuckled, largely out of schadenfreude: maybe Moggi wasn't as powerful as Capello thought.

Again, without Ibrahimovic, it was Del Piero and Trezeguet up front. And the two combined brilliantly to score the only goal. Del Piero, stuck out on the left wing and pressed by an opponent, conjured up an improbable cross with a brilliant overhead kick, which the lightning-quick Trezeguet pounced upon, beating Dida with a powerful header. The lead was back to three points. Capello drew a huge sigh of relief.

The following week, the lead increased to five points, as Milan were held at Lecce and Juventus beat Parma 2–0. And, on the penultimate day of the season, Juve became champions without kicking a ball, as Milan were held to a draw at the San Siro by Palermo, forty-eight hours ahead of Juve's home tie with Livorno.

Capello had delivered again. It was his seventh league title in thirteen seasons of management, with four different clubs. And, just as he had done at Real and Milan, he had won it on his first attempt.

But he also knew there was work to be done. He could use some help at the back, for a start. Moggi duly delivered the Croatian Robert Kovac, signed on a Bosman from

Bayern Munich, the athletic Giorgio Chiellini, back from his loan spell at Fiorentina and Federico Balzaretti, a full-back signed from local rivals Torino.

His main concern, however, was in central midfield. Emerson needed a reliable partner. The Brazilian had tailed off badly as the season went on, but Capello was not concerned about that (with hindsight, this would probably be a mistake). He seemed to trust Emerson blindly, but he needed help. Juventus thus signed Patrick Vieira from Arsenal for £13.7m.

It was a lot of money for a 29-year-old who was coming off a mediocre season. Indeed, Arsenal were delighted: they got a good transfer fee, they got his wages off the books and, crucially, they freed up a spot for their rising star, Cesc Fabregas. Capello was happy too. Twenty-nine is not old in footballing years. Vieira was tall, strong, athletic and could deliver a pass. He still remembered being impressed with him as a teenager back at Milan ten years earlier. So what if he was coming off a bad season? When he was on song, he was one of the very best in the world at his position. Besides, Juventus wanted to win here and now. Even if they got just a few years out of him, it would be worth it.

The smile would be wiped off his face rather quickly. On 15 August 2005 Milan faced Juventus in a pre-season friendly. Juventus dominated early on, took the lead with Vieira, Ibrahimovic hit the post and then, thirteen minutes into the second half, after Milan's equalizer, Buffon injured his shoulder. Capello knew immediately it was serious and the verdict was confirmed by the club doctors: his goalkeeper would be out until December at the very earliest.

What to do? Juventus couldn't take a chance on dropping points in the first part of the season, they needed a top-drawer goalkeeper, but those cost money. Lots of money, particularly when there were just two weeks to go until the close of the transfer window.

Again, Moggi came through, thanks to a bit of lateral thinking. Milan had two senior goalkeepers, Dida and Christian Abbiati, a lanky Milanese, who had kept goal for three seasons before losing his place to the Brazilian international in 2002. Dida had been in sparkling form (a far cry from what he would become after losing his way in 2005), and it made sense to give him the starting job. But Abbiati was also a very good keeper, and had been capped several times for Italy. Milan were reluctant to sell him: after two seasons on the bench, they weren't going to get anything like market value. And so they loaned him to Genoa, who had just won promotion to the top flight. Except, around the time of Buffon's injury, Genoa were demoted to Serie C after their president, Enrico Preziosi, was found guilty of match-fixing. Abbiati's loan contract was voided and Moggi pounced. He offered to take Abbiati on loan.

Initially, Milan laughed him off. Buffon's injury was unfortunate, but, clearly, it was to Milan's advantage. Why would they want to help out a direct opponent by gifting them their second-string goalkeeper? Moggi was undeterred. He used every weapon in his arsenal. For a start, it would be very difficult for Milan to find Abbiati a club at this late stage. Second, Abbiati wanted to move. Third, it was in Milan's interest to put Abbiati in the shop window; if he performed well, there would be no shortage of takers at the end of the season. And what better shop window could there be than Juventus, especially since they were also involved in the Champions League? Finally, Buffon had been injured in a collision with Kaká, Milan's star player. While there was obviously no malice or intent in Kaká's challenge, the fact was that Milan were somehow responsible. Wouldn't it be a great PR move if they sent Abbiati to Juve to make up for it?

Somehow Moggi pulled off this audacious deal. Abbiati came on board within a few days of Buffon's injury and Capello breathed a huge sigh of relief. With a reliable goalkeeper in place, Juventus came out of the gates quickly, winning their first nine Serie A games of the season, while scoring eighteen and conceding just two. These weren't swashbuckling victories as much as a slow deliberate domination of the opposition.

'Our game is based on establishing a framework of discipline within which the individuals can express themselves,' Capello told *Gazzetta dello Sport* in October 2005. 'We are a very organized side, right up until the last third of the pitch, when we turn it over to the creativity and genius of our strikers.'

Indeed, Capello rotated his three front men as much as possible, though Ibrahimovic looked a notch above the other two. By that stage of the season, Trezeguet had lasted ninety minutes just twice and Del Piero only once. But it was a way of keeping them fresh and providing a change of pace when one came on for the other.

The previous summer Del Piero and Trezeguet had both wondered what Capello had in store for them. Del Piero started twenty-seven games, Trezeguet – partly due to injury – fourteen. But Capello managed to keep him in the fold.

'When Trezeguet was linked to a move because of the lack of playing time, I came out in public and demanded that he stay on,' Capello said. 'I put my own reputation into backing him. Why? Because in sport, confidence is extraordinarily important. I call it "unconscious adrenaline". I know from my own experience as a player how important it is to feel trusted. Some things have changed, this has not: no matter how talented a player, he will always need to feel that the manager is counting on him.'

Capello was helped by the fact that, unlike Roma, Juventus were better equipped to deal with controversy.

'At Juventus there is a whole structure in place which filters and amortizes problems,' he said. 'Elsewhere [i.e. Roma] I had to deal with everything myself. And that makes a big difference. Generally I try not to talk about individuals, because, frankly, the press is a minefield. If I criticize a player I come across as looking for alibis or excuses for myself. If I praise a player I run the risk of making his teammates jealous. What I have to always remember is that a manager is one person taking on twenty-five players. The manager is constantly being observed by his players who are constantly looking for inconsistencies and chinks in his armour.'

Earlier that month Capello participated in what some described as the television event of the season: a face-to-face interview between himself and Baldini. That year, with time on his hands, Baldini had started doing a series of one-off 'chats' with people in the game. The format was simple, just some cameras, a microphone and Baldini talking football with a manager or a club official. It was informal and engaging. When the idea to put him in front of Capello was raised, few believed it could be pulled off.

But, on 13 October 2005, there they were on Italian TV screens, sitting on red sofas, inches away from each other. Capello had a perma-grin on his face, Baldini smiled nervously. Everyone wondered how the delicate issue of their falling out would be raised. They didn't have long to wait.

Capello cut to the chase immediately: 'You know, I think I'm going to take advantage of the fact that you're right here to set the record straight. You were the only one who knew everything . . . You knew everything.'

On the video, Baldini looks flustered. His facial features freeze, mouth half open. He certainly looked like a man who was not expecting this.

'Ummm . . . I would dispute that . . .' Baldini says. 'I didn't quite know much of anything . . .'

Capello jumps in, his voice rising ever so slightly, the pace of his words picking up. 'I told you on [the] Tuesday when we talked with Mexès,' he insists. 'I had received a phone call the night before. I told you that I was meeting Juve that Friday. And that it was likely that I would leave.'

Baldini stops for a beat or two. He looks on the defensive. 'Well, I figured you were leaving, but . . .'

Perhaps realizing there was no point in flogging a dead horse, Baldini moves the interview on. Capello nevertheless offers up some revealing nuggets. 'I keep relationships with people who I think are worthwhile'; 'When a relationship ends, it ends. Continuing to work becomes very difficult, no matter how creative or imaginative you try to be'; and, interestingly: 'I've never wanted to manage Italy. But I've always had a thing for England. I've come close, I've hit the post a few times. And, when I had a chance to score in front of an open goal, I knew it wasn't the right time.'

Prescient words.

Week 10 of the Serie A season saw the top-of-the-table clash everyone was waiting for: Milan v Juventus at the San Siro. The *rossoneri* were five points back, but were seen as the only side capable of stopping Juve's run. And they did. By half-time Clarence Seedorf, Kaká and Andrea Pirlo had put the home side three-up. Trezeguet scored a great goal in the second half to make it 3–1, but that was it. Milan had dominated them. A warning light for Capello? Hardly.

'After this game I am now 100 per cent convinced that we will again win the title this year,' he said in the post-match interview. Not exactly what you would expect after a resounding defeat. The press were shocked, the players too.

'Well, he came and told us, the players first,' recalls Cannavaro. 'When he said that, many looked at him like he was mad. We just lost 3–1 to Milan and he tells us this? But he wanted us to know that he had seen things he liked. He saw that we were a team, a group. We didn't give up. I think that's why he said it, to let us know that he believed in us.'

Of course, praise is something that needs to be doled out in the right doses. Do it too often and players become overconfident. Do it too seldom and they'll think you don't believe in them. It doesn't take a genius to figure this out. But it does take, if not a genius, certainly someone with a gift for man-management, to know exactly when to dish it out.

Capello's words also sent a clear message, one of sporting intimidation: we're going to win it, there is nothing you can do. And it was an important one to send, given what was happening with Moggi and Giraudo at the time. In September of that year, late one night, Moggi had been seen visiting Berlusconi at his estate in Arcore, some twenty-five miles outside Milan. He stayed for more than an hour, and the contents of their conversation remain private. The media speculated that the pair had hatched a secret plot with far-ranging implications. Moggi (and possibly Giraudo) would leave Juventus and join forces with Berlusconi at Milan (necessarily casting doubt on Galliani's future). As shocking about-turns went, this one was on a par with Capello's move to Juventus.

It's hard to say where this would have left Capello. It seems unlikely that Milan would have axed Ancelotti to make way for what would have been his third stint at Milan. A more plausible scenario would have been Moggi and Giraudo setting up shop at Milan, with Capello left behind at Juve. Some gratitude, huh?

Of course, we don't know what Berlusconi and Moggi said to each other. And it's unclear whether Capello knew: if he did, he only knew what Moggi (or, possibly, Berlusconi) told him. Maybe they just had a game of cards or traded jokes and there was no devious plot. But maybe there was. After all, the young Agnelli heirs, John and Lapo, did not have much love for the Triade. Were they planning to push them out? This was Italian football, circa 2005, a place where cloaks and daggers, suspicion and conspiracy, were rife. Was it so surprising then that Capello had taken countermeasures when he signed for Juve, insisting that, if even one member of the Triade left the club, he too would be free to leave?

The prediction Capello made after the Milan defeat proved accurate. Juventus surged ahead in the league, taking forty of a possible forty-eight points over the next four months while racing through the group stage of the Champions League, winning five of six.

They were drawn with Werder Bremen in Europe in what would prove to be a memorable two legs. Juventus gave up a first-half goal in Bremen, before storming back to take a 2–1 lead. Bremen, one of the more attacking sides in Europe, threw everything forward as Capello nervously counted down the minutes. With Zambrotta, Zebina and Chiellini all unavailable – reserve midfielder Manuele Blasi was deployed as an emergency rightback – Juventus took a battering and, incredibly, capitulated. The Germans equalized three minutes from time, before Johan Micoud conjured up an improbable winner.

The return leg saw Werder Bremen take the lead after thirteen minutes. Trezeguet equalized midway through the second half and Juve went looking for the winner, but all too often found themselves on the back foot. Werder defended high up the pitch, applied the offside trap with abandon and aggressively put bodies in the box. Capello's men struggled to find any openings (later, one former Juve scout would tell me that Capello had ignored his report on the opponents). They were saved two minutes from time when Werder goalkeeper Tim Wiese spilled a pedestrian ball into the box. Emerson – alerted by Fabio Cannavaro's cries of 'Puma! Puma!' – realized the ball was loose and tapped it into the back of the net. Juve were through. But what a scare.

If luck had, to some degree, helped Juve along against Werder Bremen, it ran out in the quarter-final against Arsenal. The Gunners dominated, Capello again appearing to get his tactics wrong. Mutu, deployed on the flank, was impalpable, Emerson looked out of gas, Vieira was crushed by the man who had replaced him in the Arsenal midfield, a gifted teenager named Cesc Fabregas. Juve didn't shoot on goal until six minutes from time, when Mauro Camoranesi fired wide. Three minutes later, however, Camoranesi himself was sent off and, less than ninety seconds after that, Zebina was also given his marching orders. Arsenal had won, 2–0.

The critics piled in. They said Capello had built a side which peaked too early. That playing with Trezeguet, when he wasn't getting service, was like playing with ten men. That Vieira and Thuram were finished. That keeping Del Piero on the bench was a crime born of Capello's arrogance and sense of omnipotence. That he was losing his grip on the dressing room.

That weekend, many felt vindicated. Juventus were held to a scoreless draw by Treviso, who were bottom of the table. What's worse, as Ibrahimovic was substituted, he directed some choice words at Capello, inevitably picked up by the TV cameras, who replayed them endlessly.

Capello's reaction? Nothing. 'Zlatan was jumpy and irritable, that's why he came off,' he said. 'There was no row. I deny it in the strongest possible terms. And, besides, everything is forgotten now.'

It was shades of what occasionally happened at Roma. Capello knew when to crack the whip and when to let things slide. But his reaction did not go down well with certain members of his squad. It was one thing to be understanding towards outstanding players. Quite another to put up with blatant insubordination. Especially when, suffering on the bench, was a true Juve hero like Del Piero. Whenever things got rough for Juventus, the Ultras began calling his name, regardless of whether he was on the pitch or not. It was more than just appreciation. It was, indirectly, a criticism of Capello. Many of them had not even been born when Capello led Juventus to three Italian titles as a player; they thought of him as an outsider, a mercenary tainted by his years at Milan and Roma.

Del Piero, not one to make waves, kept his counsel during Capello's tenure. But in August 2006 he would be brutally honest about his time under Capello's tutelage. 'He's overrated,' he told *Gazzetta dello Sport*. 'Yes, it was the kind of situation which could have pushed me to ask for a transfer. The relationship with him was not gratifying. We had different points of view on just about everything. And I disagree that his man-management was as good as everyone says.'

Brutal words from a player who most of the time delivers the blandest of pronouncements. But such were his feelings for Capello. And, in that light, it's no surprise that Del Piero's supporters seized every opportunity to invoke their hero, while lambasting Capello.

It happened again during the return leg against Arsenal.

Scarcely ten minutes in, the Del Piero chants began. This was ridiculous – he wasn't even involved that night, having picked up an injury ten days earlier against Roma. Capello didn't dwell on it for long. He had to watch his side be picked apart by Arsenal. It finished 0–0, but the Gunners' domination was absolute. Not because they created loads of chances, but because Juventus, who had to make up two goals, were constantly pushed back, physically and athletically overpowered and, basically, toothless. 'What was once called "control", can now only be called "impotence",' wrote one newspaper. Juventus went out in the meekest way. They didn't crash and burn, they fizzled and faded away.

Once again, just as in Rome, despite delivering success, Capello was an outsider. And, to make matters worse, an outsider at odds with the local hero. Outwardly, again, he did not care. Inwardly, we can only speculate, but, my guess is that he was bothered by the fact that he could not rationalize the fans' anger. Juventus had won one title and were on their way to their second in two years. Yes, they would have liked to see Del Piero on the pitch. But, one of the guys keeping him out of the side was Trezeguet, one of the most natural goalscorers around, a man who would go on to notch forty-three goals in sixty-five appearances in all competitions under Capello. The other, Ibrahimovic, was the greatest talent Juve had seen since Zinedine Zidane. Furthermore, his approach had obviously worked. And Del Piero had been productive, even in his more limited role: in his two seasons with Capello he would score thirty-seven goals in all competitions. Those were cold, hard numbers, not spin. What more did they want from him?

He was also evaluating his future in light of the rise of Lapo and John Elkann. While he was not subjected to the little barbs that Lapo would occasionally throw at the Triade, he was not particularly close to them. Indeed, he was closer to their cousin, Andrea Agnelli, just as he had been closer to Andrea's grandfather Umberto, than their grandfather, the legendary Gianni. Lapo was often going on about wanting to make Juventus more likeable, more user-friendly, more entertaining. It was hard not to see it as a kind of coded language. Likeable, user-friendly, entertaining – these were not terms people associated with Capello. There were also strong suggestions that the club would be looking to curb their spending: under Giraudo, they had made a small profit most years, except for the last two. Was there a round of belt-tightening on the horizon? After what he'd been through at Roma, it was the last thing he needed.

And then there was this business with Moggi and the meeting with Berlusconi: Capello hadn't heard anything developing from it (and he liked to think he was keeping his ear close to the ground), but, with Moggi, you never knew.

He decided therefore that, come the end of the season, he would move on, find another club, probably abroad. Real Madrid were holding presidential elections; one of the candidates would, no doubt, be in touch, especially since they were once again screwing up. Maybe Inter would come back in for him, or perhaps a Premier League side. Who knew? The point was, it was time to leave.

He communicated his intentions to Moggi and Giraudo. They told him to hang in there, that they ought to first focus on winning the title. But, they said, if he wanted to leave at the end of the season, they would not stand in his way. Once again, as he had done at Milan, Roma and Real Madrid, Capello had his 'get out of jail free' card.

Immediately after being knocked out of the Champions League, Juventus had a nine-point lead over Milan in Serie A with just six games to go – surely an insurmountable margin. But Juve were spent. Week after week they dropped points while Milan just kept on winning. Juventus drew their next three games, while Milan won theirs. All of a sudden it was down to just three.

On the last day of April, thirty-five days after their last victory, Juventus returned to their winning ways, defeating Siena away, 3–0. Milan also won, but at least the gap remained at three points, with just two games to go. For the players, it was a massive relief. In the build-up to the game, Capello had to work hard to dispel the negativity that had risen among the ranks. At one stage Ibrahimovic and Vieira had nearly come to blows in training, a heavy-weight clash which forced several teammates to steam in to separate the two big men. Worst of all, it happened in plain view of the press. Ibrahimovic, in particular, had become a problem: this was his third public spat in the past few months (previously he had insulted Capello in Treviso and slapped Zebina in the face). Moggi spun the line that there was a 'healthy intensity' at the club and that the row was actually positive. Few bought into that theory. It became clear that something was needed to defuse the tension.

The next day, with the press looking on, it looked as if history was repeating itself. This time, the combatants were somewhat more improbable. Del Piero and Cannavaro squared up in the middle of the pitch. Insults flew, there were a few shoves. Just as teammates rushed in to break it up, Cannavaro and Del Piero both burst out laughing hysterically. It had all been a set-up, a fake fight meant to relieve some of the tension. And it worked. Capello looked on and chuckled. This was what he meant when he talked about taking a step back and letting the team handle certain situations themselves.

The joy of the Siena victory lasted five days. On 2 May 2006, the Calciopoli scandal broke. Prosecutors had leaked entire volumes of wiretapped transcripts of suspicious phone calls involving Moggi and a variety of powerful figures in the Italian game, including heads of the FA, the referees' association and match officials themselves. The contents were shocking and it soon became clear that it would be bad, very bad. Especially for Juventus.

'We were in Turin when it all came out in the press,' recalls Cannavaro. 'Capello, Moggi, Giraudo and Bettega got us together and talked to us about it. They told us what was going to appear in the press, what was likely to happen, how people would jump on it, because Juventus is a club that everyone loves to hate and wants to hammer as much as they can. They told us what to expect. There were two games left and they said, "Let's finish the league and then we will explain what is going on . . . but don't worry, everything will be sorted out." '

It soon became clear that, contrary to what the players had been told, very little would be 'sorted out', at least from Juve's perspective. It was obvious to Capello too. It wasn't just the evidence – reams of transcripts which appeared daily in the newspapers – it was the gathering mood in the country. This was going to be huge. But there were two games left to play and a *scudetto* to win.

Palermo were the visitors at the Delle Alpi that Sunday. As the teams took to the pitch, the TV cameras focused on the Triade, in what would be their final appearance at the stadium. When Nedved opened the scoring after half an hour, each reacted differently. Giraudo jumped up with joy and shook his fist angrily. Bettega, holding some kind of giant handkerchief, appeared to be crying. Moggi stared ahead, unblinking, expressionless, inscrutable. Rumours were already rife that Lapo and John Elkann, the young Agnellis, would jettison the Triade. It finished 2–1 and, given Milan's victory away to Parma, everything was postponed to the final week of the season.

The following Wednesday the club's entire board of directors stood down, including Moggi and Giraudo. Any hope that the owners were going to stand by the Triade, fight the allegations and make the nightmare go away vanished.

The final act of the season pitted Juventus against Reggina in a neutral venue, Bari. A draw was sufficient, but Juventus won 2–0. Del Piero, scorer of the second, was feted, as were most of the players and even Moggi. Capello got nothing; the news that he was leaving had made it into the press, and the fans viewed him as a traitor.

He didn't care. Under his guidance, Juventus had been in first place for two whole years, seventy-six games. They had won two titles, losing just five matches along the way, while winning fifty-three. He now had won eight league titles in fourteen seasons. He had done his job and delivered as promised.

After the match, Moggi, who until that moment had kept his silence, addressed the cameras. 'They destroyed my soul. This is no longer my world,' he said, expressionless, half-man, half-corpse.

Thus began the most intense and incredible summer in the history of Italian football. A word of explanation about the scandal. It stemmed from an investigation into the activities of GEA, following a complaint from some agents who claimed their clients had been intimidated into joining the agency run by Moggi's son. As a result, magistrates authorized the wiretapping of hundreds of mobile phones. What emerged, according to prosecutors, was a web of influence where favours were traded as currency, with Moggi at the top of the pyramid.

Moggi would regularly phone anyone who mattered in the Italian game and proceed to lobby, cajole, coax, sweet-talk . . . whatever was needed to help Juventus. This could mean trying to influence the selection of a referee, perhaps trying to get a certain official – whom he believed might be more desirable for Juventus, either because of his officiating style or because he was more prone to 'psychological subjection' – to referee a certain match. Or, indeed, the opposite, he might try to avoid certain officials (as a general rule of thumb, if you're stronger than your opponent, you want the best possible referee; if your opponent is better, you're better off taking your chances with a more erratic official).

But it didn't end there. In his book *Un Calcio al Cuore* ('A Kick to the Heart'), Moggi says he made or received

400 phone calls a day. He was constantly working on his web of contacts. He might arrange a favour for someone, perhaps facilitating the loan of a player between two clubs with whom he was not involved but who, he knew, would one day owe Juventus a favour. Or ring up friendly journalists, to try and generate more pro-Juve coverage. Or, indeed, speak to the producers of television shows, getting them to highlight a certain referee's mistakes (if he was on Moggi's black list) or, perhaps, praise a certain referee (if Moggi wanted to build him up and – perhaps – be owed a favour one day).

It's important to stress that not a single penny changed hands, so even the term match-fixing is inaccurate. Influence-peddling is closer to the mark. Moggi's power stemmed from his tireless lobbying and from the perception that he was this all-powerful force orchestrating everything behind the scenes. It didn't really matter if this was actually the case or not. The aura of power around him became something of a self-fulfilling prophecy, allowing him to obtain and dole out favours, all of which would, one day, add up.

I spent several hours with Moggi in writing this book. He agreed to talk to me off the record about Capello's two seasons at Juventus and their relationship. From the moment he arrived, it was obvious he was conveying a certain image. And this was *after* his fall from grace.

I met him in Milan, in April 2008, outside the offices of *Libero*, a newspaper for whom he writes a column. A large dark SUV pulled up, straight on to the pavement. Out came Moggi, accompanied by a thirtysomething guy carrying his computer bag and two cellphones (presumably

Moggi's) and a third man, in his fifties, wearing sunglasses and a pin-striped suit. As we made our way into the office, everyone we met stopped to greet him with an obsequiousness I would have never expected. They called him *direttore* ('director', although by this point he was director of nothing), laughed at his jokes, hung on his every word. He oozed power from every pore, the kind of power that comes not from privilege, but from knowledge.

Moggi, in his book, freely admits that accumulating knowledge and influence was at the heart of his success. And he freely concedes that he is guilty as charged with one of the two violations that the Italian FA slapped on him: Article 1, which refers to unsporting and unethical conduct. He knew that ringing up FA officials and referee selectors was unethical and, under the rules of the Italian FA, illegal. But, he writes, everybody did it (in this, he is not far wide of the mark: Milan, Fiorentina, Lazio, Reggina and Arezzo were also found guilty). The difference was that he was better at it than others. And, while it may have been unethical, it was something he felt he needed to do to protect himself and Juventus: Milan, he writes, controlled sections of the media via Berlusconi's TV networks and national newspaper, *Il Giornale*; Roma did too – apparently because RAI, the state broadcaster, is packed with Roma fans; and Inter had links with Telecom, Italy's telephone provider and therefore was ideally placed to spy on everyone (the fact that Guido Rossi, a former Telecom executive, had been a member of Inter's board of directors and, later, interim head of the Italian FA when Juventus were found guilty, is part of his conspiracy theory). You can buy into his theory, but only up to a point: if Roma and Inter were so powerful, so threatening that they needed to be halted via unethical means, why had they won just one league title between them in the past fourteen seasons?

But what Moggi steadfastly denies is the second charge against him, Article 6, which involves actually influencing the outcome of matches. Here, his case is based on the fact that just one referee was actually found guilty of allowing himself to be influenced (Massimo De Santis, who actually was so bad that his officiating tended to hurt Juventus more than help them), and that prosecutors could not come up with any concrete, specific evidence.

You can make up your own mind here and decide for yourself to what degree Moggi's 'lobbying' and 'influence-peddling' constitute a criminal act deserving to be punished with relegation (and a hefty points penalty). In my mind, the equally serious charge against him – which was not a part of the Calciopoli scandal – is the conflict of interest involving GEA and the things the agency did. Such a situation should never have been allowed in a normal country (Normal? Who said Italy was normal?) and it's obvious that its very existence overstepped the bounds of common sense and best practice. That said, the people who run football in Italy allowed its creation and its existence for five long years: from the Moggis' perspective, even if it might have been ethically dubious, if the authorities allowed it to operate, why shouldn't they take advantage?

The big issue here is how much Capello knew about all this and to what degree he was involved. From my perspective, the fact that in thousands of hours of taped telephone conversations there isn't a single one implicating him in any way (or even suggesting that he knew the extent of Moggi's lobbying) rather seals the deal. He wasn't involved.

But did he know what Moggi and Giraudo were doing? And did he think it was unethical or illegal? And what does he think now?

The difficult thing for Capello is that, at Roma, he had been one of Juve's biggest accusers, which means that he either knew something was going on or was simply making everything up. In fact, some of his accusations were laid out quite neatly in the interview he granted *Corriere dello Sport* back on 7 October 2002, when he warned about the dangers of GEA and the conflict of interest.

At the GEA trial in March 2008, Capello testified that he was not aware of anything and, in fact, had only a fuzzy idea of what GEA actually did and who was in it. This, of course, directly contradicts the October 2002 interview, which is why the prosecutor asked that he be charged with perjury and obstruction of justice. From my perspective that was a major blunder on his part. Whether the 'I don't remember' defence was his idea or his lawyers', it was a very ill-advised move. It made him look like someone who had something to hide.

Having spoken to a number of people who were around Juventus at the time (and, before that, at Roma), I suspect that Capello knew that Moggi exerted his influence over anyone he could. What he probably did not know was how great that influence allegedly was, or, at least, how great an influence the prosecutors would believe it was. What is undeniable is that he did not want to know. As he said several times, 'different clubs operate in different ways'. This was not his department, it had nothing to do with him. Sometimes, as the saying goes, it's best not to know how the sausage is made. And, frankly, given his personality, he could never have done what Moggi did: it's impossible to imagine Capello, a guy who is curt on the phone to everyone, taking and making 400 calls a day in some kind of diplomatic lobbying effort.

Beyond that, to this day, Capello believes that Moggi's main crime was 'superficiality', as he told *Gazzetta dello Sport* in late May 2008. Having lots of friends and cultivating lots of relationships is not a crime, though it's not something Capello says he would do, partly because he is not cut out for it, and partly because the way it was done was unethical, as Moggi himself admitted. But when it comes to suggesting that Juventus cheated and that the two titles he had delivered were in any way helped along by what Moggi may have done behind the scenes, Capello is adamant.

'We won those on the pitch, they can't be taken away from us, as far as I'm concerned,' he told *Gazzetta*. 'The reality is that there is a witch-hunt, a concerted campaign against Juventus. I'm not suggesting mistakes were not made and that people shouldn't be punished. But why punish the club and the players?'

The Italian FA's disciplinary committee saw things rather differently. Juventus were stripped of both titles, relegated to Serie B and slapped with a nine-point penalty. Fiorentina, Lazio and Milan were docked thirty points for the 2005–06 season (which for all but the latter meant no European football), plus an additional fifteen points, three points and nine points respectively in 2006–07. Giraudo and Moggi were banned for five years, Galliani received five months.

'It wasn't fair because we had worked really hard and we had won the league because we were better than Milan, Inter, Roma and everyone else,' says Cannavaro, who still has his medals at home: nobody asked that he give them back. 'Just look at the World Cup final [in 2006]. Ten of the players involved were from Juventus. I'm glad it worked out that way, because it proved that we won because we were good, not because of Calciopoli. For two years we worked hard, we fought, we gave everything on the pitch and then, at the end, they take it away and say: "No, you cheated." Well, I didn't cheat. Neither did my teammates or the coaching staff. So, of course, we were angry.'

Capello was angry too. He offered words of support for the Triade – he wasn't going to turn his back on his friends – he knew that Moggi and Giraudo were in for some tough times. The sporting trial had concluded, now they had to face not one, but two criminal proceedings. One was the GEA trial in Naples, the other a sporting fraud trial in Rome.

Which brings me to one of the enduring mysteries of Capello: one which, after more than a hundred interviews and copious amounts of research, I still haven't fully figured out. How does Capello reconcile his friendship with Moggi with his day-to-day relationship with Baldini?

Moggi and Baldini are polar opposites and, not co-incidentally, there is a deep and public loathing between the two. And it's not just for show. In the spring of 2008,

Baldini testified at the GEA trial. During his testimony, Moggi, who was in the dock, made what the judge later described as a threatening gesture.

'Luciano, calm down,' Baldini said, interrupting his testimony. 'You've got eighteen lawyers looking after you . . . Leave me alone . . .' The judge warned Moggi and threatened to expel him from the courtroom. How can two people like that co-exist in the affections of a single man?

Capello would probably say that his relationship with one is entirely separate from his rapport with the other. It's entirely normal to have two friends who may not like each other. He doesn't judge them, he appreciates their good qualities, accepts the bad ones (largely because they don't affect him) and focuses on the common ground he has with each. Plus, he has known them for years and is loyal to his friends.

I find this explanation difficult to understand. Evidently, neither Baldini nor Moggi ever presented Capello with an ultimatum of having to choose between them; neither took a page out of George W. Bush's book and said: 'You're either with me or against me.' So I posed the question to people who know all three of them. I weighed up my own experiences in dealing with them. And I still can't find a satisfactory explanation. But I do have some interesting theories from various people.

'Baldini and Moggi are like those little cartoon angels and devils on Capello's shoulder,' one person told me. They represent 'the light and dark sides of life for Capello'; and 'Sometimes they swap roles, though obviously, most of the time, you can guess who plays the devil part. Capello simply walks between them.'

Another had a rather more biblical interpretation: 'Capello represents humanity. Moggi is temptation, earthly values, cynicism, materialism. Baldini is the Christ figure who comes down to Earth to redeem Capello. And, of course, like any self-respecting Christ, Baldini suffers and is crucified. But, ultimately, he may well rise again and lead Capello to salvation. Though that has not happened yet.'

This may have been said with tongue in cheek, but maybe there is a kernel of truth in it. And I can see why Capello would enjoy working with Moggi and Baldini on a professional level. Both are among the very best at what they do. And Capello respects and values competence immensely. I can also see why he would choose to spend time with Baldini, a guy who shares many of his interests outside football, from theatre to travel to art. But what does he get from hanging out with Moggi? Yes, he's obviously clever and can be funny and witty, but he's not the kind of person with whom Capello would discuss Kandinsky or Stoppard or pre-Colombian archaeology.

Perhaps the answer is this: Baldini represents the individual, the Renaissance Man, the humanist search for individual self-improvement, Moggi embodies the system, tribalism, compromise, the basic concept that the whole can be greater than the sum of its parts. Or maybe I'm just talking out of my backside. You be the judge.

CHAPTER 15

Sometimes Winning Is Not Enough

As the Juventus empire crumbled, Capello retreated, going about as far away from Turin as you can possibly go, without actually leaving Italy. He withdrew to his holiday home on Pantelleria, the volcanic island south of Sicily. He was still officially the Juve manager, though he had the get-out clause stashed away and ready for use. And, of course, Moggi and Giraudo knew of his intention to leave, though at this stage, they obviously had far bigger fish to fry.

Inter had contacted him back in April, before the Calciopoli scandal even broke and with Juve still in the title race. Evidently they had got wind that things were changing in Turin and that, perhaps, Capello would be amenable to a move. He wasn't thrilled with the idea, but dutifully met Massimo Moratti, the Inter chairman.

'Moratti asked me lots of questions, but then, just before the last week of the season, he told me he wasn't going to take things further,' Capello told *Gazzetta dello Sport* on 29 May 2008. 'He said that it was because of the

Calciopoli scandal, which, frankly, was just an excuse. In reality, I think that Moratti secretly wants to manage the club himself. So I gave him some advice. And I gave it for free, even though normally I like to get paid when I advise people. But I didn't mind. It feels good to be wanted and to have someone tell you how great you are.'

By my reckoning, it was at least the fourth time that Moratti had approached Capello. Clearly, the two just didn't click. The way Capello dismissed Moratti – his words imply that what the Inter president wanted was a 'yes-man' – suggested what many suspected: in his next job, he wanted wide-ranging powers. He wanted a place that would be remembered as 'Capello's club', something which he never really had. Juventus, in the time he was there, was always Moggi's domain. At Roma he found himself in a financial straitjacket. At Real, the players had already been bought for him when he arrived. And Milan would always be identified with Berlusconi and Galliani, no matter how many *scudetti* he delivered.

Meanwhile, Juventus' sentence had yet to be determined, but the owners prepared for the worst. They nominated an emergency administrator, Carlo Sant'Albano, to lay the foundations for the club's rebirth, starting with the sporting director. The fact that the first man they turned to was none other than Franco Baldini settled any doubt that they truly wanted to break with the past. Baldini had been the main accuser of the Triade, of the power structure in the Italian game, of the way the big clubs divided up the TV pie, leaving nothing but crumbs for the rest. By turning to him, they were sending a clear signal: the Triade era was over and, with it, Capello as well.

Baldini turned the job down, showing great honesty: 'How could I have taken it? I believe the way television rights are divided in Serie A is one of the greatest evils in our game. But if I had accepted the Juventus job, it would have meant serving Juventus' interests and that, in turn, would have meant maintaining the status quo on so many things, including TV rights. I could not in good conscience do that.'

Besides, Baldini had another option, one which appeared, at first, distinctly far-fetched. He received a call from Predrag Mijatovic, the former Yugoslavia international who, coincidentally, had been a key part of Capello's Liga-winning side in 1996–97. After retiring from football, Mijatovic had settled in Spain, working as a player agent. He told Baldini that he had joined forces with a lawyer by the name of Ramón Calderón, a candidate for the presidency of Real Madrid. Elections were being held in early July and Calderón had asked Mijatovic to help his campaign. Did Baldini want to lend a hand?

Why not? Baldini thought. It was something different, and, besides, he didn't have much else to do at the time. Running for Real Madrid president basically means putting together an elaborate slate of election promises and convincing the electorate that you're the man to deliver them. Just as Florentino Pérez's promise of delivering Luis Figo from arch-rival Barcelona had propelled him to an election win in 2000, the five candidates in 2006 jockeyed to assemble the most attractive manifesto, beginning, of course, with the manager.

Juan Miguel Villar Mir, the early frontrunner, said he had a commitment from Arsène Wenger, the Arsenal boss.

Juan Palacio, another strong candidate, promised to bring back the good times with a combination of Vicente Del Bosque and José Antonio Camacho. Del Bosque was also the choice of Lorenzo Sanz, who, of course, had been president during Capello's Liga win of 1996–97, while the outsider Arturo Baldasano said he would plump for Sven-Göran Eriksson. As for Calderón, his man was Bernd Schuster.

And that was a bit of a problem for Mijatovic. Schuster had been a phenomenal player, but, as a manager, he hadn't made any waves until a few months earlier, when he took little Getafe, in just their second season in the top flight, to ninth place. He earned plaudits for their style and organization, but, frankly, Mijatovic knew that Schuster was not exactly a marquee name. And so he convinced Calderón to take a different route: Capello.

In late May Calderón, Mijatovic and Baldini flew out to Pantelleria to talk to Capello. It was the first time in two years that Baldini met Capello in a professional capacity. Over some seafood and a few bottles of wine, they laid out Calderón's plans for the club. Capello listened, but, most of all, he enjoyed himself. He had missed Baldini's company, the air was warm, the breeze was sweet, the food was good and the wine flowed. He told them he would be delighted to go back to Madrid and laid out what he expected in return. But he stopped short of a full-blown commitment. He wanted to listen to other offers.

Indeed, Capello knew he was a hot commodity. Both frontrunners, Villar Mir and Palacio, had also approached him and he knew that he was the second-choice candidate for both of them. In fact, he was a bit more than that.

Capello suspected that it was highly unlikely that Wenger would leave Arsenal for Villa Mir. As for Palacio, Del Bosque was a sentimental choice, but not an automatic one.

Capello therefore knew that, with three of the five candidates having him so high on their list of preferences, there was a strong likelihood he'd be returning to his old stamping ground in 2006–07. Not so Baldini. At that stage, Calderón remained a long shot, not least because Villar Mir had spent a record £4m to woo Real's 100,000 club members who made up the electorate.

It's often said that if you make outrageous promises during your campaign, you have an excellent chance of being elected. It seemed to work for Calderón. In addition to Capello, he announced that he would bring Kaká, Cesc Fabregas and Arjen Robben to the club. Plus, of course, whoever Capello wanted. With a £65m budget – and, crucially, no indication that Kaká and Fabregas were for sale – it did seem a tad unrealistic. But the fans evidently bought into it. On 3 July Calderón was confirmed as the winner – by just 246 votes – over Palacio. Capello had a new job. And so did Baldini.

Capello returned to the Juventus headquarters on 4 July to exercise his get-out clause, which was now just a formality. The Juve fans he ran into – still shocked by Calciopoli – had neither the energy to jeer him, nor to say good-bye. That same evening he was on a plane for Madrid. Less than twenty-four hours later, he signed for Real.

There was no question that the club had lost their way in the post-Galactico era. Florentino Pérez's policy of adding one superstar per season had yielded, starting from 2000–01: Luis Figo, Zinedine Zidane, Ronaldo, David

Beckham, Michael Owen and Robinho. But the club had come up empty-handed for three consecutive seasons. And it was not just that the stars got progressively less stellar as the years went by. Real's transfer policy seemed to have no rational basis, it was a case of buying good players and throwing them together.

Baldini was on board to change that. And Capello was going to be the man to make it all work. The first thing that became obvious was that Real already had a big squad of big-name players with big personalities and even bigger wages: hardly the ideal conditions for a new boss, especially one who did not count diplomacy among his strong suits.

Capello and Baldini took stock. The obvious conclusion was that the squad was talented, but poorly assorted. The players simply did not fit well together. The first thing to do was build a strong base. Goalkeeper Iker Casillas and defender Sergio Ramos were among the best in the business, but they needed help.

Capello rang up the new regime at Juventus. With the club relegated to Serie B (and without Champions League football for at least the next two seasons), income from both gate receipts and television rights was going to plummet, which meant the club had to sell to raise some funds and to reduce the wage bill. Cannavaro needed a new home: were they ready to do business?

That summer, Cannavaro had captained Italy to the World Cup title, winning plaudits as one of the best players in the tournament. There was no way somebody like that could be playing second-tier football. Equally, Emerson, although he'd had a disappointing season, was not realistically going to feature in Serie B. The Brazilian was a player Capello loved and, more importantly, felt was needed to provide balance to a squad long on attacking flair and short on holding midfielders. A £13.7m price was agreed for the pair of veterans.

Well aware that he wouldn't have the time to give Real a distinct identity – especially in the final third – Capello wanted to keep things simple with a back-to-basics approach. In addition to a strong defence, the plan was to deploy two holding midfielders in front of the back four and give the front four freedom – at least at first – to find the back of the net on their own. Thus, in came Mahamadou Diarra, the ferocious holding midfielder from Lyon, for £18.5m.

So far, so good, except Calderón was starting to get a little bit of heat from the fans: he had promised them Kaká and Fabregas, but there was no sign of either. Capello felt that, of the two, the Brazilian had to be the priority. Fabregas was a great player, but still developing. And, tactically, he envisaged a side with two holding midfielders, rather than a marauding box-to-box type like Arsenal's Catalan.

Kaká had recently extended his contract through 2011 and Milan figured that was the end of that. Calderón had made an election promise, but it was just hot air. Or was it? Real put Baldini (hardly a favourite of Galliani) on the case and the pressure mounted, especially since Baldini was reported to have spoken directly to the player's family, telling them that Milan were likely to be relegated as a result of the Calciopoli scandal and that, in any case, they could miss out on the Champions League the following season.

Milan were furious. Galliani called Real 'a bunch of bandits' and reported the club to FIFA. He went on to say that the Madrid club's behaviour was 'smearing fifty glorious years of history' and that he did not understand why a legend and a gentleman like Alfredo Di Stefano continued to be associated with them.

Capello was unperturbed. He knew Kaká was a pipe dream, but he also understood that Baldini had a job to do. Besides, Real had enough attacking midfielders as it was. And, there was another Brazilian who was taking up a disproportionate amount of his time: Ronaldo. The Brazilian centre-forward had flown to Brazil to have a knee operation, against the wishes of club doctors. While he was out there, it emerged that he was in serious danger of losing his driving licence after committing his thirteenth traffic offence in twelve months. Given that he didn't actually live in Brazil, it was quite an impressive feat.

Capello's concerns over Ronaldo grew. Like everybody else, he admired his immense talent, but he wasn't convinced he had a logical place in this team. Capello felt the 4-2-3-1 formation was the best way to release the gifts of his attacking midfielders. But that meant having Ronaldo on his own up front. And the Brazilian had just had his worst season at the club, had recurring knee problems and his behaviour was becoming increasingly erratic off the pitch. He told Baldini to quietly see what kind of interest there might be in the former Phenomenon. And while he was at it, to get him a centre-forward: Ruud Van Nistelrooy.

Signing the Dutchman was rather straightforward. Manchester United had put him up for sale with much fanfare. Bayern Munich had actually made a more lucrative offer, but Van Nistelrooy wanted Real and a deal was done at £13m, meaning that Ronaldo was now expendable. It was a case of waiting for the offers to come in.

And, of all clubs, it was Milan who knocked on the door. Galliani and Milan's sporting director Ariedo Braida met Real officials at Puerta 57, the swanky restaurant in the Bernabéu. Calderón aimed high: he wanted £26m, plus first option on Kaká, plus a public apology from Milan for having called Real 'bandits'. I couldn't confirm it, but I'm pretty sure that when he heard this Galliani's face turned purple and smoke started coming out of his ears. Milan's counter offer was £14m. Negotiations lasted until half past three in the morning and continued the next day. But to no avail. Capello was stuck with Ronaldo.

For his part, the Brazilian swore he would get back to his best, though perhaps not in the language Capello would have liked to hear: 'If I don't go back to being the best player in the world, I will shoot myself in the head,' Ronaldo said in a Brazilian television interview.

Ronaldo wasn't Capello's only reclamation project. Antonio Cassano was being reunited with his old boss and, from day one, the former wunderkind from Bari Vecchia made all the right noises. 'He's the greatest, he's like a father to me,' Cassano told the Spanish daily *Marca*. 'Sure, we've had our rows, but it's normal between a father and a son. It's part of growing up, he knows me and he knows how to handle me.' The paternal relationship would eventually get rather Oedipal (at least the bit about killing your father) but, at least at first, Capello thought Cassano would give him an extra option.

Indeed, Cassano fell into the same category as Robinho and José Antonio Reyes, who arrived on loan from Arsenal. All three were young, hugely gifted attacking players, hybrid striker-winger types, who could be deployed both out wide and behind a centre-forward. All had big upsides, but all were coming off difficult seasons. Robinho had not lived up to the hype after arriving from Santos. Reyes struggled to settle in the Premier League. Cassano joined Real from Roma in January 2006 for a cut-rate fee, largely because his contract was expiring at the end of the season and he had refused to extend it. He landed with much fanfare, appearing in a giant fur coat and telling everyone who would listen that Alfredo Di Stefano (who retired sixteen years before Cassano was born) was his idol. Alas, injuries and poor performances slowed Cassano down, along with an ever expanding waistline. Indeed, Carlos Latre, a Spanish comedian, lampooned him regularly, depicting him as a crazed pimply-faced big-bellied bully obsessed with feeding himself Pantera Rosas – pink sweets of the kind you find in a vending machine.

Those three – plus Ronaldo – represented calculated risks, but Capello felt they were gambles worth taking, especially when Van Nistelrooy, Raúl and Guti provided known quantities going forward. The key early on, as he saw it, was to create a stable platform at the back and in the middle of the park. Cannavaro would do the former and his brand-new partnership of holding midfielders Emerson and Diarra would do the latter.

Problems arose straight away, right from the 2006–07 season opener against Villarreal. Real created very little,

Emerson and Diarra sat very deep with the former looking out of form and the latter out of sorts. Cassano was a nonfactor and was substituted. It finished 0–0, a game which the sports daily *AS* described as 'the chronicle of nothingness incarnate'. Cannavaro blamed the players' fitness, but already there was a sense that the problem was deeper.

Meanwhile, beginning to rumble in the background was another issue: David Beckham. Goldenballs was in the final season of his contract at the Bernabéu, a partnership which had proved to be a commercial boon for both parties. While Real's brand grew in Asia, where Beckham's popularity was immense, the England captain himself gained new markets in places like South America, where he was sometimes viewed with suspicion. Capello understood Beckham's commercial value to the club, but at the same time felt that, given the empty trophy cabinet, there had to be one overriding priority: bringing silverware back to the Bernabéu. And in that sense, Beckham was no different from his teammates.

Beckham's situation, though, was unique. For a start, he was coming back from an injury as well as the huge disappointment of being dropped by England boss Steve McClaren. Physically and mentally he needed to recover. Then there was the issue of formation: the 4-2-3-1 scheme was not an ideal fit for Beckham, particularly with a slower centre-forward like Van Nistelrooy up front. And finally, Capello knew that every scrap of Beckham news would be magnified no end. The last thing he needed was an ongoing and public contract negotiation involving such a high-profile footballer. He would rather limit Beckham's role in the side than have a key player embroiled in something which could potentially prove to be a massive distraction.

And so the strategy was twofold. On the one hand, the season was planned without taking Beckham into account. If he performed well enough, Capello would find a way to fit him in the side, but he would not rack his brains to devise a formation that could accommodate him. On the other, the club would make a quick decision over Beckham's future so as to cut through the uncertainty as crisply and decisively as possible.

Capello felt he had kept his side of the bargain. But, by October, negotiations were stuck. Beckham did not ask for a pay rise, but wanted a larger share of his image rights, that is, the revenue streams he directly generated. The club were looking to cut Beckham's percentage of image rights, arguing that the 'Beckham effect' was, if not ending, certainly slowing. Those people who would buy a Beckham shirt regardless of whether he played for Real Madrid or Pyongyang FC had already purchased their Beckham-related Real Madrid paraphernalia. After four years, the novelty had worn off. Any new business that Beckham would bring in would be mostly based on his footballing achievements. And, when it came to that realm, Beckham was already very handsomely paid, at around £6m a season.

'Who said anything about paying him more?' Mijatovic said in early October. 'Maybe David will stay and we will pay him less.' Around the same time, Calderón told the BBC that as far as he knew, 'Beckham has decided to retire in two years.'

Those statements annoyed both Capello and the Beckham

camp. Mijatovic's words may have been just a negotiating ploy, but they also undermined Beckham, who remained a Real Madrid asset. As for Calderón, what he said was simply not true – Beckham had made no such decision – and it left a lingering question: was Calderón just ill-informed or was he trying to send a message?

Either way, tension between Beckham's advisers and the club began to rise and it served only to annoy Capello. This was not what he meant when he told the club he wanted things resolved quickly and quietly.

Meanwhile, things were not improving on the pitch. And on 14 October they went from bad to worse. Real Madrid were beaten 1–0 by little Getafe, managed by Schuster, the man everybody knew had been Calderón's original first choice for the club. Everyone was stunned by the absolute ineptitude shown by Real Madrid. In ninety-five minutes of play, they did not have a single shot on goal. Not one. No matter what Capello did, nothing seemed to work. Van Nistelrooy began on his own up front and, judging from the service he received, might as well have been invisible. At half-time, Capello called on the cavalry, bringing on Ronaldo and Raúl for the awful Cassano (who threw one of his trademark tantrums in the dressing room) and Diarra, but to no avail. Later, he sent on Robinho for Beckham. Still nothing. No matter how many attackers were on the pitch, they just could not create anything. And, to make matters worse, Ronaldo foolishly got himself sent off in the final minute, which meant he'd be suspended for the Barcelona game a week later.

'We played very badly,' Capello said. 'There are no

excuses.' Casillas called it the 'worst Real Madrid performance he could remember'. Few would have disagreed. The
knives all came out, with Capello in the dock. When he
arrived, Capello had asked for fifty days to sort Real out
tactically. Well, now the fifty days were up and the
questions came fast and furious. Why was he playing
Beckham when he was clearly out of form? Why didn't
Ronaldo start? Why was the team so conservative in the
first half? Just how awful is Emerson and can he get any
worse?

It was hard to argue with the numbers. Real were
averaging just 3.6 shots on target up to that point in the
season. *Marca*, the local daily, put a photograph of a goal
on its cover, with the tagline: 'This is called a goal. You are
supposed to kick the ball in its direction.'

It was hardly the ideal way to prepare for the clash with
Barcelona the following weekend. Already it looked like a
match which would determine Capello's future at the
club. In fact, Mijatovic had to deny reports that Capello
had resigned immediately after the Getafe game: 'No,
those would be the actions of a coward,' he said. 'And
Fabio is not a coward.' Hardly the most encouraging vote
of confidence.

Still, Capello was unfazed. 'In Spain, they go from one
extreme to the other just like that,' he said. 'It's not difficult for them to change their mind.' He knew that, while
Barcelona could be another nail (maybe the final one) in
his coffin, it could also shift the pressure off him and on to
Rijkaard. But only, of course, if Real got the three points.
The omens weren't terrible: Barcelona had lost at Chelsea
in midweek, while Real had won away to Steaua

Bucharest. Now if only they could take that form into the *Clásico* . . .

That day, 22 October, Madrid was being pounded with rain showers. Capello knew the pitch would be heavy and laid out his team accordingly. Rijkaard, instead, stuck to his game-plan: small, quick, creative players, short-passing, technical brilliance. That day, Barcelona were 'more Barcelona' than usual, not least because Samuel Eto'o, the one forward with pace, power and work-rate, was unavailable. The purists were convinced that Barça's artistry would demolish Capello's 'caveman' football, as one paper called it. And it was obvious that Barça were both loose and confident. Perhaps far too much.

'I watched them in the warm-up and I could see they were being arrogant and over-confident,' Capello would say later: 'They were doing tricks and playing keepy-uppy, they were lying on the pitch as if they were on the beach, using the ball as a pillow . . . it was disrespectful. We wanted to make them pay.'

Capello did not mention Ronaldinho, but it was obvious he was a part of it. In fact, he spent most of the warm-up trying to emulate the famous Nike advert, the one where he hits the crossbar from distance on four consecutive occasions, each time controlling the ball and bringing it down effortlessly.

Watching their opponents behave like that at the Bernabéu – their house – was the perfect motivator for Capello's men, who came out of the gate with intensity and spirit. Raúl opened the scoring after six minutes and hit the crossbar shortly after. Van Nistelrooy added a second and Real cruised to a 2–0 win which cut

Barcelona's margin over Madrid to just two points. Crisis averted.

But there were still more fires to put out, courtesy of Cassano. The following week, Real coasted to an easy 3–1 win over Gimnàstic in Tarragona. Cassano was on the bench, but failed to catch Capello's eye after warming up for most of the second half. When he realized he wasn't going to come on, he let the manager have it. 'Have you no shame?' he shouted. 'I always defended you, I always stuck up for you and this is how you repay me? Have you no sense of decency?'

Capello simply shook his head. Cassano evidently had issues and, in another time and another place, Capello would have played Freud (or, better yet, Dr Jennifer Melfi) and tried to sort it out. But Real Madrid had far too many other problems to deal with. And, frankly, Cassano was not important enough to be a priority. Capello described the incident as 'a setback for all of us' and sent him off to train by himself for the next ten days, until Cassano apologized to him and to his teammates. It was obvious though that he had become a problem and the best thing for everyone would be to find him a new home in January.

For a while it looked like things were back on track. Real won five of six in La Liga and remained within a point of table-topping Barcelona ahead of their home fixture against Recreativo de Huelva, the last game before the Christmas break. But then, once again, things began to unravel. And again it was Cassano making headlines for the wrong reasons.

Television cameras had filmed him chatting to Diarra

and Ronaldo during a training session. Cassano was seen first imitating Capello, drawing a chuckle out of his team-mates. Then, he clearly launched himself on a mini-rant: 'For Capello only certain people exist. Ruud [Van Nistelrooy], Raúl, of course, Robinho . . . oh, and Emerson, of course. Always Emerson. Emerson always plays . . .'

Had the cameras not been there, it's unlikely that Capello would have cared what Cassano's thoughts were on his team selection. But this was different. This was a player openly questioning his manager and, indirectly, attacking a teammate, Emerson, for being the 'manager's pet'. Just as important, it underscored what the Spanish press had been writing all season, that Capello was obsessed with Emerson who, by that point, was clearly an inferior player but nevertheless seemed to start most games. Cassano was left out for the next match, against Recreativo, a horrid 3–0 defeat at the Bernabéu. As far as Capello was concerned, he couldn't leave soon enough.

It was obvious that Cassano was persona non grata at this point. And, with him, Ronaldo, who had yet to last ninety minutes in La Liga and had notched just one league goal. The press, who had never taken Cassano to their hearts, delighted in describing the ways in which Capello supposedly tortured him. Once, Cassano reportedly told the coaching staff that he wanted to take extra shooting practice after training. Upon Capello's instructions, they all left the pitch, leaving him alone and humiliated in front of an empty goal. On another occasion, when Capello elected to end training with an informal eight-a-side scrimmage, Cassano tried to get into one of the two sides:

when Capello realized he had infiltrated the kickabout, he sent him off running on his own.

'Cassano is the club's problem, not my problem,' Capello was quoted as saying in *Corriere della Sera* on 7 January 2007. He had run out of second chances as far as Capello was concerned.

Some encouragement did come from the transfer market. Capello had asked for some youthful dynamism to add to the side. Baldini and Mijatovic delivered three guys who fitted the bill: leftback Marcelo, central midfielder Fernando Gago and striker Gonzalo Higuaín. All gifted players, but the fact that Gago, at twenty, was the oldest of the three led many to conclude that they were going to be part of Real's future, not their present. Didn't the club need experience and steel to navigate through these difficult times?

Yet Real had plenty of experience, maybe too much. Sometimes players over-think things, sometimes veterans can create problems. Capello felt that to throw a bit of youth in at the deep end could be just what the side needed. That's why Marcelo and Higuaín – whose deals had been completed in November and were originally due to join the following summer – arrived that January and not later, as was originally planned.

The new year brought no immediate improvement in results. Quite the opposite. Real lost away at Deportivo La Coruña on 7 January. The 2–0 loss turned into an absolute nightmare. Real showed all their old failings. Emerson looked sluggish, Gago, alongside him, appeared lost. The strikers got little service and the defence looked shaky. Back to square one.

After the match, Mijatovic convened an emergency 'state of the club' meeting with Capello, Baldini and members of the coaching staff. Capello's line was simple: 'Some players aren't performing to their potential.' Which was undoubtedly true, though perhaps it smacked a little bit of passing the buck. Wasn't it his job to get them to the level they should be at?

Capello emerged the next day in defensive mood, battening down the hatches before the onslaught. He knew the media were going to put him through the wringer and did not back down.

'How do you feel?'

'I feel like the manager of Real Madrid.'

'Are you happy?'

'I'm not happy, because in football you're only truly happy when you win.'

'Is it your fault?'

'No, because when we win we all win and when we lose we all lose.'

'What will become of Ronaldo?'

'I don't talk about individual players.'

'What about Cassano?'

'I don't talk about individual players.'

'Beckham?'

'I don't talk about individual players.'

Tough stuff. But, in fact the media didn't even have time to get their knives out and start an inquest when another, bigger story broke: Beckham. Two days after the Deportivo loss, Madrid awoke to find *AS* reporting that Capello had included Beckham in a 'blacklist' of under-performing players (along with the usual suspects Cassano and Ronaldo) and had urged the club not to extend his deal.

This was not entirely the case. For a start, Capello was in no position to determine whether or not Beckham's contract would be renewed, not when his own job was in serious jeopardy. Capello did express the opinion – when asked by the club – that Beckham was having a poor season and that, in his current state, he was contributing little.

The numbers bear this out. Beckham had started just five league games all season, of which Real lost three and won just one. More worryingly, he seemed to have a knack for getting himself booked: he had collected eleven yellow cards in 633 Liga minutes. When a player as experienced as Beckham – who was in his fourth season in Spain and therefore had few mitigating circumstances – has such a bad disciplinary record, there must be a reason. Whether it was his physical condition or the uncertainty over his future, he simply wasn't producing.

Within forty-eight hours the Beckham saga was over. Well, in some ways: in others as we'll see it was just beginning. He signed a five-year deal with the Los Angeles Galaxy of Major League Soccer in the United States. The world's media went into overdrive, parallels were drawn with Pelé's move to the old North American Soccer League in the mid-1970s. As usually happens with Beckham, the story became about whether he could convert 280 million Americans to the religion practised by the rest of the world: football (the kind played with a round ball). And, to do this, he was being paid a reported $250m over five seasons, or £25.6m a year.

A brief detour: it was, perhaps, inevitable that a figure such as Beckham would be submerged by a wave of hype and ignorance, as usually happens whenever his name comes up (witness the stories about him wearing his wife's underwear). But, even then, the gullibility and predictability of the world's media looks shocking in hindsight. For a start, the storyline that Beckham was some kind of footballing prophet spreading the one true word among the great unwashed across the pond was as stupid as it was unfair. It was stupid because, while football is obviously not a major sport in the United States, some 15,000 people show up to each MLS game, making it one of the world's top ten leagues by average attendance. And it was unfair on Beckham: while he embraced the role of missionary, we are, ultimately, talking about a thirtysomething footballer here, not some self-appointed Messiah.

Then there was the issue of his contract, which made him far and away the highest paid athlete in team sports. The media uncritically lapped up the fact that he would supposedly be earning a quarter of a billion dollars (a nice round number), when, in fact, just a modicum of digging would have revealed that the figure was just an estimate of what Beckham might earn if a whole series of factors – from sponsorship to merchandising – went his way. In reality, Beckham's contract called for him to earn a little bit less in guaranteed money than he was on in Spain. Not that any of the parties involved went out of their way to reveal the truth about his deal. Everyone from Real Madrid (who could claim they had lost Beckham to an out-of-this-world offer) to Beckham's own camp (who could revel in the fact that their client was one of the highest paid sportsmen in the world) to MLS (which had given itself a newfound legitimacy) had an interest in keeping the myth alive.

What happened next was largely unexpected and wholly extraordinary. Capello announced that Beckham would no longer feature for Real Madrid.

'He won't play,' Capello said. 'He'll train, but he won't play. Why? Because when you sign such an important contract with another club it's difficult to have the right level of motivation. David has always been a great professional, but it's obvious that we can no longer count on him.'

Capello's decision to drop Beckham for the rest of the season seems entirely illogical. Every season hundreds of players sign with other clubs on Bosman transfers in January and then move on in June, without anything fishy going on. His words seemed petty and vindictive and clearly a case of cutting off your nose to spite your face.

'Ronaldo and Beckham were in a similar situation,' Toni Grande from Real's backroom staff recalls. 'There came a time when they weren't helpful to the club. [Beckham] was in the side, he wasn't playing well, he wasn't doing what he was told and the side weren't winning. If a player of that level helps you win games, you accept certain things. But if he doesn't, you have to be ready to make drastic decisions.'

'It was a joint decision by myself and others, but, ultimately, I had the final say, I could have kept him in the team,' Capello said after the season. 'So I have to accept responsibility. We wanted to send a certain message.'

Whatever that message was, it could have been sent in a much better way. Leaving Beckham out for the next few matches, without any kind of public pronouncement, would have done the trick (and without making Capello look like an ogre). It was a foolish statement to make, and one which he soon came to regret.

A win over Zaragoza on 14 January pulled Real to a point behind, and a further point from Sevilla. Even then, there was controversy, with Capello right in the middle of it. Having been abused by two supporters just behind his bench for much of the game, Capello turned to them at the final whistle and gave them the universal middle-finger gesture. The ubiquitous cameras caught it all and, once again, the Real Madrid manager was on trial.

'I am going to apologize to the supporters because what I did was wrong and I should not have done it,' Capello said after the game. 'Those two guys had been needling me the entire game and I simply lost control. They do this every game, in fact they were there ten years ago when I was last here. But it's no excuse. I was wrong and I apologize.'

Perhaps more would have been made of this incident had it not been for an extraordinary blunder from Calderón two days later. The Real president was address-ing a group of students at Villanueva University. He was supposed to talk about Real Madrid as a business venture, but he decided to give a fair portion of his players both barrels. In the course of his speech – which was recorded without his knowledge and aired on the radio later that night – Calderón called Real's players 'vain' and 'egotistical', while adding that they lacked 'culture and education'.

He also rubbished Guti, gave details of Casillas's

contract, effectively called the paying public at the Bernabéu 'lame' and topped it off by putting the boot into Beckham: 'He's going to Hollywood to be a half-baked actor,' he said. 'We were right not to extend his contract and that has been proved by the fact that nobody wanted him outside of Los Angeles.'

That same night word of Calderón's speech spread among the players, who were understandably incensed. They demanded an immediate meeting with their president. Calderón, fearing the worst, initially offered to meet the club's captains Raúl, Guti and Roberto Carlos, but he was quickly rebuffed. He was going to face all the players and he had better come up with a convincing apology.

And so the following day Calderón drove up to Valdebebas to face the music. Capello and Mijatovic sat in on the meeting but were largely silent. Calderón tried to explain himself, talking about such things as 'context' and 'meaning' but he was soon interrupted by one senior player who shouted: 'That's enough shit coming out of your mouth! Why don't you repeat what you said on Tuesday to our faces?' Another player asked him straight out: 'Are you with us or against us?' At this point the president understood that the only way he was getting out of the meeting was by apologizing and listening to the players' grievances. Among the most vocal was Beckham, who called Calderón a 'liar' and said he felt 'let down' by his behaviour. He also said that, while he was disappointed at being dropped, he 'respected' Capello because he was open about what he did and how he felt.

For his part, Capello was struck by the bond which had

developed among the players. He had been in crisis situations before, but he was noticing something which many had missed earlier: these players, despite their massive egos and even bigger wage packets, genuinely cared for each other. They had professional pride and dignity. He was particularly impressed with Beckham's reaction: how easy it would have been for him just to laugh it off, knowing that in a few months' time he'd be in the LA sunshine and would probably never see Calderón again. Instead, there he was, sticking up for himself and his teammates. Whatever internal battles or jealousies may have existed before, the team was pulling together. And Capello was proud of them.

It wasn't just about Calderón's comments. Mijatovic also got an earful. One player accused him of being two-faced, of not giving the manager the right kind of backing and, effectively, making his and the players' job impossible. There was no clear criticism of Capello at the meeting, but the manager understood that some players weren't happy with him. That, however, did not bother him: there was inevitably a degree of resentment towards someone they work with every day. The key, however, was that they were all pulling together, something which had been missing until that point.

Capello would say later that the Calderón face-off helped change his mind over Beckham. His professionalism and intensity on the pitch, both in training and in matches, had never been in question. However, he did not appear to be the most vocal of leaders and you were often left with the sense that he was just doing a job. That day, however, another side of Beckham emerged, that of a deeply caring teammate. To Capello this was of paramount importance. He now softened his stance and made it clear that, were it not for a slight injury, he would be considered for selection again.

Whatever unity the Calderón affair engendered, its effects were slow to manifest themselves on the pitch. Real lost two straight games and the second, at home to Levante, was particularly painful. It was the one thousandth match at the Bernabéu; supporters' clubs from all over the world had sent representatives. And yet Real were greeted with a *panolada*, a mass waving of white handkerchiefs which signals the supporters' disapproval. It did not stop there. Calderón was abused by the supporters, who asked for his resignation. Capello too came under intense fire, as Barcelona moved five points clear.

One sector of the crowd which kept up its support of the manager and his embattled players were the Ultras Sur, Real's hardcore supporters. So much so that Capello thanked them in public after the match. Not a wise thing to do. Some of the Ultras Sur have links with far-right extremists and the media jumped all over the story. He even received a slap on the wrist from the government's anti-violence commission who described his gratitude towards the Ultras Sur as 'inappropriate'. For his part, Capello wasn't making any kind of political statement and certainly didn't feel as if he was endorsing violence. He was simply thanking those supporters who stuck with him, an ever dwindling group.

And with good reason. Real had already lost seven of twenty-one matches: by comparison, in his previous stint, they had lost just four of forty-two. The only saving grace was that Barcelona were having their own troubles and thus the gap from the top stood at a manageable five points.

The side clearly needed a shake-up. Ronaldo was finally gone, off-loaded to Milan. Cassano, on the other hand, was still around (he had come close to moving to Inter) but fortunately was isolated enough that he wasn't doing too much harm. And so Capello chose the next match, at Real Sociedad, to bring Beckham back into the fold.

'The ability to change your mind is a sign of intelligence,' Capello said.

It worked perfectly: with Beckham on board, Real won 2–1 and, in fact, the equalizing goal came from a trademark Beckham free-kick (albeit one which the goalkeeper palmed into his own net). Some media outlets described it as a 'humiliating' climb-down for Capello. But he certainly didn't feel that way. The transfer window had closed, Beckham was still around, he'd be mad not to use him. The 'Beckham effect' did not last very long – he was foolishly sent off the following week – but it did show the players that Capello was a man whose mind could be changed.

'[Dropping Beckham] was obviously not one of Capello's better decisions,' says Grande. 'He tried something different, Raúl out wide on the right and it didn't work. And so he went back to Beckham. There are times when you get things wrong, the trick is recognizing your mistakes and fixing them.'

In fact, Beckham's exclusion fits in with one of the themes of Capello's career: the fact that no grudges are ever held and you are only ever judged on performance.

'It doesn't matter if you're Ronaldo, Baggio or Cannavaro,' says Cannavaro. 'If you don't train well, you're out. But players also know that with Capello they will always get a second chance. Lots of coaches have a bust-up with a player and then that player will never play again. With Capello, as long as you're working hard, what happened before becomes irrelevant. He only has one aim – to win – and if you can help his cause then the door will always be open. At the same time, he is very strong. If you want to fight him, he'll fight back. The difference is that the next day it will all be over. That's something which makes him stand out and one of the reasons I really like him as a person.'

With Beckham back in the fold, Ronaldo gone and Cassano (relatively) muzzled, one would think some measure of focus and tranquillity had returned to Real. But in fact quite the reverse took place.

On 17 February Real played out an unimpressive score-less draw with Betis at the Bernabéu. It was a frustrating night if not quite their worst performance of the season, and it did look as if they were treading water once again. After the match Mijatovic and Baldini stuck around the ground for an hour or so to discuss the situation. It was clear to both that Calderón wanted Capello out. The previous six weeks had been difficult for everyone involved. Some felt Capello's behaviour had become somewhat erratic, as evidenced by his handling of Beckham. The problem wasn't whether Calderón or the club believed in Capello (and, by this stage, they clearly didn't) or whether the players believed in him (judging by results, one would think not). The issue was whether Capello still believed in Capello. Was the fire gone? Had he lost the will and strength to react? It was felt that the subject had to be broached with Capello and, specifically, the issue of whether he wanted to continue as manager. And if he didn't, what would it take to persuade him to go?

Capello spent the next thirty-six hours pondering that very question. He had a long chat with Laura and did a fair bit of soul-searching. He was not the quitting type, but then he had never been in a situation like this before. Even in the darkest days at Roma, he felt that there was a way out and it was just a question of pushing the team through it. Now, he wasn't even sure he had the ability to search for an opening, much less make it out. He instructed Baldini and Mijatovic to tell the club's board – who were due to meet at 11 a.m. on Monday, 19 February, the day before Real's Champions League clash with Bayern Munich – that if the club felt he was the problem, he was open to going.

Predictably, discussion at the board meeting centred on Capello's words. Did it make sense for the club to take up his offer? And, if so, what kind of mutually acceptable compensation package could they put together? (This was not an insignificant issue as Capello was earning close to £4m a year and had a contract up to summer 2009.) By two o'clock, a strategy had been laid out: the club would tell Capello that he was, in fact, part of the problem and that Real Madrid would be better off without him. For all parties to save face, it would officially be a case of Capello resigning, rather than being forced out. All that remained was to iron out his severance package, which they agreed to do after their lunch break. As the meeting broke up everyone – including Baldini and Mijatovic – was convinced that this was it.

Meanwhile, Capello led the training session as normal and addressed the media ahead of the Bayern game. If he was worried or concerned by what was happening at the board meeting, he betrayed none of it. He looked confident and self-assured and talked about the long-term objectives of the club and how they were still in the running for both the Champions League and La Liga. In the back of his mind, however, he knew that Baldini, Calderón, Mijatovic and the rest of the board were discussing his departure from the club.

Something happened during that lunch break to change the minds of several board members. Just what it was is unclear. But when the meeting resumed, one of those present said: 'Are we sure we want to sack him now, the day before Bayern Munich and two and a half weeks before Barcelona? Does this really make sense? And what about his replacement? Sure, we can bring in Michel [the former Real legend was currently managing the feeder club Castilla and had been mooted as a successor] but what happens if, under him, we get knocked out of the Champions League and lose to Barcelona? Won't his credibility be shattered?'

The words did hit home. The logic was undeniable. And it struck a chord with Calderón. Acting now could destabilize the side and cost them a place in the Champions League quarter-final. Besides, he wanted Schuster at the helm and the German wasn't going to be available until the summer. Capello had been a failure, but what would be gained by changing managers at this point? It was one thing if Capello threw in the towel of his own accord. But doing it this way, the club would have to pay him close to £6m while bringing in an interim manager with no guarantee of success. And what if the new guy lost control and Real missed out on the Champions League next season? And what would people think if the president had to sack the interim boss at the end of the season? Already, after his ill-conceived speech, he was hardly flavour of the month among the Real faithful. Surely they could wait until after the Bayern clash, maybe even the Barcelona game, to let Capello go. Three weeks weren't going to make a difference.

Just like that, the mood changed. Several board members still wanted him out straight away, of course, but Calderón's mind was changed. He had to think about his image and that of the club. And this was not the right move.

While the meeting was still running, Cope, a leading Spanish radio network, broke the news that Capello had, in fact, resigned and would be stepping aside after the Bayern game. The news broke at twenty-one minutes past five o'clock. It did not take a genius to figure out that somebody – most likely someone in that boardroom – had obviously leaked the news during the lunch break. And, at the time, the news had been correct, Capello was resigning.

The media went into a frenzy, but with all of Real's higher-ups still in the board meeting there was nobody to confirm the story. The uncertainty lasted for 116 minutes. That evening, a club spokesman faced the press and steadfastly denied that Capello had offered his resignation or that, indeed, it had even been discussed.

Of course, Capello was still in the dark about all this. He had spent much of the afternoon at home, eagerly awaiting a call from Mijatovic or Baldini. That call, of course, never came. He headed off for the Somosierras, the hotel on the outskirts of Madrid where Real usually spend the night before home Champions League ties, still unsure whether he would be in charge. He had heard the news from Cope, of course, but did not know what to make of it. If the club had accepted his resignation, surely they would have been on to him by now. It wasn't until he arrived at the hotel that he was called and informed about what had happened at the meeting.

His offer to resign had been turned down. Nor were the club going to sack him. He was under no illusions: he had neither the support nor the faith of the board. But, for whatever reason, he was still there. He wasn't about to walk out without compensation. And that meant that, for better or worse, the marriage would continue.

It occurred to Capello that this kind of thing would never have happened at Juventus, where Moggi and Giraudo ran a very tight ship, or even at Milan. But Real was different, it was as much a political organization as anything else. Calderón's power stemmed from the fact that he had won the election, his mandate came from the club members. And just as they had bestowed power, they could take it back; after all, wasn't that the fate which befell both Ramón Mendoza and, more recently, Florentino Pérez?

Capello knew that Calderón was worried about how he was perceived. Was he scared to make a decision which, while popular right now, might boomerang badly in a few months' time? In fact, there wasn't too much time to think about it. Capello knew that between the Bayern tie and the Barcelona match at the Camp Nou nineteen days later, his fate would likely be decided.

He mixed things up, reverting to a basic 4-4-2, with Beckham and Raúl on the flanks, and the youngster Torres at rightback. Up front, Van Nistelrooy was joined by Higuaín. At half-time, Real were 3–1 up and fully in control. Even the Bernabéu crowd was cheering them on, proving Capello's point about just how fickle the fans could be. Bayern may have been embroiled in their worst season in thirty-one years – leading one observer to joke that 'the best way for a struggling team to turn it around is to play someone far, far worse' – but they still had the pedigree and the cachet. But then Mark Van Bommel pulled one back two minutes from time, fixing the final score at 3–2. Though pleased with the win, Capello was seething: conceding two goals at home after dominating most of the match was simply not acceptable. And it could come back to haunt them in the return leg.

Did it ever. Capello had set up the return leg with the kind of cautious, safety-first formation the Spanish press hated. The Real line-up featured three central midfielders: Gago, Diarra and the much-maligned Emerson. But there was no time to debate his tactical choices, because Real found themselves a goal down after the fastest score in Champions League history. Gago picked up the kickoff, knocked it wide to Roberto Carlos, who promptly lost it, allowing Hasan Salihamidzic to nick the ball and streak down the flank. His low cross found Roy Makaay who side-footed it past Casillas. All in just 10.2 seconds.

Capello was livid. How did things like this happen? Real chased the game and dominated possession but, without a creative force in the middle, failed to open up the opposing defence. After half an hour, he replaced Emerson with Guti – the Brazilian had, once again, underperformed – but early in the second-half Bayern made it 2–0. Van Nistelrooy pulled one back late from the penalty spot, but to no avail. Real were out on away goals. Once again, basic mental errors had cost Madrid dear.

As if that weren't enough, Mijatovic did him no favours after the game. Asked for the umpteenth time about Capello's future, he said: 'I don't know, but for the moment he is our coach.'

'For the moment': three little words which made the media's inquest all the more forceful. Real were fourth in La Liga, having scored just thirty-two goals in twenty-five league matches, the kind of average you see from sides fighting to avoid relegation. And now they were out of the Champions League as well. Still, Capello was not pleased with Mijatovic's words. Were they not in this together?

Barcelona away were up next. Another humiliation and Capello's season would be over. Cope radio – them again – had reported that the only reason Capello still had his job was that, given the size and length of his contract, it would cost Calderón €16m to sack him. And, at this stage, he would rather write off the rest of the season than fork out that kind of money.

Three times Real took the lead, three times Barcelona stormed back to equalize. It was the kind of 3–3 draw which thrilled the neutrals and showed there was plenty of life left in Madrid. Capello was proud of the character his side had shown (less so about the three goals conceded, though he had to admit that in light of Leo Messi's superlative performance, there wasn't too much they could do). More importantly, Real had proved that they could kick it up a notch when necessary. And with Sevilla losing away to little Gimnàstic, the unthinkable was becoming reality: there really was a three-way title race and Real were a part of it.

Capello was under no illusions. But the league table didn't lie. And if things went his way, he could yet walk away a victor. That was all that mattered. Not the fact that, at the Camp Nou, Cassano had once again blown his top, chastising Capello in the dressing room for not sending him on in the dying minutes, after making him warm up for a good ten minutes. Not the fact that the TV crew from a Spanish satirical programme had given an embarrassed Ronaldo a 'Capello Voodoo doll', inviting him to exact his revenge. And certainly not the comments coming from Bernd Schuster a few weeks later. 'Capello is only preoccupied with winning. You can't succeed at Real Madrid with that kind of philosophy. And that's why I'm sure he won't be in charge next season.' Not the classiest move from the German, given that it was an open secret that he was close to Calderón and had been his preferred choice the previous spring. But Capello knew that Schuster was right – his relationship with the Real president had clearly deteriorated and was almost beyond repair. The fact that Schuster's words got no public response from Calderón proved to him what everyone already knew: he wouldn't be here next season.

And yet, according to Grande, the Barcelona game was

a turning point: 'We deserved to win that game,' he says. 'We all knew that. We left the Camp Nou with a certain spirit, a certain belief ... Capello was very good at bottling that spirit and using it to carry us the rest of the way.'

Real won five of six after the draw at the Camp Nou, staying right on top of Sevilla who were the visitors on 6 May. A goal down at half-time, Real came back to win 3–2, leap-frogging Sevilla in the table and moving to within two points of Barcelona. The catalyst of the win was Guti, a player who had spent his entire career at the Bernabéu (he got his start under Capello back in 1996–97) but, most of the time, had flattered to deceive. His talent was unquestionable, his temperament was another issue. Most observers had cynically pointed out that, with Madrid sinking, Guti would be among the first to abandon ship. They were wrong.

By this point, Real were clicking. There was a self-belief and a unity there that set them apart from Sevilla and Barcelona. Guti was only part of it, Capello had also promoted a young defender from Castilla, Real's feeder team, Miguel Torres, who had been a fixture since making his Liga debut against Zaragoza in January. The way he did it was typical Capello.

'He had been keeping an eye on us at Castilla and then one day brought me up into the first team,' Torres recalls. 'He didn't say anything specific, just a few words here and there, usually focusing on specific details. He treated me like the other players. I think it's a good thing, he didn't want to overload me with information. [Had he] done that, I might have felt more of the pressure. Instead, he did not treat it like a big deal, but still made me feel like I had his confidence.'

The following weekend saw Real at home to Espanyol on Saturday, while Barcelona hosted Betis on Sunday. At half-time Real were 3–1 down to a Walter Pandiani hat-trick. The crowd began to groan: once again it looked as if Capello's crew was running out of steam just as it looked to be putting a run together. But in the second period they conjured up an improbable comeback to win 4–3 with a late Higuaín goal and left the pitch to rousing applause. Even better news came the following day, when Betis held Barcelona to a 1–1 draw. The sides were now level, but – crucially – Real Madrid had the tie-breaker, given their better record in the head-to-head (2–0 at the Bernabéu, 3–3 at the Camp Nou). If they finished level, Capello would win his ninth title.

They didn't make it easy for themselves the following week. It took a dramatic injury-time winner from Roberto Carlos, brilliantly set up by Higuaín, to take the three points away to Recreativo, while Barcelona routed Atlético 6–0 in Madrid. Grudgingly, the press was giving Capello his due. Yes, it wasn't pretty, but the fact that Real were still in the hunt was a minor miracle. And, what's more, the recent run, with its stunning comebacks and late goals, was often a function of Capello's game-changing substitutions, something even his critics had to concede.

The penultimate round of the season would prove to be one of the most dramatic in Liga history. Well into the eighty-ninth minute the title was firmly in Barcelona's hands. Rijkaard's men were leading 2–1 against crosstown rivals Espanyol, while Real were 2–1 down at Zaragoza.

But then came an incredible eighteen seconds in which everything changed. Or, rather, from the perspective of the table, stayed the same. Van Nistelrooy equalized in Zaragoza and, just eighteen ticks later, Raul Tamudo snatched the draw in Barcelona. Just like that, the two contenders were level again, with Real holding their destiny in their own hands.

Some called Capello lucky, given that it was his side's umpteenth comeback. But, as Branch Rickey, the legendary baseball manager, once said: 'Luck is the residue of preparation and design.' And, even then, given what Real had been through that season, Capello was convinced they were due a bit of good fortune. Not least because, on that day, Barça had enjoyed a fair dose of luck as well: their first goal should never have stood, Messi had clearly punched it into the back of the net. Shades of the man he was most compared to, a certain Diego Armando Maradona some twenty-one years earlier.

'God is with us,' remarked Calderón after the match. So was Capello, though, everyone knew, not for much longer. But it didn't matter. All he had to do was dispatch Mallorca – a side with nothing left to play for – and Real would be champions for the thirtieth time, regardless of what Barcelona did.

The date was 17 June, exactly six years to the day after leading Roma to the Serie A crown. Typically, it was a comeback job, as befitted the kind of season Real had had. After going a goal down, they hit back in the second half to win 3–1, scoring twice through Reyes (who had missed most of the campaign through injury) and adding a third with Diarra. Capello had given Real a title which had eluded them for 1,456 days. It was his ninth crown in fifteen seasons of management. And that was all that mattered to him. Certainly not the incessant speculation over his future, which once again he rebuffed in the usual way: 'Ask the president, I know nothing.'

The president? It was as if Calderón was in a parallel universe. After the match, rather than dropping by the dressing room to celebrate with the players and staff, he remained in the directors' box, glad-handing with club officials and celebrity fans. Then, as Real rode on an open-topped bus accompanied by several hundred thousand fans for their traditional celebration at the Cibeles fountain in central Madrid, manager and president stood side-by-side but each looked and acted as if the other were invisible. Watching footage of the trip down is remarkable: the pair's eyes never seem to meet, there is no mutual acknowledgement. Calderón was there, alongside Capello, but light years away.

Calderón had organized a celebratory dinner at Puerta 57, the exclusive club restaurant in the Bernabéu itself, but many players and staff members – including Capello – deserted it. Or, if they showed up, they grabbed a drink and left. Capello felt he had done his duty, the last thing he needed was to spend several hours schmoozing with Calderón's mates and pretending that everything was OK. Besides, by this point it was his birthday – surely on your birthday you can do what you like.

The same applied to the players. Most felt this was 'their win' and came in spite of the president's behaviour a few months earlier, which had seriously jeopardized their season. They wanted to celebrate on their own.

Capello made his way to his favourite restaurant, Meson Txistu, a Basque eaterie a few blocks away from the Bernabéu. He was overcome with emotion, as was everyone in his party: Baldini, who had endured a difficult season sharing power and responsibility with Mijatovic, while mediating the explosive triangle of Calderón, Mijatovic and Capello; Massimo Neri, the fitness coach who had somehow persuaded Real's expensive primadonnas to sweat and work their way to the title (Madrid's fitness late in the season was several notches above that of Sevilla and Barcelona); and Laura, of course, usually so understated but, on this occasion, draped in a Real Madrid flag.

Cannavaro and his wife were there too, seated a few tables away. And, in a private room, David and Victoria Beckham, Tom Cruise and Katie Holmes were having their own celebratory dinner. Both players came to greet Capello and thank him. At one point, Beckham put his hand on Capello's shoulder, leaned in, and whispered in his ear. Only they know what was said, but it was obvious that whatever tension had existed was now forgotten. Little did they know that some eight months later they would be working together again.

Around four o'clock in the morning, Calderón walked in. Realizing that his own party at Puerta 57 hadn't exactly been the evening's hotspot, he had spent the night dropping by various restaurants in search of Real players, congratulating as many of them as he could. In all the euphoria after the match, Capello and Calderón had hardly exchanged words. But now was different. Now was the perfect time for Calderón to either tell Capello that winning felt a lot better than chasing some footballing utopia and, therefore, he would be staying on at the Bernabéu. Or, alternatively, shake his hand, thank him for succeeding where so many in recent history had failed and wish him well for whatever his next job might be.

Their eyes met for a split second. Calderón strode purposefully across the room ... entirely bypassing Capello's table as if it were invisible. Just like that. Not a hello, not a wave, not a quick handshake. Capello was completely blanked. A source close to Calderón would tell me later that the president was simply 'embarrassed', 'didn't know what to say' and 'wanted to avoid a potential confrontation'. It now looked obvious that was the final nail in Capello's coffin. Or perhaps in Real's.

That night, Capello only managed a few hours' sleep. He knew he'd be facing the press the next day and had a few things to get off his chest, beginning with Calderón.

'Don't ask me if I will be here next season, ask Calderón,' he said. 'Ask Calderón whether winning the league is enough for him or whether he will be on the phone to another manager tomorrow. I don't feel that I have had Calderón's support this season. He did not come down to the dressing room to congratulate the players and me after the game.'

The line being spun from Calderón privately was the one peddled pretty much all season. Capello's brand of football simply wasn't in keeping with Real's tradition and image. Roberto Palomar, a columnist for *Marca*, neatly summed up the vitriolic feelings of a large chunk of the press:

I see no reason why Fabio Capello should continue with Real Madrid. He arrived with one objective, to win the title, and he obtained it. Mission accomplished. Now he can take his footballing avarice and go back to where he came from. The only thing linking him to the club is a contract, the same contract which, ten years ago, he failed to observe. This is the Bernabéu, my good sir, and we play football here.

The supporters themselves were split. Yes, the football was often unpalatable. But they – perhaps far more than the press – appreciated the simple fact that Real had finally won, breaking their longest drought in fifty years. This is not to say that they would have necessarily enjoyed another five years of Capello. But, rather, at that moment in time, he was the man who provided what his predecessors could not.

To paraphrase and modify Jack Nicholson's speech from *A Few Good Men*, you could almost imagine Capello in the dock, defending himself against Palomar, Calderón, the Prisa Group and the rest of his critics.

'You want the truth? You can't handle the truth! . . . I have a greater responsibility than you can possibly fathom . . . You have the luxury of not knowing what I know: that my approach, while tragic, probably won us the title . . . And my existence, while grotesque and incomprehensible to you, saves lives . . . You don't want the truth. Because deep down, in a place you don't talk about at parties, you want me on that bench. You need me on that bench . . . I have neither the time nor inclination to explain myself to a man who rises and sleeps under the blanket of the very success I provide, then questions the manner in which I provide it!'

Arrigo Sacchi was not spared either. His predecessor at Milan – the Yin to his Yang – had said that the Liga season had been a mediocre one and that Capello was ideally suited to triumphing when surrounded by mediocrity. It, most likely, wasn't a pop, just an opinion that when things are tough all around, Capello's toughness, experience and general scrappiness can make the difference.

'So Sacchi thinks I thrive on mediocrity?' he said. 'Well, I guess it's a compliment given that he twice came to Spain and twice landed on his arse. He went to Atlético Madrid and they sent him packing, he went to Real as technical director and they sent him packing. I guess a guy like him who has been beaten and battered twice evidently has yet to regain consciousness.'

Capello truly had had enough. Not just of some people in Spain, but a portion of the press in Italy as well. He felt that his feat had been underappreciated back home, that he did not get the same accolades or respect accorded others who had gone abroad. It should have been the old paradigm of the emigrant going abroad to find fame and fortune and being celebrated back home, his success becoming a triumph for a whole nation. He cited the example of Pau Gasol, a young Spanish basketball star who had moved to the NBA and who was cheered on by all of Spain. By contrast, it seemed to Capello that many in Italy wanted him to fail.

His feelings were no doubt genuine, but it was hardly a fair comparison. This was not Capello's first time abroad, and besides, the novelty of an Italian going beyond his borders to achieve success had worn off. He was hardly the luckless emigrant, setting off with a battered suitcase held together by string. Moreover, between Roma and Juventus, his legacy had left him with few supporters around the country. Yes, he was respected and admired as a winner, but he was not the kind of winner you cheered on.

Ordinarily, he couldn't have cared less what people thought. But things were a bit different now. He felt he had the respect and appreciation of a fair chunk of his squad – with the exception of the usual suspects – and that was important, because on a personal level, it was a victory. Beckham, in his final public appearance, summed up the general mood: 'Capello proved the kind of man he is. He wasn't afraid to change his mind. I will always be grateful to him. And I will never speak ill of him.'

Calderón had no such qualms. He revealed in the newspaper *AS* that, after getting knocked out by Bayern, Capello had told him that the squad 'simply wasn't good enough' and that, at best, 'Real would finish sixth'.

'But then the team came together and we won the league,' Calderón said. 'I am so proud of the players. They deserve 90 per cent of the credit.'

And, presumably, the other 10 per cent goes to the fans, the club, Calderón, Mijatovic, Baldini, the team's medical staff, the guy who drives the team bus and the old lady selling sunflower seeds outside the Bernabéu. Everyone but Capello.

Torres disputes the theory, popularized by Capello's critics, that it was all about the players winning the league, not the manager.

'I don't think it's fair,' he says. 'He created a solid bloc, a team. When I arrived there were problems, but he sorted them out and things really changed. By the end of the season there were genuine friendships and relationships within the squad, which had not been there before. It was Capello who laid the foundations. It was Capello who made us Madrid again. He gave us the pride, the spirit, the fight, the things which had always characterized the club.'

As for the style of football, there is no question in whose camp Torres lies.

'I didn't care in the slightest about the way we played,' he says. 'The only thing I cared about was Ruud [Van Nistelrooy] scoring a goal, winning 1–0 and going home with a victory. We were all very clear about that; if you're going to play great football you need time to build a team. We didn't have that luxury. We were a mix of new players and old players who were on the decline. And the expectations were very high. Results had to come first.'

Cannavaro, another Capello loyalist, puts things in no uncertain terms.

'Winning the title with Madrid was a miracle,' he says. 'No question about it, a miracle. And I think more than any other team he's worked at, we were a side where you could clearly see the coach's hand, his personality at work. This was a much greater feat than the two titles I won with him at Juventus.'

Capello wasn't about to start ranking his victories in order of difficulty. But, viewed from afar, this may well have been the most taxing title, even more than the one at Roma. Probably the most satisfying, too.

CHAPTER 16

The Ultimate Challenge

Capello spent the summer after his departure from Madrid the way he spent most summers. On holiday, far off the beaten track. As was his custom, he and Laura left soon after the victory celebration at Cibeles. They made their way to China – their sixth trip – and on to Tibet.

He wasn't trying to get away, he was merely following his routine. A time to work, a time to rest. The public sphere had disappeared and he and Laura were going to delve back into their private world. That said, he knew his time in Madrid, the city he had come to adore, was at an end. Unlike ten years earlier there was probably a greater sense of regret. He would have wanted to stay, even though he knew as early as March that this would be a one-year job.

On 28 June 2007, just eleven days after leading the club to the title, Real Madrid announced Capello's sacking. His mobile began ringing almost immediately. His reaction was typically dry.

'Really?' he told one journalist, who caught him on a

street corner in Lhasa, the capital of Tibet. 'Well, you can't say it comes as a surprise, can you?'

With that, Capello switched off his mobile and enjoyed the rest of his holiday. He obviously had no financial concerns and, professionally, he knew the offers would come in. Whatever one may have thought about events at the Bernabéu the previous season, he had delivered as promised, ending Real Madrid's trophy drought and winning his ninth league title in fifteen seasons – a strike rate which put him among the greatest in history. Now it was time to relax and, at most, check the voicemail once a day.

His son Pierfilippo, stuck at work in a typically sticky Milanese summer, was getting no such respite. Agents, clubs and national associations all wanted to know what his father's next move would be. And, given that Capello does not employ an agent, Pierfilippo was the next best thing.

The secretaries at the Guardamagna law firm became accustomed to fielding calls from around the globe. Pierfilippo dutifully noted everyone's name and number and passed it on to his father whenever he checked in. The line was always the same: 'He's in Tibet . . . No, he has no phone coverage . . . Yes, I'd be happy to take a message . . .' Pierfilippo, a successful lawyer in his mid-thirties, had turned into a glorified answering service.

And it wasn't just agents, intermediaries and clubs. Capello received a variety of commercial offers: speaking engagements, endorsements, media work. Yet when word filtered through to Tibet, the answer was always the same: 'No, I'm not going back to managing. Not now. Unless, of course, England call.'

Yes, England. The Three Lions. The country against

whom he had scored his most famous goal, that deflection at Wembley which sealed Italy's first ever win under the Twin Towers. He had been approached, of course, back in 2000. And he had never made a secret of his desire.

In a March 2006 interview with the Italian magazine *L'Espresso* he had made it about as clear as anyone could: 'My dream is managing England. It's something I have carried inside me for my entire life. In three years I'm going to quit club football and I would love for my dream to come true. After that, I'll be ready to quit for good. Maybe I'll retire to the island of Pantelleria, where I've just bought a house.'

Cynics will no doubt question the timing of those comments. Two months earlier, the Football Association had announced that Sven-Göran Eriksson would be stepping down after the World Cup that summer. This kicked off a frenzy of media speculation as the FA made their announcement without having a replacement in the bag. Capello, of course, had that clause in his contract which allowed him to leave Juventus at the end of the season. And even though the 'Calciopoli' scandal had yet to break, there were suggestions that Juventus would regardless change direction, severing ties with the trio of Antonio Giraudo, Roberto Bettega and Luciano Moggi, in which case Capello would likely move as well. Was it a case of self-promotion?

Possibly. Most likely, though, he was simply reminding everyone of a belief he had held most of his professional life. He wanted the England job and the challenge it posed. As it happened, it quickly became irrelevant as the FA looked elsewhere.

Eventually, in May 2006 the FA selected Steve McClaren, who had been doing double duty as Eriksson's assistant while also managing Middlesbrough. McClaren beat out a shortlist which included Charlton Athletic boss Alan Curbishley and Bolton Wanderers manager Sam Allardyce. His appointment hardly stoked popular enthusiasm. But, after five years of Eriksson, the FA felt that McClaren was a safe pair of hands. Plus, of course, he was English. It was almost as if the FA was saying: 'If we can't get an A-list coach like Scolari or Guus Hiddink [who had also been sounded out], we need to at least secure an Englishman.' Or, put another way, if we're going to gamble, let's gamble on one of our own.

Fast forward to July 2007 again. On his way back to Europe from Tibet, Capello had developed something of a game plan. He wasn't ruling out a return to club management, but, realistically, it wasn't going to happen before 2008 anyway. Besides, there weren't that many places where he could go, even in a year's time. Italy and Spain were improbable destinations at this point, for different, but obvious, reasons.

The Premier League might have had its appeal. But the problem was a lack of potential vacancies. Sir Alex Ferguson at Manchester United and Arsène Wenger at Arsenal were institutions only slightly less secure than Ayers Rock. Rafa Benítez had just taken Liverpool to the Champions League final and with two new owners supposedly backing him to the hilt, Merseyside was overjoyed with its continuing Rafa-lution (of course, that would change a few months later, when the two owners would fall out, but that's another story). José Mourinho remained at Chelsea, despite occasional reports suggesting that club owner Roman Abramovich was getting frustrated with the lack of entertainment on show at Stamford Bridge. 'Lack of entertainment': now there was something Capello had heard before. It did not take a genius to figure out that, after what happened in Madrid, if Mourinho did leave, Capello probably wouldn't be top of the list to replace him.

There were calls from elsewhere, touting opportunities in Major League Soccer, Australia and Asia, with at least three different national teams and half a dozen clubs around Europe. Some of them were direct, some via inter-mediaries or agents whose reliability, in some cases, was perhaps a bit dubious. Yet it was all pointless. While he was happy to listen, their words left him cold. This was going to be the last major job of his career. Capello knew what he wanted. And he was willing to wait.

He wasn't waiting for the England job to open up per se, but like anyone else, he knew the situation. Unless Steve McClaren delivered a very strong showing at Euro 2008 – which meant reaching the semi-finals at the very least – odds were that the FA would be looking for a new manager in less than twelve months.

Of course, Capello wasn't going to sit on his hands and do nothing until then. Marcello Lippi, his great rival, had genuinely taken time off after winning the 2006 World Cup. He went out on his boat, spent time with his grand-children, attended the occasional UEFA workshop. All things which had their appeal, but Capello is a man used to working long days. He wasn't ready to retire or even just take time out. Pantelleria would have to wait.

The logical thing was to go back to his role as a pundit, a job in which he had no shortage of suitors. RAI, the Italian state broadcaster, Mediaset, the leading commercial network and Sky Italia, the main satellite broadcaster, had all been in touch.

'As soon as it became clear that he was free, we went for him,' one RAI executive told me. 'There was no question about it. People can debate about whether he's the greatest living manager, but as far as I'm concerned, most would agree that he's the greatest living pundit. I believe some of our competitors actually offered him more than we did, but he had a soft spot for us. And for that, we were all very grateful.'

Capello threw himself into his punditry just as he had done before: with passion and professionalism. He was the co-commentator for the network's Champions League and national team matches and he was also a fixture on *La Domenica Sportiva*, Italy's equivalent of *Match Of The Day*. Crucially, the job also allowed him to remain in the public eye while watching football, lots of it.

Yet throughout, there was a sense that this was just a temporary assignment. Capello spearheaded RAI's coverage with an eye on the England results. And as England's qualifying campaign unfolded, it became clear that the vacancy might come sooner rather than later. By September, England were third in their qualifying group for Euro 2008. McClaren's men were on fourteen points, one behind Russia and three behind Croatia in what was not exactly a 'Group of Death': the other nations were Israel, Macedonia, Estonia and Andorra.

McClaren's men had dropped points the previous

October in a lacklustre home draw against Macedonia and a disappointing 2–0 away defeat to Croatia, in a game that would be remembered for goalkeeper Paul Robinson's flailing air-kick, an instant classic on YouTube. But they arguably hit rockbottom in March. They couldn't do better than a scoreless draw in Israel, fruitlessly trying to ram the ball home against a side which stuck nine men in the box and hung on for dear life. Things got even worse four days later against little Andorra, whose side was almost entirely made up of amateurs. At half-time, with the match deadlocked against a bunch of waiters, tour guides and forest rangers, the previously unthinkable happened. England were booed off the pitch and a number of players and staff, most notably McClaren, were roundly abused. The fact that England scored three times in the second half, securing all three points, did nothing to soften the humiliation.

The Andorra trip resonated around the world, not so much for England's poor performance, but for the way a sizeable portion of the travelling support turned on the team. No major footballing nation enjoys as much support from its fans as England. England regularly sell out all their games, even friendlies; other nations move games to smaller grounds to avoid embarrassing vistas of empty seats on television (under the guise of 'giving everyone a chance to see the national team'). England supporters take up their entire allocation for away trips and travel in numbers; other nations rely almost exclusively on ex-patriates for support on the road. But most of all, England fans do not boo their own team. And, on those rare occasions when they do, it happens at the final whistle, not during the match when there is still hope for victory. Andorra changed all that. On that day, the fabled England football fan became just a little bit more like every other supporter around the world. The spell had been broken. It was a sign of just how frustrated many had become with McClaren's tenure.

Still, amid the bleakness, there remained room for rational hope. The top two sides in each group advanced and England had a relatively manageable run-in. In September, home wins over Israel and Russia, both by a 3–0 margin, lifted England into second place, three points behind Croatia, but two ahead of Russia. Once again, McClaren's men controlled their own destiny.

It lasted just over a month. Following another 3–0 home victory, this time against Estonia, England travelled to Moscow. A draw would virtually have sent them on their way to the finals in Austria and Switzerland. Instead, after taking the lead through Wayne Rooney inside half an hour, England contrived to lose, giving up two late goals to Roman Pavluchenko.

All of a sudden, everything had changed. England's future was now in the hands of Israel, who would host Russia the following month. Croatia had qualified. England held a two-point lead over Russia – twenty-three to twenty-one – but the Russians had two games left, England just one. Given that Russia's final game was against Andorra, a team that had lost every match in qualifying, it was obvious that if Russia won in Tel Aviv, England might as well book their summer holidays.

And so a nation watched. They cheered when Elyaniv Barda gave Israel an early lead after ten minutes. They worried when Diniyar Bilyaletdinov equalized just after the hour mark. And then, in stoppage time, they despaired when Dmitri Sychev, the fleet-footed striker who had once been called 'Russia's answer to Michael Owen', cut through the Israeli positions and, with two defenders hanging off him, unleashed a shot which beat the goalkeeper and powered its way towards the target . . . only to hit the Israeli post. There was no question the ball looked goalbound. It may have been an optical illusion. It may have been a divot on the Ramat Gan pitch. Or, it may have been an act of God or fate or whatever you believe in.

The latter theory was reinforced by what happened in the next minute: Israel went straight back up the pitch, springing the offside trap and releasing Omer Golan in front of the goalkeeper. Golan calmly slotted the ball into the back of the net, giving Israel an improbable victory and lifting English hopes and spirits. If Lady Luck could smile on them like that, then maybe they really were a team of destiny.

All they needed now was a draw against Croatia at Wembley. One little, measly point would make all of Russia's efforts in vain. If England could only just get the draw, it wouldn't matter if Russia put twenty past Andorra. England had the tiebreaker in the head-to-heads with the Russians (3–0 and 1–2), which meant that finishing level on points would still send McClaren's men to Euro 2008.

True, Croatia were probably the strongest side in Group 5, but, crucially, they had already qualified as group winners. Perhaps that might prompt the Croats to treat this game as no more than a glorified friendly. After all, just a few days before, they appeared to do precisely that, losing 2–0 against Macedonia in a similarly meaningless game. Surely a draw – at the new Wembley, in front of 90,000 screaming supporters, against a side with nothing to play for but pride – was within England's reach?

We know what happened next. England 2–0 down inside fifteen minutes. Frank Lampard, from the penalty spot, and Peter Crouch put the home side back on track with less than half an hour to go. And then, fifteen minutes from time, Mladen Petric's scorching left-footed strike sunk McClaren's battleship once and for all.

Two images eloquently sum up that moment. The first is Petric, the epitome of the Croatian diaspora – born in Bosnia, raised in Switzerland, plays his club football in Germany, but fiercely proud of his heritage – sprinting to celebrate with the Croatian supporters. The other is McClaren, in what has become the much-lampooned 'wally with a brolly' photo. The England coach, standing under an oversized umbrella, looks on with a blend of disbelief and wonder. It's almost as if he's witnessed something unthinkable, something so absurd it could not have been contemplated beforehand. It's the kind of look you might have if you go to the toilet and see Roger Rabbit and Boris Johnson snorkelling around in your bowl. Too absurd and inexplicable to contemplate.

As rain and tears mixed freely at Wembley, Capello – as you read earlier – was throwing his hat in the ring on national television. In reality, his name had already come up in the previous weeks as the media, particularly after the result in Moscow, had already begun drawing up short-lists of potential successors.

Officially, the Football Association did not contemplate relieving McClaren of his duties until after the Croatia match sealed his fate. Nor was it discussed privately. But it's difficult to believe that Chief Executive Brian Barwick was not in some way thinking about the Plan B he would need if the worst-case scenario materialized.

In some ways, the FA had free rein. The taboo of a foreign manager had already been broken in 2000, when they turned to the Swede Sven-Göran Eriksson. That day, England became the first of the game's traditional powers to look overseas for its national team coach. It was a choice which shocked many. England had invented the game, they had pioneered its growth for the first fifty or so years of its existence. And, given the success of the Premier League, they were again trailblazers, at least in a commercial sense.

Appointing Eriksson was an admission of failure, a realization that something had gone badly wrong. Jeff Powell, one of the elder statesmen of the English football media, put it memorably, if virulently, writing in the *Daily Mail* in November 2000: 'So now, the mother country of football, birthplace of the greatest game, has finally gone from the cradle to the shame . . . We have sold our birthright down a fjord to a nation of seven million skiers and hammer-throwers who spend half their year living in darkness.'

Never mind the factual inaccuracies – Sweden has no fjords, unlike its neighbour Norway, the population is closer to nine million and the hammer-throw is as much of a minority pursuit as it is in England – Powell eloquently summed up the mood of a sizeable portion of the English footballing public.

Still, Eriksson had broken the glass ceiling. The public and the pundits had grown accustomed to a foreigner leading their national side, just as foreigners led most successful English clubs. Barwick was very clear on this point and he knew it was one of the few things that worked to his advantage. Back in 2006, after the failed attempt with Scolari, he did come under pressure to appoint an Englishman, or at least a Briton. But the scarcity of quality candidates in that job hunt – which resulted in the appointment of McClaren – was still fresh in everyone's minds. The factions that demanded an Englishman at all costs were severely weakened by the options – or lack thereof – available.

These circumstances quickly persuaded Barwick that this time around he really could scour the world for the best possible candidate, without excessive fear of a backlash from the Little Englanders. Hours after the England defeat, he was already thinking about the next move and how he would handle the FA's managerial search.

Back in Milan, the Capello camp waited for things to develop. They had read the papers, they knew what was going on, but solid information was hard to come by. They did not want to go out on a limb, but, at the same time, chose not to be shy about Capello's interest in the job.

The calls came in thick and furious, just as they had the previous summer. Agents, intermediaries, journalists, PR spin doctors, everyone wanted to get in on the action. The answer was always the same: 'If the FA want to speak to us, tell them to call us.'

It should be noted that the position of England manager can be a veritable gravy train for a variety of people.

Everyone knew that Capello did not have an agent, which meant that any middleman who could make the deal happen was bound to earn a nice little commission. Then there were the sponsorship opportunities, the PR guys offering to fluff his image in the English media, the journalists looking for any shred of information.

In these situations, information is scarce, but priceless, particularly since the FA were doing a good job at keeping their plans under wraps. Capello's camp, having at this point no direct line to the FA, relied on scraps gleaned from agents and journalists. They were told that there was an initial shortlist of ten names and that José Mourinho, the former Chelsea manager, was in pole position.

Either way, Capello felt it was best to get things out into the open, partly to avoid letting the situation drag on too long and partly out of respect for RAI, with whom he was under contract. Having turned down more than fifty interview requests, Capello's camp returned the BBC's phone calls and agreed to sit down for a *Football Focus* interview, to be aired on Saturday, with highlights appearing the day before on RAI.

The move shocked more than a few people. It was unusual for Capello to move so decisively without having any kind of assurances.

'I was surprised,' a long-standing associate of Capello told me. 'When he agreed to speak out so candidly I figured he must have the job in the bag. I didn't think he would expose himself like that. Because if he did not get the job, he would look silly. And Fabio has his pride.'

In fact, Capello had nothing at that point. Not even a phone call from the FA, just a bunch of hearsay and input from agents, whose reliability is often hit-or-miss. But at the same time, he knew that it was now or never. Whatever embarrassment he might have faced had he been snubbed, paled in comparison with his desire for the job. And, as you've probably figured out by now, Capello is not a guy who gets easily embarrassed or who particularly cares what others think or say about him.

The interview was well timed. As it happened, within forty-eight hours of the Croatia game, two of the names rumoured to be on the shortlist – Aston Villa boss Martin O'Neill and Sam Allardyce, both of whom had been in the running in 2006 – had ruled themselves out. Furthermore, by Friday morning, Mourinho's camp let it be known that he was 'flattered' by the FA's reported interest but reluctant to consider the job.

Mourinho had not been directly approached at that point, though his agent, Jorge Mendes, had been contacted by at least half a dozen individuals claiming to have a 'direct line' into Soho Square. But there is little question that the Portuguese manager expected a clear and direct offer from the FA. He wasn't content with the dribs and drabs, filtered by agents and journalists, that Capello was getting. Either way, how interested he genuinely was remains a matter of debate.

According to a source close to Mourinho, 'José was willing to hear them out.' But for him to say yes required a mega-offer, not just financially, but in terms of control as well. He wanted 'something black-on-white, clearly stating everything', if only to flush out other potential suitors at club level (and there was no shortage of those). When asked about Mourinho's reticence in the *Football Focus* interview, Capello did not duck the question. 'I was convinced Mourinho would have accepted,' he said. 'The fact that he has opted to step aside means that he has other objectives.'

And when asked about the job itself, he said it would be a 'challenge' but one that was, at once, 'exciting' and 'fascinating'. In Capellospeak, it's about as close to a 'come-and-get-me' plea as you can get.

It may have been the clear message Capello delivered on Friday. It may have been a bit of a surprise at the way the English media interpreted his 'reluctance' as 'ruling himself out of the job'. Either way, by Saturday, Mourinho's camp knew they needed to send a countermessage.

They briefed journalists that Mourinho considered the England job 'special' and was, in fact, very interested. But, they said, the FA needed to 'move quickly' because there were a number of high-profile job openings coming up in club football.

As for the FA, Barwick made it clear that, with England's next match some three months away, he was in no hurry. Besides, there were still a number of administrative hoops to jump through. He scrapped the interview system used in 2006, opting for a more streamlined process where most of the decision-making power rested with one man: Barwick himself. If there was one thing 2006 taught him it is that too many cooks spoil the broth. He was the chief executive, it was his rear end on the line, it was only right that he be the man making the decision.

In any case, Barwick and other FA officials were in Durban that weekend for the 2010 World Cup qualifying draw. There was a clutch of English journalists with them and they wisely engaged them in the discussion, albeit without giving anything away (not that there was much to give away at that stage) and remaining distinctly 'on message': England's next manager would be a 'world-class manager'.

Barwick may not have intended it that way, but his words certainly sent the message that the next England manager would most likely be a foreigner and that those holding out hope for Alan Shearer or Stuart Pearce were barking up the wrong tree.

Shearer was the emotional and patriotic choice. A legendary centre-forward who had excelled for England and Newcastle United, he epitomized the strong, under-stated warrior, whose charisma derives from his bearing and his actions, more than his words. He was also the choice of those who believe that good coaching is born out of stature, character and passion, rather than experience and formal training. To this day, there are many in England who see things that way, as evidenced by the number of footballers who hang up their boots and move straight into management. Having worked as a pundit for the BBC after his retirement, Shearer had zero managerial experience. In fact, he had yet to gain his UEFA Pro Licence. These factors meant he was far from meeting Barwick's definition of a 'world-class manager' and his candidacy soon waned.

Pearce, like Shearer an England hero, was in a similar situation. A hard-tackling international calibre fullback who embodied the 'bulldog spirit', he was widely admired as a player. He was nicknamed Psycho – a result of some of his more scything tackles – but, in fact, the moniker was somewhat reductive. Pearce was a genuine professional, who grew and improved as he got older. His intensity, coupled with his professionalism and the thoroughness with which he trained and took care of his body, allowed him to play at the highest level until the age of forty. Pearce's problem was that his coaching record was simply sub-standard for a job of this magnitude. After retiring, he worked under Kevin Keegan at Manchester City, before taking over the job full-time in March 2005. He finished that season well, but then, with Pearce in sole charge as manager, City severely underachieved, narrowly avoiding relegation the next two seasons.

Furthermore, he was already employed by the FA, having coached the Under 21 team part-time since February 2007. While his results at Under 21 level weren't bad – England reached the semi-finals of the European Championships – his reputation was still somewhat tarnished by his tenure at City. And, at this stage, having made an internal appointment with McClaren in 2006, the FA wanted to make a clean break with the past.

There was a third English name bandied about, one with more impressive credentials: Harry Redknapp, the Portsmouth manager. Redknapp was a larger than life figure, a man who had only ever taken charge of smaller clubs – West Ham United, Southampton, Portsmouth – but often exceeded expectations. He didn't fit the mould of the stereotypical English manager, he had long championed a progressive style of play and had a weak spot for technically gifted rather than physically over-powering players, such as Paolo Di Canio, Joe Cole and Nico Kranjcar.

On the morning that Croatia knocked England out, I sat with my colleague Guillem Balague in Redknapp's kitchen and he told us in no uncertain terms that, while he would love to have a crack at the England job, he did not think that he would ever be considered.

'But I do think that, if I had had the players that Sir Alex Ferguson [at Manchester United] or [Arsène] Wenger [at Arsenal] had, I would have won a lot of silverware as well,' he told us. 'I don't consider myself inferior to any manager in the Premier League.'

Redknapp's brand of football has been praised by – among others – Louis Van Gaal, Rafa Benitez and, yes, Fabio Capello. But his problem was one of image. With his marked East End accent and hyperactivity in the transfer market, he was regularly lampooned in the media as a cockney wide boy wheeler-dealer. And some media outlets made more serious allegations as well, none of which have been proved. Redknapp was stuck with that baggage, but worse was to come.

In the early hours of 28 November 2007, police raided his house on the south coast. Redknapp wasn't home – he was flying back from a scouting trip and would be taken into custody a few hours later – but officers removed documents and personal computers. City of London police said it was part of an investigation into corruption and illegal payments in football. Redknapp was questioned and released. No charges were brought – and the way the police acted on that day was, at best, questionable – but it certainly tarnished his image once again and, effectively, ruled him out of the running.

Thus, with three more domestic candidates effectively

struck off the list, Capello chose to lie low. He had stated his interest and, for now, there was nothing left to do. He knew that Barwick would be canvassing opinion, taking in different viewpoints and, for now, merely listening. And so, the following weekend, the entire Capello family, including sons Pierfilippo and Edoardo, went off to Istanbul for some sightseeing on the Bosphorus.

It was there that Pierfilippo received a call from Giovanni Branchini, one of Italy's most high profile agents. The bearded, low-key Branchini has a reputation for discretion and professionalism, as well as an ability to get deals done. It may be a trait he inherited from his father Umberto, a legendary boxing promoter who is enshrined in the IBF Hall of Fame. In his career, he has represented hundreds of footballers, from Ronaldo and Careca, to Romário and Seedorf. He wasn't working for Capello in any official capacity, but he nevertheless was 'in the loop' and the Capello clan appreciated his assistance and that of another agent, Capello's former teammate Oscar Damiani.

'You're going to get a call from someone at the FA in the next half-hour,' Branchini told Pierfilippo. 'Keep your phone on.'

Sure enough, less than thirty minutes, later, Pierfilippo's phone rang and the words 'Private Number' flashed on his mobile. It was Simon Johnson, the FA's director of corporate affairs. He advised Pierfilippo that half a dozen people claiming to represent Capello had been in contact with them. Not wanting to create confusion or be led up blind alleys, they were keen to 'cut through the bullshit' and speak directly to Capello's camp.

Thus, against the wintry backdrop of Istanbul's Hagia Sofia, first contact was made. Pierfilippo was told that, at this stage, there were no more than three or four names left in the running and that Capello was one of them. Was Capello interested? Pierfilippo said that 'in principle' he was, but, obviously would have to talk about contracts and other details.

The voice on the other phone seemed relieved. 'OK, then. For the next ten to fifteen days you won't hear from us. Then, once we know what the situation is, we'll call you.'

And, just like that, the FA 'went dark'. Upon reflection, Capello had no way of knowing whether the voice on the other end of the phone was genuine, beyond the fact that Branchini had told him someone would call. But, at the time, what mattered was that the wheels had started to turn.

Mourinho was waiting too. While he made no statements, members of his entourage worked the media, suggesting that the FA needed to 'hurry up' because various clubs were on his case. It was the usual mantra. Curiously, his approach was something of a turn-off to some within the FA, who believed Mourinho was using them to flush out interest from elsewhere.

This prompted one of Mourinho's advisers, speaking in the *Observer*, to issue a vehement denial: 'That is crazy. José does not need England to get a job. He knows the jobs are there for him and it is just a matter of timing. To say he has to make a decision between a Spanish club and England is more accurate.'

Six of one, half a dozen of the other. Mourinho, as you do in these situations, was playing his hand, just as Capello, in a different way, was playing his. The FA did consult John Terry, the England captain, who gave Mourinho a glowing assessment but also said he was open to other options. Media reports went further, suggesting that Terry had offered to put the two in touch, by giving the FA his 'new mobile number' as if the problem was that the FA did not know how to find Mourinho. It was a silly story – anyone with internet access can get the direct number of Jorge Mendes, Mourinho's agent – but, at times like these, with such massive interest and so little concrete information, any little scrap will do. Not to mention that such stories made another important point (at least from Mourinho's perspective): the England captain wanted Mourinho.

On 7 December the *Sun* reported that Mourinho had flown to London the previous night by executive jet, landing at Farnborough, a private airfield just outside the M25. According to the newspaper, which had championed Mourinho's cause from the beginning, he was there to hold secret talks with Barwick and the FA. The *Sun* also quoted the usual 'source close to Mourinho' as saying: 'There is no doubt that José wants the job and that England desperately want him. He is the FA's first choice. What is crucial now is for José to thrash out the fine details of a deal. That is why he is flying into London to meet Mr Barwick and other members of the FA board. It just depends on whether the FA can give him the deal he wants.'

Within hours, the FA denied the story. And later that same day, Mourinho himself agreed to appear on Sky Sports News from the front doorstep of his villa in Setúbal, confirming once and for all that the story was a dud; Mourinho has many talents, but, for now at least, the ability to be in two places at once is not among them. He did say that he had originally planned a trip to London to 'do some Christmas shopping', but cancelled it.

So where did the story come from? Contrary to what some believe, newspapers don't just go around making things up. The *Sun* may have had a bad steer. Or it may have been lured into following somebody's agenda. Either way, up to that point, Mourinho had yet to meet the FA in person to discuss the England job. Instead, discussions were held via telephone, both directly with the Portuguese manager and with his entourage.

While Mourinho never made it to London, the *Observer* reported that Mendes did show up at Soho Square on Friday, 7 December, hand-delivering Mourinho's detailed plans for what he called his 'Club England' set-up, which involved a radical overhaul of the FA and gave the new manager unprecedented and wide-ranging powers. Meanwhile, Capello's camp remained in the dark. They would get updates from journalists and agents, but generally treated them with a pinch of salt. When two different sources came up with the same 'privileged in-formation' then, and only then, would they pay it any heed. They knew Mourinho was in the driving seat, but also trusted in the fact that the FA would let them make their case before making their decision.

That same weekend, just after the FA received Mourinho's 'Club England' dossier, Pierfilippo's phone rang again. It was the FA. If you want to come up to London, we'd love to have a chat.

Sure enough, Capello was still in the running. The reasons why became even more obvious on Monday afternoon. Mourinho issued a statement on Mendes' website, ruling himself out once and for all. He said that he had had 'useful discussions' with Barwick, Sir Trevor Brooking and others about the England job. But, 'after deep and serious thinking', he was placing himself out of the running. The decision not to proceed with Mourinho had, according to a source, been made the evening before.

Forty-eight hours elapsed between the moment the FA received Mourinho's 'Club England' dossier (assuming the dossier was, in fact, delivered: FA sources would neither confirm nor deny this) and the decision not to proceed. What had prompted the climbdown? Different sources offer different explanations. Some suggest Mourinho only wanted the job under very specific conditions – that he would have those 'unprecedented powers' – and the FA simply could not meet his demands. Others maintain the FA simply looked at the situation and decided to go in a different direction. Still others insist that Capello had never been the second choice, but rather Mourinho and Capello were number 1 and number 1A on the list. And that it was Capello's experience and enthusiasm for the job that tipped the balance in his favour.

Either way, with Mourinho having removed himself from the picture, it didn't take long for the press to shift their sights on Capello. With rumours that a trip to London was imminent, photographers and spotters were dispatched to each of London's five airports. Any flight from Malpensa, Linate or Bergamo airports in Milan would be scrutinized. (Though, to be fair, the photographers stationed at Luton and Stansted probably knew theirs was a fruitless task: Capello simply isn't a low-cost, RyanAir type of guy.)

Still wishing to elude the press, Capello designed his trip carefully. He would fly from Malpensa to Zurich and then, from there, take a Swiss Air flight to City Airport. It was the aviation equivalent of driving from London to Birmingham on A roads, rather than the M1.

The FA's phone call may have described it as a 'chat', but Capello was under no illusions. This was in fact a full-fledged interview, with a likely black-or-white result. Like those one-off 'dates' prior to arranged marriages, it would either result in him moving into Soho Square or retreating to the commentary booth. Capello probably knew about as much about the English game as any foreign manager who kept abreast of things but had never worked or lived in England could know, which isn't all that much.

Capello may have an image of absolute certainty, as an uncompromising autocrat who values his own opinion above anyone else's. But, in fact, he is very conscious of his own limits. He may act, at times, like he knows everything, but the truth is that he knows what he doesn't know. Or, as Donald Rumsfeld might have put it, he's very clear on what the 'known unknowns' are. He has no qualms about asking questions when he doesn't know something. He'll take on board as much information as possible and then choose his own path.

This is where Capello and Pierfilippo really relied on Branchini. The veteran agent's web of contacts is unparalleled and, in the seventy-two hours leading up to the meeting, Capello was briefed on what to expect. Branchini painted verbal vignettes of the characters Capello would be meeting: Barwick, of course, as well as his trusted side-kick, Simon Johnson, the FA's director of corporate affairs,

Adrian Bevington, the FA's head of communications and Sir Trevor Brooking, the director of football development.

They tried to figure out what arguments would resonate with each of them, what each FA representative's priorities might be and they tried to anticipate every possible question. They also discussed what the process would entail. Barwick had ensured that he would be the focus of this manager search and that it would be far less of a communal affair than previous ones, but, ultimately, he wasn't omnipotent. He had a board to answer to and it would be important to identify, predict and neutralize whatever objections or caveats the other board members might throw at Barwick.

Armed with that information, Capello set about putting together a PowerPoint presentation for the FA. Yes, just like a middle management type flying off to try and impress clients, Capello's camp relied on good ol' PowerPoint.

Thus, on Wednesday, 12 December Capello set off from Malpensa, switched flights in Zurich and landed at City Airport just after noon. Whatever spotters were staking out the arrivals lounge evidently didn't notice him (or, more likely, were too intent on flights originating in Italy) and he easily slipped out and into the waiting car the FA had arranged.

From there, the car headed north and west to Wembley. Any fears of a media scrum were swiftly put to rest. When they arrived at Wembley Way, just before two o'clock, a couple of photographers were waiting outside, but that was it. Fabio Capello, his son Pierfilippo and Diego Rodriguez, his Spanish lawyer, strode in to meet the FA contingent which, as Branchini predicted, consisted of Barwick, Johnson, Bevington and Brooking.

One of the first things which struck the FA was Capello's command of English, which was better than they expected. The press – including me – had questioned his ability to communicate, particularly as he had never granted any interviews in English (two months earlier, I had a sit-down interview with him on behalf of UEFA.com: we spoke in Italian and it was later translated).

In fact, Capello's English on a conversational level was, even then, more than adequate. His reluctance to speak English in public had more to do with his vocabulary. He likes to choose his words with some precision and, with a limited understanding of the nuances of certain terms, he knew he could not have the same accuracy and subtlety in English. For a man who is proud of the way he speaks in Italian and Spanish, being forced to speak English in public was a little bit like making Elton John perform on a plastic Fisher Price children's keyboard: he could do it, but not to his satisfaction (or anyone else's for that matter).

At Wembley that day Capello listened intently and, only on a few occasions, did he turn to Pierfilippo to clarify what the FA crew were saying. He expressed himself in English as much as he could, deferring to Pierfilippo for the more complex concepts. The PowerPoint presentation, painstakingly put together in the previous forty-eight hours, did the rest.

It outlined Capello's vision in great detail. It covered scouting, both of English players and opponents, the type of work to be done in training, relations with the media, his assistant's specific duties, how the stays in the pre-match team hotels would be structured, physical preparations, relationships with clubs, medical support, the role of the Under 21 set-up, youth development . . . basically every aspect of the job was covered. His meticulous preparation, as well as the way it was presented, enthralled the FA.

But there were still a few issues to be resolved. Capello wanted to bring in four assistants: Italo Galbiati, his right-hand man, Franco Tancredi, his goalkeeping coach, Massimo Neri, his fitness guru and Franco Baldini, whom he called his 'general manager'. The FA were open to the first three, but required further clarification over Baldini.

Baldini was a respected figure but in the past he had been primarily responsible for transfer activities and player contracts, both of which, obviously, would not come into play at the FA (fortunately the day when the FA has to negotiate wages with players is not yet upon us). What would he be contributing to England?

Capello's camp outlined Baldini's qualities. For a start, while he was not a coach, he had a reputation as an outstanding scout and talent-spotter. Given that Capello would have to familiarize himself with a whole raft of footballers – he'd obviously seen plenty of the England stars, but he had to check out the fringe players, the youngsters and those guys in mid-career who had perhaps been overlooked – in a very short period of time, Baldini represented another expert set of eyes. He was very much on Capello's wavelength and, even though the manager always liked to make up his own mind, he trusted Baldini's opinion as much as anyone's.

But there was another reason behind wanting Baldini.

He spoke good English and, at least until Capello got up to speed, he would provide a quick and efficient conduit with the FA, club managers and the press. Capello knew that Baldini was a good complement to his skills. Where Capello can be gruff and distant with outsiders, Baldini is charming and likeable. He was the man who could smooth the edges and help resolve the external conflicts as they arose. He was liked and trusted by journalists and club managers alike, he was the man who could have a quiet, off-the-record conversation to sort things out. But he was also a savvy operator who knew, as an Italian adage goes, that you get more results with a spoonful of honey than with a barrelful of vinegar. And, if necessary, he could play 'good cop' to Capello's 'bad cop'.

Barwick was quickly convinced, some of his advisers less so, but they soon came around. Especially because, what-ever fears they may have had of a 'foreign invasion' were soon allayed when Capello's plans for a 'mirror system' flashed on the screen during the presentation. For each backroom position occupied by one of Capello's Italian assistants, he envisaged an English 'mirror' or 'shadow', who would work alongside them. Thus, Galbiati, Tancredi and Neri would each be working alongside an English assistant coach, goalkeeping coach and fitness coach. Capello said that, if offered the job, he would not im-mediately name the 'mirror' positions – apart from that of assistant coach, where he insisted that an Englishman should be appointed straight away – but that he thought it was important to have a parallel English staff under him.

Again, this won points with the FA. Capello was not coming in with the arrogance of the foreign 'Mr Fix-It'. He was not a prophet descended from the heavens to guide a wayward footballing nation towards the light. Rather, he seemed to understand the FA's needs and priorities and, especially, how – no matter what anyone says and no matter how much the Eriksson experience might have changed some perceptions – England was a proud foot-balling nation and the appointment of a foreigner was a blow to that collective ego.

Capello was open to suggestions regarding the English components of his backroom staff. While the FA was not averse to his 'mirror' idea, it was felt that, for the time being, keeping Ray Clemence, the former goalkeeping coach, in the England set-up would tick one of the boxes and that they would hold off on the English fitness coach. There remained, of course, the issue of the English number two who would shadow Galbiati.

Capello felt that it was best not to involve someone who was already working at club level, as had been the case with McClaren. This applied to the entire England set-up. It was felt that, potentially, it could upset the clubs, as the backroom staff could become privy to information about England players' injuries and other issues which could, potentially, create a conflict of interest. Capello wanted a staff who would be loyal to England and only to England. He wanted a clear 'Chinese Wall' between England and the clubs; he didn't want to risk the appearance of impropriety.

The FA agreed in principle and, to be fair, McClaren, Eriksson and other England coaches had made the same request. However, it was felt that a number of those doing 'double duty' for clubs and England – such as head physio

Gary Lewin, whose day job is at Arsenal – were so highly regarded in their field and so trustworthy that removing them would have amounted to shooting yourself in the foot. The FA simply did not see this as a massive problem and Capello went along with it.

There was another tricky issue as far as the assistant was concerned. There tend to be two varieties of assistants. Some are lifelong 'number twos' who tie themselves to a successful manager and, though they may have been head coaches in the past, clearly have no professional ambition to take over their own teams. Boro Primorac, Arsène Wenger's right-hand man at Arsenal, or John Robertson, Martin O'Neill's trusted number two, are examples of this, as is Galbiati himself. And then there are others, usually younger ones, who use the position as a springboard into full management jobs.

It was difficult for the FA to appoint a figure who fitted the former profile, for two main reasons. Such people are usually well entrenched in their clubs and unwilling to leave, especially to work for a man like Capello with whom they had no connection. Secondly, it was very much in the FA's interest to be seen to be looking forward, grooming an Englishman who could one day take over; that would not have been the case with a veteran assistant.

And so thoughts turned towards a younger coach, who might use the position as a stepping stone. Here, again, there was an issue. Having seen the McClaren experience and how the former number two was greeted with a distinct lack of enthusiasm when he moved up to the top job, the FA were somewhat wary of what might happen if Capello's tenure was seen to be a failure. Would it blacken the assistant's name as well? Would it make it that much more difficult for him to move on to other jobs?

This, obviously, wasn't Capello's concern, but it did weigh on the FA's minds. And it may have been one of the reasons why Alan Shearer, whom some sectors of the media had been touting for a role within the set-up, was not aggressively pursued, or, indeed, why Shearer didn't push his case with the FA. Despite his lack of coaching experience, he would have brought gravitas and prestige to the backroom staff (plus, he was liked and respected by much of the media). However, there was a sense that, should things go horribly wrong, his association with the England job might tarnish him to some degree.

And so the choice fell to Stuart Pearce. Capello knew Pearce by reputation and he was aware that, throughout the 1990s, he had embodied the 'patriotic England footballer'. Pearce, of course, was already employed by the FA, so he was already familiar with the inner workings. The fact that he kept his job as Under 21 boss wasn't ideal – it would mean that he would necessarily miss most pre-match training sessions – but Capello was delighted to have him as part of his team. He saw him as a valuable sounding board who came from a different footballing background and a man whose knowledge of the next generation of England players was exceptional.

Pearce's continued role with the Under 21s also made sense from the FA's perspective. They had invested time and energy in him and believed that he had a bright future. At the same time, if he was too closely linked to Capello and things went awry, his image would be damaged. By keeping him involved, but leaving him in charge of the Under 21 side, they were creating the perception of separation. And, of course, if the Under 21 side did well, Pearce's credentials as a potential future England boss would be strengthened.

After several hours of discussion, it became clear that both sides were largely in agreement. Capello had answered the FA's queries to their satisfaction and, just as importantly, had shown himself to be well prepared and proactive. For his part, Capello, of course, knew he wanted the job. But he had gone into the meeting with an open mind, ready to pick up any warning signs that might turn him off. He had been in situations before when he went to meet a club for a job and picked up little things which should have rung alarm bells. It happened with Milan, when he returned, back in 1997, it happened again when he met Inter in 2004. The first time, he ignored them and let his heart rule his head, with, as it turned out, disastrous results. The second time, even though the job appealed to him, he trusted his instincts and his brain and said 'thanks, but no thanks' to Inter's offer.

Branchini had briefed him on the FA and Capello had also done a bit of homework of his own, but, in his mind, he was interviewing them as much as they him. How did they deal with pressure from clubs? How much independence would he have? How much decision-making power did Barwick really have? How did they deal with media intrusion into the England manager's private life?

Capello had reached a stage in his life where, if the working conditions weren't right, he didn't need the aggro. He went through it at Roma after winning the title; he went through it on both occasions at Madrid. Not any more. He didn't have to like the FA representatives, but he did have to respect them and truly believe they could provide the right conditions for him.

Curiously, the one who most struck a chord with him was Barwick. The Liverpool-born former BBC executive is neither photogenic nor telegenic and often comes across as aloof and awkward in public. For a man with a media background, he keeps a relatively low profile and is extremely discreet. Quite the opposite from the bosses Capello was accustomed to working for: Ramón Calderón, Luciano Moggi, Lorenzo Sanz, Adriano Galliani and, of course, Silvio Berlusconi, to name but a few.

Capello liked Barwick's understated professionalism. But he was also looking for something else, something beyond planning, projects and negotiation, some kind of personal connection. It came in what for Barwick might have seemed a casual line, but which had a profound effect on the Capello camp.

'I believe in you.'

Those words, tumbling earnestly from Barwick's lips, helped seal the deal, at least metaphorically, in Capello's mind. The FA had addressed his practical, logistical and technical concerns to his satisfaction. The vibe he got from Barwick spoke to his heart and his soul. It felt right. Shortly thereafter, around five o'clock, the meeting was wrapped up. Capello had heard enough, the FA had too.

Capello motioned to Pierfilippo and to Rodriguez and said they would be taking over from here. In those three hours, they had covered everything; all that was left were the financial terms of his contract. He didn't need to be around for that part of the discussion. With that, he made his farewells and set off for Heathrow Airport, accompanied by Ray Whitworth, the FA's head of security. Photographers snapped him leaving, but, otherwise, he returned home, excited, satisfied and waiting for news from Pierfilippo.

Meanwhile, back at Wembley, negotiations carried on well into the night. It wasn't just a matter of determining Capello's wages and contract length, there were plenty of smaller points and clauses to resolve as well. For example, Capello's contract stipulates that his main residence must be 'no more than thirty miles' away from Soho Square. Capello was fine with this – in fact, he looked forward to experiencing a new city like London – though it did appear somewhat arcane and unusual. Then again, in a country where they drive on the left and where Black Rod opens Parliament, perhaps this wasn't so strange.

There were other stipulations too, covering in detail how disputes would be resolved. For example, if Capello somehow brought the FA into disrepute by his words or behaviour, he'd be subject to certain disciplinary proceedings.

On this point, the FA had done their homework as best they could. Previous England managers had seen their regimes clouded by non-footballing issues. Glenn Hoddle, who had some unconventional religious beliefs, had to resign the England job in 1999 after making some rather controversial remarks which suggested that people with disabilities were paying for sins in a 'former life'. Eriksson had a long laundry list of indiscretions in his private life, including dalliances with Ulrika Jonsson, a television presenter, and Faria Alam, an FA employee at Soho

Square. Plus, of course, there was the famous incident with the Fake Sheikh: Mazher Mahmood, an undercover reporter for the *News of the World*, had dressed up in Arab garb, pretended to be a wealthy sheikh from the Gulf and duped Eriksson into making all sorts of revelations, including the fact that he was willing to walk out on the England team.

The FA had, understandably, become very sensitive about this kind of non-footballing negative publicity. Indeed, just before his appointment, McClaren was urged to reveal that he had had an affair with a Middlesbrough employee during a period of separation from his wife. It was a way of getting potential skeletons out of the closet and into the open.

Taken on their own, the actions of Hoddle, Eriksson and McClaren were not earth-shattering. Hoddle, after all, had a right to his own religious views, no matter how insensitive some may have found them. Eriksson was not married and his conversations with the 'Fake Sheikh' were just that: conversations. And McClaren, of course, was separated from his wife when he had his affair. Yet public opinion can be exceptionally prurient and somewhat prudish on these issues. And, for better or worse, these men represented the FA. They may have had a right to their private lives, but they were public figures and, when the two spheres overlapped, the FA had to act.

That's why the FA felt it needed to take precautions with Capello. They had done the research and were quietly confident that there was nothing in his past that might resurface to embarrass them. But they knew they weren't omniscient. For all they knew, Capello might convert to a Satanic cult the day after his appointment, paint a pentagram on his front door and bow down before the inverted cross while drinking sow's blood. They needed a mechanism to deal with such issues should they ever come up. Every detail of this had to be examined and worked on. There was no one-size-fits-all solution.

Perhaps this is why negotiations continued to drag on. Pierfilippo and Rodriguez, having burned the midnight oil, were up early again on Thursday and spent all day at Soho Square, hammering out the deal. Capello was kept updated, but remained hands-off: he had told his son what he wanted and was happy to let him do the work.

The length of contract was sorted out rather quickly. The FA wanted the security of having Capello for two international cycles, which suited everyone. Capello was realistic about his age: four and a half years were just right. Simply signing until 2010 might not give him the time to see his work come to fruition. Pursuing a commitment up to 2014 seemed excessive.

And then there were Capello's wages. The FA had prepared a package offer which covered the remuneration of Capello and his entire Italian staff. In addition, they outlined a series of incremental bonuses, based on qualification to the World Cup and rising with each successive round. It was a similar deal to that offered to previous England managers.

Capello, however, disagreed. You brought me here for one reason and one reason only, to get to the final. I don't need a bonus for finishing fifth: that was his message. Instead, Capello suggested raising his base salary, but, in exchange, offered to forgo all bonuses, except for reaching the final of the 2010 World Cup in Johannesburg. It was the kind of move which the FA welcomed and which left no doubt that he was clear about the task in hand. Anything other than reaching the final – and, ideally, winning it – was a failure and not deserving of a bonus.

Beyond that, Capello's crew negotiated a deal which made him the highest paid manager in world football. The FA knew they had to bite the bullet. They had a reputation as being far and away the most generous employers in the game and they had to live with it. They had already set the bar very high by paying Sven-Göran Eriksson a reported four million pounds a year. And, in some ways, giving his successor, McClaren, a man with a sparse CV at best, a four-year contract worth in excess of two million pounds, came across as an even greater gesture of generosity.

In one sense, the FA were a victim of their own success. They may be the highest-paying national association in the world, but then they are also far and away the most profitable. Indeed, Barwick himself made that point at Capello's first press conference, when questioned about the wages.

'The gross income of the FA in the next four and a half years may well be in excess of one billion pounds,' he said. 'Whatever figure is put on what Fabio is earning, it is a very small percentage of the overall figure and if he turns English football around it will be money well spent for the fans.'

While Barwick may have meant well with his comment, typically, it came across as somewhat bombastic. When it comes to public speaking he is no Barack Obama. Capello knew he was dealing with a very wealthy employer who, at this stage, was desperate for his services. And he knew he could push the boat out. At this point, you may be wondering why Capello – or, indeed, why any wealthy professional footballer or manager – makes such an issue of wages when they are already rich beyond belief. This is especially true in the case of Capello, a man who has been very judicious with his investments throughout his career and has relied on some of the most prestigious wealth managers around to grow his personal fortune.

For some, it may be greed, pure and simple. But for many, and perhaps Capello is among them, the issue is also one of pride. In a world where everyone has an opinion about everything and everyone is constantly judged, wages are a way of keeping score. Simply put, if Eriksson was worth four million pounds a year, it was more than reasonable for Capello to demand at least the same.

You just had to work out the numbers. Eriksson had twenty-three seasons in club management and won six league titles. Capello had fifteen and won nine. And all of his came in Spain or Italy, whereas five of Eriksson's came in Portugal and Sweden, which is hardly the same thing. Eriksson reached one European Cup final, Capello three. There was no logical reason why Capello should earn less than Eriksson and plenty that he should earn more. Which, ultimately, is what happened.

Pierfilippo and Rodriguez returned to their hotel rooms late on Thursday night exhausted but elated. The deal was finally in place. Every detail had been examined with a fine-toothed comb (the lawyer who had negotiated McClaren's contract had also been consulted). Now it was just a question of putting pen to paper. Which, of course, was not as simple as it seemed. Capello was back in Italy. The press were getting very antsy, wanting an official announcement before the weekend. Fortunately, there was another solution.

On Friday morning, Capello left his home in Milan and headed north. Two carloads of photographers who had been staking out his residence were hot on his heels. It was a crisp sunny morning as he got on the motorway. Was he heading to Malpensa airport? Or was he off to some secret meeting with FA representatives?

Realizing he was being followed, Capello exited the motorway and headed towards the outskirts of Varese, some twenty-five miles north of the city. He knew these roads well, having lived nearby in Legnano when he was at Milan. He made a series of turns, then doubled back, then took a variety of side roads. When he looked in his rearview mirror, they were gone. He had successfully shaken off the paparazzi. Satisfied with himself, he headed for the border, crossing over into Switzerland and arriving at the Lugano offices of the Studio Severgnini, the Milanese law firm where Edoardo, his other son, worked.

It was here, on the shores of Lake Lugano, that the England contract was signed. The fax machine whirred into life and, in the presence of two certified witnesses, Capello put pen to paper. The deal was done.

CHAPTER 17

England: the Final Chapter?

Later that Friday afternoon, 14 December, the FA made its official announcement. Capello would be in London on Monday morning, when he would sign the hard copy of the contract and then, finally, meet the press.

Jeff Powell, the veteran *Daily Mail* columnist, referenced the piece he had written eight years earlier, upon Eriksson's appointment, the one that referred to 'fjords' and 'hammer-throwers'. His first line said it all: 'And so we move on from the hammer-throwing Swedish lotharios who live half their year in darkness to the spaghetti-twirling Latin lovers of football's black arts.'

More of the same mildly xenophobic, cliché-ridden little Englander jingoism? Yes and no. This time, Powell was largely tongue-in-cheek. His main point was that Capello was passé, a relic from a *catenaccio*-loving Italian past who was 'not even the best manager in Italy' (that would be – according to Powell – Marcello Lippi). Yet he was in the minority. The general consensus was that England had found the best coach money could buy, a man who was all about results, an instant-success type of guy. The phrase 'you can't argue with his record' must have been written hundreds of times and, largely, it was true. The message was simple: 'If Capello couldn't get England to win, nobody could.'

Around this time, I was also reminded that, for all the talk of convergence, global villages and shared European experiences, we Europeans really are still a bunch of little tribes, hermetically sealed within our borders. The language used to describe Capello and his assistants would probably have attracted several lawsuits in a more politically correct environment.

I'm not talking about Powell's 'spaghetti-twirling', 'Latin lovers' and 'Stromboli's travelling circus' (whatever that means) – that stuff is harmless and unimaginative cliché. Rather, it was surprising to see the number of references to the Mafia and organized crime. 'Italian Mob', 'Godfather', 'offers you can't refuse' . . . on and on it went, as if the media had been locked in a room with nothing but Don Corleone impersonators for the past decade.

It wasn't malicious and – to be fair – every nation descends into tired stereotypes – for example, many Italian newspapers routinely use the terms 'English travelling supporters' and 'hooligans' interchangeably, and any Briton who attains any degree of success instantly becomes 'Sir' or 'Lady': Sir Alan Shearer, Sir Tim Henman, Lady Victoria Beckham and so on. The difference here is that Mafia references remain deeply offensive to many Italians. Outside Italy the Mafia exists as some kind of colourful Hollywood artifice, glamorized and lampooned by *The Sopranos*, whereas in Italy it is in reality a highly dangerous criminal organization which has murdered hundreds of innocent people.

Had Martin O'Neill, who is Catholic and from Northern Ireland, been appointed manager, would the media have greeted him with jokes about the IRA, balaclavas and hunger strikes? I think not. And note that this type of thing was not just tabloid fodder, it was surfacing everywhere, from broadsheets to the BBC.

In any case, Capello was oblivious to all this. He had work to do. The FA had, at his request, couriered him DVDs of the last ten England full and Under 21 internationals and he made it his priority to watch them all in the next two weeks. If Saturday afforded him a brief respite, Sunday was a veritable tour de force. In the morning he prepared for Monday's press conference, before spending most of the afternoon watching Liverpool v Manchester United and Arsenal v Chelsea (as luck would have it, the biggest day of the Premier League fixture list coincided with his final day in Italy). Then, it was off to the television studio, for his final appearance as a pundit on *La Domenica Sportiva*. The weekly highlights show went out live on Sunday night and, naturally, his departure was the big talking point. It was there that he spoke for the first time as England manager.

When asked about England's underachievement, he said: 'They lost drive and determination. They're different psychologically. I saw it against Russia, they weren't themselves. I need to help them find their confidence, a bit like I did with Real Madrid.' He also dropped his first hints about what he planned to do with the squad. 'The players are first-rate and there are plenty to choose from,' he said.

'Plus, there are one or two who are retired, but who I hope to bring back.'

The two men in question were Paul Scholes and Jamie Carragher, two players Capello had long admired. Scholes had announced his international retirement back in August of 2004, saying he wanted to focus on his family life and club football. Nevertheless he remained a fixture for Manchester United and, despite his age – he was now thirty-three – had reinvented himself in a slightly deeper role. Capello liked the way Scholes, having lost a step in terms of quickness, had humbly transformed himself into more of a deep-lying midfielder, shutting down opponents and spreading the play. In some ways, his combination of selflessness, passing skills and positional sense was reminiscent of Emerson.

Carragher was a slightly different proposition. He was still just twenty-nine, having retired from the England team the previous summer, unhappy at playing second fiddle to Rio Ferdinand and John Terry in central defence and being shunted all across the backline as a glorified jack-of-all-trades. Carragher wasn't the second coming of Bobby Moore, but Capello loved the way he played football. With age, he had come to rely less on his athleticism and more on reading the game, establishing himself as a natural leader who rarely screwed up the big occasions. He brought to the table the kind of intangibles that Capello valued.

At that stage, Capello had no concrete idea of what his England side might look like or even what formation he would use. But already he could envisage a core of world-class players who could hold their own against any opponent. Some combination of Carragher, Ferdinand and Terry at the back; Owen Hargreaves, who had been impressive at the World Cup, and Scholes shoring up the midfield; Steven Gerrard breaking forward; Wayne Rooney up front. Plus the other stars who, if fit and at the top of their game, would be a boost to any side: Frank Lampard, Michael Owen, Joe Cole. Yes, this England thing felt good, it was going to work out.

Of course, as it happened, both Carragher and Scholes let it be known that they were not about to come out of retirement. Capello did not feel slighted, just a bit disappointed. He really believed he could coax them back into the England fold. Now he had to find alternatives. But there was no time to think about it. The next morning he was on an early flight to London, his new home.

Having signed the hard copy of his contract (which was just a formality, since the faxed version was legally binding), Capello prepared to wander into a banqueting room at the Royal Lancaster Hotel to face several hundred members of the world's media. Outside, it was a windy, blustery day. A man, evidently less than pleased at the appointment, held up a cardboard sign which read, in large letters: 'Crap-ello'. A genuine fan making his heartfelt solitary protest? Possibly. Though he would have been more credible if he hadn't also written 'We want Harry Redknap' on his sign.

When I pointed out to him that the Portsmouth manager's name is spelled with two 'p's', not one, he got annoyed and insisted I was wrong. A pair of policemen stepped in. 'Two "p"s in Redknapp,' they said. The man looked angry, then dejected. I'm pretty sure he was about to say something rude to me when one of the dozen or so camera crews started taking an interest in him.

''Arry! 'Arry for England!' he shouted, turning his back on me and wandering towards the camera. 'Crap-ello! Crap, crap, Crap-ello!'

A few steps away, two women held a giant pizza welcoming Capello, looking unhappy. Obviously some clever – and not particularly original – PR firm had duped some restaurant into thinking that this was a good way to get photographed. It wasn't. Everyone ignored them.

Inside, the buzz was about whether Capello was going to say anything at all in English. The issue was resolved soon after he walked into the room in typically Capelloesque fashion: head up, shoulders square, chest out, jaw set, purposeful strides.

'I am very proud and honoured to be the England manager. I have wanted this job for a long time but, at this moment, my English is not so well and I prefer to answer in Italian.'

He had just delivered his first public words to the English press and he had done it in English. The fact that he had made a few mistakes was not seen as a big deal. Still, the issue of language loomed large. On the one hand, the idea that command of the language is indispensable is a somewhat curious English peculiarity. Guus Hiddink, the man whose Russia side knocked out England in qualifying, does not speak Russian. Nor did he speak Korean when he took South Korea into the 2002 World Cup semi-finals. Nor, for that matter, did Terry Venables speak fluent Spanish (or Catalan) when he won a Liga title at Barcelona more than twenty years ago.

On the other hand, there is no question that the ability to speak directly, in your own carefully chosen words, without the filter of an interpreter, is a huge advantage. Not just in the dressing room, but when facing the media as well. I remember the early days of Claudio Ranieri on the Chelsea bench. He spoke no English when he arrived and relied on an interpreter. Press conferences often turned into a circus in which Ranieri would offer up a long answer, filled with clauses, caveats and hypotheticals and the interpreter would sum it up in one or two sentences, much to the bemusement of the assembled media. (Ranieri's tendency to laugh nervously when puzzled journalists stared at him did not help matters.) Some sectors of the press cruelly mocked him, depicting him as some kind of blabbering dolt whom nobody could understand.

That, of course, was the last thing the FA needed in Capello's case. To be fair, unlike Ranieri, who would smile happily when questioned, Capello's ability to deliver an icy stare from behind his designer frames would largely ensure that nobody would take the same liberties with him. Still, that very first press conference revealed the potential pitfalls that could arise when the manager and his interpreter are not in sync, as they clearly weren't on that December day.

When asked about David Beckham – with whom, by his own admission, he had had a 'contrasting' relationship – Capello replied in Italian that he is a 'great player' and a 'great man' and that he was an important player who would be given 'serious consideration'. That part was translated accurately. Then, however, the interpreter added an ill-advised, 'He said he believes David's behaviour is important.' Which, of course, lends itself to all sorts of interpretation. Behaviour? What behaviour? Fashion shoots? Being married to a pop star? Hanging out in Tom Cruise's swimming pool? In the hands of a mischievous press, it becomes a 'warning' to Beckham. Except, of course, Capello never said that.

The press did not pounce on that occasion. But it was obvious to all that Capello needed to work seriously on his English. And so Capello said his English would be fluent by the time he took charge of the side for the friendly against Switzerland, on 6 February 2008. It was a bold pronouncement but, it was felt, a necessary one.

In that sense, he was very open about the importance of learning English. Interpreters were fine for press conferences and, initially at least, on the training ground. 'But there are times when you have to step in and when your words weigh very heavily, because their importance is magnified,' he said in a TV interview shortly thereafter. 'And, at those times, just before a match and at half-time, you need to know the language inside and out.'

The FA had provided him with one of the most experienced football-specific English teachers available. Peter Clark ran a company which had taught the language to dozens of foreign footballers. His ability to relate football's specific lingo to young, highly paid men who had just set foot in England made him a sought-after commodity. Capello snapped him up right away. In fact, when he left the very next day for a holiday in Marbella, he took Clark and his family with him so that he wouldn't miss a beat. It was to be a Christmas holiday made up largely of

English lessons, DVDs of England matches and hours spent watching Premiership football. To those who knew him, it was no surprise.

On 7 January 2008, his first official day of work as England manager, Capello arrived at Soho Square to find the usual media scrum. The first few weeks were spent in meetings, both with FA officials and club managers, as well as more mundane things, like finding a place to live.

The FA's stipulation that 'the England manager shall live no more than thirty miles from the headquarters of the Football Association' – was no big deal. He had no intention of retiring to the country. He had made no secret of the fact that part of the appeal of the job was London. Over the years, Capello had turned into a very metropolitan animal. When his children were younger, he had lived in the suburbs, but now he definitely preferred the city. It was the same story in Madrid. In his first stint he lived just outside, in La Moraleja, a wealthy suburb populated by players (Beckham would find a home there as well). But the second time around, he chose to be right in the thick of things.

London was no different. The FA had put him up in a Mayfair hotel while he looked for a flat. He soon found one in Chelsea which had the attractions of central London on his doorstep. After all, with his boys all grown, it was just him and Laura and they wanted to enjoy the city.

The FA drew up a strategy to deal with Capello's private life. Adrian Bevington, the director of communications, sent a letter to all media outlets, asking them to respect his privacy. At the same time the FA worked behind the scenes to make sure newspaper editors got a clear message: the minute he stepped outside the public sphere, everyone was to steer clear of Capello.

There had already been one incident where a newspaper published pictures of Capello and his wife sunbathing. The carefully worded caption was intentionally vague regarding where and when it had been taken. But since everyone knew that Capello was on holiday in Marbella, it's not unreasonable to think that the reader was meant to believe that these were recent holiday snaps. Of course, someone with even a rudimentary grasp of geography would have seen that these were old pictures and were not taken in Marbella. Capello is standing on volcanic rock clad only in swimming trunks. Marbella does have a lovely climate, but only polar bears would go swimming there in December. Indeed, given the volcanic rock, it was most likely taken the previous summer at Capello's holiday home in Pantelleria.

Such snaps were exactly what the FA didn't want. It's not that they were negative – indeed, the caption waxed lyrical about Capello's toned physique, which would have made most thirty-year-olds envious – it's just that they were a direct invasion of privacy. Not reacting to them could have led down a slippery slope and ended up with paparazzi chasing Laura up and down the fruit and vegetable aisle at Waitrose.

The FA reached an understanding with the media and the Capellos. The press would lay off and they, in exchange, would not go out of their way to put themselves in the media spotlight. For example, if they wanted to go to the cinema, that was fine, but it would be best if they didn't go on an opening night, preening down the red carpet. Again, the Eriksson experience had left its mark. The Swede's girlfriend Nancy Dell'Olio was a fixture on the celebrity circuit and was constantly in the paparazzi's path. The FA's view was that it's rather difficult to complain about media intrusion when you thrust yourself in front of a camera at every opportunity.

Meanwhile, Capello and Baldini made the rounds among club managers. They knew their relationships with them would be very important. And they also wanted to see how they worked. Capello knew some of them personally, and with one or two, the relationship had not always been cordial in the past. But the England manager and his club counterparts knew there had to be a certain amount of give on both sides. Opening a direct channel of communication was in everyone's interest.

A club manager and the national team boss will, almost necessarily, be at odds. The former sees the latter as an intruder who swoops in, often during the busiest time of the season, and kidnaps their star players, often for meaningless friendlies. The latter views the former as a selfish entity who occasionally discourages his players from representing their country and, sometimes, even goes so far as to get them to feign injury in order to avoid a call-up.

Capello and Baldini, having worked for clubs their entire lives, knew what clubs went through. Capello had had his run-ins with national team managers before. But now the boot was on the other foot. And it was crucial to reach some kind of understanding.

Meanwhile, there was another fire to put out. On the morning of Wednesday, 16 January 2008, just nine days into his tenure, Capello awoke to news that the Italian newspaper *Il Giornale* was reporting that he was being investigated for tax fraud in Italy. According to the allegations, Capello had not reported part of his income between 1999 and 2006. Capello and the FA had both been aware of the investigation for some time. They knew that, at some point, it was likely to be leaked to the press. And they had developed a counter-strategy.

The FA issued a statement reiterating the fact that they knew about this and were satisfied with the assurances Capello's camp had given them: everything was in order. Meanwhile, Pierfilippo took the line that these were 'routine checks' and that high-profile individuals like his father were regularly targeted by tax authorities, particularly if they changed their residence regularly.

Time for some full disclosure. My mother's cousin worked until recently for the same law firm which employs Capello's son Edoardo. In fact, for a while he was Edoardo's boss. However, in preparing this book neither I nor any of my researchers nor members of my immediate family have spoken to him about Capello's tax affairs. So make of this what you like.

That said, it seems unlikely that Capello would knowingly engage in any kind of tax fraud. Rather, a bit of research reveals that Capello's approach to savings and tax planning is no different from that of bankers, entrepreneurs and other wealthy individuals. In short, he employs very clever and very expensive tax lawyers to minimize his tax liability.

These guys specialize in what is known as 'tax avoidance', which is defined as the legal use of fiscal legislation to minimize one's tax burden (as opposed to 'tax evasion' which is essentially doing the same thing, except by illegal means, such as under-reporting income or overstating deductions). At the highest level, 'tax avoidance' is done by using a variety of tools, such as foreign-registered companies, family trusts and tax shelters. According to reports in the Italian press, Capello, acting on the advice of his tax lawyers, made liberal use of such vehicles in an effort to reduce his tax burden. Sometimes, this can take you into a 'grey area', where the tax man requires further information to establish if what you've done is legal or not. Every indication is that this is what is happening with Capello's tax investigation, which, as this book goes to press, is still pending.

There is other circumstantial evidence to support Capello's case. His tax advisers are part of one of Italy's most prestigious and respected (and pricey) law firms. The negative publicity associated with doing something illegal would be a massive blow to them.

In addition, as you know, Capello was stung once before, when he tried to take residency in Campione d'Italia, the Italian enclave in Switzerland with an arcane and peculiar fiscal relationship to Italy. On that occasion, of course, he settled with the tax authorities and paid a small fine. It would seem highly unlikely that, having been stung once, Capello would want to put himself in such jeopardy again. Nobody likes paying taxes, even people like Capello, who are fabulously wealthy. But it would be bordering on the reckless for an intelligent man like the England manager to make the same mistake twice in the space of a few years.

It's also worth making another point at this stage. Italian magistrates' offices – like police departments – are notoriously leaky, to the point that the notion of 'innocent until proven guilty' is rendered almost meaningless. Whenever someone, particularly a high-profile person, comes under investigation, it routinely finds its way into the press, usually with the kind of detail which leaves no doubt over its provenance. Wiretaps, blow-by-blow accounts, witness statements, photographs . . . evidence is routinely leaked on a large scale. (It's worth noting that the transcripts of the wiretapped conversations – and in some cases the recordings themselves – which led to the 'Calciopoli' scandal and brought down Luciano Moggi, were also handed over to the press from day one.)

This, coupled with a diabolically slow legal system, is one of the peculiarities of justice in Italy. The script is simple. In a country where rumour and hearsay are omnipresent, magistrates are quick to open investigations, especially into the affairs of people in the public eye, whether they be footballers or politicians, entrepreneurs or C-list starlets. The next step is usually tapping their phone. Getting permission to listen in on someone's calls is extraordinarily easy in Italy. There are more wiretaps in Italy than any other country in the world, including the United States, whose population is four and a half times as large, and where the Patriot Act and the George W. Bush regime created fears of a 'Big Brother' state.

In 2003, the last year for which reliable data is available, more than 77,500 wiretaps were authorized in Italy. Since then, by some estimates, the number has doubled. If that's true it would mean that nearly half of one per cent of the country's adult population is being bugged by somebody. And those are just the ones we know about. The result of this is that idle chitchat sometimes gets taken out of context and turned into potentially incriminating conversations. Which is fine: if magistrates find conversations suspicious, clearly they should do their jobs and investigate further. The problem occurs when someone in a police department or magistrates' office leaks the content of these conversations to the press. Typically, a leaked story that such-and-such is being investigated will make for big headlines, especially if it's 'corroborated' (I use the term very loosely) by transcripts of wiretaps. But what happens when the investigation continues and the authorities find their suspicions are baseless? The investigation gets dropped and, at best, it rates a tiny 'news in brief' item on the inside pages.

Back to Capello. In a 'normal' country, the fact that he was being investigated would have been kept quiet until he was formally charged. But this was Italy.

News of the investigation was a distraction ahead of the naming of his first England squad, when the media would find out if he had, in fact, learned fluent English in less than fifty days. It would also be a chance to find out his stance on David Beckham, who remained a divisive figure among the press.

Steve McClaren had, of course, dropped Beckham from his early England squads after taking over, only to recall him later on. It was partly a way to signal a break from the Eriksson era (the Swede had made him captain and considered him an automatic choice in his starting eleven). But it was also motivated by performance and the state of the England team, something which the media, in crucifying McClaren, often conveniently forgot.

Beckham had a very poor start to the 2006–07 campaign at Real Madrid, a fact which was overshadowed by his subsequent row with Capello. Furthermore, the right flank was one area of the pitch where England had a number of alternatives: Joe Cole, Aaron Lennon, David Bentley and Shaun Wright-Phillips were all considerably younger than Beckham, who would be thirty-three at Euro 2008. Leaving him out with an eye to the future had a certain logic to it.

But then Beckham made his triumphant return to Real and contributed to the league title. McClaren duly recalled him in May 2007 and kept him around for the duration of England's ill-fated Euro 2008 campaign. Now, however, it was Capello's team. Given their past history, given Beckham's recent injuries, given the media circus which follows him everywhere, would the new manager keep him in the side?

The attitude of the media had turned somewhat when it came to Beckham. Absence does make the heart grow fonder. Many of the same pundits who routinely criticized him for his lifestyle and off-the-pitch distractions now urged Capello to call him up, if only because he was on ninety-nine caps, one short of the magical century mark. It would be a cruel man indeed to deny him joining legends such as Billy Wright (105 caps), Bobby Charlton (106), Bobby Moore (108) and Peter Shilton (125).

Capello, of course, didn't really care about all this. Or, rather, he only cared to the extent that it would be a distraction from the task at hand. When he said there was no problem between himself and Beckham, that what was past was past, he really meant it. Enough times throughout his career, he had shown the ability to move on, to mend bridges, not through a kiss-and-cuddle approach, but simply by making it obvious to the other party that it was mutually beneficial to get along.

At the same time, he knew that if he denied Beckham his century, it could create problems for him. Like many other countries, including Italy, England has an incredible (and somewhat irrational) ability to build people up, tear them down and then build them up again.

'When you're in the spotlight, they crucify you,' one former England international told me. 'When you step out of it, they miss you and want you to come back. So you come back. And then they crucify you all over again.'

For his part, Beckham, aided by his omnipresent PR machine, made his case firmly, but politely. With Major League Soccer in its off-season, he asked to train with Arsenal to keep his fitness up. And when asked about England, he was characteristically humble: 'I'm as fit as I can be. I'm fit and sharp and I'm ready to be selected. Hopefully I've worked hard enough this month to get picked in the squad. I've been training with one of the fittest teams in Europe, I've done everything possible to be fit and I am without a doubt ready for it . . . but it's out of my hands now.'

Yet reservations over his fitness remained. Beckham had not completed a full ninety-minute match since 23 August 2007 (when, due to a quirk in the fixture list and his own desire to meet his commitments, sporting and commercial, he played ninety minutes against Germany at

Wembley and then, the very next day, ninety minutes for the LA Galaxy against Chivas USA). That was five months earlier. And he hadn't featured in any kind of competitive game since that fateful night against Croatia, which ended England's Euro hopes.

Still, that was only part of it. Beckham's gesture to train with Arsenal was appreciated, but, in fact, it was clear that some of his other obligations were eating into his time on the training pitch. Indeed, in the week leading up to Capello's announcement, he found time to jet off to both Africa and South America. The former was to do charity work in Sierra Leone, the latter to open a football academy in Brazil. Both commendable pursuits, but not exactly the best way to impress the new boss.

The fear was that Beckham's presence and the inevitable ceremony of his hundredth cap would overshadow the match and the training sessions, Capello's first opportunity to work with and get to know his players. Besides, if there was one England player who Capello knew inside and out, it was Beckham. And, as for the hundredth cap, there would be plenty of time for that. The patriotic Beckham was not the kind of guy to retire from international duty, especially not when he was so close to his century.

Thus, Capello made the first controversial decision of his England tenure: Beckham was dropped. And, by and large, the public took it well. The FA did a good job at explaining Capello's logic, both on and off the record. Beckham too got the message: 'Don't be bitter, your time will come.'

For his part, Beckham said all the right things as well.

Capello had called him to explain his decision, something which the LA Galaxy midfielder appreciated. In return he came out and said that he 'totally' understood the decision and that, in fact, it would have been 'unfair' if he had been selected.

Capello's other headache concerned an issue which in many other countries would have been an afterthought but, in England, was of paramount importance: the captaincy. Elsewhere, the captain's armband goes to the player who has made the most appearances for the side or, in some cases, is assigned by a players' vote. Not in England. The captain is both statement and symbol. When Beckham was dropped by McClaren and the choice came down to either Steven Gerrard or John Terry, newspapers and call-in shows were dominated by the issue. Who had the most character? Who was the better leader? And – my personal favourite – which of the two was the most 'inspirational'? As if professional footballers earning millions a year would be inspired more by Gerrard or Terry just because of that little strip of cloth around their bicep.

Capello knew that an armband doesn't turn a person into a leader. Nor does the lack of an armband turn a natural leader into an anonymous bit player. Leadership is one thing, the captaincy quite another. That said, he realized that, because it was important to English football, it had to be important to him. As Capello said on more than one occasion, 'I am the one who has to adapt to English football . . . I can't expect England to adapt to me.'

However, he wasn't about to make a definitive choice. It would have been a mistake to put his eggs in one basket straight away, anointing Gerrard or Terry or Ferdinand. Immediately, he would have been second-guessed. And, there was the risk of turning players against him, particularly if he chose to change captain, stripping Terry – who was very popular, and not just among the Chelsea contingent – of the armband.

Instead, he decided to try out a different captain in each of the friendlies leading up to England's first official qualifier for the 2010 World Cup in September 2008. The official line was that he wanted to assess the different candidates before making the final choice. Most bought this argument, although, when you think about it, it's somewhat bizarre. How do you assess if an individual is doing a good job as captain on the strength of ninety minutes with the armband?

More likely, it was really just a way of buying time. Because the other great quality of a captain is that he rarely, if ever, gets dropped. The dropping of a captain is bound to have an instant deleterious effect in a country like England. It reignites the captaincy debate, it can leave the players confused, it generally opens a big can of worms.

So, in fact, what Capello was doing was taking the time to figure out which of his players would be 'automatic choices' in his starting eleven. Once he had that pool of players, he would choose from among them. Why this approach? Partly because Capello wanted to see his squad up close and how different players responded and interacted with each other. And partly because he needed to quickly establish, at least in his mind, his 'untouchables'. Three players stood head and shoulders above the others:

Wayne Rooney, Rio Ferdinand and Steven Gerrard. That part was fairly obvious. Ask a thousand England supporters to put together their best side and, odds are, all but one or two would include those three players. Initially at least, his captain would necessarily come out of that trio.

And, in reality, it came down to just Ferdinand and Gerrard. Rooney was, after all, just twenty-two. He could be shy and somewhat introverted in the dressing room. Furthermore, his uncompromising style meant that he was a higher booking risk than the other two. Indeed, the media had devoted acres of newsprint to the issue of 'Rooney's discipline', fuelling a perception that he was a ticking time bomb ready to explode. Capello knew to look past this conventional wisdom. Yes, Rooney had suffered a notorious sending off against Portugal at the 2006 World Cup. But, in fact, he had only been sent off on one other occasion in a career of five and a half years. And his book-ings were on the decline, so the idea that his discipline could not be trusted was a bit of an urban myth. Still, at this stage, he was not an option.

The logical choice for the first outing was Gerrard. He had been there before and, in fact, narrowly missed out on the captaincy under McClaren. But Ferdinand's time would come. He had matured tremendously over the last few seasons and, in terms of ability, was clearly a class apart from the other defenders at Capello's disposal.

Of course, the whole captaincy debate was a blow to Terry. He was injured for the Switzerland friendly, so it wasn't an issue there, but news that Capello would not be picking a captain for some time effectively meant he had been stripped of the armband. Terry epitomizes the old school, blood and guts English centre-half. He's also fiercely patriotic and, unlike some members of the squad, genuinely looks forward to each international, friendly or competitive.

But there were two concerns with Terry. One wasn't really an issue for Capello – who, frankly, isn't overly preoccupied with such things – but resonated with public opinion and some quarters of the FA: Terry's occasional 'bad boy' behaviour off the pitch. The other worry was far more practical. Terry had begun missing games due to injury. At twenty-seven, he wasn't getting any younger. And while his penchant for gritting his teeth, absorbing the pain, and playing while hurt was admirable, it also meant that his body had already withstood a tremendous amount of damage. These concerns, coupled with the fact that Capello wanted to see for himself who Ferdinand's ideal partner might be, prompted the decision to wait and see how things developed with the Chelsea captain.

Those who remembered Capello's pledge to be fluent in English by the time the squad got together ahead of the Switzerland friendly were curious to see how he would handle things. At the press conference, Capello cleared his throat, leaned towards the microphone and started confidently . . . speaking in Italian. What happened to the pledge? Well, as the story went, when Capello talked about being fluent in English he meant with the players and in informal conversations with the FA and the press. Facing a press conference, with its array of potential pitfalls and 'Gotcha' questions, was a different matter. The FA took pains to explain this privately to journalists ahead of the press conference and most bought into it. In any case, that story was overshadowed by another one: Capello's 'Ten Commandments'. The media – not just in England, but in Italy and elsewhere too – lapped up the fact that the new manager had supposedly introduced some kind of draconian boot camp. The *Sun* helpfully laid out Capello's ten rules and the rest of the media followed suit. What were these terrible new regulations that made Louis Gosset Jr in *An Officer And A Gentleman* look like some kind of wimp?

Tardiness won't be tolerated. The team eats together. No ordering room service. No use of mobile phones, except when you're in your hotel room. No flip flops. Dress appropriately when in public. No visits from agents, wives, girlfriends, relatives and hangers-on (bookies and call girls? Out of the question).

Capello certainly hadn't planned it as some kind of show of force. To him, they seemed like reasonable standards to ensure a professional and cohesive squad which could work productively without distractions.

'I was surprised by the reaction to this,' Marcello Lippi, the former boss, said in a March 2008 interview. 'I mean, it's common sense. Most managers have similar rules, don't they? I know I do . . .'

Capello was somewhat bemused as well. Those things seemed obvious to him. He could have added: 'No main-lining of heroin while on England duty. No conspiring with Al-Qaeda operatives to blow things up. And, most definitely, no juggling of chainsaws.' Those activities were almost as obviously unproductive as the ones he had banned. So why the fuss?

Indeed, the rules weren't too dissimilar under McClaren or Eriksson for that matter. It's just that nobody had thought to spin them into a neat little drill sergeant package. Possibly, it was because they fit Capello's image and not those of his predecessors. The affable Eriksson was – at least initially, before he became the Swedish lothario – presented as some kind of subtle psychological master, who used gentle prodding rather than whip cracking. McClaren was depicted as the smiling northern cousin, a kindly relative with twinkly eyes. But when it came to the hard-ass role, Capello, on the other hand, was more than credible.

From an image perspective, this suited everyone just fine. England fans loved the idea of a disciplinarian, as anyone browsing the internet forums and listening to radio phone-ins would have quickly realized. It suited the FA too: Capello was getting good publicity and the talk had, for now, shifted away from more controversial topics. As for Capello and his staff, he probably could not have cared less either way.

The first England side of the Capello regime was laid out in 4-1-4-1 (or 4-3-3, if you prefer) and raised more than a few eyebrows. With Terry and Ledley King out injured, West Ham's Matthew Upson – who had received very little buzz until that point – was a surprise choice to partner Ferdinand. Conventional wisdom would probably have taken any of the three defenders whose backside remained rooted to the Wembley bench all night. Jonathan Woodgate, who seemed regenerated after his move to Tottenham, Joleon Lescott, who had enjoyed plenty of playing time under McClaren, and Micah

Richards, the nineteen-year-old wunderkind who was enjoying a banner year at Manchester City, playing in central defence; all these guys seemed more credible candidates than Upson.

The midfield featured Gareth Barry and Jermaine Jenas, with Steven Gerrard just ahead of them, with licence to roam. Jenas was a bit of a surprise, as Owen Hargreaves, who had a terrible injury record, was available. But there was a logic to Capello's choices. Hargreaves was a proven quantity, tactically sound and with an ability to operate in a variety of systems. Jenas wasn't, and Capello was keen to see how he would settle. Out wide, he opted for Joe Cole, who, it was believed, could become a world-class creative force if he ironed a few kinks out of his game (Capello's staff had been impressed with his eagerness and enthusiasm), and David Bentley, who was winning only his third England cap, but was enjoying a sparkling campaign at Blackburn Rovers.

The surprise came up front, where Rooney was asked to operate on his own. It was a curious choice for several reasons. For a start, conventional wisdom had it that Rooney was not a genuine centre-forward and, in this case, it was correct. He's not at his best playing with his back to goal and tends to want a teammate nearby, for whom he can create space and with whom he can dialogue. Nor is Rooney a particularly prolific goalscorer. At the time of the Switzerland game, his Premier League record with Manchester United was 47 goals in 116 appearances, with England it was 14 in 40.

The idea was that Rooney would bring the likes of Joe Cole, Bentley and, especially, Gerrard into play and they would pick up the goalscoring slack. Alas, the first two weren't exactly goalmachines either. Cole had 19 goals in 131 Premier League games, Bentley 12 in 90. Indeed, Gerrard was, Rooney apart, the only player who presented any kind of goalscoring threat. And so, perhaps predictably, England struggled to find their feet in the first half. They held the ball, passed and moved, but lacked a cutting edge. Some individuals looked distinctly subpar at this level. Others appeared unsure of themselves, perhaps fearful of slipping up under the new boss.

Still, England had their moments. And, when they took the lead, it was after a move which clearly had Capello's stamp on it. The formation had been laid out to help Gerrard find space and he did, using it to conjure up a beautiful crossfield ball for Joe Cole, who did exactly what Capello wanted: he ran at defenders, cut inside and delivered a perfect assist for the onrushing Jenas. Pretty and effective, although such moments were too few and far between.

The experiment with Rooney as centre-forward lasted until ten minutes into the second period. Capello sent on Peter Crouch and Shaun Wright-Phillips for Jenas and Joe Cole. This led to an inevitable reshuffle. Crouch took his place up front while Rooney switched to the left flank with Wright-Phillips taking the right and Bentley switching into the midfield three, replacing Jenas.

Having tried the experimental lineup – with decidedly mixed results – Capello tried the more traditional approach. He didn't have too much time to think about it because Switzerland equalized almost immediately through Eren Derdiyok, who took his goal well but also benefited from some rather poor defending. The press rightly criticized Ferdinand for reacting too late, but England's entire midfield and back four looked out of place and sluggish during the build-up.

It didn't take long for the 'Crouch Effect' to kick in. Straight from a goal kick, the big man headed on for Rooney, who knocked it wide to Gerrard. The skipper accelerated into space, past the last defender, and squared it for Wright-Phillips who tapped it into the back of the net.

The inevitable conclusion was that the win took some pressure off, but there was plenty of work to be done. What to do with Rooney was a question that would, no doubt, preoccupy Capello and his staff right up to the competitive games in September. Defensively, they would have to do a better job at closing down the spaces and reading the opponents' play. Derdiyok's goal had exposed them: even if Ferdinand had been tighter and made a goal-saving challenge, it wouldn't have changed the fact that, on that move, England had made Switzerland look a quality team.

He was less concerned about individual mistakes (though some players had made far too many). Players will always commit errors; the key is helping them commit fewer mistakes or, at least, making sure you are organized enough to put the fires out when they start. Besides, he wasn't just evaluating a team, he was assessing individuals. If some players made mistakes regularly, he could always replace them with others, at least in those areas of the pitch where England had options.

Wright-Phillips' goal may have been the epitome of

traditional 'Route One' football, but that wasn't necessarily a bad thing. Capello liked having options. By now, you've probably figured out that he isn't wedded to a particular style or approach. In fact, the occasional hoof to the big man can be a welcome weapon in one's arsenal as it forces the opponent to adjust.

Facing the press after the game, however, much of the talk wasn't about the game per se, but instead focused on the choice of Rooney to lead the attack, with Michael Owen left on the bench for the whole ninety minutes. Owen, when fit, had been an automatic choice for both Eriksson and McClaren. His forty goals in eighty-eight international appearances made him the fourth highest England goalscorer of all time. At twenty-eight years of age, he appeared certain to break Bobby Charlton's record of forty-nine . . . but, of course, to do that, he had to get on the pitch.

Capello knew the Owen questions were coming, though, perhaps, he didn't quite appreciate the extent to which the Newcastle United striker would be a talking point. To the English public, Owen was synonymous with goalscoring, something this team desperately needed. And, Owen apart, England had not had a reliable scorer since Alan Shearer retired from international duty in 2000. How could Capello even consider leaving him out, particularly given the obvious lack of alternatives? Obviously, the manager saw things differently. Again, it was probably a function of the cultural gulf which exists between England and Italy. At the time, Owen had not reached double figures in league goals since 2005, when he notched thirteen in thirty-six appearances for Real

Madrid. His tally in the season thus far was three in sixteen league games: hardly the kind of record which demanded that Capello tear up his tactical plans to accommodate the Newcastle striker.

And then there was the issue of fitness. Owen had been out an entire year after the World Cup (and, for that matter, he wasn't fully fit in Germany either). He had missed nine Premier League games through injury in the current season. This, coupled with his poor performance in terms of goals, probably sealed the deal in Capello's mind. Owen was a great player who needed to regain form and probably fitness as well. His time, like Beckham's, would come. And above all, Capello wanted to try out a different system, one with a lone striker, Rooney first and then Crouch. In that context there simply was no room for Owen. In Italy such a decision would probably not have been a big deal. In England it was and this was another thing Capello would have to get used to: in his new job, reputations mattered.

His next squad announcement would, no doubt, be scrutinized with equal intensity. Not calling up David Beckham for his hundredth cap and snubbing Owen once again would send a definitive message about their future. By this time Owen's club performances had improved dramatically and Beckham's training regimen had intensified. It was not the kind of message Capello wanted to send, partly because he genuinely believed that the pair still had a contribution to make, partly because he didn't need another brewing controversy.

As he put together his squad for the friendly against France on 26 March, Capello reflected on how, this time, he could count on all of his big guns. John Terry and Frank Lampard, injured against Switzerland, were now fit, and the media were curious to see how he would handle it. Both had been England regulars over the past five years, but both had seen their places come under scrutiny.

One of those choices was made for him. Lampard was hit by a stomach bug upon arriving in Paris and was out of the reckoning straight away. Terry's availability, however, reopened the debate over the captaincy. With the Chelsea skipper back, was it his turn to get a shot in Capello's armband rotation? Or, given that Beckham was back, would Capello stick to tradition and hand the armband to the man making his one hundredth appearance?

It was soon obvious that the latter option was a non-starter. Capello is a man who, once given an objective, does not diverge from working towards it. And his goal was reaching the 2010 World Cup final, which meant that every ounce of energy would be devoted to meeting that expectation. Giving Beckham the armband would not bring England closer to their goal. He had said he wanted to rotate the captaincy and see how players responded and that's what he was going to do. Beckham had captained his country fifty-eight times; his place in Capello's future England plans was far from secure, so there was no point in making him captain for this fixture. No point, except the 'tradition' that previous centurions had enjoyed the captaincy, something which a few media outlets took him to task for ignoring. But, in fact, Capello knew that some traditions are legitimate, others mere constructs or the result of happenstance.

For a start, it had only occurred four times, which meant

it was hardly an age-old tradition. And, on two of those occasions, the men in question – Billy Wright and Bobby Moore – were already long-standing England captains (both would wear the armband an incredible ninety times). Peter Shilton, the last man to reach the mark, was rewarded with the captaincy on the night of his century, but then went on to skipper England another dozen or so times (including Italia 90), something Beckham was highly unlikely to do. To Capello, a closer look at the facts showed clearly that this was not a 'tradition' worth keeping if it meant deviating, even in a minimal way, from his stated objective.

But Terry was another matter. Many in the press expected him to be an automatic choice. They were wrong. On the eve of the game Capello announced that Rio Ferdinand would captain England. To some, this flew in the face of conventional wisdom. Ferdinand did not look like a traditional England captain. You could picture Gerrard or Terry in the trenches, you could see Alan Shearer or Stuart Pearce in a blood-soaked jersey (like Terry Butcher in 1989), but Ferdinand?

He was depicted as the flash, unreliable, somewhat arrogant Londoner. The guy whose attention was divided between football on the one hand, and women, music and partying on the other. Beckham had suffered some of the same scepticism when Eriksson made him captain, but this was different. Beckham's workrate and ceaseless effort eventually led most to accept him.

But there was an effortlessness and an elegance to Ferdinand's game which some were, evidently, suspicious of. Even when at full sprint, he seemed to glide, rather than pound his way across the pitch. He made difficult things look simple and turned simple things into afterthoughts (which may be why he, occasionally, made a few howlers). Because of this, when things went wrong, he was often mercilessly criticized. It was as if, because he had tremendous athletic and physical gifts, whenever he was beaten there could be only one explanation: he wasn't putting in the effort and wasn't concentrating.

Some have suggested that race may have come into it as well. But, in some ways, that's a reductive argument. England have had black captains before in Paul Ince and Sol Campbell – the difference is that they were much closer to the old-school English ideal of what a footballer should be like and act like: a tough-tackling, high-energy holding midfielder or a big, strong, no-nonsense centre-half.

Much was made of Ferdinand's behaviour off the pitch as well, though, upon examination the case against him looked extraordinarily flimsy. He had a drink-driving conviction, but that was ten years earlier, when he was nineteen. Yes, he enjoyed clubs and music, but that had never got him into trouble. He was scapegoated for organizing Manchester United's Christmas party (which had turned into a marathon drinking session for some players) a few months earlier, but all he had done was book the venue and make the reservations, something you would expect a senior player to do. He was also mocked for producing and presenting an ill-advised *Beadle's About*-type TV show, in which Ferdinand would play practical jokes on his teammates, with hidden cameras recording every moment of hilarity for posterity. Called *Rio's World*

Cup Wind-Ups, it was basically a rip-off of Ashton Kutcher's *Punk'd* on MTV, right down to the silly catch-phrase, 'You've been merked!'

The other supposed stain on his reputation was that he had missed a drug test back in 2003, for which he received an eight-month ban. Ferdinand's defence was that he had 'forgotten'. But the authorities came down hard on him, he was tested dozens of times before and after and, most importantly, he had served his time. As far as Capello was concerned, that case was closed. He could not see why any of these things should be held against Ferdinand. The United defender had matured tremendously over the past few seasons. And what mattered were his performances, not whether he had made mistakes as a teenager or pro-duced a TV show which nobody seemed to like.

And so it was the Manchester United defender who led England out at the Stade de France against the World Cup runners-up. It was bound to be a sterner test than Switzerland, not least because it was away from home and because France boss Raymond Domenech was loath to tinker or experiment with his side.

England's formation was the same as at Wembley and, for eight-elevenths, it was the same personnel as well. Terry returned to partner Ferdinand at the back. Beckham took Bentley's place on the right. And, in the middle, Owen Hargreaves was in alongside Gareth Barry. Jenas, who had scored against Switzerland, wasn't even called up, much like that night's other scorer, Wright-Phillips.

The evening soon turned into a game to forget. Neither side showed much urgency. A very muted crowd watched in near silence as the two teams seemed to be going through the motions, worrying more about hanging on to possession and filling the passing lanes. But there were two key differences. France looked more comfortable, which was understandable, as they had been working in the same system, under the same manager, for three and a half years.

The other main difference was pace. France had Nicolas Anelka, Franck Ribéry and Florent Malouda, all of whom have a quick first step and the ability to accelerate over twenty or more yards. England were comparatively sluggish. Joe Cole had quick and clever feet and his creativity made him potentially a consistent threat, but he was never going to get away from anyone. Gerrard's running is more about power than pace. Rooney, who is medium-fast, by nature tends to retreat and play teammates in, rather than attacking the space behind. And then, of course, there was Beckham, with his middle-distance runner's build: plenty of stamina, no afterburners.

What England lacked in pace, they made up for in technique. Indeed, this was probably the most talented front four England could muster. Basic footballing logic tells you that, if you can't move quickly, make sure the ball, at least, moves quickly. And vary the pace at which it moves. Much of South American football is based on this concept: the 'slow, slow, slow, fast!' as some people call it. Knock it about, find the opening, and then, conjure something up – a first-time ball, a reverse pass, a one-two – something to befuddle opponents and free your teammate in a good position. England's problem was that the build-up never found that extra gear. The ball circulated around, without ever finding that change of pace. It may have been that England had prioritized possession and, therefore, had become a little too patient as they were loath to give it away. Or it may simply have been an off-night.

As it happened, France capitalized on the one quality that set them apart: pace. Half an hour into the game, François Clerc, the French rightback, launched a deep, probing ball into the English half. Terry lost Anelka who streaked into the area where he was met by a lunging David James. The penalty was inevitable. Up stepped Ribéry and England were a goal down.

Capello stuck to the script until half-time, when he overhauled the attack. Off came Gerrard, Rooney and Joe Cole, on went Michael Owen, Peter Crouch and Stewart Downing. England promptly switched to a more familiar 4-4-2, with Downing and Beckham as traditional wingers, and the little-and-large partnership of Owen and Crouch up front. It was a more straightforward approach, but one which, nevertheless, hid a few wrinkles. Owen, who for much of his career had played on the shoulder of the last defender, floated behind Crouch, a role with which he had begun to experiment at Newcastle.

Still, the second half ticked away with little to celebrate, both for the England staff and for the supporters. And, after the game, Capello would, albeit indirectly, experience his first run-in with a member of the press. It concerned Owen, who, once again, had been left initially on the bench and who, when he came on, was used in a novel role.

The headline came out on Friday, 27 March in the *Sun* and it left little room for interpretation; the banner on the back page read: 'Clueless: Owen Bombshell Verdict on Capello'. The *Daily Mirror* was not far behind: 'Owen rift with Capello'. It was quite an attack on the England boss. And, to make matters worse, it purportedly came from Owen, a senior professional who for much of his career had strenuously avoided conflict with his bosses, resorting instead to anodyne comments. This was not a Paolo Di Canio or Roy Keane figure engaging in a trademark outburst after a match. This was Owen. If he was calling Capello 'clueless' there had to be a reason.

Except, by most accounts, that's not quite what happened. Owen was asked about his position on the pitch and why he had yet to start a game under Capello. He replied: 'In terms of what he is trying to do, you'd better ask the manager.'

According to a reporter present when Owen spoke, his tone, facial expression and the fact that he used the same line three times in answer to different questions, left little doubt that he wanted to convey his anger at Capello. Another journalist, who was also standing close to Owen at the time, strenuously disagrees with this version of events. 'He was obviously not happy that he wasn't being selected, but then no player is happy when they sit out,' he said. 'But it seemed obvious to me, he wasn't having a dig at Capello in any way. If he had, we would have run with the story. He was probably simply wary of getting into certain subjects, knowing that his words could be twisted or taken out of context. Which, in my opinion, they were.'

The FA, unsurprisingly, felt the same way. As did Owen, who that very same afternoon gave a rare exclusive interview to Sky Sports News. He strongly denied any kind of rift with Capello, reiterated that he had nothing but 'positive' things to say about the new management and claimed his words had been badly misconstrued.

'It's frustrating that you've got to come out after not saying anything in the first place and retrack and retrace and give your version of the story,' he said. 'And not only that, obviously with the technology we've got now, it's probably all over the world now – "Owen having a go at Capello".'

Capello felt that Owen was being honest. It was obvious that the Newcastle striker desperately wanted to play. Some depict Owen as a somewhat distant figure, more interested in horse-racing and golf than living up to his potential as a footballer. But there is no doubting his commitment when it comes to England. It was Owen who rushed back from injury to be a part of the 2006 World Cup squad, where he played through the pain on more than one occasion.

Capello wasn't going to fault a player for wanting to play. In fact, he expected nothing less: when you're left out, it should hurt. Had Owen said what had been attributed to him, he might have had to take action. But the way he quickly set the record straight showed that he was on board. For now, at least. Because you wouldn't blame Owen for being fearful for his England future.

The fact that Capello's first two England sides featured a lone striker – and, given that it was Rooney, a striker who was anything but a traditional front man – could be read several different ways. He either believed in this kind of system, or he thought that it was best suited to the qualities (and lack thereof) available to him. And if you bought into the second line of reasoning, what did it say about Capello's faith in the England strikers? Wasn't he effectively suggesting that his options were so limited that he'd rather have Rooney on his own than put his faith in an Owen, a Crouch or a Jermain Defoe?

That was easily the most negative way of reading the situation. And there was some historical basis to it. Over his fifteen-year club career, Capello had tried, whenever he could, to play with at least one genuine, penalty box striker: Ruud Van Nistelrooy, David Trezeguet, Gabriel Batistuta, Vincenzo Montella, Davor Suker, George Weah, Marco Van Basten. Of course, when you've got guys of that calibre at your disposal, it doesn't take a rocket scientist to put them in your side. Still, it was clearly his preferred option. For him to deviate from it meant that he felt his other striking options must have been substandard . . . or did it?

Perhaps a look at two of Capello's sides that did not feature a genuine centre-forward can offer a clue. In 1993–94, as we've seen, his Milan side went most of the season with the following strike partnership: Daniele Massaro, a speedy winger recycled as a striker and Dejan Savicevic, a vastly talented – if somewhat self-indulgent – creative player who roamed the pitch at his pleasure. And in 2003–04, with Montella injured, his striking tandem at Roma was made up of Francesco Totti and Antonio Cassano, neither of whom is a traditional centre-forward.

The implication here is that, while in an ideal world Capello would rely on a classical striker, right now he had another priority. Capello is a believer in players 'who can make a difference'. Stars, if you will. Guys whose ability and attitude lift the whole team. But, to do that, you have to put your 'difference-makers' into a position where they can be most effective, while surrounding them with players who can best serve their needs. Rather than finding a way to shoehorn the eleven best English players into a starting lineup, the priority was finding a way to maximize the production he got from his 'difference-makers'. The rest would follow.

Capello's two 'difference-makers' right now were clearly Gerrard and Rooney. Any lineup or formation had to begin with them. Five or six years ago, when Owen was among the most admired strikers in Europe, he probably would have been in that category as well. For now, however, he had to take a backseat, like everyone else, until Capello found the best way to use him.

Then there was the issue of goalkeepers. One of the mysteries of sport is how sometimes a generation of talent comes along all at once, all in similar roles. Joe Frazier, Earnie Shavers and George Foreman might all have staked a stronger case as being the best heavyweights in history if they hadn't all been born within a few years of a certain Muhammad Ali. Chris Evert had the misfortune of being Martina Navratilova's contemporary. Sometimes, they just come along, like buses. And sometimes they don't come along at all.

England, the nation which at one time could count on four goalkeepers of the calibre of Gordon Banks, Peter Bonetti, Ray Clemence and Peter Shilton, now found itself with a serious dilemma between the sticks. David James was Capello's choice in his first two matches and, indeed, he was enjoying a sparkling season. He was tall, athletic, commanding and intelligent, a quality Capello always admired in goalkeepers.

In the long term though, James had two problems. First of all, he would turn forty just after the 2010 World Cup. And while countries had won World Cups with ageing goalkeepers in the past (Italy's Dino Zoff was forty in 1982), it was far from an ideal situation and certainly no long-term solution. James's other issue seemed to be one of image. He was the kind of goalkeeper who regularly made the saves he wasn't supposed to make, but occasionally missed the more routine ones. And when this happened, he became an easy target for the press. It had happened before, at Euro 2004, it happened again in Paris. James was another player who had matured tremendously in recent years, but Capello still wanted time to get to know him better, to see exactly how he bounced back from the inevitable criticism which, occasionally, all keepers must face.

Either way, given James's age, Capello needed a Plan B. There wasn't much out there. Tottenham's Paul Robinson, the most experienced option, had been savaged after some bad errors during England's qualifying campaign and was in and out at club level. Aston Villa's Scott Carson had done well at Under 21 level, but he too had blundered badly on the big stage, getting blamed for the crucial loss to Croatia when he was suprisingly preferred to Robinson. Robert Green at West Ham United and Chris Kirkland at Wigan Athletic had fair ability, but looked a notch below international standard, at least for now. Manchester United's Ben Foster was highly regarded in some quarters of the FA, but he had played just once since returning from an injury which had kept him out for ten months. And then there was Joe Hart. Capello's staff liked him a lot, but, at the time of the France friendly, he had yet to turn twenty-one and was in his first season as a Premier League regular. He would be watched closely, but brought along slowly. If he was rushed into the first team and happened to make a bad mistake in a big game, it could seriously dent his confidence.

The other area with a dearth of options was up front. Apart from Rooney, Crouch was the only English striker at a top four side and, even then, he was very much an understudy. It only took a quick scan of the Premier League table to see just how dire the situation was. The closer you got to the top, the less playing time English strikers seemed to get. Everton's Andy Johnson and Aston Villa's Gabriel Agbonlahor played a fair bit, though often on the wing. Defoe had established himself as a starter at Portsmouth, after sitting on the bench for several years at Tottenham. Matt Derbyshire, a starlet with the Under 21s, was fourth choice at Blackburn. Dean Ashton had the physical attributes to do reasonably well, but had missed all of 2006–07 through injury and his fitness looked precarious at best.

Capello knew he had to get creative. He would try to work with the formation he put out in his first two matches, with Rooney as centre-forward, but he needed more options. Crouch or Owen might both provide one, but he needed more. Liverpool's big man simply didn't get enough playing time and Owen's injury record was not encouraging. The message was clear: find more options. This meant looking not just at young strikers, but also taking a long, hard look at some of the guys in mid-career who might have slipped through the cracks. People like Wigan's Emile Heskey (who, of course, had been an England regular before disappearing from view), Reading's Dave Kitson, Bolton's Kevin Davies, Birmingham's Cameron Jerome, West Ham's Carlton Cole . . . everyone would be looked at. Nobody would be ruled out.

Capello felt better about his options at the back and in midfield. He had some world-class footballers and he had what he felt was a deep enough talent pool of role players to complement them. One of his strengths as a manager in the past had been identifying a specific need, working with the club to formulate the profile of the type of player who could address that need and then persuading the club to go and buy the right man to plug the hole. Obviously, he could no longer do this.

'The fact is, only 38 per cent of Premier League players are English,' he said in a March 2008 interview with Sky Italia. 'So there aren't many to choose from. We have to hope that the ones we can choose from are going to be good enough.' In short, he had to make the best of what he had. The whole process of team-building was now different. It had to start from within. It was a new experience but, then again, not as new as some might suggest. After all, he had spent five years at Milan's youth academy, winning a national title, in a similar context: working with what he had. There were years at Milan when, for different reasons, he had to redesign the playing style, rather than simply acquiring new players, to address weaknesses. And, of course, when he went to Real Madrid the first time around, the club had already made their summer signings.

And so, there he was, in what was likely to be the final challenge of his managerial career. All told, he was right where he wanted to be. But there is one question left unanswered: why?

It's a question to which, after months of studying Capello intensely, I'm still not confident I have the answer. I hope this book offers some clues. When asked, Capello answered only in part.

'I want to win the World Cup with England,' he said in a March 2008 interview. 'This country may seem cold and aloof. But there is a mass participation, a general sense of belonging when it comes to the England team which is truly extraordinary. I want to be a part of that. And I hope to make history.'

Yes, history. In some ways it's a bit unusual. If there is one person who – one would think – could live perfectly happily without football, it would be Capello. He has his travels, his books, his contemporary art collection, a whole galaxy of interests far beyond the pitch. And if he wanted to stay in the game, he could probably walk into any top pundit's job in Italy or Spain. He had already proven himself in that capacity and it was something he seemed to truly enjoy.

Beyond that, his place in football lore was already secured. His teams had set records which could never be bettered, they had won nine league titles (forget the two which had been stripped by the Italian FA when he was at Juventus: Capello always insisted that he won those on the pitch, regardless of what happened elsewhere). He had triumphed in the most adverse of circumstances.

And yet maybe, just maybe, even if he denies it, there is,

in Capello, a competitive spirit which spurs him on and which can't be extinguished. He will, inevitably, forever be placed alongside Marcello Lippi as the outstanding coach of his generation. Their numbers are, in many ways, comparable. Lippi has won five league titles to Capello's nine. He has won a domestic cup, Capello hasn't. Both have won a Champions League title, but Lippi reached the final four times to Capello's three. But what tipped the balance in Lippi's favour was the World Cup he won in 2006 with Italy.

Sure, Capello could have lobbied hard for the Italy job and, odds are, he would have had it in time to lead the Azzurri to the 2010 World Cup. But then what? Even if he won it, he'd be doing it four years after Lippi. And, at best, becoming world champion with Italy would have seen him only equal Lippi.

England, however, were another matter. Winning the World Cup with England meant becoming the first foreign manager in history to become world champion. It was a feat which could never be erased. True, England had won it before, but that was on home soil and as far back as 1966, which meant that most people with clear memories of that triumph are either dead or of pensionable age. Imagine what triumphing in 2010 – in Africa! – would mean.

The issue came up indirectly when Capello and Lippi met one afternoon in March. The Sky Italia cameras were there, but it was nevertheless a relaxed conversation, between two of the most successful men in football.

'You know, Fabio, no matter how much you might enjoy winning the World Cup with England, you will never experience what I felt,' said Lippi, referring to his role in Italy's triumph in 2006.

Capello pursed his lips. 'I told you,' he said. 'I will never manage Italy.'

Lippi looked at him in wonder, mouth slightly open. He shook his head and said: 'Well, you don't know what you're missing . . .'

Capello's head turned to look straight at Lippi. His expression didn't change, though his jaw looked firmer than usual.

'Envy is a feeling that does not exist in my being,' he said. It was his way of moving on to the next topic. 'I wish happiness and good things to everyone. When you won the World Cup, I was happy too. I'm Italian, after all. But I don't envy anything. Nothing at all.'

Lippi's expression spoke volumes. It screamed: 'You're not like the rest of us.' And, in fact, he isn't.

Career Record

As a player	Club	Major Honours
1962–67	Spal	Promoted to Serie A, 1964–65
1967–70	Roma	Coppa Italia 1968–69
1970–76	Juventus	Serie A 1971–72 Serie A 1972–73 Serie A 1974–75
1976–80	Milan	Coppa Italia 1976–77 Serie A 1978–79
National team		
1972–76	Italy	32 caps, 8 goals

As a manager	Club	Major Honours
1991–96	Milan	Serie A 1991–92 Serie A 1992–93 Serie A 1993–94 Champions League 1993–94 European Super Cup 1994 Serie A 1995–96
1996–97	Real Madrid	La Liga 1996–97
1997–98	Milan	
1999–2004	Roma	Serie A 2000–01
2004–06	Juventus	Serie A 2004–05* Serie A 2005–06*
2006–07	Real Madrid	La Liga 2006–07

* Titles later stripped from records

National team

2008–	England	

Picture Acknowledgements

FIRST SECTION

FC in the 60s: Cesare Galimberti/Rex Features

FC playing for Roma: Cesare Galimberti/Rex Features; FC changing, FC training and FC with Roberto Tancredi: all Offside/Grazianeri; FC and Pietro Anastasi; FC and Gianni Rureva both Offside/Farabolafoto; FC with Giancarlo Antonioni, 1970s: Alinari/Rex Features

FC scores goal v England, Turin, 14 June 1973: AP/PA photos; FC by goal-post, Wembley, 14 November 1973: mirrorpix; FC scores, Wembley, 14 November 1974: PA Archive/PA Photos; FC hugged by manager Enzo Bearzot (left): Popperfoto/Getty Images; World Cup 1974, Italian team to play Haiti: John Varley/Offside; FC reprimanded by referee Pavel Kass, Italy vs Argentina, 19 June 1974: DPA/PA Photos

FC, AC Milan player, 1976: Cesare Galimberti/Rex Features; AC Milan team, 1979: Carlo Fumagalli/AP Photo; FC playing for AC Milan, 1978 and 1979: both Cesare Galimberti/Rex Features

FC at home with Laura and sons, mid-70s: Cesare Galimberti/Rex Features

SECOND SECTION

FC with President Silvio Berlusconi, 1 July 1977: Claudio Villa/Offside/Grazianeri

FC, and new signings, 20 July 1995: AP Photo/Carlo Fumagalli; FC celebrates victory over Fiorentina with (l. to r.) Alessandro Costacurta, Marcel Desailly, George Weah, Sebastiano Rossi, Paolo Maldini, 28 April 1995: AP Photo/Luca Bruno; FC in Real Madrid kit, 29 July 1996: Eric Lafargue/PA Photos; FC shouts at Poncaro during Milan/Lazio game, 13 September 1997: AP/Carlo Fumagalli; AC Milan fans protest against club directors, 10 May 1998: Marco Buzzi/PA Photos

FC and Francesco Sensi, 7 June 1999: AP/Domenico Stinellis; FC and pitch invaders, Rome, 17 June 2001: Getty Images; FC and Francesco Totti after substitution, 25 August 2003: Offside/Grazianeri; FC at Roma v Lazio game, 21 November, 1999: Gabriel Bouys/AFP/Getty Images; FC and Adriano Galliano, 15 May 2005; and celebration of Juventus victory v Cagliari, 15 May 2005:

both Offside/Grazianeri; Antonio Giraudi, Luciano Moggi, FC and Andrea Agnelli, 2 November 2005: AP Photo/Luca Bruno

FC arrives at Barajas airport, 5 July 2006: Paul White/AP/PA Photos; FC and David Beckham during training, 18 August 2006: Offside/Marca; Franco Tancredi and FC celebrate Real Madrid winning La Liga, 17 June 2007: Grazianeri/PA Photo; Fabio Cannavaro, FC and David Beckham celebrate La Liga victory: Offside/Marca; Adrian Bevington, FA Director of Communications, Brian Barwick, chief executive of the English Football Association, FC and translator at press conference, 17 December 2007: Alastair Grant/AP/PA Photos; protester 14 December 2007: Getty Images; Capello supporters, 6 February 2008: Mike Egerton/EMPICS Sport/PA Photos

England's general manager, Franco Baldini, manager, FC, assistant coach, Italo Galbiati and coach, Stuart Pearce: Mike Egerton/EMPICS Sport/PA Photos; FC at England v Switzerland friendly, 6 February 2008, with Wayne Rooney: Mark Leech/Offside; Michael Owen: Action Images/Andrew Coulridge; Shaun Wright-Phillips: Mike Egerton/EMPICS Sport/PA Photos

Index

Capello, Fabio
   Management Career [*see also*
   individual clubs]
      ability to move on and not
      dwell on victories/defeats
      78, 108–9, 154, 168, 175,
      225
      announcing of starting
      lineups 168
      belief that players can con-
      tinue to improve skills
      209–10
      coaching style 121–2
      comparison with Lippi 514
      face-to-face interview with
      Baldini (2005) 366–8
      feels unappreciated back
      home in Italy 429–30
      gets full coaching badge at
      Coverciano 116
      management style 62
      qualities and strengths
      110, 512
      public image of 47
      record and achievements
      514, 518
      relations with media 247,
      322–3
      and television punditry
      244–8, 437, 473
      testifies at GEA trial
      (2008) 306, 382
      view of English football in
      1983 113–14
      ENGLAND (2008–)aim of
      winning World Cup
      467–8, 513, 514
      assistants issue and 'mirror
      system' 459–62

Beckham issue 477–8,
485–9, 500
captaincy issue 489–92,
500–1
choosing squad for friendly
against France 499–504
contract negotiations and
signing of 464–70
dearth of options up front
problem 511–12
featuring of lone striker in
sides 507–8
first press conference
475–8
first side named and tactical approach in
Switzerland match 494–8
goalkeeper issue 509–11
interview and meeting
with FA officials 455–64
language issue 476–7, 478,
492–3
and media/press 471–2,
479–81, 505–6
Owen issue 498–9, 505–6,
506–7
plans for 473–5
problems to sort out 497
public announcement on
appointment and reaction
471–3
relationship with club
managers 481
road to appointment
443–50
tactical approach 507–9
and team-building 512
'Ten Commandments'
493–4

Udinese 123–4
UEFA Cup
  (1972) 68
  (1975) 92
  (1996) 196
  (1999) 262, 266
  (2001) 280
Ultras Sur 412
Upson, Matthew 494

Valcareggi, Ferruccio 68, 88, 89
Van Basten, Marco 128, 133,
  144, 145, 148, 149, 152,157,
  158, 159, 160, 173, 177
Van der Sar, Edwin 296
Van Nistelrooy, Ruud 394–5,
  396, 397, 399
Vassallo, Gustavo 329
Venables, Terry 319, 476
Venditti, Antonello 293
Verona 73–4
Vialli, Gianluca 124, 297
Viani, Gipo 30–1
Vieira, Patrick 37, 363, 371, 375
Villar Mir, Juan Miguel 389,
  390–1
Völler, Rudi 157
Volpi, Jacopo 245
Vycpalek, Cestmir 62, 63, 64,
  68, 70, 74–5, 90
Vycpalek, Cestmir Jr 68

Walsh, Paul 114

Weah, George 189–90, 192,
  193, 235, 238
Wenger, Arsène 141, 389, 391,
  435
Werder Bremen 370–1
Whitworth, Ray 465
Wilkins, Ray 121, 122
Windass, Dean 235
Wolverhampton Wanderers 68
Woodgate, Jonathan 494
World Club Cup
  (1993) 165–7
  (1995) 182
World Cup
  (1974) 69, 85–90
  (1994) 178
Wright, Billy 501
Wright-Phillips, Shaun 486, 496,
  497–8

Zago 257, 296–7, 314
Zambrotta, Gianluca 353
Zanetti, Cristiano 260, 272, 298
Zanoncelli, Francesco 121
Zebina, Jonathan 270, 271, 272,
  276, 277–8, 297, 316, 353
Zeman, Zdenek 249–50, 251
Zenga, Walter 102
Zidane, Zinedine 196, 258, 391
Ziege, Christian 230, 234, 242
Zoff, Dino 69, 71, 82, 86, 88,
  89, 90, 169, 246–7
zonal marking system 103–4

The Italian Job
Gianluca Vialli & Gabriele Marcotti

A journey to the heart of two great footballing cultures

FOOTBALL IS A vital part of popular culture in both England and Italy. It is played, watched, written about and talked to death by millions, every day of every year. But how do the characteristics of England and Italy affect the game in these two great footballing nations? Do the national stereotypes of Italians as passionate, stylish lotharios and the English as cold-hearted eccentrics still hold true when they kick a ball around?

In *The Italian Job*, Gianluca Vialli, in conjunction with sportswriter and broadcaster Gabriele Marcotti, tackles this debate head on. And they have invited some of the biggest names in the sport to join in their discussion. Sir Alex Ferguson, Jose Mourinho, Arsène Wenger, Sven-Göran Eriksson, Fabio Capello and Marcello Lippi, amongst others, add their not inconsiderable weight to the highest-profile symposium on football ever convened.

Stuffed full of controversial opinions and gripping revelations, and fully updated to cover World Cup 2006 and the Italian football league controversy, *The Italian Job* takes you on a journey to the very heart of two of the world's great footballing cultures.

'The most thoughtful book by a footballer I can remember reading'
INDEPENDENT

'Provocative and well researched'
THE TIMES

9780553817874